Also by **Ashgate**

ANDRZEJ GARLICKI and JOHN COUTOUVIDIS
JozefPilsudski, 1867–1965

DAVID ABULAFIA and NORA BEREND
Medieval Frontiers: Concepts and Practices

ANDREW POPP
Business Structure, Business Culture and the Industrial District: The Potteries, c. 1850–1914

SAM A. MUSTAFA
Merchants and Migrations: Germans and Americans in Connection, 1776–1835

BERNARD CRONIN
Technology, Industrial Conflict and the Development of Technical Education in 19th-Century England

and in the Collected Studies Series

PETER F. SUGAR
Nationality and Society in Habsburg and Ottoman Europe

PETER F. SUGAR
East European Nationalism, Politics and Religion

PÉTER GUNST
Agrarian Development and Social Change in Eastern Europe, 14th–19th Centuries

ANTONI MACZAK
Money, Prices and Power in Poland, 16th–17th Centuries

ZSIGMOND PÁUL PACH
Hungary and the European Economy in Early Modern Times

NIKOLAI TODOROV
Society, the City and Industry in the Balkans, 15th–19th Centuries

JERZY TOPOLSKI
The Manorial Economy in Early-Modern East-Central Europe: Origins, Development and Consequences

ERIK FÜGEDI edited by J. M. BAK
Kings, Bishops, Nobles and Burghers in Medieval Hungary

VARIORUM COLLECTED STUDIES SERIES

Studies in East-Central Europe
General Editor: Ivan T. Berend

Studies on Central and Eastern Europe in the Twentieth Century

Professors Ivan T. Berend and Györgi Ránki

Ivan T. Berend and György Ránki

Studies on Central and Eastern Europe in the Twentieth Century

Regional Crises and the Case of Hungary

Routledge
Taylor & Francis Group
LONDON AND NEW YORK

First published 2002 by Ashgate Publishing

Published 2016 by Routledge
2 Park Square, Milton Park, Abingdon, Oxon OX14 4RN
52 Vanderbilt Avenue, New York, NY 10017

Routledge is an imprint of the Taylor & Francis Group, an informa business

British Library Cataloguing-in-Publication Data
Berend, Ivan T. (Ivan Tibor), 1930–
Studies on Central and Eastern Europe in the Twentieth Century: Regional Crises and the Case of Hungary . (Variorum Collected Studies Series: CS739).
1. Europe, Eastern – Politics and Government – 20th Century. 2. Europe, Central – Politics and Government – 20th Century. 3. Hungary – Politics and Government – 20th Century. 4. Hungary – Foreign Relations – Germany. 5. Germany – Foreign Relations – Hungary. 6. Hungary – Foreign Relations – 1918–1945. 7. Germany – Foreign Relations – 1933–1945.
I. Title. II. Ránki, Györgi, 1930–1988
943'.000904

US Library of Congress Cataloging-in-Publication Data
Berend, Ivan T. (Ivan Tibor), 1930–
Studies on Central and Eastern Europe in the Twentieth Century: Regional Crises and the Case of Hungary / Ivan T. Berend and Györgi Ránki.
p. cm. – (Variorum Collected Studies Series: CS739).
Includes bibliographical references (p.)
1. Hungary – Economic Conditions. 2. Hungary – Politics and Government.
I. Ránki, Györgi, 1930–1988. II. Title. III. Collected Studies.
HC300.24.B465 2002
330.9439'05–dc21 2001048702

ISBN 978-0-86078-887-4 (hbk)

VARIORUM COLLECTED STUDIES SERIES CS739

CONTENTS

* = written by I.T. Berend and G. Ránki
† = written by I.T. Berend
§ = written by G. Ránki

This volume contains x + 348 pages

PREFACE

This is a joint volume by two historians whose works and names became known together. Our joint work began in the early 1950s and our first joint book was published in 1955. For a while, we worked and published only together. From the 1960s, however, besides having continued our joint work until the late 1980s, we also initiated separate projects and published separately as well.

I met György Ránki after the war at the age of 16 and studied together in high school. This period became decisive in both our lives. First of all, we became closest friends, whose lives, ways of thinking, and work were closely connected and strikingly similar.

Our high school history teacher, Zsigmond Pál Pach, turned our interests towards history, and when he was appointed Professor of Economic History at the Budapest University of Economics, both of us, having graduated in high school, enrolled in this institution and began to study with him. Studying together, both of us graduated in Economics and in History. During these university years, we started a joint research project on early twentieth century Hungarian industry, developed a method to work and write together, and published our first book together. Since that time we have naturally continued our joint research and published a series of books, first on Hungarian economic development, and then, from the late 1960s, on Central and Eastern European economic and social history during the nineteenth and twentieth centuries. During the decades of harmonious collaboration between 1950 and 1988, we published ten books together. Four of them were translated and published in Britain, the United States, Italy, Japan, and Croatia. The last joint book, an Economic History of Europe 1780–1914, came out a few months before the unexpected early death of György Ránki.

During the nearly forty years of closest friendship and joint work, both of us continued our separate research and publications. György Ránki as well as myself published several works alone. His special field of interest led him to diplomatic history, while I mostly concentrated to contemporary economic problems.

This volume contains three studies, written together, four by György Ránki, and four by me. The first article was published in 1958, the last one in 2000. The reader should not forget that our early works were written in Stalinist Hungary, during the harsh years of the fifties. I gladly include two of those studies in this volume, partly because they belong to our lives, partly because of their rich and original archival sources, which are still useful.

***

This volume consists of three parts. The first contains four articles on the troubled German – Hungarian relations during Hitler's rule. Although it relates to Hungary, it also provides an understanding of German – Central and Eastern European economic ties in general during the turbulent war years.

The second part contains three studies on the economic and political problems of the Central and Eastern European area during the interwar decades.

Two of the four studies of the third part present the efforts and strict limitations of reforms in state socialist Hungary. The other two analyse post-communist economic transformation in Central and Eastern Europe in a broad international context during the 1990s.

The selected studies cover more than forty years of research, a document of a life-long friendship and joint work.

IVAN T. BEREND

Los Angeles
December, 2000

ACKNOWLEDGEMENTS

For permission to reprint these essays I am grateful to following publishers, institutions and individuals: *The Journal for Contemorary History*, London (V); *The Journal of European Economic History*, Rome (VIII); the Südosteuropa Gesellschaft, Munich (X); the United Nations, Geneva and New York (XI).

PUBLISHER'S NOTE

The articles in this volume, as in all others in the Collected Studies Series, have not been given a new, continuous pagination. In order to avoid confusion, and to facilitate their use where these same studies have been referred to elsewhere, the original pagination has been maintained wherever possible.

Each article has been given a Roman numeral in order of appearance, as listed in the Contents. This number is repeated on each page and quoted in the index entries.

PART I
NAZI GERMANY AND HUNGARY

The four studies in this chapter discuss the German-Hungarian economic and political relations during the nazi period between 1933 and 1944. The topic reflects the focus of the first period of our career between the 1950s and mid-1960s, the economic history of modern Hungary. The first and third articles were written during the 1950s when we were at the beginning of our career in our twenties and Hungary was closed. We could not travel and get access to modern Western publications that time. The terminology we used also reflects the situation.

One to one-and-half decades after World War II research was not conducted yet on German-Hungarian relations. We felt a professional mission to study the history of the fatal and devastating economic and political connections between Hitler-Germany and Horthy-Hungary. Furthermore, both of us as young boys had the worst possible experiences in German concentration camps and wanted to understand the history of the near past.

The two articles – second and fourth – of György Ránki clearly express his special interest in diplomatic history. The fourth study, written in the mid-1980s, became a major contribution to the national and international debate on the topic.

I

German-Hungarian Relations Following Hitler's Rise to Power (1933—34)

Her alliance with Hitler's Germany was pivotal in Hungary's inter-war history, both political and economic. If there was an event during those twenty years or so which may be said to have been fateful for the further development of Hungary, that event was by all odds her alignment with Nazi Germany. That historic association, which so catastrophically determined Hungary's position, formed a process that went on for years, culminating in the military occupation and ruthless fleecing of Hungary by the Germans during the second world war. It is not by chance that our historians have tended so far to turn the searchlight upon the fast-moving, dramatic events of the second world war rather than the preceding period, and, even in their investigation of the fatal consequences of German influence in Hungary, confined their enquiry to those hectic years. They have failed to give due attention to the events — less dramatic and lower-moving, perhaps, but crucial for Hungary's subsequent subjection, political as well as economic — of the years following Hitler's accession to power. There were two circumstances in German-Hungarian relations in the years 1933—34 which, in our opinion, were of crucial importance as determining the whole course of future development. One was the establishment of political relations between Hitler's Germany and Admiral Horthy's Hungary by raising to the status of official policy the connexion that had for some time been maintained between Gyula Gömbös and Hitler. The other circumstances was the strengthening of economic ties between the two countries through a modification in 1934 of the trade agreements which had earlier been in force between Germany and Hungary. In this paper we shall investigate these two factors, so decisive for eventual developments, political as well as economic.

Hitler's accession to power and Gömbös's pro-German policy in 1933

Of the leading capitalist countries it was in Germany that the impact of the economic world crisis was most acutely felt. At the nadir of the crisis, in 1932, overall industrial output had slumped to 53 per cent, and the output of heavy industry — the stronghold of German Big Businesses — to 30 per cent of the pre-crisis level. Unemployment assumes extraordinary proportions: at the end of 1932 and early in 1933, it rose above the six-million mark.[1] In this catastrophic economic situation the bottom fell out of the German stabilisation of the twenties. The spirit of resistance and a revolutionary mood were growing stronger in the ranks of the working class, finding expression in the growing influence of the Communist Party and in the spectacular increase of communist votes in the elections. The five million communist and seven million social-democrat votes cast at the elections in the autumn of 1932 were evidence of a high degree of political activation among the working class and, through the sweeping advance made by the Communist Party, constituted the threat of a new revolution for the German ruling classes. The realization came home to German Monopoly Capital and the Prussian militarists that it was no longer possible to maintain their class rule in the old ways. They therefore pressed for the establishment of a political system which would resort to brutal terror for the supression of any action by the toiling masses. They demanded an administration which would throw overboard the foreign policy of the Weimar Republic and launch forth on overtly aggressive actions in preparation of a new war of revanche. The German monopoly capitalists were increasingly putting their trust in the Nazi Party. Hitler's *Nazionalsozialistische Partei*, enjoying the financial support of the great capitalists, was steadily gaining ground during the period of crisis. By means of unbridled social and nacionalistic propaganda, it secured a mass following especially among the lower middle-class and the peasantry whose conditions went from bad to worse; it gained also ground among some backward sections of the working class. The large mass following of the Nazi Party and a full agreement concluded with the monopoly capitalists in 1932, made it possible to play the power into Hitler's hands. The nazis' accession to power meant the establishment of a ruthless and openly fascist dictatorship by the most reactionary sections of German Monopoly Capital; it meant that the aggressive schemes of German imperialism would once more be made part of the official German policy. Nazism's rise to power in Germany constituted an open threat of war to the European nations.

The coming into power in Germany of openly aggressive forces was hailed unanimously by the Hungarian ruling classes which, in their efforts to undermine the system of the Versailles peace treaties were looking for support to German imperialism above all. The Hungarian ruling classes saw in the downfall of the Weimar Republic and the accession of German nazism an international consolidation of their own semi- fascist régime. This attitude was further strengthened by the fact that a large section of the Hungarian ruling classes looked upon a continued drift into fascism as the only possible means of con-

[1] René Erbe, *Die nationalsozialistische Wirtschaftspolitik 1933—1938 im Lichte der modernen Theorie.* Zürich, 1958. pp. 9—10.

solidating their class rule after the severe shock it had sustained under the crisis. This political trend rose to ascendency when Gyula Gömbös took over the government in October 1932.

As in other countries, the grave economic crisis shock, of course, the Hungarian policy of consolidation in its very foundations and led, in August 1931, to the downfall of Bethlen's government after a rule of ten years. Gyula Károlyi's interim government was powerless in the face of the political and economic problems, and attempts to install a "strong-handed" government were growing in intensity. Mounting popular discontent, from September 1930 onward, terified the ruling classes with visions of a revolution. "We are heading fast for the precipice," András Mecsér, a well known politician of the extreme right, wrote in a letter "where only social issues prevail. Under such conditions centre tend to disintegrate which is what's going to happen to the United Party as well. The Christian Socialist Party smells too much of incense to be the big stick against the Marxists. Therefore we have in this country no viable anti-Marxist party with a mass following. What's going to happen, then?... As I see it, some drastic operations are called for."[2]

The need for "drastic operations" was universally recognized by the ruling classes. This provided an opportunity of increased political activity for those ex-army officers and government officials — many of them of gentry stock — who, by taking the lead in the White Terror, had played an important part in the establishment of the counter-revolutionary régime, and, as supporters of the racialist, anti-Semitic policy of the twenties, formed the most extremist wing of Hungarian Fascism which stood for totalitarian Fascist dictatorship. The leader and most typical representative of these groups had now come to power in the person of Gyula Gömbös. In the cabinet as well as in Parliament and the governmental party, leadership continued to be vested in Count Bethlen's men, the political old guard of the big industrial and landed interests.

Gömbös's government involved certain changes in Hungary's foreign policy. Trends which under Gyula Károlyi's premiership had favoured a pro-French orientation were now swept away. What had made it possible for the pro-French line to assert itself in 1931 was the circumstance that, unaffected by the crisis as she was then, France had seemed at the time the most secure of the capitalist great powers, and the Hungarian ruling classes had hoped to achieve economic and political consolidation by a cooperation with that power. However, the grave world crisis soon engulfed France also, killing all hopes that had been pinned on French support. Károlyi's administration, out of consideration for France, had gone out of its way to soft-pedal the clamour of the ruling classes for a revision of the peace treaty; now, Gömbös's government were once more beating the revisionist drums and stepping up jingoist

[2] The Hungarian Public Record Office (H.P.R.O.), Kozma papers file No. 3. Mecsér's letter to Miklós Kozma.

propaganda, thus tying Hungarian foreign policy irrevocably to that of the Fascist and Nazi great powers, which discontent with the Versailles peace settlements, were pushing for a repartition of the world. Count Bethlen, as has been pointed out had, from the late twenties, declared Hungary's adherence to the German-Italian alliance as the only way in which to pursue the objectives of Hungarian foreign policy — the eventual revision of the Versailles (*i. e.* Trianon) Peace Treaty. The first steps taken in this direction — resulting in an agreement with Fascist Italy — are associated with Bethlen's name, though it was Gömbös, who translated this policy into actual practice. Both the intensification of the allience with Fascist Italy and — more important still — the realization of the disastrous political alliance with Nazi Germany are connected with Gömbös's name. While the pro-Italian line continued to form the main trend of foreign policy through the early years of Gömbös's government, these years nevertheless witnessed the strengthening and predominance of the pro-German trend; it was in these years, that Hungarian foreign policy was coming to serve the interests of German Nazism to a steadily greater extent.

A bare 24 hours passed since news agencies spread abroad the news of Hitler's appointment to the chancellorship when Premier Gömbös, through the Foreign Ministry, cabled the following instructions to Kálmán Kánya, the Hungarian Minister in Berlin: "By making a formal call, enter into communication with Chancellor Hitler as soon as possible. Present my compliments and congratulations to Chancellor Hitler. Remind him of the time when 10 years ago, he and I were in touch, through Herr Scheubner-Richter, on a basis of common principles and Weltanschauung... Express my desire that... he honour me by maintaining contact even now he has assumed office, since I firmly believe that our two countries should cooperate in the field of both foreign and economic policy. Draw his attention to our close cooperation at the disarmament conference and in particular to the fact that I regret to find that commercial ties between Hungary and Germany are rather slack. A point of particularly great concern to me is the fact, that Germany is not available for Hungary's agriculture to the extent that our common fate should involve... I should like to see a lively trade to and from Germany, such as would promote that aim, get started as early as next July."[3] On 7. February 1933, Hitler received Minister Kánya who delivered Premier Gömbös's message conformed to Gömbös's instructions as quoted above,[4] and in the course of his interview with Hitler, Kánya also gave utterance to Gömbös 's view that steps should

[3] H. P. R. O., Min. of For. Affr. Pol. Dept., file No. 158, 21/7, 306. Feb. 1. 1933: Gömbös's letter to Under-Secretary of State for Foreign Affairs Sándor Khuen-Héderváry, asking for instructions to be given to Minister Kánya.

[4] Notes taken of the interview are available: Deutsches Zentral Archiv (D. Z. A.) Potsdam, Auswärtiges Amt. — Abt. II. 40834/3. Gömbös's message is also quoted in the volume of documents from the German Foreign Ministry files captured by the Western Allies (*Documents on German Policy*, C. I. 34).

be taken to promote "closer cooperation between the German and the Hungarian minorities in the Succession States of the Austro-Hungarian Monarchy."[5]

According to Kánya's strictly confidential report, Hitler, who had received the Hungarian minister in an extremely friendly manner, replied to Gömbös's message as follows: "In the field of foreign policy, one of his principal aims was to place Italian-German friendship on a solid basis and make it intimate. He would always make a point of this and was confident that Hungarian-German relations too were going to develop on increasingly friendly lines and on ever closer terms... The economic situation of Germany, owing to the present extremely widespread unemployment and the serious state of agriculture, was critical. This fact must to some extent be appreciated by all governments, including his own. Nevertheless, as it was his intention that in matters economic, political as well as economic points of view should be given consideration, be deplored as utterly wrong the practice of applying the same methods to all agricultural countries. He would bring his influence to bear in order to have German policy modified on the lines outlined by him. It would take some time, of course, before his view could prevail, for in 14 years of Marxist-pacifist administration that spirit... had become a habit so deeply ingrained, that it was bound to take quite an effort to alter the shape of things. However, he, Hitler had entered the Chancellor's office not for four weeks or six, but for a very long time, and so he felt sure, that he would succeed in changing the present state of affairs in due time."[6]

Both Gömbös's message and Hitler's reply make it clear that an economic settlement — above all the creation of openings for Hungarian agricultural exports — was a vital condition in 1933 for the political alliance so eagerly desired by both parties. For though Hungary's chief foreign-policy aspirations might bind the Hungarian ruling classes to German Nazism, no opportunity could have been found, in that most precarious situation caused by the economic crisis, of building a solid basis for the proposed political alliance, had that alliance brought no solution of the most urgent economic problems, above all the widening of markets for the produce of Hungarian latifundia.

Yet, against the expectations of the Hungarian landowning class, the Nazis' accession to power failed to provide export outlets in the first half of 1933. On the contrary, further substantial German tariff rise — mainly for pork and beef (M55— to M100-per l quintal), lard, goose-fat (M5—to M20) and other items affecting Hungarian agricultural exports — were put into force as early as February 1933.[7]

[5] D. Z. A. Potsdam. AA. Abt. II. 41289.

[6] H. P. R. O., Min. of For. Affs. Pol. Dept. File No. 158. 21/7. 306/1933.

[7] H. P. R. O., Min. of. For. Affs. Pol. Dept., German file. 654. Misc. II/3 1415/1933. 23 Feb. report of Hungarian Legation in Berlin; KARSTEN ANDERSEN: *Die Deutsch-Ungarischen Wirtschaftsbeziehungen und das Problem ihrer engeren Ausgestaltung.* Rostock, 1935., p. 67.

Several factors has combined to produce these new German tariff rises. Above all, they were a result of the chief political aim pursued by the Hitlerites. For from the very moment of having seized power, the Nazis worked for the preparation of a new war and began accordingly, to build up a system of autarchy. Seeking to isolate German economy from the world market, this policy of national self-sufficiency permitted no imports except for products indispensable for the national industry. Also, this autarkic isolationalism had something to do with the short-term political objectives of the Nazis. Right in the early years of the crisis, the National Socialist Party had drawn up a programme for agriculture, and made considerable — by no means unsuccessful — efforts to win over the German peasantry.[8] Established in power, they now put into effect a series of tariff increases favouring domestic market prices in an attempt further to extend their influence among the masess, making the peasants believe that they were actually protecting their interests. The Hungarian Legation in Berlin made it clear that "the increased agricultural tariffs, put into force with such speed and thoroughness during the last fortnight, had been designed with an eye to the approaching elections."[9]

At the same time, the Nazi policy of agricultural isolationism concurred with the economic aspirations of the *junker* landowning class which had been badly hit by the crisis. These aspirations were represented by the German National Party, which had much weight in the early months of Hitler's administration. Early in 1933, the portfolio of Food Supply and Economic Affairs in the Hitler Government was actually held by Hugenberg, leader of the National Party.

Last but not least, the tightening up of the isolationist policy was in some measure due to Germany's critical foreign-exchange situation. Germany's gold and exchange reserves dropped by 50 per cent during the first half of 1933. The balance of trade developed unfavourably — against a monthly export surplus of 240 million marks in the first five month of 1931, there was a monthly surplus of only 50 million in the first five month of 1933. These circumstances led to the tightening of the foreign-exchange policy and to import restrictions.[10]

Besides tariff rises, the German Government impeded Hungarian exports in other was, *e. g.* by refusing to grant barter deal permits, thereby excluding from the German market articles — poultry, eggs — which had earlier figured as the chief items of Hungarian exports.[11] This situation, on Hitler's accession to power, threatened with an all but total cessation of Hungarian-German eco-

[8] K. Diek Hoeft: *Die Agrarpolitik des deutschen Fascismus als Mittel zur Vorbereitung des Zweiten Weltkrieges.* Zeitschrift für Geschichtswissenschaft, 1959, No. 6, p. 1212.

[9] H. P. R. O., Min. of. For. Affs. Pol. Dept., German file. 654. Misc. II/3. 1415/1933.

[10] H. Lossos: *Bilanz der deutschen Devisenbewirtschaftung.* Jena 1940. pp. 18, 30.

[11] H. P. R. O. Min. of. For. Affs. Pol. Dept., file No. 640. I/2. 287"2 adm. 29. Legation report dated 25 Feb. 1933.

nomic relations. As the Hungarian Ministry of Foreign Affairs noted, "the tendency for autarky and agricultural protectionism steadily gaining ground in Germany... which has manifestated itself so strikingly through the recently published German tariff rises, bears most closely upon Hungarian export interests and is bound to affect our commercial policy towards Germany. For this reason, this office will instruct our Legation in Berlin to inform the German Government of the following. It is vitaly important for us to be able to sell the surplus of our agricultural products and to preserve the balance of trade. The tendency, recently manifested by the German Government to exclude foodstaffs coming from Hungary by withholding their consent to barter deals except in the case of a few raw materials, means — view of the present difficulties on exports with no premium on price — that our exports to Germany will shrink to almost nil. It will in all probability soon force this country to restrict its imports from Germany to such items — primarily likewise raw materials — as are absolutely necessary here."[12]

The economic differences became so acute in the early months of 1933 that the Hungarian Government availing themselves of a recommendation made by the League of Nations' Financial Commission concerning the annulment of clearing agreements, took some measures directed against Germany and, with effect from May 31, denounced the clearing agreement concluded the year before.[13] For Germany, this was an unwelcome move economically, as it represented the threat of a fruther drop in German industrial exports. But it was even more so politically, since in that period Hungary was only country to flaunt, in its foreign policy, open sympathy for German Nazism. Discontinuance of Germany's economic relations with Hungary would have been politically demaging to German Nazism. For this reason, Neurath, the Minister of Foreign Affairs, wrote a letter to Hugenberg in which, stressing that, were the clearing denounced, it would put them in a very awkward position in the

[12] H. P. R. O., Min. of. For. Affs. Pol. Dept., File No. 640. I/2. 312/4 adm. res.

[13] H. P. R. O., Min. of For. Affs. Pol. Dept. German file 645. II/a. 141/4 adm. res. 1933, II/b. 55. 035/4—1934.

In connection with the counter-measures to be taken by Hungary, the possibility was considered of bringing pressure to bear upon cabinet minister Hugenberg, through his personal interests, in order to obtain better conditions for Hungarian agricultural exports. For Hugenberg — as we read in a proposal put forward on 2 March 1933 by the Hungarian Minister in Berlin — "is not only an agriculturist but . . . has highly divergent industrial holdings, is the principal shareholder of the UFA film corporation, and as such, closely interested in that company's exports to Hungary. The recently published official statistics for the year 1932 put the value of German export to Hungary at round one million Marks. I take the liberty to suggest that Your Excellency give his consideration to the matter of wether, in view of the actual constellation, it would not be a politic move to let a possible restriction of the sales of German films as a reprisal for the restrictive measures in German agricultural imports be discussed by the press in Hungary, thus making Hugenberg understand that the agricultural policy with which he is identified may, even in countries sympathetic to the German cause, produce counter-measures that are liable to prove damaging not only to economic, but also to private interests which — as in the present case — are generally known to be protected energetically and with uncommon ingenuity." — H. P. R. O., Min. of For. Affs. Pol. Dept. German file. 640. cs. D I/2 345/4. adm. res.

field of foreign policy, solicited compliance with some of Hungary's wishes concerning agricultural exports.[14] At the same time, the German government made representations at the Hungarian Ministry of Foreign Affairs and asked the Hungarian government to relinquish its project of denouncing the clearing agreement. Naturally, the Hungarian government hastened to meet the German request — the cleering agreement continued in force.[15]

The Hungarian ruling classes were extremely anxious to prevent the acute economic differences from leading to estrangement in the political field and from becoming an obstacle to political alliance. This is not to say that the Nazi leaders did not promote these relations, for Hungary — and Southeast Europe in general — was meant to play an important role in Hitler's plans. But whereas a close alliance with German Nazism was a vital condition which had to be fulfilled of the agressive designs of Hungarian foreign policy were to be realized, Hungary was but one of the pieces on the Hitler's chessboard. This is why in the spring of 1933, when economic differences became acute, Hungarian politicians once more took the initiative to build up a German-Hungarian alliance. Bethlen's trip to Germany in March 1933 must be regarded as having been if utmost importance in this connection. The ex-Premier, who at the time was still the most eminent politician of the governing party, held lectures on international politics in Berlin, Hamburg, Frankfurt an Munich; he attacked the Little Entente in these lectures, and solicited official German support for a revision of the Hungarian peace treaty. Altough Bethlen was not a member of the Hungarian government, and had not gone to Germany in an official capacity, his trip may be considered as a political move of great importance, not only because it was the first time a leading Hungarian politician was visiting Hitler's Germany, but also because it was an unmistakable demonstration to show that the Hungarian ruling classes were unanimously supporting Gömbös in the matter of an alliance between Hungary and Nazi Germany. While in Germany, Bethlen did not restrict his activities to holding lectures: he also met Hitler, and had talks with Foreign Minister Neurath and Minister of War Blomberg.[16]

A few weeks after Bethlen's general exploratory trip and political talks, Premier Gömbös, this time in an official capacity, made certain opening moves to bring about a political *rapprochement* and to remove the economic differences that were an obstacle in the path of such a development. On 21 April 1933 he received the German Minister, Herr Schön, and told him that Germany's new agricultural tariffs had produced a very unfavourable impression in Hungary, and that a strong sentiment demanding countermeasures had developed in the country. Gömbös assured the German Minister of his determination to

[14] *Documents on German Foreign Policy*. C. I. 455. Neurath's letter of 17 May, 1933.
[15] H. P. R. O., Min. of For. Affs. Pol. Dept. 645. II/b 55.035/4—1934.
[16] H. P. R. O., Min. of. For. Affs. Pol. Dept., File 159, 21/7. 805/1933.

abide by his pro-German policy, but, he said, to make it possible for him to do so, it was essential that Germany made some economic concessions without delay. For, he pointed out, in spite of political differences, Hungary was enjoying more export possibilities in Czechoslovakia and France. Finally, Gömbös told the Minister, that in order to discuss these problems, he would welcome an opportunity of meeting Hitler in person at the earliest date possible.[17]

Next day, Gömbös wrote a letter to Hitler. In this letter he discussed the need for and the possibilities of political and economic cooperation between Hungary and Germany. He wrote:

Your Excellency,

When I had the honour to express my best wishes on Your Excellency's taking over of the government, I stressed the necessity of straightforward discussion, and to such straightforwardness I mean to adhere in the future. In my view, the regulation of the relations between Germany and Hungary — in the first place, as regards our economic situation — is an urgent necessity.

Nationalist Hungary, now governed with a strong hand, has always looked to Berlin with some expectation and sympathy. It is, I believe, also in Germany's interest to prevent unstable economic relations from undermining this sympathy. The circumstance, however, that little or no agricultural produce from Hungary has of late been allowed to enter Germany has already drawn forth some criticism, not totally unfounded, attacking my policy towards Germany. Your Excellency will have received information that I have brought to heel the Jewish racialist newspaper which attacked Your Excellency and the government of Germany, thereby supplying proof that I am standing by Your Excellency not only in matters of principle and ideology, but also for motives of real-politik.

I would therefore request urgently that the German government take a decision to come to our assistance in matters of agricultural export. I am convinced that Your Excellency's strong will will be obeyed over this issue as well, all the more so as I know that Your Excellency holds views that are identical with mine : viz. that politics and economic policy should be coordinated as far as possible.

Agricultural export, as I view it, is not merely an economic problem but one which has a bearing upon politics ; and as my political line would be strengthened if this were appreciated on the part of Germany, I should request Your Excellency to take urgent measures of fundamental importance, and perhaps it would be possible for prominent experts to be sent to Budapest as soon as possible . . .

In conclusion Gömbös emphasizes that he feels sure that

we fellow-racialists of long standing, who hold a common ideology, shall understand and back each other on economic policy as well.

[17] D. Z. A. Potsdam. AA. Abt. II. 41283. Minister Schön's telephone report of 21 April, 1933.

[18] One copy of Gömbös's letter, written in German is to be found among the documents both of the Hungarian and the German Ministry of Foreign Affairs: H. P. R. O., Min. of For. Affs. Trade Dpt. File 158, 21/7 206/1933, and D. Z. A. Potsdam. AA. Abt.—II. 41288. The original german text of the letter is as follows:

In answering Gömbös's letter on 28 April, Hitler once again expressed his readiness for political and economic cooperation. He wrote —

Let me assure you that there is nothing that the men of the National Government would desire more fervently than the deepening of the spiritual understanding that exists in the political leadership of both sides into an actual political one. So long as there are economic difficulties that are liable to trouble these relations, we shall not slacken our efforts to ensure and find ways and means of clarification and improvement.

.... We are determined not to look upon this issue as one of a purely economic nature, but, in dealing with it, to regard its political aspects as decisive.

Indeed in May 1933, both the German Foreign Ministry and the National Socialist Party's Department of Foreign Trade declared their sympathy for and appreciation of the Hungarian requests. In order to prove their readiness to negotiate, the Germans informed the Hungarian Legation in Berlin that Dr. Werner Daitz, head of the National Socialist Party's Department of Foreign

---

Eure Exzellenz!

Als ich die Ehre hatte bei Ihrem Regierungsantritt Sie zu begrüssen, betonte ich die Notwendigkeit der offenen Aussprache und will ich in der Zukunft mich selbst auch an diese Offenheit halten. Ich glaube nämlich, dass es dringend notwendig ist die Beziehungen zwischen Deutschland und Ungarn zu regeln, in der ersten Linie was unsere Wirtschaftslage anbetrifft.

Hier wird mit fester Hand das nationale Ungarn regiert, welches immer mit einer gewissen Hoffnung und Sympathie nach Berlin blickte. Es liegt auch, glaube ich, im Interesse Deutschlands, dass diese Sympathie keinesfalls durch unsichere wirtschaftliche Beziehungen gestört wird. Der Umstand aber, dass in der letzten Zeit ungarische Agrarprodukte überhaupt nicht, oder nur in sehr geringem Masse nach Deutschland kommen können, lässt bereits Stimmen hören, die gegen meine Politik Deutschland gegenüber eine Kritik üben, die nicht ganz unbegründet ist. Exzellenz haben bestimmt Meldung erhalten, dass ich das jüdische rassenschützlerische Blatt, welches Eure Exzellenz und die Regierung Deutschlands angegriffen hat, gemassregelt habe, womit ich bewies, dass ich nicht nur aus prinzipiellen weltanschaulichen Rücksichten, sondern auch aus realpolitischen Erwägungen Eurer Exzellenz zur Seite stehe.

Ich möchte daher dringend bitten, dass die deutsche Regierung sich entschliesst uns in Agrarexportfragen zur Hilfe zu kommen. Ich bin überzeugt, dass sich der starke Wille Eurer Exzellenz auch in dieser Lage durchsetzen wird, um so mehr, da ich weiss, dass Eurer Exzellenz Prinzipien mit meinen übereinstimmen; nämlich dass Politik und Wirtschafts-Linienführung womöglich dasselbe sein muss.

Da die Agrarexportfrage bei mir nicht nur eine Wirtschaftsfrage, sondern eine Frage der politischen Erwägungen darstellt und meine politische Linienführung stärken würde, würde sie von deutscher Stelle verstanden, bitte ich Eurer Exzellenz dringende Verfügungen prinzipieller Natur und vielleicht könnten bedeutende Referenten ehebaldigst hier in Budapest erscheinen...

... Wir alte rassenschützlerische Kameraden, die wir in derselben Weltanschauung und auch auf der wirtschaftlichen Linie verstehen und uns gegenseitig unterstützen werden.

[19] Hitler's answer is likewise to be found among the documents of both Ministries of Foreign Affairs: H. P. R. O., Min. of For. Affs. Pol. Dpt. 158 21/7. 306/1933; and D. Z. A. Potsdam AA. Abt II. 41283. In original German, the quoted passages are as follows:

»Lassen Sie mich Ihnen versichern, dass die Männer der nationalen Regierung nichts sehnlicher wünschen als die in der beiderseitigen politischen Führung gegebene geistige Übereinstimmung zu einer tatsächlichen politischen zu vertiefen. Soweit wirtschaftliche Schwierigkeiten dieses Verhältnis zu trüben geeignet sein könnten, werden wir nichts unterlassen um Mittel und Wege zur Klärung und Besserung zu sichern und zu finden.

... sind wir entschlossen diese Frage nicht als eine wirtschaftliche anzusehehen, sondern bei ihrer Behandlung die politischen Gesichtspunkte als ausschlaggebende zu berücksichtigen.«

Trade, intended to visit Hungary before long. According to the legation, there could be no doubt that Daitz anxious to improve Hungarian-German economic relations, so severely strained of late.[20] A few days after Under-Secretary of State Bülow told Minister Masirevich in Berlin that he felt sure that some kind of agreement in the-economic field would be reached between the two countries. At the same time, Bülow pointed out that „for the time being... nothing more is likely to be made than some arrangements designed to document the friendly disposition of Germany in the economic field, in accordance with the spirit of political friendship between you and us."[21]

Daitz visit to Budapest and his negotiations there seemed to give the Germans the desires chance to iron out economic differences and remove the obstacles that were hindering a political *rapprochement* by announcing several minor and immediate concessions while holding out the prospect of major ones to follow. What sounded particularly reassuring to Hungary's big landowners was one point in Daitz's Budapest address, in which though coming out strong for Germany's drive for autarky, he said that, in meeting Germany's import needs, the experience of World War I would not be overlooked and Hungary would be given preference over oversea countries.[22] The fundamental principle of National Socialist foreign-trade policy required, Daitz stressed that „if possible, imports should come from a *Lebensraum* which has been made secure through a lasting political alliance and friendship and which is accessible even in time of trouble."[23]

Thus, acting on instructions from Hitler, it was the Nazi Party itself which undertook the task of regulating Hungarian-German commercial relations. By that time, successive Hungarian requests and protests had driven home to the Nazi leaders the need for a slight revision of their extremely rigid system of foreign-trade policy. At the same time the leaders of the Nazi Party turned to good advantage the circumstance that, in the first few month after their assumption of power, the economic ministries had not yet been brought under direct Nazi control, a circumstance which made it posible for them to pretend that the official German foreign trade policy had not been fully sanctioned by them. It was in the context of this pretence that Daitz made his pledges which held out the prospect of a possible volte-face in German foreign-trade policy. "The efforts of the National Socialist Party are directed towards the gradual deepening of the economic relations between the two countries, with due regard for actual possibilities. The National Socialist Party is confident that by duly asserting its influence it will soon succeed in quen-

[20] H. P. R. O., Min. of For. Affs. Trade, Pol. Dpt. German file 640. I/2. 742/4. adm. res.

[21] H. P. R. O., Min. of For. Affs. Dept. 158. 21/7. 1718/1933. Masirevich's letter of 31. May to Foreign. Minister Kánya.

[22] Köztelek, 4. June, 1933.

[23] Cf. W. Daitz: *Vortrag vor der ungarischen Regierung und Wirtschaft in Budapest*, May, 1933.

ching the spirit of liberalism which throughout the long Weimar era dominated German commercial policy and which, at the expense of the German national economy, recognized the most-favoured-nation-clause as its guiding principle. A *volte-face* in the economic policy will be so achieved and it would facilitate the forging of still closer economic links between Germany and Southeast Europe, Hungary in particular."[24]

Already during Daitz's preparatory talks, Waldeck, an official expert of the German Foreign Ministry, came to Budapest where he concluded a preliminary agreement providing for the purchase of some Hungarian wheat and fruit. Under the agreement concluded between the Hungarian "Futura" and German "Getreide Industrie & Commission" and approved by the German Government, Germany undertook to purchase from Hungary 5 million guilders-worth of wheat and 4 million guilders-worth of maize, or rye and barley. The other major stipulated item concerned the purchase of 5 million marks-worth of Hungarian fruit, but this was bought for "commodity pengoes,"[25] *i.e.* it meant the amortization of German frozen assets in Hungary. At the same time, the German delegates held out the prospect of purchases of eggs, butter, poultry and fish. These agreements were contained in the Budapest protocols, signed 2 June.[26]

After the preliminary negotiations, German-Hungarian trade talks — designed to complement the 1931 agreement — were held in Berlin from 14 to 22 July, 1933. In these trade talks, the German delegation, acting on the principles enunciated by Hitler and voiced by Daitz, behaved in a way that suggested as though they were willing to make unselfish concessions to Hungary. But even while making this apparent political gesture, they never lost sight of their principal short-term goal: to make the Hungarians repay their frozen commercial debts. In his report of 23. July, 1933, dealing with the result of the negotiations, the Hungarian Minister pointed out: "It became clear, at the very outset of the negotiations, that the chief objective the government of the Reich tried to achieve was to grant to Hungary concessions which would appear to the outside world as actual aid, and which, at the same time, would promote the release of nontransferable German frozen assets."[27]

[24] H. P. R. O., Dept. of Trade Pol. Min. Foreign Affairs. German file 640. I/2. 918/4 adm, res. Minister Masirevich's report from Berlin, 27. June, 1933.

[25] The National Bank of Hungary distinguished between debts and repayments arising from commercial transactions on the one hand, and those arising from financial transactions on the other hand. Debts and payments of the first category came under the head of "commodity pengoes", those of the second category were registered as "financial pengoes".

[26] H. P. R. O. Dpt. of Trade pol. Min. Foreign Affs. German file 640/13. Alfred Nickl's memorandum of 28 December, 1933 on transactions exceeding the usual exchange of goods.

[27] H. P. R. O. Dept. of Trade pol. Min. of For. Affs. German file No. 640. I/2. 967/4 adm. res. Minister Masirevich's report of 23 July, 1933.

[28] D. Z. A. Potsdam. AA. Abt. II. 41284.

As the only tangible result of the Berlin negotiations, duty concessions were granted to Hungary for three categories of goods: vegetables and vegetable seeds, fish and apricot brandy.[28] The Hungarian request for major tariff concessions was rejected from the very first on the ground that, were these granted, they would have to be extended to other states because of the still existing most-favoured-nation-clause. The actual result of the negotiations consisted in the conclusion of a few barter agreements. The I. G. Farbenindustrie, in order to further their exports to Hungary, undertook two barter transactions, and these constituted the main point of the agreement. The I. G. Farbenindustrie pledged themselves to secure the realization of the quota for 6,000 cattle which was granted to Hungary back in 1931 but had never been actually made available to her. The other barter agreement procured by the same big chemical concern concerned the Hungarian export of eggs to the tune of M 500,000. In addition, some openings were obtained for the exportation of comparatively large consigments of butter, and, subsequently, of horses.

The agreements, concluded as the result of the Berlin negotiations and styled Supplement No. 1. to the 1931 Agreement, took face as early as August of the same year. The 1931 trade agreement — and the supplementary protocols signed since — were then ratified in November, 1933.

Under the effect of the agreements, concluded in the summer of 1933, the serious decline during the firts half of the year was now followed by a slight recovery which did compensate in some measure for the earlier setback, and, as a result, made for a slighter drop to be registered for the whole of the year. Hungarian exports dropped by 7 million pengoes compared with the previous year, thus hitting their lowest point during the crisis.

Germany's Share in Hungarian Foreign Trade 1929—33.*

Year	Imports		Exports	
	in 1000 pengoes	% of total imports	in 1000 pengoes	% of total exports
1929	212,515	20,0	121,197	11,7
1930	174,975	21,1	94,124	10,3
1931	131,385	24,1	78,620	12,7
1932	73,938	22,5	50,661	15,2
1933	61,505	19,7	43,701	11,2

Thus, in the years of the crisis, Hungarian imports of German goods dropped sharply in value, more sharply in fact than Hungarian exports to

* Statistical Year-Book of Hungary 1931 (p. 129) and 1933 (p. 149).

Germany. The resulting tendency towards a certain equilistrium between imports and exports had the effect of sharply reducing the enormous passivity of the trade balance between Hungary and Germany.

Nevertheless, the slump in Hungry's trade with Germany was not greater in proportion than the general decline in Hungary's foreign trade, and when the crisis ended, Germany's share of Hungarian exports and imports stood, essentially, on its pre-crisis level (in fact, it had even surpassed it in some years of the crisis).

Although Germany had, during the years of the crisis, increased its share in Hungary's foreign trade; although the dwindling of Czechoslovakia's importance in the same respect had atached Hungary still closer to the German market, with the result that Germany emerged as Hungary's second biggest business partner behind Austria; the volume of actual trade yet diminished dramatically so that by the end of the crisis, in 1933, the exchange of goods between Hungary and Germany had reached its lowest point.

The year 1933, besides seeing German-Hungarian trade touch bottom, also brought a turning-point in German-Hungarian economic relations. Nazism, now established in power, gradually consolidated its positions in the course of 1933 both at home and internationally. Simultaneously, it set to drawing up its plans for world conquest and made the first steps in that direction. A most important part of these plans consisted in the economic enslavement and subsequent political conquest of Southeast Europe. So, after 1933, German imperialism stepped up its economic and political activities in that area, and thus also in Hungary. Under the Weimar Republic, its weakness prevented German imperialism from drawing these countries once more into its economic orbit as intensively as it had done before World War I — those Weimar years witnessed a loosening of economic relations. Things were changed radically after Hitler had taken over. Far more energetically than ever before, Nazi Germany buckled down to the business of incorporating the countries of Southeast Europe in the German "*Lebensraum,*" and continued expansion of commercial relations provided one of principal means of achieving that aim.

Of course, the building up of the German *Lebensraum* in Southeast Europe meant a long process of economic and political development; but with Admiral Horthy's Hungary — which looked upon German Nazism as a natural ally — Germany, as we have seen, found a common language directly after Hitler's rise to power. And if, as they did, the economic differences that had become unusually acute during the first half of the year presented a barrier in the way of full cooperation in the political sphere, the very first moves made to overcome these differences afforded a way towards and the means, of constructing a political alliance. Succesive steps of political and economic *rapprochement* paved the way for the incorporation of Hungary into the *Lebensraum* of German imperialism.

The first German steps to compose economic differences coincided with the actual opening of German—Hungarian political negotiations, with which they were closely related. Werner Daitz, as has been pointed out, came to Budapest to do the spadework for economic negotiations; yet it was he who, on behalf of the National Socialist Party, invited Premier Gömbös to visit Germany.[29] Naturally, Gömbös accepted the invitation made on behalf of the Nazi Party and Hitler himself. The trip came suddenly and in a remarkable manner. Gömbös met Hitler on 16 June, 1933; he travelled as a private person, and neither the press nor the Hungarian legation in Berlin had been previously informed of his visit. It was at that highly important meeting that the foundation of the alliance between the Horthy régime and Nazism was laid. Because of its strictly confidential nature, only indirect sources of information are available concerning this conference, Hitler and Gömbös discussed the most fundamental issues involved by the alliance between the German and the Hungarian ruling classes. Gömbös proposed the closest cooperation in the political, military as well as economic spheres, and dwelt particularly in the Hungarian territorial claims, explaining the views of the Hungarian ruling classes concerning a revision of the peace treaty, for which he solicited Hitler's support.

Hitler told the Hungarian Prime Minister plainly that he, Hitler, could only support Hungary's revisionist aspirations as part of Germany's plans of aggression. He emphasized that, although he sympathized with Hungary's territorial claims, it was impossible to meet them fully. He pointed out, that a weakening of Yugoslavia and Rumania was contrary to Germany's anti-Soviet designs. The German conception envisaged the incorporation of these two states into the German system of alliances through the medium of German political and economic influence. Therefore, Hitler suggested that Hungary should refrain from voicing her territorial claims with regard to these countries and that moreover, she should try to pursue a policy of rapprochement towards them in order to weaken and disrupt the Little Entente. Hungary, Hitler advised, should direct her revisionist demands and foreign-policy activity against Czechoslovakia — that would fit in perfectly with the aims of German foreign policy; Hungary could count here on full German support. Gömbös was delighted at the prospect of receiving far-reaching Nazi support against Czechoslovakia, the leading member of the Little Entente, but he could not yet reconcile himself to Hitler's attitude regarding to Yugoslavia and Rumania.

Austria was another key issue discussed by Hitler and Gömbös. The rise to power of the most aggressive section of German imperialism automatically raised the question of Austria's independence or her incorporation into the German Reich. As the Nazi general staff did not think the time had come to take up the question of the Anschluss, they applied to tactics of weakening

[29] H. P. R. O. Min. of For. Affs, Dpt. 158. 21/7. 1983/1933.

independent Austria internally as well as externally by supporting the Austrian Nazis. For this reason, Hitler touched upon the question of the Anschluss only as a matter of principle and as a distant possibility. Gömbös was actually against the Anschluss but stressed that he fully appreciated and supported the actual German Attitude towards Austria. He pledged himself that Hungary would exert pressure on Chancellor Dollfuss of Austria and prevent any possible rapprochement between Austria on the one hand and France and Czechoslovakia on the other. He also promised his intervention in order to compose the differences that had arisen about the Anschluss between Germany and Italy and undertook to explain to Mussolini that what the Germans wanted was just a participation of Austrian National Socialists in the power; Gömbös further promised to persuade Mussolini to give his support to and promote these plans.

Although foreign policy questions constituted the main subject under discussions, several problems of Hungarian domestic policy came on the *tapis* too. Hitler said that, fundamentally, he approved of Gömbös's policy and did not wish to raise difficulties for him in the field of domestic policy. He accordingly promised not to support the various National Socialist groups that formed Gömbös's rightist opposition, and to raise no difficulties by organizing the German minority in Hungary.

Finally, as regards economic matters, Hitler once again promised to ease some of the bans on imports.[30]

Contemporary public opinion learned very little about the conference of Hitler and Gömbös. The Hungarian prime Minister did not even inform the members of his own cabinet about his conversations. Yet, the meeting had a tremendous reaction throughout the world, as this was the first time that the head of another government had called on Hitler.

The exchange of messages and letters following Hitler's rise to power had evolved a common attitude and common views. Now, at the meeting in June 1933, this common attitude and these common views were applied in a positive form to current political questions. In the domain of domestic and foreign policy there was agreement, if not on every issue, at least on the few most important matters. This was a guarantee for the Hungarian ruling classes, that in Nazi Germany, they could count on solid support for their *foreign-policy* aspirations. Therefore, the Hungarian ruling classes hailed the meeting between Gömbös and Hitler and acclaimed it as a great success of Hungarian foreign policy, one that consolidated the international status of their régime. All this did not mean, however, that official Hungarian policy had at this early date already abandoned the principle of a priority of the pro-Italian policy. Such a development could not be contemplated at the time because Ger-

[30] This account of the meeting between Hitler and Gömbös is based on reports recorded in *Documents on German Foreign Policy* C. I., pp. 580 and 586 and on C. A. MACARTNEY: *October Fifteenth — A History of Modern Hungary*. Edinburgh 1957. Pp. 138—140.

many was still weak both militarily and economically, and isolated internationally; and altough the eventual spread of German Nazism was reckoned with, it was believed that Hungary must continue to base her policies primarily on Italy which was playing a more important part in the international political arena, and which had been an active supporter of Hungary ever since 1927. Accordingly Hitler's suggestion that Hungary should limit her revisionist aspirations to Czechoslovakia was not yet considered decisive. The notion was entertained — and it continued to dominate Hungarian foreign policy for next two years or three — that it was securing Hitler's support against Czechoslovakia and Mussolini's against Yugoslavia and Rumania that, the Hungarian ruling classes would be able to assert their territorial claims. "Hungary," Gömbös pointed out a month later to Hassel, the German ambassador in Rome, "sees at present no reason why she should waive part of her claims."[31]

A few weeks after he had met Hitler, Gömbös went to Vienna and Rome. This was intended as a demonstration that, in foreign policy, Hungary did not wish to change her earlier relations with Italy and Austria. On the other hand — and this was the principal motive behind his visit — Gömbös meant to promote a German-Italian *rapprochement* as something that suited Hungary's aggressive aspirations. In Vienna, where Gömbös's visit to Germany had elicited a rather unfavourable reaction,[32] Gömbös, true to his promise to Hitler, strove to reassure the Austrian government and emphasized that Hitler entertained no designs for the annexation of Austria. On the other hand, he warned Dollfuss against a possible pro-French policy or a rapprochement with the Little Entente.[33] His negotiations with Mussolini likewise pivoted round the future of Austria and the crucial issue of an Italian-German rapprochement. Gömbös and Foreign Minister Kánya, who was present at these conferences, expressed their fears that any further deterioration in German-Italian relations might cause Italian foreign policy to drift closer to France and the Little Entente. They feared that Italy might coordinate her foreign policy with France, instead of Germany, a development which would of necessity have entailed the withdrawal of Italian support from Hungary in her controversy with the states of the Little Entente, which were allied with France. After Mussolini had assured the Hungarian statesmen that their fears were unfounded, the latter proceeded to acquaint him with Hitler's proposals for a German-Italian

[31] *Documents on German Foreign Policy*. C. I., p. 691. Ambassador Hassel's report of 28 July, 1933.

[32] Chancellor Dollfuss of Austria regarded, according to the report of the British ambassador in Vienna, Gömbös's visit to Germany as a stab in the back. He feared that Gömbös had come to terms with Hitler concerning the annexation of Austria by Germany, in return for the province of Burgenland. *Documents on British Foreign Policy*, Second Series. Vol. V. p. 397. Report from Austria, 29 June, 1933.

[33] D. Z. A. Potsdam, AA. Abt. II. 41009. A report of 14 July, 1933, on Gömbös's visit to Vienna; and *Documents on German Foreign Policy* C. I. p. 653.

rapprochement for which they endeavoured to win his support.[34] Agreement was reached on all major issues. It was resolved to expand Italian-Austrian-Hungarian economic cooperation into a treaty, and to jointly oppose the Anschluss. At the same time, however, it was laid down as a general principle that both Italy and Hungary should cooperate with Germany both economically and politically. Further, Rome and Budapest would combine their efforts to promote a *rapprochement* between Austria and Germany.[35]

The negotiations with Hitler and the subsequent mediation between German Nazism and Italian Fascism in the summer of 1933 laid the foundation for a new phase in Hungarian foreign policy. The beginning of this new phase was characterized by simultaneous pursuance of pro-Italian and pro-German policies; after that, the pro-German policy gradually achieved ascendancy to end in Hungarian foreign policy being reduced to the status of a satellite of German Nazism. The German-Hungarian political alliance which led to Hungary's political subjection to Germany, was economically based upon the agreement of 1934. This agreement prepared the ground for Hungary's economic integration with the southeast European "*Lebensraum*" of German imperialism.

The new principles of German economic policy and the German-Hungarian supplementary trade agreement of 1934

The consolidation of the Nazi régime made it possible to reorganize German national economy in accordance with Nazi aims and to adapt it to war requirements. Some of the measures made under the Nazi programme of 1933 with a view to creating opportunities of work had already been connected in an indirect way with military preparations; the full-scale rearmament of Nazi Germany began in 1934. The rearmament programme, in keeping with the requirements of modern warfare, extended, of course, not only to the armaments industries proper, but included also other branches of industry, agriculture, banking and commerce, *i. e.* affected economic life as a whole. The economic readjustment for war brougth in its train state-control of economic life on an unprecedented scale. It was in Nazi Germany that the system of a state-monopoly capitalism of warlike character was first evolved. State control, which created a most vigorous boom for German monopoly capital, covered, as from the middle of 1934, the following three areas: huge military contracts, direct and indirect; the reorganization of national economy for autarky; and strictest control of foreign-trade and international payments. The two last

[34] *Documents on German Foreign Policy* C. I. p. 691. Ambassador Hassel's report of 28. July, 1933, from Rome.

[35] D. Z. A. Potsdam. AA. Abt. II. 41284. Ambassadorial report of 2 August, 1933 and *Documents on German Foreign Policy* C. I., p. 702: Ambassador Hassel's reports of 30. July and 2 August, 1933, respectively.

represent the principal elements of so-called economic rearmament. While autarkic economic policy was designed to make the German national economy independent of sources of raw materials inaccessible in time of war, the tight government control of foreign trade and payments was, in part, supplementary to the policy of autarky; in part, it was destined to supply a remedy for the extremely grave difficulties existing in respect of foreign trade and the balance of payments.[36]

The policy of autarky could never have been carried out without a strict government control, for, as regards foreign trade, autarky required a restriction of imports and a considerable shift in the traditional direction of foreign commercial relationships. Thus, although state control of foreign trade as a whole formed part and parcel of the autarkic policy of building up a war economy, its short-term aim was to ease the difficulties of foreign trade and the balance of payments where very great deficits were registered. Germany's foreign trade and payments reacted their most critical phase in the spring of 1934. The condition of the balance payments was aggravated by the emerging state-investments policy as well as by the currency devaluation carried out in the two principal trading nations of the world, the United Kingdom and the United States. On top of it all, foreign trade ran into a deficit for the first time in years — the deficit of the balance of trade for the second quarter of 1934 amounted to more than 160 million marks.[37]

As an attempt to solve the difficulties that beset both the economic rearmement programme and foreign trade Schacht produced his 'Neuer Plan' in September 1934. This 'New Plan' was designed as a prop for the Nazi policy of preparing for war on the side of international economic relations.

The 'Neuer Plan' introduced full government control of foreign trade and international payments, and was, in essence, based on the following fundamental principles. The quantity of imports was curtailed intensively, and a quota fixed for the volume of total imports, by Nazi authorities mindful of the desired switchover to war economy. Foreign trade, in a drastic reversal of earlier trading principles, was placed, vis-à-vis most trading partners, on a basis of bilateral agreements concerning trade and payments. The cardinal principle governing the 'Neuer Plan' required Germany to purchase possibly from countries only which did not insist on payments in foreign currency but were willing to accept German goods in exchange. Naturally, these changes

[36] It should be remarked here that it is impossible to subscribe to the view propounded in recent West German historical studies that recognizes Hitlerite economic policy as one for war only after 1936, or still worse, after 1938, and refuses to regard the measures taken in 1934 — including the Neuer Plan — as anything but parts of a foreign-exchange policy. This erroneous view is represented by Knut Borchardt in Ein neues Urteil über die deutsche Währungs- und Handelspolitik von 1931 bis 1938, published in Vierteljahrschrift für Sozial- und Wirtschaftsgeschichte. Vol. 46. December, 1959, No. 4.

[37] Cf. A. Schweitzer: *Die wirtschaftliche Wiederaufrüstung Deutschlands von 1934—36.* Zeitschrift für die gesamte Staatswissenschaft. 1958 No. 4, pp. 594—639.

in imports went hand in hand with the state-control of exports subsidies through barter transactions, and the introduction of a system of export premiums, some openly given, others disguised.[38]

The system of the 'Neuer Plan,' as implemented, provided an effective support for the economic programme of the Nazis. Import restrictions led to an upswing in the domestic output of strategic products. In conformity with a rigorious austerity policy (designed to permit the maximum utilization of domestic resources for the purpose of rearmament, *i. e.* preparation for war), the wide application of the bilateral principle restricted imports to raw materials of strategic importance and to foodstuffs that were not available in sufficient quantities in Germany. With the aid of payment through German deliveries, Schacht's economic policy solved the foreign-exchange problem, a cardial prerequisite of war economy, for, foreign-exchange expenditure having been severely cut down, the available reserves of foreign-exchange could be used to cover purchases of strategic raw materials unobtainable otherwise.

The foreign-trade and payments system of the 'Neuer Plan' automatically directed the flow of Germany's foreign trade towards Southeast Europe, making its countries the chief suppliers of raw materials for the German war economy. The rigorously applied new principles of German foreign trade led to an isolation of German economy, since the West European and oversea countries rejected bilateral agreements, were unwilling to accept German goods in payment and refused to do business on such basis. On the other hand, the Hitler—Schacht economic policy was eminently suited for deepening Germany's economic relations with countries of Southeast Europe. Years before, Southeast Europe has already been assigned an important part in German economic policy — a drive to conquer the market of these countries had figured high in the plans of German monopoly capital in the twenties. Under Nazism, Germany not only strove to increase her trade with these countries but also wanted to place her economic relations with them on new lines. Under the 'Neuer Plan' Southeast Europe was looked upon not merely as a market — for the time being, not even primarily as a market — but as the chief supplier of raw materials and food, as an organic, integral part of German war economy.

What were the factors that enabled the Nazis to count on Southeast Europe in their economic policy? They were able to do so above all because the Southeast-European states — most of them agricultural countries — regarded the actual difficulties of marketing their farm products as the chief source of serious economic troubles. There could be no doubt that these countries would welcome any initiative that might promote the marketing of their agricultural produce: the experience of earlier years had supplied ample evidence to the effect. This alone sufficed for the Danubian states readily to accept

[38] Erbe, op. cit., p. 71.

the bilateral principle so persistently pursued by the Germans. Considering moreover the fact that, besides Germany, these countries as debtor states were worst hit by the financial crisis, and that, beset by a serious shortage of foreign currency, it was these very countries that had interoduced the policy of foreign-exchange control, it will seem natural that they welcomed bilateral trade based on payments in kind.

The Southeast-European countries possessed that surplus of foodstuffs and raw materials — *e. g.* Yugoslav cereals and non-ferrous metals, Rumanian maize and oil, Hungarian meat, fats, cereals and bauxite, Bulgarian tobacco, *etc.* — which was needed for the German war machine already in the period of rearmament, and might become doubly necessary later on. These countries are not distant from Germany, can be reached by land routes, and there was no reason to fear that, in time of war, they might be cut off from Germany by a sea-blocade. Nazi Germany had sufficient reason, therefore, to look upon the countries of Southeast Europe as her economic and strategic storehouse. Furthermore, Germany as a great power was in a position to exert political pressure, and although at this early stage only Hungary did as yet side with Hitler's Germany, the Nazis could count on extending their political influence — through close economic relations, among other things — upon the other small, economically and politically weak nations also.

All this goes to show that the new economic policy launched under the 'Neuer Plan' furthered the German imperialist aspirations for world hegemony not only by promoting the German preparations for war, but also in that it began to tie the countries of Southeast Europe — always Stage One in German expansionist plans — to the German Nazi economy, to integrate them with the German 'Grossraumwirtschaft' system. That this was one of the objectives of the 'Neuer Plan' the German rulers left the world in no doubt. In 1934, one German wrote: "The co-ordinated development of the German internal economic area — the paramount task of the first year of the National Socialist Government — having been completed, the time has now come for us to regard the integration of the German economy with the organically emerging Grosswirtschafsraum as the principal task of our economic policy."[39]

The new trend in Nazi economic policy began about the middle of 1934 to be developed into an integrated system; yet some elements of it, or some

[39] The article entitled Möglichkeiten der Grossraumwirtschaft by Under-Secretary of State Hans Ernst Posse, published in Die nationale Wirtschaft, vol. 2, is quoted in Andersen, op. cit., p. 86. In his essay Die deutsche Aussenhandelspolitik von 1879 bis 1948 (published in Zeitschrift für die gesamte Staatswissenschaft, 1948, No. 1.) Heinrich Rittershausen, though pointing out that the economic policy aimed at the establishment of regional economy is connected with monopoly capital, grossly blurs the characteristics of the Nazi "Grossraumwirtschaft" by placing Hitlerite economic policy on a footing of equality with British economic policy as evolved at the Ottawa Conference. The apologetic nature of his arguments emerges still more clearly in his placing a sign of equality between Nazi policy of Grossraumwirtschaft and the attempts made by the small agricultural countries of Southeast Europe at forming agricultural blocs, claiming that both were working for the development of "Grossraumwirtschaft."

related concepts, had made their influence felt in German economic policy before. Already in the autumn of 1933, certain signs became apparent which indicated a relaxation of the rigid agricultural autarky towards the countries of Southeast Europe. It was at that time that leading officials of the German Foreign Ministry's Department of Economic Policy gave the first indication of their readiness to promote Hungary's agricultural exports by disguised premiums. The head of the Hungarian commercial delegation reported in a confidential memorandum that Vice-Chancellor Papen as well as Waldeck, the expert of Hungarian affairs in the Foreign Ministry, had thrown out some hints to the effect that "we should strike the German iron while it is hot and, the way things are now, we can get everything from the German Government, even things that were out of question before.«[40]

In November 1933, a German-Hungarian mixed committee was set up, and preliminary conversations were begun at the end of the month.

The opening of trade negotiations with the Germans coincided with Italian-Austrian-Hungarian negotiations of a similar nature. Among Italy, Austria and Hungary, closer economic relations had been established since 1931, and, under the so-called Brocchi system, disguised tariff concessions were reciprocally granted. At the negotiations between Mussolini and Gömbös in Rome in the summer of 1933, agreement was reached in principle that the strengthening relations would be developed into a mutual economic and political treaty. Preparatory work on this project also was done at the end of 1933 and at the beginning of 1934.

It was with some anxiety that Nazi Germany viewed these negotiations. Relations between her and Italy, in whom she saw a rival threatening her drive to Southeast Europe, were, as has been pointed out, somewhat strained about this time. It was feared that Hungary, very well suited as the base German expansion in Southeast Europe, might, under an Italian-Austrian-Hungarian tripartite agreement, and in return for substantial economic concessions by Italy, go too far in committing herself on the side of the latter. Now that the newly emergent German economic policy had brought up the issue of a revision of German economic policy with regard to the countries of Southeast Europe anyway, it now acquired urgency in respect of Hungary; in order to be able to counteract Italian influence. At a conference on 17 January, 1934, of the Nazi Ministers of Foreign Affairs, Finance and Economy, special emphasis was laid on the political importance of the intended negotiations with Hungary.[41] They noted that "the Italian Government, as it is well known, is experimenting with the establishment of an Italian-Austrian-Hungarian customs union. It is in our interest to secure strong political positions in Hungary so

[40] H. P. R. O., Dept. of Trade Policy, Min. of For. Affs., German file 640. I/3. Memorandum by István Winckler, of 11 October, 1933.

[41] D. Z. A. Potsdam. AA. Abt. II. 41285. Minutes taken at the conference.

as to counteract these endeavours."[42] The German minister in Budapest points out the following in a report sent to Berlin a few weeks later: the purpose of the intended German-Hungarian agreement is "the strengthening of Gömbös's internal and external position, and — beyond this — Hungary's economic independence of Italian influences."

Early in February, Mackensen, the German minister to Hungary, solicited an interview with Premier Gömbös, and gave him to understand in a diplomatic manner, that the German government would disapprove of a customs union of Italy, Austria and Hungary, news of which had been received. It is clear from Gömbös's reply to Mackensen that Hungarian government circles were aware of the benefits to be derived from the German-Italian rivalry; of the fact, namely, that in the actual situation, not only was Hungary anxious to secure the political and economic support of the two aggressive great powers but that both Germany and Italy were making intensive efforts to win over Hungary in their attempt to obtain hegemony in the Danube Basin. The Hungarians meant to make the most of this situation for obtaining economic concessions. "There can be no doubt," Gömbös is reported to have told Mackensen, "that, in view of the circumstance that the serious plight of agriculture is primarily due to the exceedingly low price of cereals, public opinion in Hungary is almost unanimous in regarding the creation of a large economic area as the road to the economic prosperity of this country. These sentiments are too strong to be ignored by the Hungarian government. He took therefore the opportunity which his conversation with Dollfuss had afforded, to discuss ways and means of further expanding the economic relations already existing between the two countries. These issues will be brought up also on the occasion (Italian Foreign Minister) Suvich's imminent visit to Budapest. However, much as the Hungarian Government feel themselves bound to meet the universal desire for the establishment of a wider economic area, they are ready to conduct negotiations with the Italians, so as to prevent the actual establishment of a formal customs union yet, such procedure is conditional on Germany pledging herself to take a substantial proportion of Hungarian agricultural surplus... The necessity of maintaining Hungarian-German friendship is too obvious to require emphasis. The further development of these at present very good relations depends on the attitude to be taken by Germany regarding German imports of Hungarian farm products."[43]

Against the background of the development of the Nazi's expansionist economic policy for Southeast Europe, and promoted by the actual political situation that had arisen about the turn of the years 1933—34, German-Hun-

[42] *Documents on German Foreign Policy* C. II., p. 372. The volume does not contain the minutes of the ministerial conference but only a memorandum made by a Thomsen, an official of the Reich Chancellor's Office.

[43] H. P. R. O., Pol. Dept., Min. of For. Affs. File 159, 21/7. 29,134.

garian trade negotiations were held in January-February 1934 and resulted in the conclusion of an agreement.

The competent German government organs took a decision in January 1934. It is stated there that "concerning the agreement that is to be concluded, it is the intention of Germany, that, by increasing the amount of reciprocal deliveries, the Hungarian economy be closely and inseparably integrated with German economy."[44] A resolution of fundamental importance was adopted according to which, contrary to the principles that had governed foreign trade before, the method of open tariff reductions which would have to be granted to other states as well wants to be replaced by a system of drawbacks so as to make German imports of Hungarian agricultural produce possible. Thus, while the high agricultural tariff were maintained, it was resolved to grant import concessions to Hungary alone, undertaking to pay back part of the import duties. To this end, a government fund of 15 million marks was to be created.[45]

The Hungarian government, although they considered Italian-Austrian relations to be of paramount importance from the point of view of economic policy, attached extraordinary signifiance to the agreement with Germany. The Hungarian-German agreement was looked upon as complementary to the expected Italian-Austrian agreement.

The negotiations were begun in mid-January. At the initial stage, the Hungarian Government submitted their list of demands which urged the annual exportation of 100.000 tons of wheat, 25,000 tons of barley, 50,000 tons of maize, 18,000 head of cattle, 10,000 horses ant other agricultural produce. As for the major items, the German delegation declared immediately that they were closely interdependent with import duty reductions which Hungary would grant for German manufactures. Though some dispute arose over certain items, and although the Germans were prepared to meet the principal Hungarian demand for the exportation of 100,000 tons of wheat only half-way (*i. e.* taking only 50,000 tons), contrary to earlier trade negotiations, agreement was reached quite easily over the majority of items. This was greatly facilitated by Hungary's readiness to meet nearly all demands concerning German manufactures.[46] The agreement was signed on 21 February and it took effect on 1 April as the Second Supplementary Agreement to the 1931 Commercial Treaty.

Articles 1 and 2 of the Second Supplementary Agreement laid down that the German Government pledged themselves to promote Hungarian exports,

[44] D. Z. A. Potsdam. AA. Abt. II. 41, 288.

[45] D. Z. A. Potsdam. AA. Abt. II. 41, 285.

[46] Cf. e. g. H. P. R. O. Dep. of Trade Policy Min. of For. Affs. German file. 640 i/3—15, 311. Under-Secretary of State Patai's telephone report of 31 January 1934 on new German demands for export openings. The Minister of Commerce hastened to meet these demands, although they were contrary to Hungarian interests. According to a German Legation report, Gömbös should have gone on record as saying that he was only protecting those industries which were important for rearmament — other industries fell behind agriculture in importance. — D. Z. A. Potsdam. AA. Abt. II. 41288.

and that the Hungarian Government should pay due regard to German interests for Hungarian imports. As the implementation of these provisions, a German-Hungarian agreement creating opportunities for exports to Germany of substantial quantities of Hungarian farm products was concluded for the first time since the first world war. The German commitment for the year 1934 included the importation of 50,000 tons of wheat, 75,000 tons of fodder grain (Barley and maize), 6,000 head of cattle for slaughter, 3,000 tons of pork, 1,500 tons of bacon and 3,000 tons of lard. Under the agreement, the German party bound themselves to take considerable quantities of Hungarian pulse crops, small seed as well as butter, eggs, etc.

But the Second Supplementary Agreement of 1934 did more than just granting export quotas for Hungarian agricultural products; contrary to the practice of earlier trade agreements, and in harmony with the resolutions adopted in January, the quota system was supplemented with a system of drawbacks. The drawback system meant that the Hungarian Government was able to appropriate 22 million pengoes a year for price subsidies on agricultural products exported to Germany. Under the circumstances, the subsidies articles became competitive on the German market, and at the same time, this arrangement ensured for the Hungarian latifundie marketing possibilities at a price higher than the price level of the world market. The government subsidies for items exported to Germany amounted to 4.2 to 5.5 pengoes per quintal of wheat, 4 pengoes for maize, 27 pengoes for cattle for slaughter, 56 pengoes for bacon, 74 pengoes for lard, etc. In annual total, this amounted to 6.5 million pengoes for cereals, 2 million pengoes for oil-seeds, 8.5 million pengoes for bacon and lard, and 5 million pengoes for other items.

The export subsidies paid by the Hungarian Government were refunded by the German State, that is to say, the drawbacks paid by the German Government from their own funds made it possible for the Hungarians to avail themselves of the export quotas.[47]

In return for the German concessions, the Hungarian Government eased or removed the restrictions on imports of German manufactures. Above all, the 1934 agreement put into force, in full measure, all those tariff concessions which had been stipulated earlier, in the commercial treaty of 1931. These concessions concerned, above all, paper products, textiles, metal products, machinery and a large number of consumer goods. The rate of tariff reductions amounted to as much as 20% to 30%.[48] Even more important, however, was the fact that the ban on imports was lifted, and that import quotas were granted for a number of items for which import licences had hardly ever been gran-

[47] H. P. R. O. Dep. of Trade Policy. Min. of For. Affs. German file. 640. I/3. For an account of the drawback system see also: D. Z. A. Potsdam. AA. Abt. II. 41288.
[48] D. Z. A. Potsdam. AA. Abt. II. 40833.

ted since 1931. Thus, import quotas were granted for yarns and threads, cotton fabrics, shoes, machinery, etc.

The Supplementary Agreement itself was supplemented by exchanges of several confidential diplomatic notes. The Germans, "in view of the remarkable favours granted by Hungary to encourage German exports to Hungary," undertook to take, over and above the quotas stipulated for in the agreement, quantities of butter, cheese, lard, eggs, bacon, etc.[49] There were several more exchanges of diplomatic notes in the course of the year, expanding German-Hungarian trade.[50]

The new trade agreement of February 1934 was complemented with a new payments agreement concluded in March. Under this agreement, German importers were enabled to pay for their purchases of Hungarian goods in German Marks, and the sums would have to be paid into the Reichbank, for the account of the National Bank of Hungary. Payments into the Reichsbank would be entered on two separate accounts, according to the type of Hungarian goods exported. From these sums, the National Bank of Hungary would pay the German exporters for their deliveries to Hungary. By the terms of the new clearing agreement, the excess which under the 1932 clearing agreement had accrued to the Germans from Hungarian liabilities for German goods would be excepted from the clearing procedure and be made the subject of a special settlement.[51]

No change was made in that clearing arrangement by which only 90 per cent of the countervalue of Hungarian exports would be used for paying for German deliveries, with the remaining 10 per cent beind made available, on the so-called *conto-ordinario,* for free disposal by the National Bank of Hungary. By the terms of the agreement, the balance of 10 per cent would not be used for the purpose of commodity clearing, but was to be employed to pay for other, foreign exchange, purchases. The new agreement divided the *conto ordinario* into two parts. One was the "*unbeschraenkte freie Quote*" (Unlimited free quote), which consisted in the fixed sum (M 2,000,000) part of the *conto ordinario.* This sum of 2 million marks the National Bank of Hungary was free to use for buying hard currency with, and that might be employed for any purpose whatever. Accumulating on the *conto ordinario* would be the remaining, greater, part of the 10 per cent, the "*beschraenkte freie Quote*" (limited free quota). Under the agreement, these sums could be used for purchasing German raw materials or transit goods — *i. e.* likewise foreign exchange items

[49] H. P. R. O. Dep. of Trade Policy Min. of For. Affs. German file 640 I/3.

[50] 23 July: Exchange of notes concerning extension of tariff reductions to include Hungarian export of horses; 28 April: exchange of notes to supplement tariff concession for rushes; 14 August: exchange of notes for further enlargement of rushes quota; 4 December: arrangement providing for Hungarian export of flax-seeds; etc. — H. P. R. O. Dep. of Trade Policy Min, of For. Affs. German file. p. 641. I/3-A.

[51] H. P. R. O. Dep. of Trade Policy Min. of For. Affs. 645. II/b. 55035/4—1934.

— not specified in the trade agreement.[52] Considering that the 1934 trade agreement was expected to bring about an upturn in Hungarian-German trade, the unlimited free part of the sum of marks was likely to acquire increasing importance in Hungary's foreign exchange policy.

Hungarian economists and experts were expecting a sweeping expansion of Hungarian-German trade to result from the conclusion of the supplementary agreement. An Institute of Economic Research estimate forecast an increase of 50 per cent, *i. e.* round 22 million pengoes.[53] The Ministry of Foreign Affairs Department of Economic Policy put the perspective increase of trade at a higher sum — 41 million pengoes, broken down into round 13 million for imports of German manufactures, and 28 million for exports of Hungarian farm products.[54]

In reality, the agreement of February 1934 boosted Hungarian-German trade beyond expectation. Hungarian agricultural exports increased by leaps and bounds. Items which had figured on top of the export list before, such as poultry and feathers, more than doubled on quantity from 1933 to 1934. The exported quantities of fresh fruits, fodder-crop seeds, etc. registered increases of one-third and 50 per cent, respectively. Apart from these, spectacular increases were registered by items that had been exported in extremely small quantities before: Lard and fats — more than 20-fold; cattle — more than 7-fold; wool — more than 6-fold; pulse crops — more than 4-fold; and butter — more than 3-fold. Hungarian exports as a whole were more than doubled between 1933 and 1934, and their value shot up by more than 46 million pengoes to a total of nearly 90 million.

While the rise in value of Hungarian exports far exceeded all expectations, the increase of Hungarian imports of German manufactures remained far below them, and their value, rising by a mere 2 million pengoes, totalled little more than 63 million pengoes.[55]

The tale that the above figures tell is not only one of a spectacular rise in Hungarian exports to Germany in 1934; they also reveal that, for the first time since World War I, annual balance of Hungarian-German trade showed an excess. Germany had strengthened her position as a trading partner of Hungary and, after imports, had now risen to almost the same level with Austria in exports as well. Germany's share in Hungarian exports went up from 11.2% in 1933 to 22.2% in 1934.

The turn that 1934 brought in Hungarian-German trade was hailed by the Hungarian ruling classes. *Köztelek,* the organ of the big landowners, commented: "...the expansion and pick-up in our exports to Germany will be a

[52] H. P. R. O. Dep. of Trade Policy Min. of For. Affs. German file. 642 I/3—A 80/1935.
[53] The Hungarian Institut of Economic Research's Report No. 22 of 1934, pp. 43—44.
[54] H. P. R. O. Dep. of Trade Policy Min. of For. Affs. German file. 640. III. Memorandum from Department IV. 22 February 1934.
[55] The Hungarian Statistical Year-book 1934, pp. 157—158.

shot in the arm to our agriculture, which is in the throes of a serious marketing crisis."[56]

What produced particularly much satisfaction was the fact that not only did the agreement with Germany open an outlet for the Hungarian latifundium (a most auspicious development in itself, considering the persistent buyer's market caused by the Agricultural crisis); but it also helped to counterbalance, in part, the slump of prices, ensured prices higher than the world market level. Undoubtedly, the Hungarian-German trade agreement went a long way towards enabling Hungary to recover from the agricultural crisis.

Of course, the Hungarian capitalists would complain that for this agreement, so advantageous for agriculture, industry had to foot the bill, because of the increased imports of German manufactures. Nevertheless, they welcomed the agreement, as they believed that, by improving the conditions of the latifundia, it would put some pep into economic life as a whole, speeding up recovery from the crisis.

Thus, in heavily agricultural Hungary, the big capitalists, too, were interested in getting the agricultural crisis cleared up. Besides, Hungarian official economic policy was quite lavish in its use of means and devices beneficial to industrial capital — the bans on imports, the whole system of foreign exchange control and the foreign currency policy of the National Bank of Hungary alike were designed to promote the big capitalist interests.[57]

In view of the fact that official economic policy was far-reachingly adapted to capitalist interests, the industrialists could not possibly protest now that an opportunity presented itself for concluding a commercial agreement that was so important and advantageous for the large landed interests. They could not have protested all the less because they considered the economic agreement to be of *political* value, hailing it as a step towards a German—Hungarian political alliance. In this sense, an organ of GyOSz (Hungarian initials for National Association of Manufacturers) commented: "If, despite the sacrifices (tariff reductions, expansion of import quotas) it is required to accept, Hungarian industry does not toll the alarm-bell, it is because.... it views the conclusion of the Hungarian—German agreement as a brilliant political move by Hungarian nationalist statecraft to counter Czechoslovak policies."[58]

Government circles in Nazi Germany regarded the new economic policy directed at the Balkan states — and, in that context, the new Hungarian—German agreement of 1934 — as evidence to the effect that Germany and the

[56] Köztelek, 25 February 1934.

[57] No attempt is made in this paper at a searching analysis of the ways in which Hungarian official economic policy benefited big capitalists interests. For a treatment of this subject see I. Berend and Gy. Ránki: *Magyarország gyáripara a második világháború előtt és a háború időszakában (1933—1944)*, Budapest 1958. pp. 17—40; in English: *The Development of Hungarian Manufacturing Industry before and during World War II (1933—1944)* Budapest 1960.

[58] Honi Ipar, 1 March 1934.

small countries of Southeast Europe are interdependent and economically complementary. They tried to present their policy as a "friendly gesture," "generous concession" to these small nations at the time they were beset by economic depression. The much-publicised views of the Nazi politicians and the entire German economic literature were formulated by Ernst Wagemann, director of the German Institute of Economic Research, who, in a book (*Der neue Balkan* — The New Balkans), asks, "Who but Germany could have stretched out a hand" to these countries in their need? and claims that by means of making her assistance available to them Germany drew the countries of Southeast Europe "into the trail of her impetuous development".[59] This German view is formulated still more pointedly in the following passage: "Germany was the only industrial nation that, in order to help the agricultural countries of Southeast Europe, magnanimously favoured and muliplied its purchases of the products of these countries."[60]

The claim that the 1934 German—Hungarian agreement as though the purchase by Germany of Hungarian agricultural surpluses, and, in particular, her payment of prices higher than the world market level, had been, in effect, a politically motivated act to accept sacrifices is, as a matter of fact, yet to find its refutation in Hungarian political economy and historical literature. Contemporary economic writing, quite naturally, did not attempt to go beyond echoing the German propagande line unequivocally idealising German—Hungarian commercial relations. Neither has a refutation come from authors who did not fully identify themselves with the German attitude, for their criticism consisted largely in complaints about the disadvantages arising from the agreement for Hungary. Historical research since the war, insofar as it has touched upon the issue, has tended to dwell on the serious political consequences of German-Hungarian economic cooperation and, in the economic field, to point out merely that, for all the benefits it be stowed upon the latifundia, the agreement had a damaging effect on Hungarian economic life because it retarded industrial development and helped to preserve Hungary's economic vulnerability.

Searching analysis, examination of the 1934 agreement in the context of German economic policy as a whole, as well as investigation of available Public Record Office material on the subject, make it sufficiently clear, we believe, that by signing the agreement the German Government did in point of fact make no economic concessions whatever and, far from accepting sacrifices, did, in fact, strike a most profitable bargain.

As we intend on the next few pages to carry our analysis of the true nature of the agreement, so crucially important for the subsequent develop-

[59] E. WAGEMANN: *Der neue Balkan.* Hamburg 1939. pp. 119—121.
[60] H. GROSS: *Die wirtschaftliche Bedeutung Südosteuropas für das Deutsche Reich*, Stuttgart— Berlin 1938. p. 18.

ment of Hungarian-German relations, into the very economic sphere, it would be irrelevant now to go into details about the political considerations which must have guided Nazi Germany in concluding the agreement, and which are, of course, very important factors in forming a judgment of the nature of the agreement. In concluding this economic agreement, the Nazis were led by their desire to extend and safeguard their political influence; and although the Nazi politicians, and economists voicing the opinions of the former, strove to disguise or deny the fact,[61] today, viewed against the background of the crushing historical experience of the second world war, that objective of Nazi policies may be taken as proven without any doubt whatever.

There is no doubt that the 1934 agreement was aimed, above all, precisely at laying foundations for the German expansionist *political* aspirations. But that does by no means imply that the Nazi Government did not combine that move with steps to guarantee German *short-term* economic interests. As for their long-term political objectives, the Nazis wanted to attain them by trying to secure the possibility of exploiting the resources of the Southeast European countries to maximum capacity already in the given situation, and of utilising them for promoting their policy of rearmament.

In speaking of German economic "sacrifices" and "gestures", people usually refer to two circumstances to support their thesis — the purchase by Germany of Hungarian agricultural surpluses and the payment by her of prices above the world market level; therefore, we shall turn our attention to these matters in the passages that follow. As to the providing of a market, we have already pointed to Germany's extremely adverse commercial and foreign exchange conditions, which made it increasingly impossible for her to meet her needs for agricultural products, as she had been doing in earlier years, from purchases made in oversea countries. The prices of oversea products might by a good deal lower — it was of no avail as long as you had to have foreign exchange to pay for most of them; foreign exchange was something Germany had in short supply, and her available meagre stocks, or sources, of foreign exchange were set aside for making payments for purchases of strategic raw materials. In meeting her needs for food, Nazi Germany, as has been pointed out at the beginning of this chapter, was of necessity becoming increasingly dependent on imports from such countries as were ready to take German manufactures in exchange for their deliveries on a bilateral, clearing basis. This circumstance alone would show convincingly that the readiness of Nazi government circles to take Hungarian agricultural surplus produce under the 1934 agreement, far from being motivated by indulgence in economic matters, did in fact spring also from their pursuance of a vital economic interest of Germany.

[61] Cf. e.g. R. Weiner Krugmann: *Südosteuropa und Großdeutschland.* R. P. 1939. P. 13.

The afore-mentioned circumstance puts a different complexion on questions of price. Whereas, in the 1920s, price had been the key factor in German purchases, now, under the changed conditions of the Nazi era, as far as the Nazi Government was concerned, the importance of prices was overshadowed by the actual shortage of foreign currency. For the German economy, the chance to buy cheap was less advantageous a proposition — and this was indeed formulated as a principle governing economic policy[62] — than the chance to purchases on a barter basis, with no foreign currency.[63] Buying agricultural products at higher prices from the the countries of Southeast Europe, because it eliminated the expenditure of foreign currency and — which was inseparable — because it promoted German industrial exports, was an arrangement as advantageous for Germany from a directly economic point of view also as she could possibly make in the given situation.

The sources from which the subsidy was derived which served to ensure a price level higher than the world market are by no means an irrelevant factor in forming a judgment of this matter. It is known from the facts of the agreement that the sum the Germany Government pledged themselves to pay as drawback during the year 1934 amounted to 22 million pengoes. Yet, in actual fact, this sum did not burden the German economy, for the Nazi Government very cleverly linked the bounties on Hungarian agricultural exports with the mobilisation of the German assets that had been frozen in Hungary. German capitalists, as has been pointed out, had a claim for some 50 to 60 million pengoes on Hungarian debtors. These sums, because of the foreign exchange control policy introduced in Hungary in 1931 and of a transfer moratorium that had been granted, had been unavailable for the German creditors. Now, in 1934, it was from these frozen German assets in Hungary that the German Government created the necessary fund for paying bounties on Hungarian agricultural exports. The German capitalists were delighted to have the opportunity to sell these claims, which must have seemed to them as good as lost, to the German Government for cash (although at a reduction on the nominal price of 25%). In this manner, the German assets which had accumulated in pengoes on a separate account of the National Bank of Hungary, but which were non-transferable, had passed into the hands of the German State. It was this sum that the Nazi Government made available to the Hungarian Government as a fund from which to pay bounties on exports. Thanks to the drawback

[62] Cf. Lossos op. cit., p. 97.

[63] In view of the fact that since September 1933, when the Food Supply Act (Naehrstand) took force, the price control policy as a whole had been taken over by the State, and that the price level was entirely independent of the world market, there was no reason to fear that Hungarian farm products, lower-priced, in spite even of the bounty system, than the German ones, would force down prices. German home market prices stood on a fair higher level, even so, than the Hungarian export prices. — Cf. W. Darre: *A Német Birodalom és a délkeleteurópai államok együttműködése a mezőgazdaság terén* (Cooperation between the German Reich and the Southeast European States in the Field of Agriculture). Budapest, 1940.

system used for maintaining a high price level, therefore, the German economy could now get what it had been unable to obtain before — mobilisation of the German assets that had been frozen in Hungary. In this way, under pretext of aiding Hungarian agriculture, Germany got hold of assets which — as we have seen it happen in the cases of most other creditor nations — otherwise she would never have been able to obtain the release of.

Thus, the maintenance of the higher-than-the-world-market price level involved no burden on the German economy. Although the German Government spent 17 million marks in buying up the frozen German assets, the full sum was paid to German capitalists who had assets in Hungary, that is to say, these payments did not go to any foreign country. On the other hand, even this expenditure, which, on a national scale, constituted no loss whatever, was recovered, since the boost in foreign trade that resulted from the drawbacks brought in a duty excess of about 10 million marks. Add to this the fact that German manufactures exported to Hungary, under the clearing arrangement, in exchange for Hungarian farm products could be sold at prices higher than the world market level, without export subsidies, and it will become unambiguously clear that the German Government really accepted no material sacrifices under the supplementary trade agreement of 1934.[64]

An analysis of the circumstances and facts of the agreement shows convincingly, therefore, that, however advantageous it appeared for the Hungarian big landowners, and although it did help them sell their surplus produce, the German—Hungarian trade agreement greatly promoted the economic interests of Nazi Germany from the outset. It was not long before, as the agreement began to function, this point became still more markedly manifest

In the foregoing, we have attempted to show the way the German—Hungarian agreement of 1934 — which was of paramount significance as an expedient promoting the expansion of economic and political ties between the German and the Hungarian ruling classes — was made part and parcel of the German expansion through Southeast Europe by furthering German short-term economic intereste. It follows even from what has been set forth so far that, as the Germans repeatedly declared, the conclusion of this agreement did not mean, of course, that Germany was establishing closer economic ties with their Hungarian political allies alone. The agreement which was signed in February 1934 was only the first of a number of similar agreements soon to be concluded with the other countries of Southeast Europe.[65] When all is said and done, the German—Hungarian agreement cannot therefore be regarded as

[64] H. P. R. O. Dep. of Trade Policy Min. of For. Affs. German file. 642. I—3—A. 50811/4 1955, 332/4 adm. res. 1935. Confidential report of 6 Feb. 1935 and a memorandum of 19 Oct. 1935.

[65] New commercial agreements were concluded with Yugoslavia, in May 1934, and with Rumania, in March 1935, while the agreement concluded with Bulgaria at an earlier date was likewise revised in 1934. Cf. KRUGMANN, op. cit., pp. 76, 83 and 85.

anything else but the first step in the practical application of the Nazi policy of "Großraumwirtschaft". In this context, the German student of this agreement makes the to-the-point observation that it was "the prototype of agreements aimed at the *Großraumwirtschaft*".[66]

Thus the German—Hungarian trade agreement of 1934 created the forms under which the Hungarian economy was gradually integrated with the Nazi "*Lebensraum*". However, the agreement, the year 1934, was only the beginning. The struggle was at the time still going on for hegemony in the Danube Valley, which found expression in other agreements besides the agreement with Germany. A few weeks after the conclusion of the agreement with Germany, Hungary, still predominantly pro-Italian in her foreign policy, in spite of the growing pro-German trend, signed the so-called Roman Protocols. The political treaty of the Italian-Austrian-Hungarian Tripartite Agreement, concluded in Rome, March 1934, was supplemented in May with an economic agreement. The Agreement, which had been initiated by Mussolini, was intended to consolidate Italy's leading position in the Southeast European area, in opposition to the French-leaning Little Entente states and in the face of the increasingly intensive German expansionist aspirations. Italian Fascism, therefore, meant to give the Agreement an anti-German edge as well. Austria, too, saw in the Agreement a barrier in the way of Hitler's ambition for an Anschluß. The Hungarian ruling classes wanted from the very first to take off the anti-German edge of the Agreement by mediating between Hitler and Mussolini. For them, the tripartite agreement was a political weapon against the Little Entente which dovetailed perfectly with the alliance with Germany. Shortly before the signing of the Roman agreement, Mackensen, the German Minister in Budapest, was invited to appear before Horthy, who, as the minister reported, told him that "So long as he remains in his post, the pivot of Hungarian policies — that is, friendship with Germany — shall remain unchanged as the fundamental principle."[67] And on the day following the signing of the Italian-Austrian-Hungarian tripartite agreement, Premier Gömbös, still in Rome, asked the German ambassador, Hassel, to talk with him, gave him detailed information on the agreement, emphasising that it was in no way directed against Germany. He told Hassel that, in the words of the said report, "He had told Mussolini that Hungary had a friend both north and south of the Danube — Germany and Italy. These two factors had equal ties with Hungary".[68]

The same thougth Gömbös evolved in a still more graphic form in an address in Parliament: "Hungary feels called to pursue her own independent

[66] ANDRESEN, op. cit., p. 93.

[67] *Documents on German Foreign Policy*. C.II. Minister Mackensen's confidential report of 28 February 1934.

[68] Ibid., p. 628.

policies in the Carpathian Basin, relying, south of the Danube, on Italy, and, north of it, on Germany."[69]

One reason why the Rome Tripartite Agreement could at this time still form main pillar of Hungarian foreign policy was the circumstance that it seemed well-founded economically. It was laid down in the agreement that the three countries should assist one another in their efforts to boost exports, in particular, Hungarian exports of wheat. Under the commercial agreement, which was to take force on 1 July 1934, Italy was bound to take 100,000 tons of wheat annually, at prices higher than the world market level, and Austria pledged herself to purchase 220,000 tons of wheat and wheat flour, respectively. Over and above this quantitiy, Italy held out the prospect of purchasing another 100,000 tons, or, if she failed to do so, to help marketing that quantity by granting subsidies in the form of bounties. The Rome Agreement, on account of the opening for 320,000 tons of wheat guaranteed by the Rome Protocols as compared with the 50,000 tons stipulated in the Hungarian-German agreement, as it concerned Hungary's chief export item, promised to acquire greater importance than the agreement with Germany. This was underlined by the fact that the agreement was supplemented with a secret preferential agreement, which provided for the exportation of more Hungarian farm products, such as livestock, egges, fruit, vegetables, etc. These export favours were compensated for by the Hungarian Government by creating import possibilities for industrial products, mainly in the lines of timber, paper and textiles.[70]

In the course of 1933-34, the Hungarian ruling classes managed to build up the system of alliances, both in the political and the economic spheres, which for several years they had been busy laying the foundations of. Under that system, which rested on the two totalitarian great powers, Italy and Germany would (so they envisaged) have complemented — and balanced — each other in an ideal way as two forces working in Hungary's foreign and economic policies. Such complementary and counter-balancing functions were, indeed, still actually present in 1934. However, the vast differences in economic, political as well as military power which existed between the two totalitarian great powers (and which became still more accentuated as the strength of German Nazism built up over the years), spelled failure for these two-pillar foreign and economic policies from the outset. As Italy's political influence waned, and her economic might diminished, in 1935—36, as a result of the war in Abyssinia; and as the Tripartite Agreement of Rome gradually lost its significance; so did the real function of the German-Hungarian agreement as an instrument for tying Hungary to Nazi Germany in the economic and the political fields come into play with increasing force.

[69] *Magyarország és a második világháború* (Hungary and World War II), Budapest 1959. pp. 36—37.

[70] Basch, The Danube Basin and the German Economic Sphere. London 1944., pp. 158—160; *Year-Book of Hungary* 1934, p. 118.

II

The German Occupation of Hungary

"Every Hungarian, whether a peasant, a workman, or a soldier, who by his activity reduces our burdens, strengthens the führer's reserves within the Reich. Every Hungarian who bleeds for us, reduces our own losses and reinforces our own reserves for further military efforts",[1] stated the report of SS Standartenführer Edmund Veesenmayer who had been sent to Budapest in autumn, 1943, by the German Ministry of Foreign Affairs to study the political situation.

From the autumn of 1943, the German military command and the German Ministry of Foreign Affairs had been viewing developments in Hungary with a certain uneasiness. A decision was made to take violent action should it appear necessary. The aim of Veesenmayer's mission was to sound the possibilities and elaborate the best political methods for the purpose.

Veesenmayer expounded his opinion of the Hungarian situation in an extraordinarily extensive report. He emphasized that, first of all, the time of occupation would have to be carefully chosen. At the moment it was still too early, the time would be more appropriate when the Red Army will have made a further advance. Veesenmayer made it clear that a Hungarian solution would have to be found, so that certain sovereign rights of the Hungarian state should be maintained despite occupation. The best method would be for Hitler to invite Horthy and . . ."by skilful application of the method of honey-cake and the whip" persuade him to appoint a new government whose head would naturally have to be designated by the Germans. Veesenmayer indicated the arguments suited to convince Horthy. The Bolshevist menace was to be emphasized, then a few anti-Hapsburg statements might follow, and finally a promise could be held out to spare so-called "court Jews" (Hofjuden).

When Horthy was convinced — and Veesenmayer entertained no doubt as to its success — a German plenipotentiary would have to be sent to Hungary.

In February, 1944, Horthy wrote a letter to Hitler repeating his request that the Hungarian formations on the eastern front be allowed to return to

[1] Public Record Office, London. German Foreign Ministry (GFM) 2—93—106872.

Hungary. Horthy's letter explained that Hungarian troops would go into action against Soviet forces along the line of the Carpathians.[2] This letter accelerated Hitler's preparations, although on February 10 the Hungarian government decided to issue an order of general mobilization when the Soviet army reached Lemberg.[3] The Hungarian government continued to take utmost care to maintain friendly connections with the Germans. In February, 1944, feverish preparations to celebrate the 50th anniversary of Kossuth's death were already in full swing, for these celebrations were to be devoted to the idea of Hungarian independence. The Reichsjugendführer, the leader of youth in the Reich, was also sent an invitation to the festivities of March 15.[4]

These moves failed to influence the German preparations for the occupation of the country. From the autumn of 1943, not only the German Ministry of Foreign Affairs watched Hungarian developments with growing concern; the general staff, too, thought that the Hungarian government was inclined to make an agreement with the western powers. Although they were informed about the negotiations with the western powers, they could not tell whether these talks had not progressed beyond the stage known to them. Their opinion was that . . ."it was only on account of the enemy's refusal that the efforts tolerated and even supported by the Hungarian government failed to succeed".[5]

It became clear to the Germans that even if the Kállay government refrained from withdrawing the troops from the Soviet front, no further units could be expected, while steadily increasing difficulties were encountered in connection with economic supplies.[6]

The defection of Italy matured the decision that precaution was indicated lest Hungary and Rumania follow a similar course; therefore, the Wehrmachtsführungsstab submitted a project on September 30, 1943 for the occupation of Hungary and the disarmament of the Hungarian forces. The project provided the participation of Rumanian and Slovak troops in the occupation.

The idea was to divide the country into three areas of military operation. The first zone was to include Transdanubia and the territory between the rivers Danube and Tisza with Budapest; this operation would be carried out by the Wehrmacht. Eastern Hungary was to be a theatre of Rumanian military opera-

[2] *Horthy Miklós titkos iratai* (Secret Documents of Miklós Horthy). Edited and enlightened by M. Szinai and L. Szücs. Budapest, 1963. p. 409.

[3] GFM 2—99, 109743. Report of Jagow (German Minister in Hungary) from February 10, 1944.

[4] GFM 2—99, 109766. February 23, 1944.

[5] *Kriegstagebuch des Oberkommandos der Wehrmacht* vol. IV, January 1, 1944—May 22, 1945. Eingeleitet und erläutert von P. E. Schramm. (Kriegstagebuch des OKW). Frankfurt am Main 1961, p. 181. The military aspects of the German occupation have treated by J. Kun in *The Preparation and the Execution of the German Occupation of Hungary* (September, 1953—March, 1944) Hadtörténelmi Közlemények, 1963, I.

[6] *Kriegstagebuch des OKW*, p. 198. These views are mentioned as the antecedents of Operation Margarethe.

tions. In the third zone, North-Eastern Hungary, resistance, if any, was to be put down by joint operations of German and Slovak forces.[7]

In the first plan, the details of occupation were laid down for the first and the third zone; the required contingents could be concentrated in eight days to attack Hungary from the south, the west, and the north. Designating the divisions to be employed, the project laid it down that notwithstanding the political hazards involved by the use of Rumanian troops, in view of the balance of forces their cooperation could not be dispensed with.[8] It was decided that the attitude towards the Hungarian army was to depend on the political situation; should the Hungarian so-called occupational divisions on Soviet territory have to be disarmed, they were to be employed for labour service.

The project soon underwent numerous changes. The offensive of the Red Army pinned down large forces, while Hungarian developments were such as not to make the operation urgent; without abandoning the plan, it was decided to desist from designating the units which were to take part in the occupation.

Moreover, on November 7 the general staff declared that owing to the necessity of fresh eastern reinforcements the available forces would be insufficient to ensure occupation in case of resistance. By November 11 a new project was drawn up, the execution of which could be started on December 10. It was now the general intention to carry out the occupation with German forces. Unless Rumania and Hungary made simultaneous attempts at defection, the plan seemed practicable.

For the time being, no order was issued for its execution, but General Foertsch, chief of the south-eastern army staff, was informed about the project at the beginning of December.[9]

At the end of January and the beginning of February, Operation Margarethe I was once more supervised by the general staff and it came again to the conclusion that, without Rumanian cooperation, the available forces did not suffice for an occupation. The number of SS units which were to take part in the operation was increased, but even so it was found necessary to bring about a split in the Hungarian army (stationed in Hungary) estimated to total about 360,000.

On his visit to Hitler (on February 26—28, 1944) Antonescu, the Rumanian fascist prime minister, was informed about the imminent occupation of Hungary and the possible participation of Rumania. The general was very glad but, naturally, weighed the question only from the aspect of Rumanian territorial claims. Since he refused to relinquish them, the führer deemed it

[7] Ibid. p. 190.
[8] Ibid.
[9] Not long afterwards Margarethe II was devised for the occupation of Rumania. In this case Hungarian cooperation was contemplated.

preferable to dispense with Rumanian cooperation. The only reassuring feature of Antonescu's visit was that all fears of a Rumanian defection were now allayed so that the plans for Margarathe II could be set aside and full energy concentrated on the execution of Operation Margarethe I.

On February 28, 1944, Hitler gave orders for the elaboration of the final variant of Margarethe I with due regard to be paid to the following points.

1. Deployment of troops was to be preferably carried out inside the country (Hungary), in the form of transit contingents (in the manner of "the wooden horse of Troy").

2. Military movements should be camouflaged as if they served some other purpose.

3. Assaulting units should be reinforced with parachutists, armoured and motorized forces, several police units, and the Luftwaffe.

4. The most important military-economic and political targets should be marked out.[10]

The concentration of motorized forces was accordingly started in the outskirts of Vienna on February 29. At the same time it was decided what troops to send, apparently on transit through Hungary — partly from the West, partly from the Balkans — that they might go into action at the appointed time.

Military operations were originally planned for the end of March, but on March 3 Hitler suddenly declared this to be too late, and he accelerated preparations by throwing in another two divisions. The general staff did not think the troops could be drawn up before March 12, but the attack could be launched only with limited forces even at that date. This plan was approved by Hitler on March 4. On the 4th and 5th, appropriate orders were issued to the army and to various SS units. The orders said that troops were to be concentrated for the purpose of manoeuvres in the environment of Vienna.

The successful attack of Soviet troops on March 4 against Tarnopol created new difficulties. Part of the contingents destined for Hungary had to be directed to the Soviet front. They were replaced by units withdrawn from the western occupational forces. Hitler wanted to finish with the occupation of Hungary as soon as possible in order to be able to move the forces deployed here to the eastern front at the earliest moment.

On March 7, General Foertsch re-appeared at Hitler's G. H. Q. The general who was to conduct military operations, indicated March 18 as the possible zero hour. It was decided that the end of the week, Sunday, March 19, was more favourable for the occupation.

On March 8, General Foertsch set up his headquarters at Vienna from where he was to command the military operations against Hungary. Being

[10] *Kriegstagebuch des OKW*, p. 193.

afraid of betrayal, the Germans refrained from informing the other possible participants. It was deemed enough to occupy the first operational zone of the original project, i.e. the area to the river Tisza.

The operational order, issued on March 12, foresaw an attack from four sides against Budapest and emphasized the necessity of disarming the Hungarian forces and of putting down mercilessly any resistance. Two divisions and various SS units were to go into action from the Bánát, from Újvidék and Eszék; two other divisions were to attack from the west, the area of Croatia and Slavonia. Unlike the original plan, the main attack was to be launched not from the south but from the northeast whence three divisions, including motorized and armoured units as well as auxiliary troops, were to advance with the support of a few regiments from Slovakia.

The plan, prepared with utmost precision, contained accurate instructions concerning the conduct of the troops in Hungary and how to win over Hungarian soldiers, furthermore concerning the temporary suspension of oil supplies from Rumania, and the diversion of railway connection with the troops in the Balkan to the Zagreb—Belgrade line, etc.[11]

General Stahl was detailed to the general headquarters of General Foertsch to supervise the distribution of the plunder. It was decided to take only military booty, "in order to cause the possibly smallest economic disturbance", because it was necessary that economic activity should continue undisturbed. First 100, than 250 aeroplanes were to make a flight over Budapest and to throw down propaganda material.

Was the Hungarian government aware of the impending German occupation? There can be no doubt that the possibility of such a move had been envisaged by Premier Kállay since the autumn of 1943. It figured in his thoughts as a factor which was to be avoided if possible.

At the beginning of 1944, the possibility of German occupation ceased to be a theoretical contingency. During Papen's visit to Budapest in January, 1944, Kállay remarked on the fact that reports of German agents working in Hungary had fallen into his hands, and that they contained accounts of talks with arrow-cross men who demanded the occupation of Hungary and its integration into the Reich. Papen naturally declared the whole thing to be a gross forgery.[12] However, by the beginning of March, 1944, Kállay was already in possession of more positive data on the imminence of German occupation. Extensive concentration of troops had been reported from the Burgenland. Kállay's cabinet never even thought of taking preventive measures or putting up defence. It was found enough to address an inquiry to some officials of the German legation asking for an explanation of the concentration

[11] *Kriegstagebuch des OKW*, pp. 196—197.
[12] GFM 2—99, 109738. Record of Ribbentrop, January 7, 1944.

of troops. In reply to an inquiry made by the deputy chief of the Hungarian general staff, Fütterer, the German air attaché, first denied all knowledge of any such move; on the instructions of the Wehrmacht high command he later gave a reassuring reply, explaining that German troops were being trained in the vicinity of the Hungarian border; he "indignantly" rejected all insinuations concerning any plan concerning the suspected use of these troops. He went so far as to go into the offensive, emphasizing that the evident excitement of the Hungarian government over German military moves gave food for reflection. The Hungarian deputy chief of staff, Bajnóczy, was terrified at the idea of having offended the "great ally"; he hurriedly declared that it was not the soldiers who were to blame for the assumption, since the general staff felt no uneasiness, and that only civilian circles showed some nervousness.[13]

The German reply can hardly have been reassuring for realistic politicians. However, Kállay and his entourage thought that . . ."an invasion of Hungary by the Germans would be a strategical mistake politically, and a military blunder tactically". Therefore, the Germans could not be making preparations for occupying the country, they wanted only to make threats. According to Kállay's book, Keresztes-Fischer (Minister for Home Affairs) and Szombathelyi (Chief of the General Staff) shared his opinion that for the moment there was no reason to fear a German occupation.[14]

The question arises here as to whether Hungarian politicians could really have been so blind. Although in knowledge of the facts there is little justification for attributing too much foresight to any member of Kállay's government, it is beyond doubt that they were not, and could not be, so undiscerning as not to reckon with a military occupation. What Kállay wanted to do in his memoirs was to explain why nothing was done to defend the country, although positive information about the concentration of German forces had been received 10 to 12 days before the occupation. Kállay at least deemed it necessary to offer some explanation for this inexplicable impotence. Not so Horthy: he was content to record the negative answers of the German minister and the military attaché.[15]

Kállay mentions another reason why he was unable to do anything to defend the country: there were two army corps in a fighting condition, one in the northern Carpathians, the other in Transylvania; their removal to the west would have taken several weeks. This argument does not sound very convincing

[13] GFM 2—99, 109813. Jagow's report dated March 13, 1944.

[14] M. Kállay: *Hungarian Premier. A personal account of a nation's struggle in the Second World War*. New York, 1954. pp. 408—409.

[15] M. Horthy: *Emlékirataim* (Memoirs). Buenos Aires, 1953. p. 249. According to Adonyi "We watched with dismay the events at various sectors of the Hungarian border, particularly in the area of the Burgenland; news of the concentration of German forces, started in February, 1944, were promptly passed on by the general staff to the government" (F .Adonyi: *A magyar katona a második világháborúban* (The Hungarian Soldier in the Second World War). Klagenfurt, 1954. p. 59.)

either, though it is put forward also by Adonyi.[16] It is hard to believe that the necessary regrouping of forces would have taken weeks, since the mobilization and deployment of the attacking German forces was accomplished in a week. On the other hand, Kállay himself says that he did not expect an *immediate* occupation; if this is true the question arises why he did not try to counterbalance the menacing moves of the German army by a concentration of Hungarian troops.

Had the Hungarian government resolved to resist, it had means to do so. The first news of a concentration of German troops arrived at the end of February, so that more than three weeks elapsed until the attack. During this time the forces might have been regrouped; according to German sources there were 350,000 men in arms at the moment in Hungary, though their equipment was inferior to that of the Germans. Resistance would not have been hopeless because the Soviet Army was barely a hundred kilometres from the border, and the Germans had grave difficulty in mustering the units required for the occupation. Apart from the units on the Soviet front, Hungary disposed over two armoured divisions, one cavalry and nine infantry divisions, as well as two mountain brigades at the beginning of 1944. Of these, one armoured and two infantry divisions as well as the two mountain brigades had been marched to the Carpathians in February, but even so there were inside the country nine so-called active divisions which might moreover have drawn on certain reserve divisions. Even without calling up any more reserves, the Hungarian army would have numerically equalled the German forces of occupation. However, the Hungarian government did nothing. So on March 14, when Foertsch's staff met for a last conference in Vienna, the German military commanders were satisfied that the action could be speedily accomplished, since the Hungarians had so far not taken any measure and because no organized resistance could be improvised.[17]

The German Ministry of Foreign Affairs had however not yet abandoned their earlier view, shared by Veesenmayer, that the situation was by no means so hopeless in Hungary as to call for a military attack as the only solution. The Hungarian experts of the Ministry and the Security Service maintained that it would be better — and certainly more expedient and useful for the Germans — to try to take over the power together with the pro-German elements of the Hungarian ruling classes and government circles so that the occupation should be carried out along these lines. The aim should not be an open military move but the acquisition of Hungary by evolution (i.e. not by violence). This conception allotted the key role to Horthy because if he could be retained in his office the Germans might expect

[16] Adonyi, op. cit., p. 60.
[17] *Kriegstagebuch des OKW*, p. 198.

a) a pro-German Hungary with a politically stable internal situation;

b) the Hungarian Army and armed police detachments would remain at the disposal of the Reich;

c) the total economic exploitation of the entire Hungarian territory would be ensured;

d) the acquisition of Rumanian and Hungarian troops would save numerous German divisions.

"These far-reaching results can be achieved by relatively simple means" the report submitted to Hitler continued; the starting point was to be a message from the Führer addressed personally to Horthy who was known to have always been deeply impressed by the Führer's personality . . . "legalized by the Regent, a government should be formed on a wide basis, including the right wing of the existing government, the Hungarian Revival Party, the Hungarian National Socialist Party, as also the arrow-cross people . . ."[18]

The memorandum was essentially a repetition of Veesenmayer's earlier suggestions. Veesenmayer had, on December 19, already stated his opinion concerning the occupation. He had emphasized that Horthy was quite useful from the German viewpoint, and that only his clique would have to be got rid of, of whom Bethlen — who were premier between 1921 and 1931, and had a great political influence — and Keresztes-Fischer were "dangerous". In his opinion, the situation in Hungary demanded rapid intervention, but the problem would have to be solved with Horthy and preferably with Imrédy the prominent fascist, the leader of the Hungarian Revival Party — as prime minister.[19] Hitler discussed the problem once more with Ribbentrop and Himmler in the afternoon of March 15. It was decided to make use of both methods by trying to obtain Horthy's consent to a military occupation. Horthy was invited the same day to pay Hitler a visit not later than the 18th (the zero hour of military operations having been timed for the 19th, as pointed out before).[20]

Early in the afternoom of March 15 Ribbentrop instructed minister Jagow by wire to call on Horthy that same evening. He was to inform Horthy that Hitler was staying at Obersalzberg and was discussing military matters with the heads of the allied powers. Antonescu and Pavelič had already been to Hitler, and the Bulgarian prime minister was expected. Horthy was requested to come too. During his visit also the still unanswered letter of February

[18] *Procès des grands criminels de guerre devant le Tribunal Militaire Internationale. (Procès . . .)* Nuremberg, 1947. Published in Hungarian by L. Zsigmond: *Két dátum* (Two Dates) Történelmi Szemle, 1958, p. 226. The mentioned parties were openly fascist and nazi parties in Hungary.

[19] GFM 2—94, 106842. Jagow, the German minister, gave the same advice to Ribbentrop; he stressed the necessity of persuading Horthy to appoint a new government (GFM 2—94).

[20] *Kriegstagebuch des OKW*, pp. 198—199.

would be discussed. Ribbentrop furthermore instructed the minister to emphasize that the invitation had been planned for the week after, but the events of the eastern front urgently required the presence of Hitler at the G. H. Q. He would therefore like to meet Horthy on Friday (the 17th) or Saturday morning (the 18th), at the latest.[21]

That very evening, in the Opera house, Jagow asked for a private audience with Horthy, and late in the evening transmitted Hitler's request that the Regent should pay him a visit at Klessheim.[22] Horthy summoned next morning Kállay, the prime minister, Ghyczy, the minister of Foreign Affairs, Csatay, the minister of National Defence, and Szombathelyi, the Chief of Staff, to a conference at which Kállay expressed his fear of a German occupation.

A minor debate arose as to whether the Regent should accept Hitler's invitation. As stated in his book, Kállay was against it, and there is no reason to doubt his words.[23] According to Horthy, it was chiefly Szombathelyi who persuaded him to accept the invitation. As Horthy puts it, Szombathelyi hoped that the Regent might persuade Hitler to let the Hungarian troops come home.[24] Kállay, too, asserts that this idea played a role in Szombathelyi's argumentation. What gives food for thought in this matter is that not even under the existing conditions did the head of the state, the prime minister and the chief of staff took a German occupation into account but hoped rather to wring new concessions from Hitler.

Before his departure, Horthy promised not to consent to sacrificing Kállay for "political" reasons; he would not even discuss the matter. He was going to emphasize that under no conditions would he brook an interference with his own rights or those of parliament.[25]

Horthy does not mention this promise in his memoirs. As a matter of fact, Hitler knew much better what to expect of Horthy. The draft of the common protocol laying down the results of the talks was already prepared.

In the first paragraph of this protocol it was stated that the new Hungarian government, formed with German consent, undertook to stand by Germany to the end of the war. The prime minister of the new cabinet would be Béla Imrédy, the Minister of National Defence Jenő Rátz. The Germans claimed the right to appoint also the other leading personalities of the new government, or to approve such appointments.

German troops would arrive in the country for the internal and the external support of the new government, said the second paragraph.

It was laid down in further paragraphs that the new government was to conduct affairs . . . "in close agreement with the Reich government" —

[21] GFM 2—99, 109815. Telegram sent by Ribbentrop on March 15.
[22] Ibid. 109816. Jagow's report from March 16, 1944.
[23] Kállay, op. cit. p. 414.
[24] Horthy, op. cit. p. 250.
[25] Kállay, op. cit. p. 416.

"...in engstem Einvernehmen mit der Reichsregierung". To control and promote this cooperation, a German plenipotentiary (Reichsbevollmächtigter) was to be appointed. In future, the Hungarian army was to act in accordance with instructions from the German Supreme Command. Finally, the Regent was to address a proclamation to the Hungarian people, the soldiers and the authorities, calling on them to receive the German forces friendly.

An enclosure contained further demands. In the East, Hungarian troops were to be subordinated to German units; preparations along the Rumanian border were to be cancelled; the army was to be reorganized with German assistance, the Air Force was to be completely integrated into the Luftwaffe; finally, the German war machine was to be supported by increased transport activities.[26]

On March 17, Hitler received the demands of the German General Staff which were to be put before the new Hungarian government.

1. The leading military posts were to be filled with pro-German officers;

2. the army was to be reorganized in compliance with the instructions of the German Supreme Command;

3. the occupational forces on the eastern front were to be subordinated to the German army;

4. the Lemberg command was to cease;

5. all military preparations along the Hungarian—Rumanian border were to be discontinued;

6. 4 or 5 reliable, active divisions suitable for warfare were to be set up with German support;

7. conscription was to be extended; further occupational and fighting units would be set up for service in the East, perhaps in Istria or in France;

8. increasing labour efforts were to be made in order to raise the production of the Hungarian war industry; war material and oil production as well as agricultural exports were to be increased in the first place;

9. growing demands on transport facilities were to be complied with reliably.[27]

Hitler opened the conference of March 18 in the spirit of these projects. "Instead of beginning with reassurances as to ordering our troops home" Horthy writes with pretended ingenuousness, "he spoke about Italian defection and informed me that he was ... compelled to take measures in order to prevent such a contingency". Horthy rejected the accusation of defection and asked whether Hitler's measures implied occupation. Hitler replied in the affirmative, whereupon Horthy left the room in indignation.[28]

[26] GFM 2—99, 109832. Record of March 18, 1944.

[27] *Kriegstagebuch des OKW*, p. 199.

[28] Horthy, op. cit. pp. 251—252. The records of the Crown Council of March 19, 1944, are to be found among Horthy's secret documents; Horthy gives there partly different account of his first conversation with Hitler. He is alleged to have declared that he had regarded the threat of a German occupation as bluff. (*Secret Documents of Miklós Horthy*, p. 429.)

As described in his book, Horthy then informed his retinue about what had happened. It was decided to leave Klessheim at once. The records of Szombathelyi, written directly after the interview, throw light on Horthy's distortion also at this point: "We noted the statement of His Highness and asked him to resume conversation with Hitler once more in the afternoon, and to endeavour to convince him that we were entirely on his side and would do our utmost to promote their victory."[29]

After lunching together in a . . .„far from convivial atmosphere" there followed, according to Szombathelyi, another two hours' conversation between Hitler and Horthy. (Horthy makes no mention of this talk.) Hitler insisted on the occupation, and it seems that Horthy still refused to give his consent.[30]

After this conversation, at 5 p.m. on March 18, Hitler gave orders for the execution of Operation Margarethe.[31]

After a conference of the ministers of foreign affairs, the ministers of national defence, and the chiefs of staff Szombathelyi tried to dissuade Hitler from the occupation. Hitler asked Keitel whether it was still possible to countermand the orders; Keitel replied in the negative. According to Szombathelyi, this took place between 16.45 and 18.40, which shows that the orders issued at 17 hours could have been countermanded, since the German troops could not have crossed yet the Hungarian border.[32]

Of the remaining events of the day, Horthy mentions two more episodes in his memoirs. The first was his renewed conversation with Hitler, the other was Ribbentrop's visit.

Horthy writes he declared to Hitler that he would resign in case of an occupation; he maintained this attitude even when Hitler said „I give you my word, I shall withdraw the German troops as soon as there is a Hungarian government which I can trust".[33]

Then came the visit of Ribbentrop when the German minister requested Horthy to sign the joint communiqué. According to it, "the German troops have come into the country by mutual agreement". Horthy refused to sign the statement.[34]

Szombathelyi's records make it evident that Horthy glossed over his own role by reversing the chronological order of these two events. In fact, it was between 7 and 7.30 p.m. that Ribbentrop asked Horthy to sign the communiqué which Horthy actually refused. However, thereafter Szombathelyi

[29] *Magyarország és a II. világháború* (Hungary and the Second World War). Edited and introduced by M. Ádám, Gy. Juhász, L. Kerekes. Budapest, 1961. p. 451.

[30] At the Crown Council on March 19, Horthy gave a detailed account of this second interview emphasizing that he had refused the Germans wish to sign a proclamation to the effect that . . . „the German occupational forces marched into Hungary with his consent".

[31] GFM 2—99, 109839. Record of March 19, 1944.

[32] See *Hungary and the Second World War*, p. 453.

[33] Horthy, op. cit. p. 253.

[34] Ibid. p. 255.

and Sztójay declared to Ribbentrop "His Excelleney does not wish to break off negotiations, he is willing to go into further talks on these matters, but he is worried because he does not know what concrete demands are to be made on him". Thereupon, Ribbentrop arranged another meeting between Horthy and Hitler. According to Szombathelyi, the tone of this conversation was more measured, and Hitler promised that no Rumanian troops would take part in the occupation.[35]

Kertész, too, reports on two meetings between Horthy and Hitler. However, Horthy consented at the second interview to remain in his place provided the occupation would be of a purely military character, without affecting certain aspects of the political supremacy.[36]

An accurate reconstruction of the details is rather difficult, since the majority of available sources consists of the accounts of the Hungarian politicians who took part in the conversations, and they were surely not above a tendency to whitewashing. The journal of the German general staff is a better guide in this respect. It records three interviews between Hitler and Horthy; after a report on two fruitless conversations, the third is summarized as follows: "Contrary to expectations, around 8 p.m. the Regent went once more to the Führer. In the course of this new conversation he declared that, having completely grasped the Führer's intentions, he was willing to comply with his demands."[37]

There can, thus, be no doubt that during the last conference of Horthy and Hitler, the former gave his consent to the military occupation of the country and was willing to continue as regent. It is, on the other hand, certain that no further details were settled. In the journal of the German general staff this is summed up in the words "The negotiations having taken this course, there was no opportunity for presenting the military demands of the general staff, nor was there time for the signature of the prepared protocol".[38]

Horthy naturally omits to record that he actually consented to the occupation; on the other hand, he admits that during the journey home, in the train, Edmund Veesenmayer, the new German minister and "Reichsbevollmächtigter", requested an audience and immediately began his negotiations concerning the person of a new prime minister. Had Horthy refused to give his consent to the occupation, why should Veesenmayer have started a conversation on the appointment of a new prime minister, since formally Veesenmayer had no right to do so. (Let us remember here Horthy's vociferation

[35] *Hungary and the Second World War*, p. 455. An approximately similar account was given in the report submitted to the Crown Council according to the *Secret Documents of Miklós Horthy* (p. 427).

[36] S. D. Kertész: *Diplomacy in a Whirlpool. Hungary between Nazi Germany and Sovjet-Russia.* Notre Dame (USA), 1953. p. 73.

[37] *Kriegstagebuch des OKW*, p. 201.

[38] Ibid.

before his departure that he would not tolerate any interference with his own or the parliament's authority.)

As an excuse for his attitude, Horthy adduces two factors: first, that resistance was anyway hopeless; second, that he hoped that if he remained in his place and appointed a cabinet acceptable to the Germans, Hitler would withdraw his troops from the country.[39]

As regards the hopelessness of resistance, it has already been pointed out that no preparations were made although there was over ten days' time for them. According to Adonyi, three out of the country's nine divisions were stationed in Transdanubia; the 16th mobilized division was concentrated around Szolnok and the 2nd armoured division in the precincts of Kecskemét. Their transport to the western border would not have been more difficult than moving German troops from the Burgenland to Budapest. As a matter of fact, it was done in a few hours.[40]

Kertész explains that, among others, resistance was out of the question because the Hungarian military commanders were all staying in Germany.[41]

Kállay quotes both reasons, adding that the military commanders would not have obeyed anyway. (He obviously forgets that half a year before the 19th of March, he had made an agreement with Great Britain to replace all military commanders who were German hirelings.)

All these are, however, only extrinsic, formal arguments. Kállay himself admits that, relying on the working classes, resistance might still have been possible. In view of the army's inertia he dared not follow such a course because ..."it would have separated the people from their masters".[42]

The attitude of the leading Hungarian military circles of the day is reflected most faithfully by the statement of Adonyi who still openly approves of collaboration with Hitler; in his view, resistance ..."would not have served Hungarian interests".[43]

Indeed, who could have judged Hungarian interests better than Adonyi of whom Veesenmayer's report said "Major Adonyi is of a thoroughly pro-German mentality".[44]

Hitler looked on his projects as virtually realized after his conversation with Horthy. He decided to cancel the propaganda flight over Budapest, and to desist from occupying the fortress of Buda. The so-called transmit contingents commanded by General Pfuhlstein were to advance peacefully, converging in the direction of Budapest, while the main strategical points were to be taken by paratroopers. He thought that, having secured Horthy's

[39] Horthy, op. cit. p. 254.
[40] Adonyi, op. cit. pp. 58—60.
[41] Kertész, op. cit. p. 73.
[42] Kállay, op. cit. p. 423.
[43] Adonyi, op. cit. p. 60.
[44] GFM 2—99. 110 437.

consent, he could reduce the number of the occupational forces. He refrained from throwing in the chasseur division assembled around Belgrade, and sent back a few specialized units to Denmark.[45]

Thus, at 4 a.m. on March 19, 1944, three divisions from Belgrade, two divisions from Zagreb, two armoured divisions from the outskirts of Vienna, and a motorized division from the region of Cracow invaded Hungary.

"No resistance was encountered anywhere" states the OKW journal. A part of the Hungarian army had received instructions in this sense, while another part declared its readiness to join the Wehrmacht. As planned, the paratroopers landed, and the so-called "transit" troops took part in the occupation.[46]

Not only did the German occupation encounter no resistance, but, owing to the unpreparedness of the antifascist front, the occupational forces did not have to fight any spontaneous resistance of the people either.

With the assistance of arrow-cross and other extreme right-wing agents, the Gestapo units which accompanied the German forces immediately began to arrest left wing elements. Not only communists were persecuted, but many of the leaders of the Smallholders' Party and the Social Democratic Party were also arrested. Their organizations and press were destroyed. The leaders of pro-British groups in the ruling classes suffered the same fate; members of Parliament, members of the Upper House, journalists, and well-known leading capitalists of Jewish extraction were imprisoned by the Germans.

The German project was a complete success: owing to the behaviour of Horthy and the Hungarian ruling classes, the Germans contrived to occupy the country without any resistance, amidst the complete passivity of the masses.

By March 21, the northern and southern divisions established contact, and the occupation was accomplished to the line of the river Tisza. This line was closed at the same time, because the Germans thought their military power insufficient for a systematic occupation of the whole country.

The occupation was, thus, undisturbed from a military point of view. Political developments were far from being equally unequivocal. According to the German general staff, when Horthy, though only after lengthy debate, finally consented at Klessheim to the occupation of Hungary, he spoke in a positive tone, and adopted an equally positive attitude when Veesenmayer requested an interview in the night of March 18 on the home journey and informed the Regent that he was to be the future German minister and also the German plenipotentiary in Hungary.[47] Horthy, after his arrival in Budapest, fell once more under the influence of his evil advisers and refused to

[45] *Kriegstagebuch des OKW*, p. 202. According to German records, only the garnison of Ujvidék had to be disarmed.

[46] Ibid.

[47] GFM 2—99, 109841, Veesenmayer's first report from Budapest, March 19, 1944.

appoint Imrédy as prime minister.[48] The delay in the appointment of a new cabinet induced Hitler to send the division from Belgrade to Hungary after all.

Horthy declared on the 20th of March that he wished to have a caretaker government which Veesenmayer, in accordance with his instructions from Berlin, declined to accept.[49] By March 22, the German attitude had stiffened; if no cabinet was formed within a given time the German troops were to take Buda by force,[50] disband the Hungarian army, reorganize it under German command and leave only two minor Hungarian units west of the Tisza, while five divisions would be set up east of the river.[51] All this became superfluous, for Döme Sztójay, former Hungarian minister in Berlin formed a new government on the 23rd of March. Although the government failed to earn the unanimous approval of the Germans, they trusted that it would be subsequently completed by other strong personalities of the extreme right.

The question of the army still remained open. Veesenmayer who had already championed a cautious and skilful policy, suggested on March 21 that, instead of being liquidated, the Hungarian army should be thrown into active service against the Soviet Union. In his memorandum of March 21, he wrote this: "Obviously, my most important task is to release as many German troops stationed at present in Hungary as possible." In this respect, he continued to explain, the decisive point was the utilizability of the Hungarian army. The existing situation created the impression of the sovereignty having been left unaffected and this had made it possible to form a new government, so that the slogans of the day were still "Kameradschaft" and "Waffenbruderschaft" sounded on both sides. This situation would be badly disturbed by the disarmament of the Hungarian forces — which was technically certainly practicable. Such a step would involve the danger of

a) resignation by the government and the regent;

b) an unanimous opposition being formed that would include the parties of both the left and the right side;

c) such a step might elicit passive resistance, a line of conduct in which Hungarians were highly experienced;

d) it might even lead to a general strike;

e) resistance would not be strong, but it would nevertheless pin down German troops.

Therefore, Veesenmayer was against the disarmament of the Hungarian army — an opinion shared by Weichs, the commander of the occupational forces, and by Greiffenberg, the military attaché. Every German demand could

[48] *Kriegstagebuch des OKW*, p. 203.

[49] GFM 2—99, 109866, Veesenmayer's report of March 20, 1944.

[50] As stated in Veesenmayer's report, this could be accomplished in three hours. GFM 2—99, 109886, report from March 22.

[51] *Kriegstagebuch des OKW*, p. 204.

undoubtedly be satisfied by a reference to the common war. "I shall go on raising new demands" so Veesenmayer continued; he concluded his memorandum in the following terms: "It is more important to keep Hungary quiet and exploit her forces to the utmost on the basis of voluntary cooperation than create a completely new and radical situation by dangerous measures."[52]

However, the Ministry of Foreign Affairs failed to see eye with Veesenmayer. After two days, Ribbentrop sent his reply to Veesenmayer's report through Rittern, the representative of the Ministry of Foreign Affairs at the Führer's headquarters: ..."the whole line suggested in connection with the disarmament is wrong." In Ribbentrop's view, the aim of Operation Margarethe was to eliminate the Hungarian army from this important strategical point and to forestall any political change by "rendering it harmless".

The Ministry of Foreign Affairs did not believe that by a "conversion" of the Hungarians, by Horthy's continued regentship, by the appointment of a new government and by voicing the slogans of Kameradschaft and Waffenbruderschaft all would be well.

"Your most important task" the German foreign minister continued, "namely the possibly earliest liquidation of the Hungarian army, should always form the kernel of your activities, and it is inadmissible that you should be diverted from this target by secondary considerations such as the maintenance of the Regent and the new government or by contrary influences emanating from the German Wehrmacht."

Of course, also the German Ministry of Foreign Affairs did not mean disarmament in a "primitive sense"; the army was not to be disarmed to the last man, only in a degree to bar the possibility of a stab in the back. The Waffenbruderschaftpropaganda proposed by Veesenmayer was likewise decried as mistaken. Ribbentrop made it clear that the word "kameradschaftlich" was used not by the Germans but by Szombathelyi when instructing the Hungarian army not to shoot at the invading Germans. In the endeavour to accomplish the occupation with utmost speed this was naturally useful for the moment, but it would be wrong to create an illusion by insisting on the use of the term.[53]

After the appointment of Sztójay's cabinet it became evident that leading German circles disagreed concerning the future fate of the Hungarian army. The development of the matter was greatly influenced by the circumstance that not only were Veesenmayer and Ribbentrop at odds, but the German general staff inclined to Veesenmayer's opinion. The rapidly deteriorating position of the German army on the eastern front played a decisive role in

[52] GFM 2—99, 109911, Veesenmayer's report of March 21, 1944.
[53] GFM 2—99, 109965, Ritter's communication of March 23, 1944.

this development. While the Germans were busy with the occupation of Hungary, Soviet troops had made a break-through at Tarnopol.[54]

In two or three days an extremely perilous situation had developed which made it imperative for the German high command to send new reinforcements to this section of the front. On March 25, Hitler sent two of the occupational divisions from Hungary to the environs of Lemberg. The menacing military situation was, thus, one of the factors which induced the German general staff to decide in favour of making use of the Hungarian army. The attitude of the German general staff was obviously strongly influenced by the remarkably good impression created by cooperation with the Hungarian general staff, whereas the German Ministry of Foreign Affairs had no reason to be satisfied with the corresponding Hungarian ministry. The Hungarian general staff was at once ready to serve the Germans. It declared on March 25 that mobilization could be carried out in ten days if necessary, and that eight divisions would be put at the disposal of the Germans for being sent to the eastern front.[55]

While these considerations assumed a growing weight with the general staff in connection with the Hungarian army, Veesenmayer tried to induce the Ministry of Foreign Affairs to change their mind. On March 25, he sent a report regarding an interview which he had had with Sztójay in the presence of the other cabinet members. Sztójay informed him that the detention of Hungarian troops in their baracks exerted a depressing effect and caused uneasiness. Veesenmayer did not comment on this information, but continued, obviously not without intention, to describe the results of the new government's activities: considerable quantities of corn had been forwarded to Germany, anti-Jewish measures had been put into force, and steps had been taken to speed up production in war industries, etc.[56]

On March 26, Veesenmayer despatched two reports dealing with these issues. The first contained an account of his conversation with Horthy, made together with general Weichs.

The principal subject of this conference, attended also by the German Greifenberg and the Hungarians Csatay and Szombathelyi, were military questions first and foremost the disarmament of the Hungarian army. Horthy declared that the confinement of Hungarian soldiers to their barracks and the closing of the Tisza line had hitherto seemed reasonable but were now beginning to jeopardize the cooperation. The Hungarian army was beginning

[54] *Kriegstagebuch des OKW*, p. 205.

[55] *Kriegstagebuch des OKW*, p. 240. Reference is made here to the eight divisions which, as has been noted, had stood ready for action in February already. This disproves the assertion that military resistance was impossible. Before the German occupation there were actually more than two weeks in which the eight divisions could have been mobilized if the general staff had wanted it.

[56] GFM 2—99, 109926. Veesenmayer's report of March 25, 1944.

to show strong unrest which the regent was unable to allay since he, too, failed to understand these measures. Horthy emphasized that his cooperation had certain limits beyond which he would be compelled to resign. "He would like to help the German troops in overthrowing bolshevism, and was willing to mobilize the forces at his disposal on the condition that the Hungarian troops would be treated in the traditional spirit of brotherhood."[57]

The second report stated that the commander of the occupational forces, General Weichs, too, shared the Reich commissioner's opinion. In this report, Veesenmayer gave an account of his conversation with Weichs who thought that tension was increasing between the German and Hungarian troops. The minister informed his superiors about the opinion of Weichs to the effect that the disarmament of the Hungarian army could be accomplished only at the cost of fighting for which the general lacked adequate forces.[58]

Hitler was presumably informed of Veesenmayer's report, but it is likewise possible that it was the grave situation which induced him to alter his attitude. At all events, he decided in the afternoon of March 26 that the use of the Hungarian troops was of utmost significance; although he did not wish to decide definitely the problem regarding the disarmament, Hungarian units were to be thrown in for the time being. Hitler sent a personal message through the military attaché, Greiffenberg, to the Hungarian general staff emphasizing that ..."the situation on the eastern front calls for serious decisions and prompt action. The Russian advance has to be stopped by throwing in all available forces, and a closed front has to be formed in order to save the Southeast from the horrors of war and bolshevism".[59] He stated that he had commanded all his forces to the south wing of the eastern front and desired his allies to do the same. He therefore demanded that the Hungarian units stationed in the Carpathians (two infantry divisions, one motorized division and two battalions of mountain chasseurs) should join the 7th Hungarian army corps fighting in Galicia under the command of Heeresgruppe Süd. Too, he urgently recommended the elaboration of a new plan of mobilization.

Hitler lifted the restrictions imposed on the Hungarian army and also terminated the blockade of the Tisza line. Veesenmayer reported that these measures had found a favourable reception with the Hungarian general staff.[60]

[57] GFM 2—99, 109958, Veesenmayer's report of March 26, 1944.

[58] Ibid., 109972, telegram of March 26.

[59] *Kriegstagebuch des OKW*, p. 240.

[60] GFM 2—99, 109974. Veesenmayer, March 26, 1944, report at 23.30 hours. — On Keitel's instructions, Greiffenberg had informed the Hungarian general staff on the 24th March already that the part of Hungary east of the river Tisza was declared to be a theatre of war. The Hungarian troops stationed in this area were to be placed under German command, and a German military commander of the East-Hungarian theatre of military operations would be appointed. (GFM 2—99, 109933, Veesenmayer's report of March 25, 1944.)

This decision was connected with Antonescu's visit to Hitler on March 23. Antonescu demanded the evacuation of Northern Transylvania by Hungarian troops, first of all that of the Székely-land, and the return of these parts to Rumania. Hitler evaded this demand by

The final decision was still pending, but the prospects were becoming increasingly manifest. On March 27, the C. I. C. of the southeastern units stated his disapproval of disarmament declaring that . . .„after an adequate purge, no organized betrayal need be feared; such a contingency was highly improbable inside the army even under the former government".[61] Moreover, further bad news had arrived from Bucovina which made it imperative to send new reinforcement to that sector. It was under such conditions that Ribbentrop, Veesenmayer, Himmler, Keitel (chief of the general staff), Jodl (chief of the operational staff), General Warlimont, his deputy, and General Weichs appeared before Hitler in the afternoon of March 28 for a conference.

Weichs submitted the following:

a) strong nationalist propaganda should be started with German support;

b) the body of Hungarian officers was to be purged;

c) military equipment was to be improved;

d) training should be conducted under German control;

e) the Hungarian army was to be maintained under strong German influence, but the largest unit should be a division. Those present at the meeting were in favour of mobilizing the Hungarian forces, and Hitler decided in this sense. He was far from being satisfied with the situation, but — referring to the regent's and the "nobility's" fear of bolshevism, he declared that . . ."disarmament shall not be carried out, but Hungarian units should be thrown in only gradually so that they may be held in hand; the chief thing is that they should not pin down too numerous German forces".[62] Ribbentrop and Himmler, who had professed a contrary opinion, now accepted the Führer's decision. Ribbentrop instructed Veesenmayer that very evening that . . ."henceforward the slogan of Waffenbruderschaft was to be the key-note of German—Hungarian relations".[63]

The Hungarian government and general staff were informed next day about the decision, and it was emphasized that for the moment it would be enough to set up and send to the front three more divisions; instead of the promised additional five divisions, industrial and agricultural supplies were to be increased and new SS units to be formed from the Germans living in Hungary. The mobilized units were to be put under German command, while four or five German divisions would remain in the country.[64] The idea was that after all these steps, after the purge among the leaders of the Hungarian army,

---

declaring the territory east of the Tisza to be a theatre of German military operations. *(Kriegstagebuch des OKW*, pp. 238—239.)

[61] *Kriegstagebuch des OKW*, p. 241.

[62] Ibid., pp. 242—243.

[63] GFM 2—99, 109981, instructions from Ritter on March 28. 1944.

[64] As a matter of fact, only two complete German armoured divisions were in Hungary, four other divisions were only cadres *(Kriegstagebuch des OKW*, p. 829.)

the Hungarian forces left in the country should have no fighting value. The Hungarians were pleased with these new instructions, their hidden purpose having apparently escaped notice.[65]

Steps were taken next day to throw in some of the German occupational divisions on the eastern front and others against the Yugoslav partisans of Tito. On the same day, the Hungarian units stationed in the Carpathians crossed the border on their way to the front.

The Hungarian situation was now stabilized — in the most favourable form for Hitler. Not only had the country been occupied without fighting, but — with the assistance of right-wing politicians and the leaders of the army — Horthy had created a situation in which half of the occupational divisions could be spared, while the Hungarian army was engaged in the war against the Soviet Union.

Let us now weigh the statements of Kállay and Horthy in the light of the foregoing. It is asserted by both, particularly by Horthy, that by remaining in office the government at least contrived to retain control over the army.[66] Emigration literature endeavours to preserve this appearance by omitting to mention the discussions and the problems which arose in connection with the Hungarian army after the occupation.

Adonyi may have been ignorant of these discussions, but it is also possible that these conversations were incompatible with Adonyi's concept of the "loyalty of allies", for it was in the course of these conversations that the Germans refused to treat as Waffenbrüder the soldiers who were sent to their death for German interests by Adonyi and other leaders of the Hungarian general staff.

Horthy, on the other hand, did take part in these conversations which were too important to have simply been forgotten. An account of these talks would, however, immediately have raised the point of how the conduct of Horthy on March 18 and 19 could be justified if, as evidenced by subsequent events, he did not even obtain Hitler's promise to maintain the Hungarian army. Moreover, it was undesirable for him to describe these talks because it was not Hitler but Horthy who made a promise. He promised to give the Germans still more soldiers for the fight against the Soviet Union, although he must have been fully aware of the senselessness of such an act.

Adonyi's pro-German attitude, attested also by Veesenmayer, has already been noted. His comment to the effect that . . ."it is a misrepresentation to say that after the 19th of March, 1944, the German high command made exaggerated military demands" is, therefore, not surprising.[67]

[65] *Kriegstagebuch des OKW*, p. 243.

[66] Kállay, op. cit. p. 443. — Kállay first tried to persuade Horthy to resign. (Horthy, op. cit. p. 266.)

[67] Adonyi, op. cit.

A later part of Adonyi's book includes a table showing that, while in 1943 the Hungarian army took part in the war against the Soviet Union with six occupational divisions (nine so-called light divisions), by the summer of 1944 fourteen fighting and three occupational divisions had been thrown in.[68] Adonyi estimates the total number of Hungarian soldiers on the front in 1944 at about half a million, and the records of the German general staff mention a similar figure. This figure still left Adonyi discontented; his attitude may have been due to his appointment as A. D. C. of the chief of staff at the wish of the Germans in 1944.

And who became the chief of the general staff? Let us quote two reports of Veesenmayer's. The first is dated May 2, 1944; Veesenmayer informs his superiors that by means of political pressure he has managed to have János Vörös appointed chief of the general staff, although there were about thirty officers his seniors in service.[69] Cooperation was excellent with Vörös since he was willing to comply with every German demand. In his report, dated May 11, Veesenmayer describes the first results: assisted by Vörös, he had succeeded in inducing the crown council to place a great number of pro-German officers to the most important posts of the Hungarian army and supplant in this way men who had shown a more reserved attitude toward the Germans.

It was with the aid of this manoeuvre that Dezső László was substituted for Bajnóczy as deputy chief of the general staff. (László was earlier the chief of the mobilization department and it was to him that General Himer had written the "Merkzettel" in June, 1941, which induced the general staff to demand the declaration of war.) The commander of the first army corps, Géza Lakatos, was to be replaced by the arrow-cross man Beregffy. Four elderly generals who had not been sufficiently willing to serve the Germans were to be replaced; the 5th army corps was to receive a new commander; a new chief of personnel was to be appointed in the War Ministry, and a new chief of general staff in the 1st army.[70]

With the assistance of János Vörös, Veesenmayer thus succeeded in readjusting the Hungarian army according to German pattern. There was, however, someone else who, too, promoted this readjustment. Personal changes

[68] The 16th and 24th infantry divisions, the 1st and 2nd mountain brigades and the 2nd armoured division stationed in the Carpathians were sent to the front in April. The 20th and 25th infantry divisions and the 27th light division (i.e. the three divisions demanded by Hitler on March 24) were sent in May; the 7th infantry division and the 1st cavalry division in June; the 6th, 10th and 13th infantry divisions in July. All the Hungarian forces available on March 19, 1944, were thus sent to the front. (*Kriegstagebuch des OKW*, pp. 822—836.)

[69] It is known that, in November, 1944, Vörös went over to the Soviet troops and even became a member of the provisional Hungarian government.

[70] GFM 2—99, 110280, Veesenmayer's reports of May 2 and 11, 1944. — The German general staff recorded with satisfaction that "The Hungarian general staff has fully complied with the demands of the Germans, and the mobilization of the army has been carried out more speedily than was to be expected". (*Kriegstagebuch des OKW*, p. 829.)

were decided by the crown councils, and it was Miklós Horthy who presided over them. The same Horthy who, six weeks earlier, at the time of the German occupation, had remained in office in order to "retain a hold over the army". Yet he now consented to have all military commanders replaced who might have stood nearer to him than to the Germans. He consented to have a cavalry army corps — provided with armoured units and equipped with motorized heavy artillery, allegedly the elite of the Hungarian army — sent to the front. Of course, he made conditions, but why should the Germans have kept their promise in this particular instance? This is how the most valuable unit of Horthy's army was lost to the last man in the Pripjet marshes in order to cover the retreat of the Germans.

Miklós Horthy's stimulating order of the day of April 15 was found with some of the fallen soldiers . . .

III

Die deutsche wirtschaftliche Expansion und das ungarische Wirtschaftsleben zur Zeit des zweiten Weltkrieges

Nach der Machtergreifung durch den Faschismus (nach dem nationalsozialistischen Umsturz) wurde die deutsche Wirtschaftspolitik in den Dienst der Vorbereitung eines neuen imperialistischen Krieges gestellt. Diese brachte einen bedeutenden Anstieg der Industriekapazität, in erster Reihe natürlich den der Kriegsproduktion, sowie die Einführung einer Wirtschaftsautarkie mit sich. Ein wichtiges Moment der letzteren bestand in der schnellen Entwicklung der deutschen landwirtschaftlichen Produktion und in der Aufspeicherung bedeutsamer Vorräte an landwirtschaftlichen und industriellen Rohstoffen. Die Verwirklichung dieser Maßnahmen stand aber im engsten Zusammenhang mit der Modifizierung der deutschen Außenhandelspolitik zu Beginn der dreißiger Jahre. Ein wichtiger Faktor der deutschen Kriegsvorbereitung bestand nämlich in der Schaffung eines entsprechenden Hinterlandes für die deutsche Kriegswirtschaft in den südosteuropäischen Ländern, die für diese Rolle aus mehrfachen Gründen als geeignet befunden wurden. Diese Gebiete bildeten eine alte Interessensphäre des deutschen Imperialismus, und die Deutschen verfügten hier — trotz der starken Zurückdrängung seit den zwanziger Jahren — noch immer über zahlreiche wirtschaftliche Positionen. Die südosteuropäischen Kleinstaaten erschienen für Deutschland schon wegen ihrer geographischen Lage günstig, da die Benützung der wirtschaftlichen Quellen dieser Länder im Laufe eines geplanten Krieges selbst im Falle einer vermeintlichen Seeblokade als gesichert schien, und dies um so mehr, als auf diese Länder verhältnismäßig leicht ein politischer, militärischer, sowie wirtschaftlicher Druck ausgeübt werden konnte. Die südosteuropäischen Staaten waren größtenteils Agrarländer, verfügten aber auch über außerordentlich wichtige strategische Rohstoffe: in Ungarn Bauxit, in Rumänien Öl, in Jugoslawien verschiedene Buntmetalle, Holz usw. Gleichzeitig waren sie aber infolge ihrer verhältnismäßigen industriellen Rückständigkeit auf einen bedeutenden Import von zahlreichen Industrieartikeln angewiesen und kamen daher — nach den Vorstellungen des deutschen Finanzkapitals — als organische Ergänzung der deutschen faschistischen Kriegswirtschaft in Betracht. Bekräftigt wurde die Aussicht auch dadurch, daß Deutschland, über eine ungünstige Zahlungsbilanz und nur geringfügige Gold- und Valutenvorräte verfügend, das Prinzip des multilateralen Handelsverträge aufgab und den Abschluß von bilateralen Handelsabkommen erstrebte. Da die erwähnten Länder ähnliche Valutenschwierigkeiten hatten, waren sie ebenfalls geneigt, Clearingabkommen abzuschließen.

Deutschland gab seine, in den zwanziger Jahren verwirklichte protektionistische Zollpolitik gegenüber dem Agrarexport der südosteuropäischen Länder auf und sicherte den Ausfuhrländern auf diesem Gebiet Begünstigungen. Für die mit schwerer Agrarkrise und Verwertungsschwierigkeiten ringenden südosteuropäischen Länder war das sehr wichtig, selbst wenn sie als Gegenleistung große Importbegünstigungen beim Industrieimport gewähren mußten. Infolgedessen nahmen die Handelsbeziehungen Deutschlands mit Südosteuropa und dadurch auch der deutsche Einfluß in diesen Ländern in den dreißiger Jahren in hohem Maße zu. Ohne uns im Rahmen dieses Artikels auf eine ausführliche Untersuchung des Problems einzulassen, möchten wir kurz darauf hinweisen, daß während der deutsche Außenhandel im Jahre 1937 im ganzen erst 40% seines Standes von 1929 betrug, er in den südosteuropäischen Ländern bereits das Niveau des Jahres 1929 erreichte. Die Beteiligung dieser Länder an der deutschen Ausfuhr stieg von 4,3% des Jahres 1929 auf 9,4% im Jahre 1937, an der Einfuhr hingegen von 3,8% auf 10,5%.[1]

Die schon anfangs der dreißiger Jahre beginnende Expansion des »deutschen Lebensraumes« erfuhr nach dem Abschluß des Münchener Abkommens und später nach der Entfesselung des zweiten Weltkrieges zweifelsohne einen größeren Auftrieb. Die politische Bedeutung Münchens bestand darin, daß das faschistische Deutschland nach Osten hin freie Hand erhielt, und das bedeutete unter anderem auch die stillschweigende Preisgabe Osteuropas. Für den deutschen Vorstoß war selbstverständlich ausschlaggebend, daß Deutschland durch die Einverleibung Österreichs und der Tschechoslowakei seine Positionen den südosteuropäischen Ländern gegenüber sowohl wirtschaftlich als auch politisch weiter hin bedeutend verstärkte. Der veränderten Lage entschprechend begann Deutschland 1939 eine umfangreiche Wirtschaftsoffensive gegen die südosteuropäischen Länder. Deutschen Plänen gemäß sollte Südosteuropa im Rahmen der »Großwirtschaftsraum-Theorie« offen in eine deutsche Lebensmittel- und Rohstoffbasis verwandelt werden und den ganzen diesbezüglichen Bedarf decken. Die Frage stand nunmehr nicht so, welche Mengen Deutschland von den landwirtschaftlichen Überschüssen dieser Länder übernimmt, sondern wieweit die betreffenden Länder den deutschen Bedarf befriedigen können. Die Deutschen erstrebten mit allen

[1] Antonin Basch: The Danube Basin and the German Economic Sphere. London. S. 180—181. Die Angaben beziehen sich auf Ungarn, Jugoslawien, Bulgarien, Rumänien und Griechenland.

Mitteln eine erhöhte Einfuhr von landwirtschaftlichen Erzeugnissen, bei unveränderten Preisen. Diese Offensive war Rumänien und Jugoslawien gegenüber besonders stark, weil sich diese Länder damals politisch noch nicht unter dem unmittelbaren deutschen Einfluß befanden. In Ungarn hatten sie leichteres Spiel, stand doch Ungarn von allen südosteuropäischen Staaten schon seit Jahren in den engsten wirtschaftlichen und noch mehr politischen Beziehungen zu Deutschland.

*

Anfang 1939 machte Ungarn dem nazionalsozialistischen Deutschland auch politisch neue Zugeständnisse. Horthy-Ungarn, das sich als erstes auf die Seite des faschistischen Deutschlands gestellt hatte, unterstützte Hitler in seiner agressiven Politik. Ungeachtet dessen, daß Ungarn durch den Römischen Dreierpakt eng mit Österreich verbunden war, versicherte man Hitler bereits im Herbst 1937, daß Ungarn keine Einwände gegen eine Einverleibung Österreichs habe.[2] Im Herbst 1937 bzw. im Frühjahr 1938 schlossen sich die Regierungskreise den gegen die Tschechoslowakei geschmiedeten deutschen Pläne an. Dem Rate Hitlers folgend richteten sie ihre Revisionsforderungen in erster Reihe gegen die Tschechoslowakei. Im Sommer 1938 — eine westliche Einmischung befürchtend — waren sie zwar noch nicht bereit, sich uneingeschränkt zur Teilnahme an einem bewaffneten Angriff gegen die Tschechoslowakei zu verpflichten.[3] Als jedoch die Richtlinien der westlichen Politik bereits offenbar wurden, flogen Ministerpresident Imrédy und Außenminister Kánya in der Hoffnung auf Beute am 20. September zu Hitler. Ungarn enger an das deutschen Bündnis fesselnd, kündigten sie ihre Ansprüche auf tschechoslowakisches Gebiet noch während der Verhandlungen zwischen Hitler und Chamberlain an. Im Laufe der Beschprechungen äußerte Hitler seine Unzufriedenheit mit der ungarischen Außenpolitik, worauf die Vertreter der ungarischen Regierung eine aktivere Außenpolitik und militärische Vorbereitungen in Aussicht stellten.[4] Als Ergebnis der engeren deutsch—ungarischen Beziehungen wurde im November 1938 auf Grund eines Schiedsspruches (»Erster Wiener Schiedsspruch«) der an Ungarn grenzende Landstreifen der Slowakei an Ungarn zurückgegliedert.

Der mit deutscher Hilfe erfolgte Gebietszuwachs festigte den bedingungslos deutschfreundlichen Flügel der ungarischen herrschenden Klasse, die der bedingungslosen deutschen wirtschaftlichen und politischen Unterwerfung bereitwillig zustimmte. Die Positionsstärkung der absoluten Anhänger der Nazipolitik und das zunehmende Hervortreten der deutschen Bestre-

[2] Documents of German Foreign Policy. Series D Volume V. S. 203 und 242.
[3] Ebendort S. 301.
[4] Ebendort.

bungen innerhalb des Landes ging mit einer Neubelebung des deutschen Kapitals in Ungarn einher. Der ungarische Außenhandel mit Österreich und der Tschechoslowakei wurde nunmehr als ungarisch-deutscher Außenhandel weiter geführt, wodurch Deutschland sozusagen eine *Monopolstellung* erlangte. Sándor Knob, einer der Leiter des Landesverbandes der Ungarländischen Fabrikindustriellen (GYOSZ) bezeichnete die ungarisch-deutschen Außenhandelsbeziehungen folgendermaßen: »Fast 50% der ungarischen Ausfuhr kommt gegenwärtig auf den deutschen Markt. Ein 48%iges Verhältnis steht also einem dreiprozentigen gegenüber . . .« (Das war nämlich die Verhältniszahl der ungarischen Ausfuhr innerhalb der deutschen Einfuhr.) »Dieses Verhältnis bzw. Mißverhältnis, bedeutet meiner Überzeugung nach ein solches Maß der wirtschaftlichen Ausgeliefertheit und Abhängigkeit, das schon an diejenigen Gefahren grenzt, die nicht ganz unbegründet erwähnt werden, wenn wir über die wirtschaftliche und politische Unabhängigkeit des Landes sprechen.«[5]

Diese Monopolstellung im Außenhandel wurde überdies durch einen sich auf dem Gebiet der Kapitalinteressen geltend machenden deutschen Einfluß ergänzt. Die deutschen Kapitalbeteiligungen betrugen nach der Besitzergreifung der österreichischen und tschechischen Kapitalanlagen 12% des ungarischen industriellen Aktienkapitals. Selbstverständlich wäre dieses Verhältnis an und für sich noch nicht sehr bedeutend gewesen, obwohl die deutschen Kapitalanlagen die entscheidenden industriellen Schlüsselstellungen an sich gebracht haben. Wenn wir aber in Betracht ziehen, daß diese verhältnismäßig kleine Kapitalbeteiligungen von einem wirtschaftlichen Druck im Außenhandel und, was noch entscheidender ist, von einem immer stärker werdenden politischen Druck begleitet waren, so wird uns klar, daß der deutsche wirtschaftliche Einfluß in Ungarn große Ausmaße annahm. Pál Teleki, Imrédys Nachfolger, hat im Jahre 1939 im Zusammenhang mit dem deutschen wirtschaftlichen Einfluß in einem Brief folgende Feststellungen gemacht: »Das deutsche Reich verfügt in unserem Vaterland über so großangelegte und weitverzweigte wirtschaftliche Interessen, daß durch diese das ganze ungarische Wirtschaftsleben kontrolliert, bis zu einem gewissen Maße sogar beeinflußt werden kann.« Teleki wies darauf hin, daß diese Interessen nicht neueren Ursprungs sind, doch »seit dem Machtantritt der nationalsozialistischen deutschen Regierung, insbesondere seit der Entfaltung der nach dem Südostraum gerichteten Lebensraumpolitik einerseits neue Interessen entstanden, andererseits sich die alten Beziehungen erweiterten und eine *politische Bedeutung* erhielten«.[6]

Das faschistische Deutschland wollte seinen in jeder Beziehung erhöhten Einfluß durch die Verwirklichung seiner immer mehr wachsenden politi-

[5] Landesarchiv. Parlamentsausschuß. VII. 170—171.

[6] L. A. Außenministerium. Wirtschaftspolitische Sektion (= Wp S.) 1939. Deutsches Dossier. 358. Res.

schen und wirtschaftlichen Ansprüche realisieren und noch mehr steigern. Sie erzielten auch immer neue und neue Erfolge. So war z. B. der Anschluß Ungarns an den Antikominternpakt ein bedeutsamer Schritt auf politischem Gebiet. Auf wirtschaftlichem Gebiet aber schnitten die deutschen Expansionsbestrebungen direkt ins lebendige Fleisch der wichtigen, die Wirtschaftsmacht des Landes in ihren Händen haltenden Gruppen der ungarischen herrschenden Klassen. Dennoch brachten die deutschen Monopolisten — mit voller Unterstützung ihrer ungarischen Vasallen — zu jener Zeit ihre diesbezüglichen Forderungen unmißverständlich zum Ausdruck.

Der laut des Handelsabkommens vom Jahre 1931 alljährlich tagende Deutsch-Ungarische Gemischte Ausschuß hielt seine Jahreskonferenz im Frühjahr 1939 in München ab, zwecks Beschprechung der mit dem Warenverkehr des Jahres 1939 zusammenhängenden Fragen. Auf dieser Konferenz forderte die deutsche Regierung größere Lieferungen von landwirtschaftlichen Produkten, was ihnen seitens der ungarischen Delegation auch zugesagt wurde. So wurden 50% des Weizenexportüberschusses (höchstens 2,5 Millionen Doppelzentner), 35% des Roggenexportüberschusses und 60% des Maisexportüberschusses den Deutschen angeboten. Die Deutschen erklärten, sie wären geneigt jede Menge Gerste, Hafer und Mais zu übernehmen. Außerdem verpflichtete sich Ungarn selbstverständlich, die Tier- und Tierprodukten-, Obst-, Gemüseausfuhr usw. zu intensivieren.

Gleichzeitig mit der Forderung nach einer Steigerung der Ausfuhr von landwirtschaftlichen Erzeugnissen erklärte Deutschland, daß es im weiteren nicht geneigt sei, die hohen ungarischen Weizenpreise zu bezahlen[7] und daß der neue Preis aus einer Kombination der ungarischen und der Weltmarktpreise festgelegt werden müsse. Das war der erste Schritt zur späteren ungünstigen Entwicklung der Ausfuhr-Einfuhrpreise während des Krieges.

Noch nachteiliger als die Frage des Preisniveaus war aber die Ankündigung über die Steigerung des deutschen Exports von Industriewaren. Und dies um so mehr, als die deutschen Monopolisten hauptsächlich Kraftwagen, Kunstdünger, Glas- und Porzellanwaren zu exportieren wünschten, hingegen die Ausfuhr von Werkzeugmaschinen und Roheisen, was die ungarischen Kapitalisten dringend benötigten, ganz oder teilweise verweigerten. Da aber die wachsende Ausfuhr von landwirtschaftlichen Erzeugnissen den Außenhandelssaldo notwendigerweise zugunsten Ungarns vergrößerte, war die ungarische Delegation gezwungen, einer Erhöhung des industriellen Einfuhrkontingents zuzustimmen.[7a] Es ist nur zu natürlich, daß nach alldem die Dele-

[7] Zu Beginn der dreißiger Jahre hat Deutschland — um für die politischen und späteren wirtschaftlichen Vorteile seines Handelsverkehrs mit Ungarn eine Grundlage zu schaffen — von Ungarn das Getreide zu höheren Preisen als der damalige Weltmarktpreis übernommen.

[7a] L. A. A. M. Wp. S. Res. 30—1939.

gation ihren Bericht über die Verhandlungen in einem erbitterten Ton erstattete, wonach »die Tendenz zu beobachten gewesen sei, Ungarn auf das Niveau eines Rohproduzentenlandes herabzudrücken«.[8]

Kurz danach überreichte die deutsche Regierung den ungarischen Behörden ein Memorandum, in dem im wesentlichen Ungarns Platz und Rolle in den deutschen Plänen festgelegt wurde. Der erste Teil des Memorandums behandelte Fragen der ungarischen Landwirtschaft. Die wichtigsten deutschen Forderungen wurden folgendermaßen zusammengefaßt: »Die ungarische Landwirtschaft muß sich stärker als bisher den Bedürfnissen des deutschen Marktes anpassen.« Unter einer stärkeren Anpassung an die Bedürfnisse des deutschen Marktes verstand man, daß die ungarische Landwirtschaft ihre Produktion besonders von solchen Waren heben müsse, die die deutsche Kriegswirtschaft brauchte, vorwiegend Ölsamen, Weizen, Fettstoffen und Futterpflanzen. Die Deutschen waren geneigt die ganze ungarische Ausfuhr dieser Waren zu übernehmen. Gleichzeitig wurde auch darauf hingewiesen, daß eine Hebung des ungarischen Exports von landwirtschaftlichen Erzeugnissen — der ein erstrangiges Interesse der ungarischen Groß- und Mittelgrundbesitzer bildete — nur dann möglich sei, wenn als Gegenleistung Ungarn von Deutschland mehr Industrieprodukte übernimmt. Es wurde klipp und klar erklärt, daß parallel mit der zunehmenden Agrarausfuhr ». . . bei jeder Verhandlung die Notwendigkeit einer Steigerung der deutschen Einfuhr nach Ungarn in den Vordergrund zu stellen ist«. Im Interesse einer erhöhten Einfuhr von Industriewaren wurde sogar »eine Revidierung der ganzen ungarischen Einfuhrpolitik« gefordert, was die Aufhebung des Systems von Schutzzöllen und Einfuhrbeschränkungen nach sich gezogen hätte. Das wäre einer Auslieferung der ungarischen Industrie an die Interessen des deutschen Finanzkapitals gleichbedeutend gewesen. Bezüglich der ungarischen Industrie erhielt der zweite Teil des Memorandums völlig extreme »Vorschläge«. Vielsagend ist schon der Titel dieses Kapitels im Memorandum: »Anpassung der ungarischen industriellen Produktion an die deutschen Ausfuhrbedürfnisse«. Unter »Anpassung an die deutschen Ausfuhrbedürfnisse« verstand man folgendes: Da die Einfuhr der deutschen Industrieartikel sehr wichtig sei, ist für Ungarn die Entwicklung der landwirtschaftlichen Industrie am zweckmäßigsten, und das stünde auch in keinem Gegensatz zu den deutschen Einfuhrinteressen! Außer den Zoll- und anderen Forderungen gingen sie in der Einmischung in die inneren ungarischen Angelegenheiten so weit, daß sie die Abschaffung der Steuer- und Kreditbegünstigungen für ungarische Fabriken verlangten, da diese — wie offen erklärt wurde — der deutschen Konkurrenz auf dem ungarischen Markt Schwierigkeiten bereiten.[9]

[8] L. A. A. M. Wp. S. Res. 30. — 1939.
[9] Zentralwirtschaftsarchiv. Ungarische Nationalbank 7/1940.

Die deutschen Ansprüche waren darum so gefährlich, weil sie — selbst in ihren extremsten Formen — auch ungarische Fürsprecher fanden, und zwar gerade in den Regierungskreisen unter den Leitern der zuständigen Ministerien. Industrieminister Antal Kunder schlug z. B. in seiner Eigenschaft als Sprachrohr des deutschen Finanzkapitals den ungarischen Fabriksbesitzern vor, sie sollen mit den Vertretern der entsprechenden deutschen Industriezweige ein Abkommen abschließen, und feststellen, für welche Artikel »die Produktionsbedingungen in Ungarn am günstigsten seien und bei welchen eine Einfuhr aus Deutschland zweckmäßiger wäre«. Kunder verkündete auch die deutsche Forderung, wonach »der deutsche Import von den bisherigen Beschränkungen zu befreien sei«.

Der Landesverband der Ungarländischen Fabrikindustriellen verwahrte sich aufs schärfste dagegen. Unter anderem wurde darauf hingewiesen, es hänge davon ab, ob deutsche oder ungarische Industrievertreter feststellen, was für die ungarische Industrieproduktion als rentabel zu betrachten sei. Das deutsche Finanzkapital wendet nämlich Ungarn gegenüber oft besondere Exportpreise an, um auf die Weise die ungarische Industrie bewußt zu untergraben. Diese Preise sind aber nicht rentabel und im Falle der Stillegung der ungarischen Fabriken würden sie zweifelsohne sofort erhöht werden. Gleichzeitig sehen sie aber klar — und das war meistens bestimmend für die Stellungnahme der deutschfeindlichen Gruppen in den ungarischen herrschenden Klassen —, daß »die Zeit der prinzipiellen Ablehnung vorbei ist . . . und . . . wir die bestehende Lage in Betracht ziehen müssen«. Ebendeshalb traten sie mit Überbrückungsvorschlägen auf: sie schlugen Marktsicherungsabkommen vor, bezogen den Standpunkt, daß »die zukünftigen Industrieentwicklungsmöglichkeiten nicht geopfert werden dürfen . . . Es kann nur von einer Aufschiebung der Industrieentwicklung die Rede sein, und gerade auf diesem Gebiet könnten wir den Deutschen wesentliche Zugeständnisse machen«.[10] Diese Konzeption — Positionssicherung durch Zugeständnisse — war ebenfalls für die Stellungnahme derjenigen Vertreter der herrschenden Klassen bestimmend, die sich um den Landesverband der Ungarländischen Fabrikindustriellen gruppiert hatten.

Das Finanzkapital erkannte in dem gegen die Industrie gerichteten Angriff auch die politischen Bestrebungen, István Bethlen hat in diesem Zusammenhang erklärt: ». . . Bei den unlängst stattgefundenen Verhandlungen zog sich wie ein roter Faden die seitens unserer Verhandlungspartner an uns gerichtete Warnung: Forcieren Sie die ungarische Industrie nicht . . . Sie sind doch ein Agrarland, bleiben Sie auch weiterhin ein Bauernland und verkaufen Sie uns ihre landwirtschaftlichen Produkte . . . Wir werden Sie schon mit Industrieartikeln versehen . . . Das bedeutet eine völlige wirtschaftliche

[10] Honi Ipar (Heimische Industrie) in den Nummern vom 15. März. 1., April und 1. Mai 1939.

Abhängigkeit, eine völlige wirtschaftliche Penetration seitens Deutschlands, der nur eine politische Abhängigkeit folgen kann.«[11]

Über die drohende Gefahr der deutschen wirtschaftlichen Expansion hinaus erkannten das Finanzkapital und die Großgrundbesitzerkreise in den deutschen Großmachtbestrebungen die Schranken ihrer eigenen politischen Bestrebungen.

Am 1. September 1939 entfesselte Hitler-Deutschland durch den Angriff auf Polen den zweiten Weltkrieg. Die deutschen militärischen Anfangserfolge in Polen und später in Westeuropa gingen mit einer Steigerung der Ansprüche und des Druckes einher. Nach Kriegsbeginn forderten die nazistischen Führerkreise — gestützt auf ihre treuen Vasallen — immer dringlicher die Verwirklichung ihrer Ungarnpläne. 1940 war die oben angedeutete Wandlung im deutschen Verhalten bei den damaligen Handelsverkehrsverhandlungen bereits klar zu beobachten. Die deutsche Regierung kündigte schon damals an, daß sie ihren Lieferungsverpflichtungen bei einer ganzen Reihe von wichtigen Artikeln nicht nachkommen würde, die ungarische Ausfuhraber dessen ungeachtet bis zur Grenze des Möglichen zu steigern wäre! Nun wird das Programm der völligen Ausraubung des Landes zum erstenmal offen in Worte gefaßt. Dieses Programm wurde in den folgenden Jahren unzähligemal wiederholt: »Die beiden Länder, von denen das eine in einem Kampf auf Leben und Tod steht, das andere aber keinen Krieg führt, haben einander in allem zu helfen, was das eine dem anderen geben kann, ohne die Lieferungen momentan in ein genaues Gleichgewicht zu bringen, so wie es unter guten Freunden üblich ist, jeder bis zur äußersten Grenze seiner Leistungsfähigkeit, eingedenk dessen, daß der andere die erhaltene Hilfe rückerstatten werde, wenn er sich wieder in einer leichteren Lage befinde.«[12]

Die immer agressiveren Aktionen gegen Ungarn bildeten natürlich einen organischen Teil der nach allen südosteuropäischen Ländern gerichteten Expansion, die bereits zur Zeit der Kriegsvorbereitungen zur Geltung kam. Nach der Entfesselung des Krieges ist für das Dritte Reich die völlige Verwirklichung seiner Pläne dringend notwendig geworden. Zu diesem Zweck wurde im Frühjahr 1940 die Südosteuropäische Gesellschaft ins Leben gerufen. Der Berliner ungarische Gesandte stellte in seinem Bericht fest, daß die deutschen Wirtschaftskreise infolge der Einführung der Seeblokade mit erhöhter Intensität auf die weitere Entwicklung ihrer wirtschaftlichen Beziehungen mit Südosteuropa hinarbeiten.

Auf dem Gebiet der Landwirtschaft wurde im Interesse des Ausfuhrvolumens der auf Ungarn lastende Druck immer mehr verstärkt. Im Herbst

[11] L. A. Parlamentsausschuß. XVII. — 84. — I. 23. 1939.
[12] L. A. A. M. Wp. S. Res. 1940. 12.

1940 wurden die Moritz—Jurcsekschen Besprechungen geführt. In dem Abkommen vom 9. Oktober wurde zwischen Deutschland und Ungarn eine engere wissenschaftliche und praktische Zusammenarbeit auf dem Gebiet der Landwirtschaft festgelegt. Die Agrarexperten beider Länder sollten unter Anleitung der deutschen Versorgungs- und Landwirtschaftsminister sowie des ungarischen Ackerbauministers einen gemeinsamen Versuchs- und Forschungsplan ausarbeiten und dessen Ergebnisse gegenseitig austauschen. Ferner wurden laut der Vereinbarung deutsch—ungarische gemischte Ausschüsse gebildet, deren Aufgabe darin bestand, die Qualität der nach Deutschland gehenden und in dem Abkommen erwähnten Agrarprodukte zu verbessern und im Interesse der Mehrproduktion — aber im Einklang mit den Verbrauchstraditionen — neue Saatkörner und Produktionsmethoden einzuführen. In einem Punkt wurde die stufenweise Vergrößerung der ungarländischen Ölsamensaatgebiete und parallel damit eine bestimmte Steigerung der nach Deutschland gerichteten Ölsamenausfuhr auch zahlenmäßig festgestellt, während ein anderer Punkt ähnliche Vereinbarungen in bezug auf die Futtersamen enthielt[12a]. Trotz des immer empfindlicher werdenden deutschen Druckes hat die landwirtschaftliche Ausfuhr selbst im Jahre 1940 nicht zugenommen, sondern abgenommen. Die Ursache davon lag in einer katastrophalen Mißernte. Nicht nur daß von bedeutenden Produktionsüberschüssen keine Rede sein konnte, nicht einmal die einheimischen Bedürfnisse vermochten befriedigt zu werden, und dies um so weniger, als im Herbst 1940 die Bevölkerung des Landes durch die Eingliederung eines Teils von Siebenbürgen wesentlich gewachsen ist und diese Territorien selbst auf einen Agrarimport angewiesen waren.

Die Lage in der Industrie war vor allem dadurch gekennzeichnet, daß zu jener Zeit keine bedeutenden Operationen zu Lande im Gange waren. In Deutschland wurde die Kriegsproduktion nicht gesteigert,[13] ein Teil der mächtigen deutschen Schwerindustrie ist frei geworden. Das deutsche Finanzkapital war demzufolge bestrebt, seine Märkte zu erweitern, die Fertigwarenausfuhr zu vergrößern, um auf diese Weise eine Vollbeschäftigung zu sichern. Die früher bemerkbaren deutschen Eroberungsbestrebungen und die wirtschaftliche Expansion wurden jetzt unverhüllter. Gleichzeitig verstärkte sich der politische Terror des deutschen Faschismus, der besonders nach dem Überrennen Südosteuropas bedrohlicher und für Ungarn noch dadurch unheilvoller wurde, daß er auch innerhalb des Landes eine starke Basis besaß. Der deutsche Faschismus verlieh seinen maßlosen Ansprüchen durch eine zynisch offene Formulierung seiner schon früher bemerkbaren Tendenzen Ausdruck. Im Frühjahr 1941 teilte der provisorische ungarische Geschäfts-

[12a] L. A. A. M. Wp. S. Res. 336—1942.
[13] Vgl.: Die deutsche Industrie im Kriege. 1939—1945. Berlin 1954.

träger in Berlin, Szentmiklóssy, in einem Geheimschreiben an den ungarischen Ministerpresidenten Bárdossy mit, daß die Deutschen in der Frage der »Neuordnung Europas« durch den halbamtlichen Sprecher des Außenamtes ihr Wirtschaftsprinzip ganz offen und klar dargelegt hätten. Unmißverständlich haben sie dort ihre dahingehende Meinung zum Ausdruck gebracht, daß sich die südosteuropäischen Staaten »an ihre natürlichen Bedingungen anzupassen hätten« und daß die Industrialisierung »im Gegensatz zum landwirtschaftlichen Charakter dieser Länder stünde. Als eine brutale Abfassung ihrer Kolonialisierungsinteressen wurde folgendes erklärt : »Gleichzeitig mit der politischen Revision haben sich die südosteuropäischen Länder auch wirtschaftlich den Anforderungen der kontinentalen Ökonomie (d. h. des deutschen Finanzkapitals) anzupassen. Ihre landwirtschaftliche Produktion wird von den Bedürfnissen der anderen Teile des Kontinents gelenkt. Als Hauptprodukte kommen Getreide und Ölsamen in Betracht, ergänzungsweise sind auch andere Industriepflanzen anzubauen, und in diesem Zusammenhang kann sich auch eine landwirtschaftliche Industrie entfalten... Die Rohstoffproduktion (gemeint sind Öl, Erze und Leichtmetalle) wird unter Ausnützung von Wasserkräften durch ihre örtliche Verarbeitung zu Halbfabrikaten ergänzt« wurde jetzt nun viel gebieterischer, als in den Jahren 1938 und 1939 erklärt. Zum Abschluß machte Geschäftsträger Szentmiklóssy auf Folgendes aufmerksam : »In industrieller Hinsicht können wir vom ungarischen Gesichtspunkt aus mit dreierlei deutschen Plänen rechnen, die sich in kleinerem Maße auch bisher geoffenbart hatten : Bei der Schaffung und Entwicklung der landwirtschaftlichen Industriezweige arbeiten die Deutschen auf eine »gelenkte Zusammenarbeit« hin, was bedeuten würde, daß sie durch ihre ständig zu gewärtigenden Einmischungen die Entwicklung auf diesem Gebiete den Bedürfnissen des deutschen Marktes gemäß gestalten würden. Bei den schon bestehenden Industriezweigen hingegen besteht die Absicht, diese in die deutschen Interessensphären einzubeziehen. Schließlich wird die Entstehung von vom deutschen Gesichtspunkt aus ungünstigen Industrieunternehmungen mit allen Mitteln hintangehalten, die als nützlich erachteten aber mit deutschem Kapital oder zumindest mit deutscher Kapitalbeteiligung gegründet werden«.[14]

Die immer hemmungsloseren imperialistischen Eroberungsbestrebungen gingen zu dieser Zeit schon weit über die prinzipiellen Erklärungen hinaus und zielten darauf hin, die für sie unnötigen, sogar unvorteilhaften Zweige der ungarischen Industrie durch einen verschärfteren Wirtschaftswettbewerb zugrunde zu richten bzw. eine Entfaltung ihrer Produktionskapazität zu vereiteln. Demzufolge wurde der deutsche Warenimport nach Ungarn im Laufe des Jahres 1940 *erheblich gesteigert*. Unter Berufung auf die ungarischen

[14] I. A. A. M. Wp. S. Res. 466—1941.

bzw. deutschen Gebietserweiterungen ist es den Deutschen mehrmals gelungen, ihre Einfuhrkontingente beträchtlich zu erhöhen. So z. B. im Januar 1940 und laut des für das folgende Wirtschaftsjahr gültigen Vertrags vom Juli 1940 unter Berufung auf die Eingliederung der Karpato-Ukraine an Ungarn und auf die Gebietserweiterungen Deutschlands, sowie am 15. September 1940 unter Bezugnahme auf die Einverleibung Nordsiebenbürgens und 1941 der Südgebiete. Demzufolge ist der schon an sich enorme deutsche Warenimport im Laufe eines einzigen Jahres (1940) um 35% gewachsen und die deutsch—ungarischen Außenhandelsbilanz war seit langen Jahren zum erstenmal wieder passiv.[15] Dazu trug auch der Umstand bei, daß auf deutsche Forderung der Preiszuschlag der deutschen Mark erhöht wurde.

Über den, auf dem inneren Markt ausgetragenen erbitterten Konkurrenzkampf hinaus, bei dem die deutschen Monopolisten von den Schleuderpreisen bis zur Industriespionage zu allen Mitteln griffen, trat das deutsche Finanzkapital *auch auf dem Balkan* gegen die ungarischen Unternehmen, insbesondere die ungarische Schwerindustrie auf. Obwohl die ungarische Delegation bereits anläßlich der deutsch—ungarischen Wirtschaftsverhandlungen im Jahre 1939 zur Sprache brachte, daß die ungarische Industrie für die durch den deutschen Fertigwarenimport verursachten Schäden in der Form zu entschädigen wäre, daß »Deutschland uns auf den Balkanmärkten keine Konkurrenz machte«...[16], wurde die deutsche Konkurrenz auch auf diesem Gebiet immer rücksichtsloser. So hat sie den ungarischen Industrieexport nach Jugoslawien zurückgedrängt, wodurch für Ungarn ein Passivsaldo von mehreren Millionen entstand.[17] Kennzeichnend für die deutsche Konkurrenz und ihre Methoden ist folgendes : Als die bulgarische Regierung bei der ungarischen Firma »Standard« Fernsprechzentralen und Apparate im Werte von 100 Millionen Leva bestellte, intervenierten die zuständigen deutschen Ministerien bei der bulgarischen Regierung und verlangten die Bestellung für sich selbst, wobei sie ihre Forderungen sogar mit militärischen Lieferungen verbanden, so daß die bulgarische Regierung nachzugeben gezwungen war.[18] Die ungarische Gesandtschaft in Ankara teilte in ihrem Bericht mit, daß die Deutschen billigere Eisenhalbfabrikate zu liefern versprachen, als dies in der Weiss-Manfred—Sumer-Bank-Abmachung vorgesehen war.[19] Ein Bericht der Berliner ungarischen Gesandtschaft besagt über die mächtige deutsche Konkurrenz folgendes : »In letzterer Zeit erleiden wir nicht nur bei unseren konkreten Bitten eine Abfuhr, sondern ich muß auf Schritt und Tritt die Erfahrung machen, daß uns deutscherseits

[15] Magyar Gyáripar (Ungarische Industrie). Nr. 12, 1940. Statisztikai Évkönyv (Statistisches Jahrbuch) 1940.
[16] L. A. A. M. Wp. S. Deutsches Dossier. 101.
[17] ZWA. Industriesekretariat der Commerzbank 39.
[18] L. A. A. M. Wp. S. Chiffredepesche vom 28. Januar 1941.
[19] L. A. A. M. Wp. S. Res. 1941.

auch in dritten Ländern . . . durch die dort angewandten politischen Erpressungmaßnahmen Konkurrenz gemacht wird . . .«[20]

Es wäre aber irrig, aus alldem die Schlußfolgerung zu ziehen, daß es den deutschen Monopolisten in den Jahren 1939 und 1940 gelungen wäre, die ungarische Industrieproduktion zurückzudrängen. Die große Kriegskonjunktur hat der ungarischen Industrie wachsende Produktionsmöglichkeiten gesichert, die durch den zunehmenden deutschen Export nur in geringem Maße gestört werden konnten. Den Deutschen ist es zwar gelungen, einige Gebiete der ungarischen Wirtschaft — Landwirtschaft, Rohstofferzeugung — vor 1941 in den Dienst der Interessen der deutschen Kriegswirtschaft zu stellen, doch vermochte das wirtschaftlich mächtige ungarische Finanzkapital trotz des großen Druckes seine Positionen in Bezug auf die Industrie, an die sich keine unmittelbaren deutschen kriegswirtschaftlichen Interessen knüpften, weiterhin zu wahren.

Nachdem die ganze Wirtschaft der unterjochten Länder Europas in den Dienst der eigenen Kriegswirtschaft gestellt wurde, brachen die hitlerfaschistischen Truppen am 22. Juni 1941 treubrüchig in das Gebiet der Sowjetunion ein. Mit dem Angriff gegen die Sowjetunion trat der Krieg in eine neue Phase. Die deutsche Kriegsführung, die — von ihren bisherigen Erfolgen geblendet — auch hier mit einem Blitzkrieg rechnete, machte ungeheuere Vorbereitungen zur raschen Niederwerfung der Sowjetunion. Hitler-Deutschland verlangte, daß das Wirtschaftsleben der Vasallenstaaten noch mehr in den Dienst der deutschen Kriegsmaschinerie gestellt werde. Die Teilnahme an dem antisowjetischen Krieg bedeutete für Horthy-Ungarn, daß es noch mehr zu einem Vasallenstaat herabsank und sich wirtschaftlich und politisch Deutschland auslieferte. Dieser Schritt der ungarischen herrschenden Klassen war der Gipfel landesverräterischer Politik und trieb das Land an den Rand der unvermeidlichen Katastrophe.

Die deutsche Kriegsführung war sich schon vor der Entfesselung des antisowjetischen Krieges bewußt, daß dieser Angriff eine alles bisherige übersteigende Anstrengung von der deutschen Kriegsmaschinerie und vom deutschen Wirtschaftsleben erfordern würde. Deshalb wurde die ganze Wirtschaft der unterjochten und Vasallenländer in die Kriegsvorbereitungen mit einbezogen. So wurden vor allem die Ausfuhrtransporte der Rohstoffe und Lebensmittel bedeutend gesteigert. Im Laufe der deutsch—ungarischen Wirtschaftsverhandlungen vom Juli 1941 für die Jahre 1941 und 1942, verpflichtete sich die ungarische Abordnung, daß Ungarn 5% seiner »Weizen- und Roggenüberschüsse« — was nach der Befriedigung der dürftigen Rationen noch übrigbleibt — Deutschland sichern werde. Außerdem verpflichtete sich die ungarische Regierung, bis zur Beendigung des Krieges die Agrarüberschüsse

[20] L. A. A. M. Wp. S. Res. 1941. — 111.

aus den einverleibten Südgebieten auszuführen. Der Vertrag gestattete Ungarn nur die Deckung des eigenen Ölkuchen- und Hanfbedarfes, und zwar lediglich in einer, der früheren jugoslawischen Einfuhr entsprechenden Menge. Außer den Geitreideüberschüssen wurden die gesamten Ölsamen und 80% der Maisüberschüsse nach Deutschland ausgeführt. Zur Sicherstellung der großen »Überschußmengen« erschien am 15. August eine Verordnung, die das Getreideausmahlen regelte, höheres Ausmahlprozent vorsah und eine sparsame Mehlwirtschaft vorschrieb. Dieser Verordnung folgte aber bald eine noch strengere »Sparsamkeitsverordnung« : am 6. September wurde in Budapest und Umgebung — also in erster Reihe zuungunsten der breitesten Arbeitermassen — das Mehl- und Brotkartensystem eingeführt. Die Ration wurde auf monatlich 2 kg Mehl und täglich 250 g Brot festgestellt.

Auf dem Gebiet der Tierausfuhr wurde eine Ausfuhrverpflichtung von jährlich 56 000 Rindern und ebensoviel Schafen übernommen. Entgegen dem ungarischen Angebot, 100 000 Schweine zu liefern, forderten die Deutschen 175 000 Stück.[21]

Innerhalb von wenigen Monaten ist aber infolge der Niederlage der deutschen Truppen bei Moskau klar geworden, daß die Aussichten auf einen Blitzkrieg zusammenstürzten und die faschistischen Eindringlinge noch harte, langwierige Kämpfe werden bestehen müssen. Dieser Umstand stellte das deutsche Wirtschaftsleben vor immer größere Schwierigkeiten, denen es nicht mehr gewachsen war. In dem Maße, wie die deutschen Schwierigkeiten wuchsen, wurden auch die Maßnahmen gegen die unterjochten und Vasallenstaaten drückender. Im Dezember 1941 beordnete Ribbentrop den ungarischen Ministerpresidenten Bárdossy zu sich und forderte mit unmißverständlicher Offenheit eine weitere Steigerung der Ausfuhr. In seinen vertraulichen Aufzeichnungen berichtete Bárdossy über sein Gespräch mit Ribbentrop : »Er berief sich darauf, daß sie gegenwärtig auf dem Maximum ihrer Kraftanstrengungen stünden und er zugeben müsse, daß sie jetzt alles bedürften, um das augenblickliche gigantische Ringen mit Erfolg zu Ende führen zu können. Er sage es mir offen, daß es in erster Reihe auf Öl und Getreide ankomme! Er bittet uns, alles zu tun, wir müßten doch selbst einsehen, daß in den jetzigen Kämpfen sie die größten Opfer brächten, und alle, die über entbehrliche Vorräte verfügen, müßten dem Deutschen Reich zu Hilfe eilen . . .« Zwei Tage später waren schon konkrete Verhandlungen über die Erhöhung der Ausfuhrtransporte im Gange. Die Verhandlungen wurden deutscherseits von Clodius und Moritz, ungarischerseits vom Staatssekretär im Versorgungsministerium István Losonczy geführt. Im Laufe dieser Verhandlungen begnügte sich die Nazi- Regierung schon nicht mehr mit den sogenannten »Überschüssen«, sondern for-

[21] L. A. A. M. Wp. S. Geheimprotokoll Nr. 21 über die deutsch—ungarischen Besprechungen 7—29. Juli 1941.

derte weitere Opfer. Und was in der Ribbentropschen Abfassung noch als Übergabe von »entbehrlichen Überschüssen« figurierte, wurde hier schon mit brutaler Offenheit folgendermaßen gefordert : ». . . wir mögen uns nicht darauf berufen, daß wir von dem einen oder anderen Produkt heute oder im folgenden Jahr keine Überschüsse hätten, sondern eilen wir ihnen selbst um den Preis einer gewissen Beschränkung der einheimischen Versorgung zu Hilfe«.[22] Wie es in dem Bericht des Berliner ungarischen Gesandten Döme Sztójay über die Verhandlungen heißt, »gab Losonczy sein Versprechen, daß er das berücksichtigen würde, und daß die ungarische Regierung deshalb beabsichtigte, bei wichtigen Versorgungsgütern noch weitere Beschränkungen und Rationen einzuführen, um einem solchen Ersuchen gerecht werden zu können«.[23] Demzufolge wurde im Februar 1942 und in den folgenden Monaten die Brotration auf 200 g, die monatliche Mehlration auf 1,6 kg herabgesetzt. Im Sommer 1942 wurden noch weitere Einschränkungen eingeführt und die Brotration auf 150 g gesenkt. Die bedingungslose Auslieferung der ungarischen Wirtschaft dem deutschen Faschismus brachte die ungarischen Arbeiter und Werktätigen in eine sehr schwere Lage. Die Bevölkerung Ungarns war selbst in europäischer Relation am schlechtesten versorgt. Im Frühjahr 1942 betrug die tägliche Brotration in Deutschland 286 g, die monatliche Zucker- bzw. Fettration 1012 bzw. 927 g — in Ungarn hingegen war die Brotration nur 200 g, die monatliche Zuckerration 600 g und die Fettration 720 g.[24]

In den Jahren 1942—43 vermochte man trotz äußerster Einschränkung des einheimischen Verbrauchs den deutschen Ansprüchen immer weniger gerecht werden. Der Grund hierfür lag aber nicht etwa darin, als ob die Politiker Horthy-Ungarns die Lieferungen sabotiert hätten, wie einige emigrierte Politiker nachträglich zu erklären suchten, sondern ganz entschieden darin, daß Ungarn während der Kriegsjahre einige Mißernten hatte. Wenn wir die Durchschnittsziffer der Brotgetreideproduktion in den Jahren 1929 bis 1938 mit 100 annehmen, so betrug sie 1940 — 83,1, 1941 — 84,1 und 1942 insgesamt nur 76,2. Eine gute Ernte hatte das Land nur in den Jahren 1943 und 1944. Ähnlich gestaltete sich die Lage bei Gerste, Mais und anderen landwirtschaftlichen Produkten. Hinzu kam der Bedarf der angeschwollenen Armee und die Deckung der Bedürfnisse der an Ungarn gegliederten Territorien. Diese Gebiete konnten nämlich ihre eigenen Bedürfnisse nur in geringem Maße decken (Siebenbürgen, Karpato-Ukraine). Wo aber Überschüsse vorhanden waren (Batschka), wurden diese — wie erwähnt — samt und sonders von den Deutschen beschlagnahmt. Unter solchen Umständen war die Auf-

[22] L. A. A. M. Wp. S. Res. 996. vom 10.12. 1941.
[23] L. A. A. M. Wp. S. Res. 1006. vom 12.12. 1941.
[24] Lagebericht Nr. 50 des Ungarischen Wirtschaftsinstituts, S. 111.

rechterhaltung der früheren Exportquoten — ohne im Lande eine katastrophale Hungersnot hervorzurufen — ein Ding der Unmöglichkeit geworden.

Man war aber bestrebt, auf zahlreichen anderen Gebieten Entschädigungen zu bieten, und zu diesem Zweck wurden in der bisherigen Struktur der ungarischen Landwirtschaft einige Abänderungen vorgenommen. Das Saatgebiet der von den Deutschen geforderten Ölpflanzen wurde im Verordnungswege erweitert, der Sonnenblumenanbau wurde auf Landgütern von über 50 Joch für obligatorisch erklärt, und zwar auf 5% des gesamten Saatgebietes ; hinzu kam ein weiterer 2prozentiger Rizinusanbau auf Landgütern von über 200 Joch. Im Jahre 1942 wurde der Pflichtanbau für Ölpflanzen auch auf Landgüter von über 15 Joch ausgedehnt, und zwar in einem noch höheren Maße als früher (7%). Demzufolge sind während des Krieges auch in der Struktur der Saatgebiete bedeutende Verschiebungen eingetreten. Am meisten ist das Saatgebiet der Industriepflanzen gewachsen : im Vergleich zu 1931—1939 stieg es bis zum Jahre 1944 fast auf das 3,2fache. Besonders erfuhr der Anbau von Ölsamen einen stürmischen Auftrieb. Wenn wir das Sonnenblumensaatgebiet der Jahre 1936—1938 als 100 annehmen, so war es 1944 schon 1858, für Flachs 407 usw. Im Zusammenhang mit der Ablieferungsverordnung war die Entwicklung der Halmfutterproduktion ebenfalls bedeutend.[25]

Die im Krieg vorgenommenen Veränderungen kamen in der gegebenen Lage in erster Reihe den Interessen der deutschen Kriegswirtschaft zustatten und haben zur Sicherung der deutschen Rohstoffversorgung beigetragen.

Außer der Ausfuhr von Getreide, Fleisch, Fett usw. traten die deutschen Monopolisten auch in Bezug auf die Ausfuhr von militärisch lebenswichtigen ungarländischen Rohstoffen (z. B. Öl und Bauxit) mit immer höheren, enormen Forderungen auf. Die ungarische Abordnung verpflichtete sich bereits bei den im Juli 1941 stattgefundenen Verhandlungen zur Lieferung großer Mengen der erwähnten Rohstoffe. Laut Vereinbarung sollten im nächsten Jahr 830 000 Tonnen Bauxit sichergestellt werden. Tatsächlich wurden im Jahre 1942 865 000 Tonnen exportiert, wobei die Gesamtproduktion 988 547 Tonnen betrug. Am 1. August 1942 verpflichtete sich die ungarische Regierung auf Grund zwischenstaatlicher Vereinbarungen zu einer jährlichen Ausfuhr von einer Million Tonnen Bauxit. Die gesamte Produktion lag damals noch unter dieser Ziffer, und das erwünschte Ausfuhrniveau wurde erst 1943 erreicht. Fast die gesamte Produktion wurde auch in jenem Jahr Deutschland zur Verfügung gestellt, doch genügte sie nicht mehr. In einer Vereinbarung von 1943 wurde eine weitere Steigerung der Bauxitproduktion im Wirtschaftsjahr 1943/44 bis auf 1,5 Millionen Tonnen, und im Wirtschaftsjahr 1944/45 sogar bis auf 2 Millionen

[25] *Miklós Szuhay*, Staatliche Einmischung und die ungarische Wirtschaftsproduktion im zweiten Weltkriege (Manuskript).

Tonnen vorgesehen, um diese Mengen sogleich nach Deutschland exportieren zu können.[26]

In gleichem Maße wuchsen die deutschen Ansprüche auf einen immer größeren Teil des ungarischen Ölschatzes. In Ungarn nahm die Ölproduktion erst am Vorabend des Krieges (1937) ihren Anfang. Die amerikanisch interessierte MAORT (Ungarisch—Amerikanische Ölindustrie-Aktiengesellschaft) trieb ihre Produktion in den Kriegsjahren immer mehr in die Höhe und trug damit zur Versorgung der Wehrmacht bei. Der Großteil der jährlich wachsenden Ölproduktion wanderte nämlich nach Deutschland. Im Jahre 1937 betrug die Ölproduktion noch kaum mehr, als 2000 Tonnen, und selbst 1938 bewegte sie sich noch um 43 000 Tonnen. In den Kriegsjahren nahm die Produktion einen stürmischen Anlauf. 1939 wurden 143 000, 1941 bereits 422 000, und 1943 bereits 842 000 Tonnen Öl erzeugt.[26a] Wie sich der Industrieminister 1942 auf einer Geheimkonferenz äußerte, »könnte diese Politik den ganzen Landesbedarf auch ohne Beschränkungen reichlich decken. Der Grund der Einschränkungen liegt im Kriegsbedarf und darin, daß wir zu Zwecken der gemeinsamen Kriegsführung nach Deutschland und Italien beträchtliche Mengen von verarbeitetem Rohöl und sogar auch Rohöl ausführen.«[27] Ende 1941 konnte zum Beispiel ein außerordentlicher Öltransport von 80 000 Tonnen erst nach völliger Lahmlegung des privaten Kraftwagenverkehrs nach Deutschland ausgeführt werden. Als bei der erwähnten Besprechung zwischen Bárdossy und Ribbentrop der ungarische Ministerpresident sich hierauf berief, »holte Ribbentrop eine Aufzeichnung hervor, warf einen Blick darauf und bemerkte, daß die Deutschen tatsächlich von uns unlängst 80 000 Tonnen erhalten hätten und sehr dankbar dafür seien. Seines Erachtens könnte aber diese Menge auf 120 000 Tonnen erhöht werden«.[28] Im Jahre 1942 wurden rund 300, 1944 400 000 Tonnen Öl nach Deutschland ausgeführt — größtenteils raffiniert. Das war ungefähr die Hälfte der gesamten ungarischen Ölproduktion.[29]

Neben Bauxit und Öl legten die Deutschen großes Gewicht auf die Ausfuhr jedes auffindbaren und transportfähigen Rohstoffes. Stark forcierten sie zum Beispiel die ungarische Manganerzproduktion. Deutschland konnte seinen Bedarf an Manganerz bei weitem nicht aus eigenen Mitteln decken und bedurfte eines Imports von ungefähr 500 000 Tonnen. Während der zeitweiligen Besetzung der Ukraine konnten sie sich an den sowjetischen Mineralschätzen

[26] L. A. A. M. Material des Ausschusses für Friedensvorbereitung II/2—28/13 und I/1—3/1—24/20. L. A. A. M. Wp. S. Geheimprotokoll Nr. 25 über die deutsch—ungarischen Besprechungen. 13.2—7.8. 1943.

[26a] Auf Grund der Statistischen Jahrbücher.

[27] L. A. Parlamentsakten. Protokoll des 42er Ausschusses vom 19.10. 1942. XXX. S. 349.

[28] L. A. A. M. Wp. S. Res. 996. vom 10.12. 1941.

[29] L. A. A. M. Wp. S. Paket 706. Geheimprotokoll Nr. 25 über die deutsch—ungarischen Besprechungen. S. 71—73.

schadlos halten, nach dem deutschen Rückzug und nach dem Verlust der geraubten Gebiete war der Mangel an Manganerz besonders spürbar. In jener Zeit hat das deutsche Finanzkapital die ungarische Manganproduktion auch mit eigenen Kapitalinvestitionen gefördert. Im Jahre 1938 machte die Produktion alles in allem nur 15 000 Tonnen aus, nach Kriegsausbruch belief sie sich auf 60 000, 1941 auf 70 000, 1942 auf 87 000 Tonnen, während sie 1943 schon 102 000 Tonnen erreichte.[30]

Auch ein Großteil der ungarischen Holzschätze wurde von den Deutschen ausgebeutet. Im Jahre 1942 wurden 110 000 m^3 Holz nach Deutschland exportiert, darüber hinaus wurde noch um weitere 80 000 m^3 Nadelholz für den Bedarf der Wehrmacht ersucht. »Obzwar uns der von den Deutschen gewünschte Rahmen als zu hoch erscheint...« stellte der ungarische Außenhandelsausschuß fest, »... werden sie mit Rücksicht auf höhere Interessen den Deutschen bewilligt, es kommt sogar die Schaffung einiger, ausschließlich für die Wehrmacht arbeitender Sägewerke in den Ostkarpaten in Betracht.« Selbst auf Kosten des »Zivilkontingents« sollten den Deutschen gewisse Holzmengen zur Verfügung gestellt werden.[31]

All das bedeutete, daß die entscheidenden rohstoffproduzierenden Industriezweige in hohem Maße mit der Erfüllung deutscher Bestellungen beschäftigt waren.

Die gesteigerte Ausfuhr von Lebensmitteln, landwirtschaftlichen und industriellen Rohstoffen stimmte vollkommen mit jenem schon früher bemerkbaren deutschen Wunsch überein, wonach Ungarn auf das Niveau eines rohstoffproduzierenden Landes herabgedrückt werden sollte. Hierin brachte der Krieg nur insofern eine Änderung, daß die deutschen Forderungen *quantitativ* außerordentlich anstiegen und die Ausfuhr bis zur maximalen Grenze anwuchs. Der antisowjetische Krieg erforderte aber vom faschistischen Deutschland solche Anstrengungen, die seine Kräfte überstiegen. Es genügte nicht mehr, die Wirtschaftsquellen der besetzten Teile Europas mit allen Mitteln in den Dienst der eigenen Kriegsmaschinerie gestellt zu haben. Deutschland war gezwungen, in diesen Gebieten weitere Schritte zur Erweiterung der ihm zur Verfügung stehenden Industriekapazität zu unternehmen. So sah sich Deutschland bemüßigt, Ungarns *Industrie* ebenfalls in die industrielle Versorgung der deutschen Armee einzuschalten. Das Wesen der Dinge bestand darin, daß — obwohl sie unverändert, ja sogar in gesteigertem Maß eine völlige wirtschaftliche Unterwerfung Ungarns erstrebten und bezüglich der ferneren wirtschaftlichen Entwicklung Ungarns im Grunde genommen ihre alten Pläne

[30] L. A. A. M. Material des Ausschusses für Friedensvorbereitung I/1—3/1—24/20 und II/2—28/13.

[31] L. A. A. M. Wp. S. Protokoll 697 des außenpolitischen Ausschusses über die Sitzung vom 10.12.

aufrechterhielten — sie zumindest für *die Dauer des Krieges gezwungen waren, die ungarische Industrie*, hauptsächlich die Kriegsindustrie, *zu fördern.* Auch solche Industriezweige waren darunter, deren Entwicklung sie früher mit allen Mitteln zu hintertreiben versuchten: jetzt aber benötigten sie die Produkte dieser Industriezweige und waren auch ihrerseits bestrebt, ihren Ausbau zu fördern. In diesem Zusammenhang schreibt der Berliner ungarische Gesandte Sztójay in einem Bericht, daß durch den antisowjetischen Krieg »der wirtschaftliche und politische Schwerpunkt sich von Südosten nach Osten verschiebt und die Pression nach Südosten hin vielleicht nicht so intensiv wird. Eine Bekräftigung dieser These erblickte ich auch darin, daß die früheren wirtschaftspolitischen Grundsätze, wonach der Südosten seine Industrie abzurüsten und sich immer mehr auf eine reine Agrarproduktion einzurichten habe, jetzt aufgegeben worden sind und die Deutschen damit vorlieb nehmen, daß die mittel- und südosteuropäische Industrieproduktion — wenigstens vorläufig — Deutschland versorgt.«[32]

Seit der Entfesselung des antisowjetischen Krieges erhielt die ungarische Industrie — von früherer Regel abweichend — von der deutschen Kriegsführung große Aufträge. Im Sommer 1941 begannen die deutsch—ungarischen Industrieverhandlungen, bei denen die ungarische Industrie von einem deutschen Ausschuß einer Prüfung unterzogen wurde, welche Kapazität sie für die deutsche Armee sichern könnte.[33] Während der Verhandlungen wurde ungarischerseits erklärt: »Wir sind gern bereit, die bisher frei gewordene bzw. in der Zukunft frei werdende Kapazität zur Deckung des Bedarfs der Wehrmacht zu überlassen. Ungarn« — wird später nochmals wiederholt — »überläßt einen bedeutenden Teil seiner Industriekapazität dem Deutschen Reich.«[34] Vereinbart wurde auch folgendes: »Jede neue Kapazität, die Ungarn in der nahen Zukunft mit deutscher Hilfe ausbauen kann, soll ständig bis zu 70% für deutsche Lieferungen vorbehalten bleiben.«

Die ungarischen Schwerindustriebetriebe, Waffen- und Munitionsfabriken erhielten immer größere Bestellungen von den Deutschen. So übernahmen hauptsächlich die Weiss-Manfred-Werke und die MÁVAG (Ungarische Staatliche Eisen-, Stahl- und Maschinenfabriken) bereits 1941 die Lieferung von monatlich 300 000 Stück Munition. Sehr bald genügte das nicht, und zur Deckung der steigenden deutschen Bestellungen stellten die Weiss-Manfred-Werke eine neue Munitionsfabrik in Betrieb. Die Monatskapazität der neuen Fabrik belief sich auf 125 000 Stück, und 100 000 Stück wurden davon den Deutschen vorbehalten.[35] Die bedeutendsten Kriegsbetriebe führten den größ-

[32] L. A. A. M. Wp. S. Res. 751. — 1941.
[33] ZWA. Weiss-Manfred-Munitions-Fabrik 85., MÁVAG 3467/res.—1941. Allgemeine Korrespondenz. Aufzeichnung über die Sitzung vom 25.8. 1941.
[34] L. A. A. M. Wp. S. Res. 402/1941—3—29.
[35] ZWA. Weiss-Manfred-Munitionsfabrik 85.

ten Teil ihrer Produktion nach Deutschland aus. So bekamen z. B. die MÁVAG im Herbst 1941 eine Bestellung auf Patronenhülsen im Werte von 5 Millionen Mark, auf Granaten im Werte von 8 Millionen Mark und auf Fliegerabwehrkanonen FLAK im Werte vom mehr als 10 Millionen Mark usw.[36] Allein dieser Betrieb lieferte den Deutschen im Jahre 1942 300 44-mm-Automatenkanonen, eine Million Geschosse und 100 000 15-cm-Granaten.[37]

Über die Ausfuhr des Kriegsmaterials nach Deutschland stehen uns keine vollständigen, die ganze Kriegsperiode umfassenden Ziffern zur Verfügung. Doch ist es sehr aufschlußreich, daß — nach den Angaben einer zusammenfassenden Statistik — bis April 1942 allein die Kriegsmaterialausfuhr 425,8 Millionen Pengő und die übrigen militärischen Lieferungen (in Form von Halbfabrikaten) 319,2 Millionen Pengő betrugen. Dazu kommen noch die enormen Summen für Flugzeuglieferungen.[38]

Im Jahre 1942 diente die ungarische Kriegsindustrieproduktion zum weitaus größeren Teil der deutschen als der ungarischen Armee. Das geht aus einem Bericht des Industrieministers hervor, den er Ende 1942 vor dem sogenannten 42-er Ausschuß erstattete. (Die Mitglieder dieses Ausschusses rekrutierten sich aus den führenden Abgeordneten der Nationalversammlung.) Der Industrieminister führte aus : »Die Frage, was von der Landesverteidigungsproduktion für uns bleibt, und was die anderen erhalten, kann ich nur später beantworten. Doch möchte ich wiederholen, was ich von einem ziemlich bedeutenden Industriellen gehört hatte, und zwar daß nur 15% (von der gesamten Kriegsproduktion) uns verbleibe, alles andere Fremde erhalten. Diese Ziffer muß ich dementieren, denn es bleiben doch in sehr bedeutsamen Produktionszweigen volle 100% für uns . . .«[39] Auch aus diesem Dementi geht klar hervor, daß — wenn auch die 15% irreal sind — der größere Teil der ungarischen industriellen Produkten zweifelsohne den Deutschen zufiel. Nach der Niederlage der deutschen Armee bei Stalingrad verschärfte sich die Lage noch mehr. Im Jahre 1943 wurde auf Ungarn ein wachsender Druck ausgeübt, durch den sich die Deutschen einen noch größeren Teil der ungarischen Kriegsproduktion sicherten. Zum Anlaß wurde der Untergang der bestausgerüsteten ungarischen militärischen Einheit, der 2. ungarischen Armee, bei Woronesh genommen, wo mehr als die Hälfte der Kriegsausrüstung der Horthy-Armee vernichtet wurde. Diesen Umstand benützten die Deutschen, als Entschädigung für die Übernahme gewisser Verpflichtungen — wie die Lieferung einzelner Kriegsmaterialien, die Übergabe von Konstruktionsentwürfen und technologischen Verfahren usw. — einen noch größeren Teil der ungarischen

[36] L. A. Finanzministerium, H-res. 1943. 962/1941., 53.222/1941.
[37] L. A. Industrieministerium. 82.366/1946.
[38] L. A. A. M. Wp. S. Res. 336/42.
[39] L. A. Protokoll des 42-er Ausschusses vom 14.10. 1942. S. 429.

Industriekapazität für sich in Anspruch zu nehmen. So wurden zum Beispiel 80% der Produktion der Waffenfabrik (Fegyvergyár), 50% der Artillerie- und Munitionskapazität der MÁVAG und 60—90% der Kapazität der neugegründeten Kriegsbetriebe der deutschen Armee zugesichert.[40]

Eine wichtige Form der Inanspruchnahme der ungarischen Kriegsindustriekapazität bestand im *System der für die deutsche Armee verrichteten Aufträge.* Die deutschen Armeelieferanten erteilten den ungarischen Fabriken große Arbeitsaufträge und stellten sehr oft auch die zur Ausführung der Aufträge erforderlichen Patente und Entwürfe zur Verfügung. Das militärische Lohnarbeitssystem wurde stufenweise ausgebaut. Anfangs diente es hauptsächlich der Versorgung der deutschen Landesarmee mit leichten Gewehren und Munition. Bis September 1941 war die Übernahme von Arbeitsaufträgen für ein ausländisches Heer an eine besondere Erlaubnis des Ministerpresidenten gebunden, entsprechend der juristischen Lage, wonach Ungarn bis Mitte 1941 dem Krieg nicht beigetreten war und formell seine Neutralität aufrechterhielt. Vor dem antisowjetischen Kriege erteilten die Deutschen keine bedeutenden Aufträge für Lohnarbeiten. Bis zum 30. September 1941 vergaben sie nur einen Arbeitsauftrag im Werte von 130 Millionen Pengő. Seit der zweiten Hälfte des Jahres 1941 waren die deutschen Monopolisten in gesteigertem Maße bestrebt, das Lohnarbeitssystem auszudehnen, worauf auch die ungarischen Kapitalisten gern eingingen. In Verbindung damit wurde die Verordnung über eine besondere Erlaubnis des Ministerpresidenten abgeschafft. Man bestimmte die ziemlich hohe Rahmenziffer von 580 Millionen Pengő, die im Juli 1943 auf 660 Millionen, und im Mai 1944 abermals auf 825 Millionen Pengő erhöht wurde.[41]

Das deutsche Finanzkapital und die faschistische Kriegsführung haben zur Kontrolle der Lohnarbeit der ungarischen Industrie einen Sonderausschuß, die sogenannte DIKO (Deutsche Industrie-Kommission in Ungarn) ins Leben gerufen. Diese übte — unter dem Vorwand der Kontrolle — eine amtliche Aufsicht über die ganze ungarische Industrie aus, da sich ja die Lohnarbeit auf die gesamte ungarische Kriegsindustrie erstreckte. Der Wirkungskreis der DIKO ging weit über die Kontrolle der Lohnarbeit hinaus. Und so führte das Lohnarbeitssystem, obzwar es den ungarischen Kapitalisten einen enormen Profit sicherte und ihnen dadurch auch gewisse Betriebserweiterungen ermöglichte — letzten Endes zur verstärkten wirtschaftlichen Unterwerfung Ungarns. Das kam nicht nur in der deutschen Kontrolle der Industrie zum Ausdruck, sondern auch darin, daß die Rohstoff- und Arbeitsmaschinenversorgung der ungarischen Industrie infolge des Lohnarbeitssystems in erhöhtem Maße von den Deutschen abhängig, und die Lieferung dieser Rohstoffe bzw. Arbeits-

[40] L. A. A. M. Material des Ausschusses für Friedensvorbereitung I/1—12—B/28.
[41] L. A. A. M. Material des Ausschusses für Friedensvorbereitung II/2—28/13.

maschinen ausschließlich von deutschen Interessen bestimmt wurden. Die Deutschen schränkten Ungarns Rohstoffversorgung auf der ganzen Linie ein und drückten die ungarische Industrie hauptsächlich zur Verrichtung von Lohnarbeit herab.[42]

Das Lohnarbeitssystem nahm aber nicht selten solche Formen an, daß die Deutschen die zur Ausführung des Auftrages benötigten Rohstoffe gar nicht lieferten, sondern diese einfach aus den ungarischen militärischen Reserven »ausliehen«. Das geschah bei Lieferungen seitens der MÁVAG, der Ungarischen Optischen Werke (Magyar Optikai Művek) und anderer Firmen.[43] Selbstverständlich wurden diese Anleihen nicht zurückerstattet — später kam es sogar des öfteren vor, daß selbst die Löhne für die verrichtete Arbeit nicht ausbezahlt wurden. Und so gestaltete sich das Lohnarbeitssystem zu einem weiteren Mittel der völligen Ausplünderung Ungarns und da der Staat den ungarischen Kapitalisten einen großen Teil der deutschen Schulden auszahlte, trug er in großem Maße zur sich entfaltenden Inflation bei, die in erster Reihe die Volksmassen traf.

Im Lohnarbeitssystem nahm das sogenannte *gemeinsame Flugzeugbauprogramm* einen besonderen Platz ein. Flugzeuge wurden in Ungarn seit der zweiten Hälfte der dreißiger Jahre hauptsächlich in der Weiss-Manfred-Flugzeugfabrik hergestellt, aber nur in sehr geringem Maße, was auch daraus ersichtlich ist, daß die Fabrik auf Serienproduktion gar nicht eingerichtet war und vorwiegend nach italienischen Mustern nur veraltete Schultypen baute. Im Jahre 1940 wurde mit der deutschen Regierung auf zwischenstaatlichen Verhandlungen eine Vereinbarung getroffen, die den Ausbau der ungarischen Flugzeugbauindustrie vorsah. Angeregt wurde diese Vereinbarung seitens der ungarischen finanzkapitalistischen Kreise, und zwar in erster Linie seitens der Pester Ungarischen Commerz-Bank (Pesti Magyar Kereskedelmi Bank) und dem Barone Weiss, da der Flugzeugbau hauptsächlich für die Weiss-Manfred-Werke ein enormes Geschäft bedeutet hätte. Die Bestellung des ungarischen Verteidigungsministeriums und die im Budget angewiesenen Vorschüsse ermöglichten schon im Herbst 1940, die Flugzeugbaukapazität durch eine 12-Millionen-Pengő-Investition zu erweitern.[44]

Die ungarische Flugzeugindustrie wurde erst beim Ausbruch des antisowjetischen Krieges rascher ausgebaut. Im Sommer 1941 verpflichtete sich das Verteidigungsministerium in einem erneuten zwischenstaatlichen Vertrag, die ungarische Flugzeugindustrie außer zur Befriedigung des eigenen Bedarfes auch auf die Ergänzung der deutschen Flugzeugindustrie umzustellen. Der Flugzeugbau machte den Großteil des deutschen Lohnarbeitssystems aus.

[42] L. A. A. M. Wp. S. Res. 703, 252—1942.
[43] L. A. A. M. Wp. S. Res. 400—1941.
[44] ZWA. Urkundensammlung Weiss Manfred. 55—1048/2—31.

Diese Form der Lohnarbeit paßte im wesentlichen in jenen deutschen Plan hinein, welcher — zwecks Steigerung und Sicherung der Kriegsproduktion und um sie vor Luftangriffen zu bewahren — eine umfassendere Dezentralisation der deutschen Kriegsindustrie vorsah. Die deutschen Pläne zogen nicht nur die deutschen Gebiete in Betracht, sondern wollten die Aktion auch auf die Gebiete der Vasallenstaaten des deutschen »Lebensraumes« ausdehnen, und dies um so mehr, als sie damit rechneten, daß diese Länder von Luftangriffen weniger heimgesucht würden. Im Laufe dieser Aktion waren die Deutschen bestrebt, nicht nur in Deutschland, sondern auch in den Vasallenstaaten eine Erweiterung gewisser Produktionszweige in die Wege zu leiten, selbstverständlich völlig unter deutscher Kontrolle.

Um vor allem die deutschen Bedürfnisse zu befriedigen, genügte der Ausbau der Flugzeugproduktion der Weiss-Manfred-Werke schon nicht mehr. In der Vereinbarung vom Jahre 1941 war ein Flugzeugbauprogramm festgelegt, der sogenannte Messerschmidt-Plan, mit einem ursprünglichen Kostenvoranschlag von einer Milliarde Pengő.[45] Bezeichnend für die Ausmaße dieses Planes war, daß er *in seiner Endsumme dem Investitionsplan des berüchtigten Győrer Programms gleichkam.* Selbstverständlich wurde der Löwenanteil in der Ausführung dieses Programms wiederum dem Weiss-Manfred-Konzern übertragen. Demgemäß begannen die Weiss-Manfred-Werke und die Commerz-Bank — unter Beteiligung von bedeutendem deutschem Kapital — mit der Errichtung der Donau Flugzeugbau Aktiengesellschaft (Dunai Repülőgépgyár Részvénytársaság) mit einem Kostenaufwand von 95 Millionen Pengő. Laut Vertrag wurde in das Unternehmen auch die schon früher in geringem Maße Flugzeugbau betreibende Ungarische Waggon- und Maschinenfabrik Aktiengesellschaft (Magyar Waggon- és Gépgyár Részvénytársaság) zugezogen. Hier wurde die Abteilung für Flugzeugreparatur mit einem Kostenaufwand von 43 Millionen Pengő erweitert. In der Ungarischen Waggon- und Maschinenfabrik wurden dem Programm gemäß anfangs monatlich 50 Flugzeugrümpfe Typ Messerschmidt (ME) 109 hergestellt, in der Donau Flugzeugbau A. G. hingegen wurden monatlich 50 Stück vom Typ ME 120 und 700 Flugzeugmotore Typ Daimler-Benz (DB) eingeplant. Die Motoren zu den in der Győrer Fabrik hergestellten Flugzeugrümpfen wurden teilweise in den Wienerneustädter Flugzeugwerken gebaut. Im Sommer 1941 wurden insgesamt 1800 Rümpfe und 3100 Motore bestellt.[46] In diesen Plan wurden gleichzeitig mehrere andere Unternehmungen als Subunternehmer für einige Detailarbeiten eingeschaltet. In diese Unternehmungen wurden

[45] ZWA. Urkundensammlung Weiss-Manfred. 55—1048/2—31.

[46] ZWA. Urkundensammlung Weiss-Manfred. Ungarische Waggon- und Maschinenfabrik 26.; Landesarchiv. Außenministerium. Wirtschaftspolitische Sektion. Res. 238—1941.; Landesarchiv. Außenministerium, Material des Ausschusses für Friedensvorbereitung II/2—28/13.

12 Millionen Pengő investiert. Wie ersichtlich, wurde ein großzügiger Ausbau der ungarischen Flugzeugindustrie auf Grund der diesbezüglichen deutsch—ungarischen Verhandlungen vom Jahre 1941 mit einem Kostenaufwand von 150 Millionen Pengő in Angriff genommen, aber nicht zu Gunsten Ungarns, sondern ausschließlich zum Vorteil des deutschen Finanzkapitals.

Im Februar 1943 wurden auf deutsche Aufforderung die Investierungen von ursprünglich 1 Milliarde *durch eine Erweiterung der Programms auf 2,7 Milliarden Pengő erhöht.* Das bedeutete eine 50prozentige Steigerung der Kapazität der Donau Flugzeugbau A. G. und der Ungarischen Waggon- und Maschinenfabrik durch eine neuere Investition von 50 Millionen Pengő. Im Zusammenhang damit wurde auch die unlängst ins Leben gerufene Pestszentlőrincer Industrieanlagen-Aktiengesellschaft (Pestszentlőrinci Iparteleрek Részvénytársaság) in das Flugzeugbauprogramm eingeschaltet. Sie richtete sich mit einer Investition von 50 Millionen Pengő auf die Herstellung von monatlich 30 Flugzeugrümpfen Typ Junkers (JU) 52 ein. Bis Ende 1943 wurden die Donau Flugzeugbau A. G. und die Flugzeugabteilung der Ungarischen Waggon- und Maschinenfabrik ebenfalls völlig ausgebaut und seitdem wurden dort die Maschinen in voller Serie hergestellt.[47]

An das Flugzeugbauprogramm knüpfte sich ein »gemeinsames Programm für die fernmeldetechnische Einrichtung der Flugzeuge«. Außerdem wurde die Standard Elektrizitäts-Aktiengesellschaft (Standard Villamossági Részvénytársaság) — die schon früher fernmeldetechnische Ausrüstungen für Focke-Wulf Maschinen verfertigt hatte — zusammen mit der Telephonfabrik Aktiengesellschaft (Telefongyár Részvénytársaság) in das sogenannte Gustav-Programm einbezogen. Sie stellte Instrumente für Rundfunkausrüstungen für die in Ungarn gebauten Flugzeuge her, wozu sie auch die entsprechende deutsche Lizenz erhielt.[48] Zwecks Produktion von Flugzeugbordwaffen und Munition schlossen sich dem Flugzeugbauprogramm auch die »Danuvia« Waffen- und Munitions-Fabrik Aktiengesellschaft (»Danuvia« Fegyver- és Lőszergyár Részvénytársaság), die »Elzett« Eisenwarenfabrik Aktiengesellschaft (»Elzett« Vasárugyár Részvénytársaság) und die Weiss-Manfred-Munitionsfabrik usw.an.

Die im März 1944 erfolgte Besetzung Ungarns durch die deutschen Faschisten, die Ungarn auf Gnade und Ungnade dem faschistischen Unwesen auslieferte und eine offene Ausplünderung des Landes ermöglichte, offenbarte sich auf dem Gebiete der Flugzeugindustrie in der Form, daß sie nunmehr einer unbeschränkten deutschen Kontrolle unterstellt wurde. Die deutsche Heeresleitung vereinigte die ungarischen und einige deutsche Flugzeugfabriken in zwei sogenannte »Arbeitsgemeinschaften«. Die eine Arbeitsgemein-

[47] Archiv des Instituts für Parteigeschichte. II/2. Betriebsmaterial. Donau Flugzeugbau A. G. *und* Zentralwirtschaftsarchiv. Ungarische Waggon- und Maschinenfabrik. 122.

[48] Archiv des Instituts für Parteigeschichte. II/2. Betriebsmaterial. Standard.

schaft — die Wienerneustädter Flugzeugwerke, die Donau Flugzeugbau A. G., die Ungarische Waggon- und Maschinenfabrik — baute Flugzeugrümpfe, die andere hingegen — die Steyer-Daimler-Puch A. G., die Donau Flugzeugbau A. G. — Flugzeugmotoren. Der Produktionsplan beider Arbeitsgemeinschaften sah den Bau von monatlich 550 Flugzeugrümpfen und 650 Flugzeugmotoren vor. In der »Arbeitsgemeinschaft« lag sowohl die politische als auch technische Leitung in deutscher Hand. Im diesbezüglichen Vertrag war sogar festgelegt, daß der Maschinenpark der einzelnen Unternehmungen nach Belieben aus einem Land ins andere *überführt werden könne.* Dies bedeutete im Endergebnis, daß die ungarischen Kapitalisten sich mit dem eventuellen Abtransport des Maschinenparks ihrer Betriebe nach Deutschland einverstanden erklärten. Die deutschen Faschisten ließen durch die Sztójay-Marionettenregierung einen Regierungskommissar für Flugwesen ernennen, der einen sehr ausgedehnten Wirkungskreis hatte und bevollmächtigt war, die Kontinuität des Flugzeugbaus auch auf Kosten anderer Kriegsproduktionen sicherzustellen. Im Sinne des Abkommens wurde der Betrieb in den Felsenkeller der »Steinbrucher Bierbrauerei« (Kőbányai Serfőző) verlegt.[49]

Auch die Entwicklung der Aluminiumindustrie während des Krieges hängt teilweise mit dem erhöhten Flugzeugbau, mit dem »gemeinsamen« Flugbauprogramm zusammen — deutet aber gleichzeitig auch darauf hin, daß die Deutschen jetzt schon nicht nur die ungarischen Rohstoffschätze, sondern auch die Industriekapazität des Landes benötigten. Das deutsche Finanzkapital drängte bereits in den dreißiger Jahren auf eine Ausweitung der Bauxitförderung in Ungarn, wiedersetzte sich aber der weiteren einheimischen Verarbeitung des Bauxits und hintertrieb den Ausbau einer Aluminiumindustrie in Ungarn. Vor dem Krieg wurde der Bauxit nur in der Magyaróvárer Tonerdefabrik (Magyaróvári Timföldgyár) — mit einer minimalen Kapazität von 10 000 Tonnen — und in der Csepeler Aluminiumhütte verarbeitet. In den ersten Kriegsjahren begann man in Ajka eine zweite Tonerdefabrik (20 000 Tonnen) sowie eine Aluminiumhütte und in Felsőgalla eine weitere Hütte zu errichten. Alle diese Betriebe vermochten aber nur einen Bruchteil des einheimischen Bauxits zu verarbeiten. Bis zum Ausbruch des Krieges gegen die Sowjetunion »haben bestimmte fremde industrielle Kreise uns darauf aufmerksam gemacht, daß die ungarischen Aluminiumfabriken nicht rentabel sein würden . . .«,[50] erklärte der Industrieminister. »Nach dem Ausbruch des antisowjetischen Krieges hingegen fielen die Deutschen — die jahrelang gegen die Errichtung einer ungarischen Aluminiumfabrik gekämpft hatten — ins andere Extrem.«[51] Auf deutsche Anregung ist im März 1942

[49] ZWA. Ungarische Waggon- und Maschinenfabrik, Akte Nr. 23 *und* Landesarchiv. Außenministerium. Material des Ausschusses für Friedensvorbereitung. II/2—28/13.
[50] L. A. Protokoll der Parlamentsausschüsse vom 4.11. 1941. V. S. 132.
[51] L. A. Protokoll des 42er Ausschusses vom 19.10. 1942. XXX. S. 416.

eine Vereinbarung zur Gründung der Donautaler Tonerde-Industrie-Aktiengesellschaft (Dunavölgyi Timföld-Ipar Részvénytársaság) zustande gekommen, wodurch eine bedeutende Erweiterung der ungarischen Tonerde- und Aluminiumproduktion bezweckt wurde. Man wollte mit einer Investition von 70 Millionen eine Tonerdefabrik mit einer Jahreskapazität von 60 000 Tonnen einrichten und diese auch mit einer Aluminiumfabrik versehen. Da die deutsche Heeresleitung diese Fabrik benötigte, übernahmen die deutschen Vereinigten Aluminiumwerke die Lieferung der Einrichtung, doch behielt sich das deutsche Kapital beim neuen Unternehmen eine führende Rolle vor. Somit wurde dafür gesorgt, daß selbst eine ungarische Tonerde- und Aluminiumindustrie unter der Kontrolle des deutschen Kapitals stehe. Es wurde verträglich festgelegt, daß der Ausbau der ungarischen Aluminiumindustrie in einem solchen Rahmen zu halten sei, der die ungarischen Rohstoffe der deutschen Aluminiumindustrie nicht entziehen würde. Die am Unternehmen beteiligte ungarische Kapitalistengruppe, die Aluminiumerz Bergbau- und Industrie Aktiengesellschaft (Aluminiumércbánya és Ipar Részvénytársaság), verpflichtete sich, »mit allen ihr zur Verfügung stehenden Mitteln danach zu streben, daß der Bauxitbedarf der Donautaler Tonerde-Industrie A. G. die Bauxitversorgung der deutschen Tonerdefabriken weder qualitativ, noch quantitativ beeinflusse«. Zur Bekräftigung dessen verpflichtete sich die ungarische Regierung, daß »Ungarn 25 Jahre lang, vom 1. August 1942 angefangen, die Ausfuhr von einer Million Tonnen Bauxit nach Deutschland bewilligen und auf diese Ausfuhr weder Zoll noch irgendwelche andere Gebühr erheben werde«.[52]

Die deutschen Bestellungen nahmen neben der Schwerindustrie auch einen bedeutenden Teil der Kapazität der Lebensmittelindustrie in Anspruch.

Die Produktion für die ungarische Armee, insbesondere aber für die deutsche Kriegsmaschinerie hat die Entwicklung der ungarischen Schwerindustrie bis 1943 erheblich beschleunigt. Die Produktion der Eisen- und Metallindustrie, der Maschinenfabrikation, der Elektrizitätswerke und der chemischen Industrie überstieg 1943 um beinahe 50% das Niveau des Jahres 1938. Dessenungeachtet wurden die für den Zivilverbrauch produzierenden Industriezweige zurückgedrängt, was eine kriegsbedingte Verschiebung in der Struktur der Industrie mit sich brachte.

Es entstand also die merkwürdige Lage, daß obwohl die kolonisatorischen Bestrebungen des deutschen Finanzkapitals die Entwicklung der ungarischen Industrie mit allen Mitteln hintertrieben, sich die Deutschen gerade zu einer Periode, als sich Ungarns Abhängigkeit vom faschistischen Deutschland immer mehr vertiefte, gezwungen sahen, die Entwicklung der ungarischen Industrie mit Rücksicht auf ihre militärischen Interessen vorübergehend zu fördern. Da die deutsche Industrie selbst durch eine totale Mobilisation nicht

[52] L. A. A. M. Wp. S. Res. 30/1942.

mehr imstande war, die eigenen Kriegsbedürfnisse zu decken, erforderten ihre Kriegsinteressen, daß Ungarns Unterwerfung *vorläufig* nicht in einer völligen Verkümmerung der ungarischen Industrie, sondern eher in einem immer vollständigeren Einbau in die deutsche Kriegsmaschinerie zum Ausdruck komme. Dieser Umwandlungsprozeß spiegelte sich in der Gestaltung des deutsch—ungarischen Außenhandelsverkehrs während des Krieges, was bei einer beständigen quantitativen Steigerung der ungarischen Ausfuhr gleichzeitig auch eine Vergrößerung der Verhältniszahl der ungarischen Industrieartikel innerhalb der gesamten ungarischen Ausfuhr aufweist.

Deutsch-ungarischer Außenhandelsverkehr 1938—1944

Jahr	Einfuhr (Mill. Pengő)	% der gesamten Einfuhr	Ausfuhr (Mill. Pengő)	% der gesamten Ausfuhr
1938*.......	171	40,9	239	45,7
1939.......	237	48,4	304	50,3
1940.......	316	52,4	249	49,4
1941.......	429	58,5	475	61,4
1942.......	483	51,5	632	54,9
1943.......	612	53,4	776	60,3
1944.......	568	70,3	628	73,6

* Österreich mitinbegriffen[53]

Es muß noch bemerkt werden, daß der Außenhandel mit Deutschland in Wirklichkeit noch bedeutsamer war, da obige Daten die geheime Ausfuhr nicht beinhalten. Sie kann auf 15% der gesamten Ausfuhr geschätzt werden.

Die Warenzusammensetzung der Deutschlandausfuhr belegt die Hebung der Industrieausfuhr mit folgenden Zahlen :

	1940	1941	1942	1943
Landwirtschaft	82,1%	76,4%	68,9%	69,0%
Industrie	17,9%	23,6%	31,1%	31,0%
	100,0%	100,0%	100,0%	100,0%

[53] Auf Grund der Daten der Statistischen Jahrbücher.

Da die Geheimausfuhr ausschließlich nach Deutschland ging und aus Industrieartikeln und Kriegsmaterial bestand, würden ihre Angaben das Konto der Industrie noch mehr belasten. Die Unterwerfung unter die deutsche Kriegswirtschaft drückte ihren Stempel auch der Industrieentwicklung und damit der Gestaltung ihrer Struktur während des Krieges auf. Die Entwicklung der Industrie während des Krieges ruft im allgemeinen strukturelle Veränderungen hervor. Die Industrie stellt sich nämlich auf die Produktion von größtenteils improduktiven Artikeln um, während die Bedarfsartikel und Produktionsmittel erzeugenden Industriezweige der Schwerindustrie zurückfallen. Diese strukturellen Verschiebungen kamen in der ungarischen Industrie besonders anschaulich zum Ausdruck und riefen große Mißverhältnisse hervor, war sie doch schon im Voraus in erster Linie als ein Bestandteil der *deutschen* Kriegsmaschinerie ausgebaut worden. Die kriegsbedingten Mißverhältnisse der Industrie machen sich in den kapitalistischen Ländern durch die Ausgestaltung gewisser »Kriegsproportionen« bemerkbar, indem die Kapitalisten bestrebt sind, die Industrie auf eine allseitige Befriedigung der Heeresbedürfnisse umzustellen.

Die ganze Industrie des Vasallenstaates Ungarn wurde als eine Ergänzung der deutschen Kriegsindustrie betrachtet. Demzufolge wurden gewisse Relationen der Kriegsbedürfnisse — nach deutschen Bedürfnissen — ungeheuer überentwickelt (so beispielsweise der Flugzeugbau, die Munitionserzeugung usw.), andere Relationen hingegen — wenn es die deutschen Interessen erforderten — sind weit hinter dem damaligen Stand der Kriegstechnik zurückgeblieben (so z. B. die Produktion von Militärfahrzeugen und schweren Waffen). Die deutsche wirtschaftliche Expansion verschärfte also nur noch mehr die kriegsbedingten Verschiebungen der ungarischen Industrie, und ungeachtet der erheblichen Entwicklung der Schwerindustrie entstanden in der gesamten Struktur der ungarischen Industrie besonders eklatante Mißproportionen.

Aus der Entwicklung gewisser Zweige der Schwerindustrie konnte aber nicht darauf geschlossen werden, daß die deutschen Monopolisten auf ihren früheren Plan verzichtet hätten, wonach Ungarn die Rolle eines rohstoffproduzierenden, lebensmittelliefernden, und höchstens über eine bescheidene Lebesmittelindustrie verfügenden Landes innerhalb des Lebensraumes des faschistischen Deutschlands zufiel. Das deutsche Finanzkapital setzte nämlich selbst während des Krieges alles daran, diesen Plan — nach der, ihres Erachtens, siegreichen Beendigung des Krieges — in die Tat umzusetzen.

Diese Bestrebung äußerte sich auch darin, daß die Deutschen hauptsächlich die Produktion solcher kriegswichtigen Artikel förderten und dem Ausbau solcher kriegsindustriellen Kapazitäten zustimmten, deren Brauchbarkeit unter den Bedingungen einer Friedensproduktion als am wenigsten wahrscheinlich erschien. Sie hintertrieben aber gleichzeitig mit allen Mitteln die Weiterentwicklung von zahlreichen wichtigen Industriezweigen, die zwar zur Steigerung der ungarischen Kriegsindustrie außerordentlich wichtig, für Deutschland aber von weniger Interesse waren. Die gleichen Industriezweige hätten einen wichtigen Bestadnteil der ungarischen Friedensproduktion bilden können, hätten zur Verstärkung der ungarischen Industrie beigetragen und das Erlangen ihrer Unabhängigkeit vom Ausland zur Folge gehabt. Die besondere kriegsbedingte Verschiebung der Industrie, als Folge der deutschen kolonisatorischen Bestrebungen, bezweckte auch die Erdrosselung der weiteren Entfaltung der ungarischen Industrie.

Auf dem Gebiete der Eisenmetallurgie warfen die ungarischen herrschenden Klassen den Plan zur Errichtung einer neuen Hütte auf, da die Kapazität der bestehenden Hochöfen schon maximal ausgenützt und eine Steigerung der Produktion ohne die Aufstellung einer neuen Hütte nicht mehr möglich war. Sie rechneten damit, daß die deutschen Kapitalisten, die damals die Erweiterung der Industriekapazität in mehreren Beziehungen ermöglichten, auch bezüglich des neuen Hochofens keine Schwierigkeiten bereiten würden. Ende 1942 äußerte sich der Industrieminister diesbezüglich folgendermaßen: »... jene Abneigung, sogar Angst, die Deutschland der ungarischen Industrie gegenüber früher an den Tag legte, ist völlig im Erlöschen begriffen, so daß wir eventuell auch eine Eisenhütte erlangen können.«[53a]

Man wollte die neue Hütte an der Donau aufbauen, und darin das Eisenerz aus dem zeitweilig besetzten Kriwoj-Rog verarbeiten. Da die Deutschen das Eisenerz in großen Mengen zu Wasser nach Deutschland zu befördern beabsichtigten, »... war die Daseinsberechtigung einer solchen Hütte hinsichtlich des Erzes gegeben«,[54] stellte der Industrieminister des weiteren fest. Der Ministerrat hat am 6. Januar 1943 sogar einen Beschluß über die Errichtung der neuen Hütte gefaßt.

Man rechnete damit, daß die Hütte verhältnismäßig schnell in Betrieb gesetzt werden könne, »da sich dazu durch den Ankauf zweier, in Deutschland schon im Bau befindlicher, wegen des Krieges aber nicht gelieferter Hochöfen eine günstige Gelegenheit bot«.[55] Die Verhandlungen zum Ankauf der Hochöfen sind auch in Gang gesetzt worden, die deutschen finanzkapitalistischen Kreise waren jedoch nicht geneigt, die schon fertiggestellten, in Deutschland aber ungebraucht liegenden Hochöfen an Ungarn zu verkaufen.

Dieselben Erscheinungen können wir auch bei anderen wichtigen Industriezweigen beobachten. Auf ähnliche Weise ist auch die Aufnahme der ungarischen Sodafabrikation hintertrieben worden. Die ungarischen industriellen Kreise waren auch hier der Meinung, daß sie infolge des Krieges deutscher-

[53a] L. A. Parlamentsakten. Protokoll des 42er Ausschusses vom 10.10. 1942. XXX. S. 414.

[54] Ebendort.

[55] L. A. Parlamentsakten. Protokoll des 42er Ausschusses von 19.8. 1942. XXX. S. 334 ff.

seits keinen Widerstand zu gewärtigen hätten, und die Deutschen der Errichtung einer Sodafabrik in Ungarn zustimmen würden, »obzwar sie früher lange bestritten hatten, daß wir tatsächlich eine bedürfen«,[56] fügte der Industrieminister hinzu. Auch hier bestand die Möglichkeit, eine von der deutschen Ferrostahl-Firma für Iran fertiggestellte, aber infolge des Ausbruchs des Krieges nicht mehr gelieferte Sodafabrik mit einer Kapazität von 18 000 Tonnen für Ungarn zu übernehmen. Die Ende 1942 stattgefundenen Verhandlungen sind aber erfolglos geblieben, da der ungarische Markt im Sinne des internationalen Kartellvertrages von deutschen Firmen mit Soda versehen wurde und das deutsche Finanzkapital nicht geneigt war, darauf zu verzichten.[57]

In der chemischen Industrie haben die deutschen finanzindustriellen Kreise den Ausbau der Kunstkautschukerzeugung bis zu Ende verhindert. Auch diesbezüglich sind ungarischerseits Versuche eingeleitet worden, da die Kapitalisten darin sehr große Profitmöglichkeiten erblickten. Die dazu erforderlichen Maschinen, Materialien und technische Hilfe wollten die Deutschen nur unter der Bedingung zur Verfügung stellen, wenn die Regierung sich verpflichtet hätte, den ungarischen Kunstkautschukbedarf nach dem Kriege noch 5 Jahre hindurch ausschließlich aus Deutschland zu beziehen. Die Verhandlungen verzogen sich deshalb und blieben ergebnisten.

Man könnte noch in der Aufzählung fortfahren. Nehmen wir z. B. die Frage der Schwarzplattenfabrikation. Im Laufe des Krieges sind die Rohstoffvorräte für Konservenbüchsen der ungarischen Konservenindustrie, die größtenteils für die Versorgung der deutschen Armee arbeitete, völlig erschöpft. Die Weiss-Manfred-Werke wollten deshalb die Lizenz der Schwarzplattenfabrikation von den Deutschen erkaufen, um die einheimische Produktion in Angriff nehmen zu können. Die Deutschen wollten aber die Lizenz nur in dem Falle überlassen, wenn die in Ungarn zu errichtende Fabrik mit Beteiligung des deutschen Kapitals aufgebaut worden wäre. Ungeachtet dessen, daß die Überlassung der Lizenz auch von der deutschen Heeresleitung mehrmals urgiert wurde, haben die deutschen Finanzkapitalisten den Verkauf der Lizenz und damit die Inangriffnahme der Schwarzplattenfabrikation in Ungarn bis zum Ende des Krieges unmöglich gemacht.[58]

Die Siemens-Werke verhinderten die für die deutsche Armee arbeitende Standard-Elektrizitäts-A. G. daran, sich auf Staubeisenkernfabrikation einzurichten, obwohl dies zur Herstellung gewisser Spezialrundfunkapparate notwendig gewesen wäre und der erforderliche Rohstoff (das Carbonil) nur von der I. G. Farbenindustrie hätte bezogen werden können. Die I. G. Farbenindustrie exportierte zwar diesen Artikel in die verschiedenen Länder, »die

[56] Ebendort S. 414.
[57] L. A. A. M. Material des Ausschusses für Friedensvorbereitung II/2—28/13.
[58] L. A. A. M. Wp. S. Res. 283.—1942.

Siemens-Werke ließen es aber auf Grund einer mit der I. G. Farbenindustrie abgeschlossenen Vereinbarung nicht zu, daß die Firma auch uns liefert«.[59]

Die Entwicklung der ungarischen Industrie während des Krieges stand also in unmittelbarem Zusammenhang mit den deutschen militärischen Interessen und richtete sich nach diesen. Den Ansprüchen der deutschen Kriegswirtschaft gemäß wurde ihr Entwicklungsweg einerseits von weiten Entwicklungsmöglichkeiten, andererseits aber von enggezogenen Schranken bestimmt. Die bedeutende Hebung der Industrie trug in erster Linie zur weiteren Stärkung der Wirtschaftsmacht des seine Positionen fest in den Händen haltenden ungarischen Finanzkapitals bei. Dessenungeachtet kam aber in Form der *Eroberungsbestrebungen des deutschen Finanzkapitals* eine entgegengesetzte Tendenz während des Krieges in der Entwicklung der ungarischen Industrie zur Geltung. Die deutschen finanzindustriellen Kreise strebten danach, immer mehr Wirtschaftspositionen an sich zu reißen und vermochten im Interesse der Verwirklichung dieser Zielsetzung die politische Abhängigkeit Ungarns in hohem Maße auszunützen. Es ist sehr bezeichnend und gleichzeitig vom Gesichtspunkt der Wirtschaftsexpansion des deutschen Finanzkapitals sehr wesentlich, in welch hohem Maße die deutschen Industrie- und Bankkreise die ungarischen Gebietseingliederungen sich zunutze machen konnten. In den Ungarn einverleibten Gebieten konnten sie durch Enteignung von ehemals in serbischem, kroatischem und tschechischem Besitz befindlichen Aktien zahlreiche Unternehmungen erwerben bzw. an diesen für sich eine Beteiligung sichern. So geriet zum Beispiel die Ujverbászer Heimische Ölfabriks-Aktiengesellschaft, die früher die größte Pflanzenöl produzierende Unternehmung Jugoslawiens war, in deutsche Hände. Die interessierten ungarischen Kapitalisten konnten bei dieser Unternehmung nur 20% der Aktien erwerben. Die dem Skoda-Konzern angehörende Karpatische Elektrizitätswerke A. G. wurde einem Unternehmen des Göring-Konzerns angeschlossen. Die Özörenyer Zellulosefabrik war vor dem ersten Weltkrieg eine Unternehmung der Ungarischen Escompte- und Wechsler-Bank (Magyar Leszámitoló és Pénzváltó Bank). Die Bank wollte sie nun wieder in Besitz nehmen, das deutsche Kapital trat aber dazwischen, indem es das Eigentumsrecht von den Slowaken übernahm. So geriet auch diese Unternehmung völlig in die Hände des deutschen Kapitals. Eine geheime schriftliche Information des Außenministeriums stellte in diesem Zusammenhang fest, daß »dieser Prozeß Erbitterung in den ungarischen großindustriellen Kreisen hervorrufe, da er der ganzen Sache den Anschein verleihe, als hätten die Ungarn diese Gebiete nur zur Hälfte wieder in Besitz genommen«.[60]

[59] L. A. A. M. Wp. S. Res. 450.—1941.
[60] L. A. A. M. Wp. S. Res. 83.—1942.

Das deutsche Finanzkapital gab sich damit freilich nicht zufrieden, daß es in den Ungarn einverleibten Gebieten wertvolle Positionen erwarb. In seinen imperialistischen Plänen gehörte doch Ungarn dem deutschen »Lebensraum« an, und obwohl es während des Krieges seine ursprünglichen Bestrebungen zur Erdrosselung der ungarischen Industrie nicht geltend machen konnte, so wollte es sich wenigstens in der ungarischen Industrie einen immer größeren Einfluß sichern. Natürlich verletzten diese Bestrebungen die Interessen der ungarischen Finanzkapitalisten, obzwar sofort hinzugefügt werden muß, daß auf gewissen Gebieten für sie zweifelsohne auch einige Vorteile erwachsen waren. Dies bezieht sich vor allem auf die neuentwickelten Kriegsindustriezweige. Zu den enormen Investitionen hatten nämlich — gerade zwecks Ausdehnung ihres Einflusses — auch die Deutschen erheblich beigetragen, oft lag sogar die führende Rolle bei ihnen. All das — wie schon oben erwähnt — hat zwar den größten ungarischen finanzkapitalistischen Gruppen gewisse Möglichkeiten gesichert, war aber im Grunde genommen ein wichtiges Moment der deutschen Expansion. So hatte z. B. beim Ausbau des ungarischen Flugzeugbaus nebst der Weiss-Manfred — Commercial-Bank-Gruppe — wie wir eben gesehen haben — auch das deutsche Kapital einen sehr großen Einfluß inne. Bei der Errichtung und Einrichtung der Donau Flugzeugbau A. G. spielte das deutsche Kapital die führende Rolle.[61]

Die Ungarische Bauxitgruben Aktiengesellschaft (Magyar Bauxitbánya Részvénytársaság) wurde ebenfalls auf deutsche Initiative gegründet, wobei die Dürener Metallwerke A. G. eine große Rolle spielte.[62] Ebenfalls auf Grund einer Vereinbarung mit den deutschen Kapitalisten kam es zur Gründung der Donautaler Tonerde-Industrie Aktiengesellschaft (Dunavölgyi Timföldgyár Részvénytársaság), woran nebst den ungarischen finanzkapitalistischen Gruppen und dem ungarischen Staat auch die deutschen Vereinigten Aluminium Werke bis zu einem Drittel beteiligt waren, und laut den Vereinbarungen im wesentlichen das ganze Unternehmen beherrschten.[63] Die Deutschen waren bestrebt, ihre Hand auch auf die ungarischen Ölförderungsindustrie zu legen. Daran war aber auf Grund eines Vorkriegsvertrages bereits die amerikanische Standard Oil interessiert. Die deutsche I. G. Farbenindustrie A. G. wollte schon im Juli 1941 mit der amerikanischen Unternehmung über die Übernahme der MAORT-Aktien (MAORT = Magyar—Amerikai Olajipari Részvénytársaság = Ungarisch—Amerikanische Ölindustrie Aktiengesellschaft) Verhandlungen führen und sie war bereit, als Gegenleistung ihre südamerikanischen Kapitalbeteiligungen abzutreten. Die Standard Oil war geneigt, auf dieses Geschäft einzugehen, hat aber schließlich infolge der Mißbilligung

[61] ZWA. Weiss-Manfred-Urkundensammlung 55. 1048/2.
[62] L. A. A. M. Wp. S. II/2—28/13.
[63] L. A. A. M. Wp. S. Res. 30/42.

seitens der amerikanischen Behörden ihre MAORT-Aktien doch nicht abgetreten.[64]

Über den Versuch hinaus, die schon bestehenden Ölförderungsunternehmungen für sich zu erwerben, wollte sich das deutsche Finanzkapital die Beschlagnahme etwaiger neuer Rohstoffquellen sichern. In diesem Zusammenhang schloß die deutsche Winterschall-A. G. bereits im August 1940 mit der Regierung einen Vertrag zur Erdölschürfung ab und erhielt gleichzeitig Vorkaufs- und Konzessionsrechte darauf. Schon in diesem Vertrag wurde ausbedingt, daß »das an das Vertragsgebiet im Süden angrenzende Territorium, sollte es an Ungarn rückgegliedert werden, ebenfalls der Firma Winterschall überlassen wird«.[65] Die Deutsch—Ungarische Mineralöl-Werke Aktiengesellschaft (Magyar—Német Ásványolaj-Művek Részvénytársaság) nahm im Südteil des Alföld (Große Ungarische Tiefebene) in der Umgebung der Gemeinde Tótkomlós Bohrungen vor. Ein geheimer Gesandtschaftsbericht von 1942 setzt uns darüber in Kenntnis, daß unter dem Vorwand eines kulturellen Abkommens die Ankunft einer deutschen Forschungsgruppe erwartet wurde, um in der Umgebung der Stadt Gyula Ausgrabungen vorzunehmen, wie aber hinzugefügt wird, »verbirgt sich hinter den Ausgrabungen irgendeine Petroleumforschungsaktion. Unseres Wissens hielten sich in Ungarn schon auch andere unter dem Vorwand von archäologischen Forschungen auf, und wenn sie zu Petroleumbohrungen geeignete Landstücke entdeckten, ließen sie die betreffenden Gebiete durch Strohmänner aufkaufen.«[66] Auf diese Weise wurde die deutsche Erdölschürfung in Ungarn nicht nur offen, sondern auch im Geheimen fortgesetzt.

Außerdem war das deutsche Finanzkapital bestrebt, auch auf anderen Gebieten der ungarischen Industrie Fuß zu fassen oder seine Positionen zu erweitern. Es versuchte, die wichtigsten Gebiete und Unternehmungen der Industrie in seinen Einflußkreis einzubeziehen. In einem seiner Berichte an den ungarischen Ministerpräsidenten Bárdossy teilte der Berliner ungarische Gesandte Sztójay darüber folgendes mit: »Die Reichsgruppe für Industrie hat Auftrag zur eingehenden Ausarbeitung von Propositionen erhalten, die sich auf die Beteiligung einiger deutscher Industriezweige und Kapitalistengruppen an ungarischen Unternehmungen oder aber auf die Beteiligung an Kapitalerhöhungen schon bestehender Unternehmungen beziehen.«[67]

Einer der wichtigsten Wege zum Eindringen des deutschen Kapitals und zur Erweiterung seiner Interessensphären bestand in der Ergatterung eines Teils des Aktienbestandes der ungarischen Unternehmungen. Das ungarische Finanzkapital überließ natürlich den Deutschen nicht freiwillig die

[64] L. A. A. M. Wp. S. Chiffretelegramme vom 22.7. und 2.8. 1941.
[65] L. A. A. M. Wp. S. Res. 41.—1942 *und* Zentralwirtschaftsarchiv. Korrespondenz des Industriesekretariats der Commerzbank. Auslandspressemeldungen.
[66] L. A. A. M. Wp. S. Res. 249.—1942.
[67] L. A. A. M. Wp. S. Res. 572.—1941.

bestehenden eigenen Positionen und die deutsche Expansion ergab sich im wesentlichen daraus, daß die in ungarischen Kreditorganisationen und in der ungarischen Industrie vorhandenen österreichischen, französischen usw. Kapitalbeteiligungen durch die Unterwerfung Europas in deutsche Hände gerieten. Vom Gesichtspunkt des Eindringens des deutschen Kapitals war besonders bedeutsam, daß fast 140 000 Aktien der Ungarischen Allgemeinen Creditbank (Magyar Általános Hitelbank) in den Jahren 1941 und 1942 aus französischen Banken zur Dresdner Bank gelangten, denn dadurch war — zusammen mit den von den Wiener Rotschilds schon früher erworbenen rund 20 000 Aktien — eine mehr als 18prozentige Kapitalbeteiligung für die Dresdner Bank gesichert. Demzufolge konnten sich die Vertreter des deutschen Kapitals auch unmittelbar in die Direktion der Creditbank hineinsetzen und sie erlangten Einfluß im ungarischen Wirtschaftsleben. Außer der Beteiligung an der Errichtung neuer Industriezweige waren eben diese Aktionen der bedeutsamste Schritt auf dem Wege der deutschen Kapitalexpansion.[68]

Das deutsche Kapital war überdies bestrebt, sich in den meisten Großunternehmungen Positionen zu erwerben. Es muß in diesem Zusammenhang hervorgehoben werden, daß es auch an der Ganz & Co. Elektrizitäts-, Maschinen-, Waggon- und Schiffbau-Aktiengesellschaft (Ganz és Társa Villamossági, Gép-, Waggon- és Hajógyár Részvénytársaság) erhebliche Beteiligung erlangte, da die amerikanischen Aktionäre — nach einer Mitteilung des Handelsattachés der englischen Gesandtschaft aus dem Jahre 1940 —, ihre Aktien an die Deutschen verkauft hätten.[69]

Seitens des deutschen Finanzkapitals waren selbstverständlich auch andere Bemühungen zur Erwerbung von wichtigen Unternehmungen zu beobachten. So machte z. B. die I. G. Farbenindustrie Schritte zur Beteiligung an der Chemisch-Pharmazeutischen »Chinoin« Fabrik (»Chinoin« Gyógyszer- és Vegyészeti Termékek Gyára Részvénytársaság), und dies um so mehr, als »Chinoin« auch eine weitverzweigte Exporttätigkeit entfaltete. Im Sommer 1941 wurden in der Fabrik Verhandlungen geführt, ». . . die deutschen Fabriken und Exporteure belegen unser Unternehmen seit einigen Wochen mit einem Materiallieferungsverbot . . . Dieses Materiallieferungsverbot läßt sich auf eine Anordnung des deutschen Wirtschaftsministeriums zurückführen . . . Es läßt sich auch mit den früheren Versuchen in Zusammenhang bringen, die schon immer darauf gerichtet waren, daß sich die großen deutschen Firmen, in erster Linie die I. G. Farbenindustrie und die Schering-Werke, bei der Chinoin eine Kapitalbeteiligung und einen entscheidenden Einfluß sichern.«[70] Zur Abwehr des deutschen Druckes ließ die an der Spitze der Chinoin stehende

[68] ZWA. Creditbanksekretariat. 1. Paket und Metallwaren-, Waffen- und Maschinenfabrik A. G. Material von I. Perényi.
[69] ZWA. Ganz-Fabrik. Protokoll der Präsidialsitzungen. 19.6. 1940.
[70] ZWA. Chinoin. Protokoll des Exkutiv-Komitees vom 21. 8. 1941.

Kapitalistengruppe die Vertreter einer kleineren deutschen Firma (Walter Haupt) und Hitlers Hausarzt in die Direktion wählen.[71]

Das deutsche Finanzkapital konnte aber außer den neuentwickelten Industriezweigen und der Erwerbung von im österreichischen, tschechischen, französichen usw. Besitz befindlichen ungarischen Aktien trotz seiner ständigen Versuche, nicht so große Kapitalbeteiligungen erwerben, wie es erstrebt hatte, demnach spielte es in der ungarischen Industrie während des Krieges keine große Rolle. Die meisten deutschen Positionen bestanden aus früheren deutschen, österreichischen und tschechischen Kapitalbeteiligungen. Nach einem Ende 1942 von den Großbanken verfertigten *internen Ausweis*[72] belief sich die deutsche Aktienbeteiligung in der ungarischen Industrie auf mehr als 200 Millionen Pengő. Das deutsche Kapital war sozusagen an allen größeren Unternehmen mehr oder minder beteiligt. Die deutsche Aktienbeteiligung erstreckte sich auf die folgenden wichtigsten Unternehmungen:

Name der Unternehmung	Aktien %
Ganz-Fabrik (Ganz-Gyár)	17,3
Rimamurányer Eisenwerk (Rimamurányi Vasmű)	18,3
Vereinigte Glühlampen (Egyesült Izzó)	15,3
Elektrotrust (Villamos Tröszt)	34,0
Salgótarjáner Steinkohlenbergbau (Salgótarjáni Kőszénbánya)	13,1
Urikány—Zsiltaler Steinkohlenbergbau (Urikány—Zsilvölgyi Kőszénbánya)	8,7
Ungarischer Allgemeiner Kohlenbergbau (Magyar Általános Kőszénbánya)	6,7
»Hungária« Chemische Werke (»Hungária« Vegyiművek)	17,5
Gummiwarenfabrik (Ruggyantagyár)	22,8

Außerdem besaßen die deutschen Kapitalisten noch bei folgenden Unternehmungen Kapitalbeteiligungen:

Hundertprozentig in deutscher Hand befanden sich die Angyalfölder Textilwerke A. G. (Angyalföldi Textilművek RT.), Bantlinsche Chemische Fabriken A. G. (Bantlin-féle Vegyigyárak RT.), Baumwolltextilwerke A. G. (Pamuttextilművek RT.), Budanil A. G. (Budanil RT.), Erste Ungarische Schriftgießerei A. G. (Első Magyar Betűöntöde RT.), Stephan Felmayer & Söhne Blaufärberei und Kattundruckfabrik A. G. (Felmayer István és Fiai Kékfestő és Kartonnyomógyár RT.), Albert Förster Steinindustrie A. G. (Albert Förster Kőipari RT.), Philipp Haas und Söhne A. G. (Haas Fülöp és Fiai-féle RT.), Kispester Seidenweberei Gebrüder Schiel A. G. (Kispesti Selyemszövőgyár Schiel testvérek RT.), Julius Meinl Kaffeeimport A. G. (Meinl Gyula Kávébehozatali RT.) mit den zu ihr gehörenden kleineren Unternehmungen für Lebensmittel, Mercedes Benz Automobil A. G. (Mercedes-

[71] ZWA. Chinoin. Protokoll des Exkutiv-Komitees vom 21. August 1941. Protokoll vom April 1944. Nach der deutschen Besetzung ist Dr. Morell zum stellvertretenden Generaldirektor ernannt worden.

[72] ZWA. Material der Creditbankdirektion. Deutsch—ungarischer Aktientausch. Liste der deutschen Kapitalbeteiligungen.

Benz Automobil RT.), Neusiedler Papierhandel A. G. (Neusiedler Papírkereskedelmi RT.), die Firma Ohrenstein & Koppel, N. Rella & Neffe Bauunternehmung A. G. (Rella N. és Unokaöccse Építési Vállalat RT.), Guido Rütgers Holzimprägnierungs- und Holzpflasterungs A. G. (Rütgers Guido Fatelítő és Faburkoló RT.), Schimmel & Co A. G. (Schimmel és Társa RT.), Stölzles Söhne Ungarische Aktiengesellschaft für Glaswaren (Stölzle C. Fiai Üvegáruk Magyar RT.), »Tudor« Akkumulatorenfabrik A. G. (»Tudor« Accumulatorgyár RT.), Ungarische Siemens-Werke Elektrizitäts-A. G. (Magyar Siemens Művek Villamossági RT.), Papier- und Rohpappenfabrik A. G. (Papír- és Nyersfedéllemezgyár RT.), Ford Motor A. G. (Ford Motor RT.), Naxos Polierwarenfabrik A. G. (Naxos Csiszolóárugyár RT.), Újvidéker Schrauben- und Eisenwarenfabrik A. G. (Újvidéki Csavar- és Vasárugyár RT.), Ungarische Siemens-Reiniger-Werke A. G. (Magyar Siemens-Reiniger Művek RT.), Zinkwalzwerk A. G. (Horganyhengermű RT.).

Auch an vielen anderen Fabriken hatte das deutsche Finanzkapital bedeutende Beteiligungen (vgl. Anmerkung[73]).

[73] Das deutsche Kapital war an folgenden Fabriken und Betrieben beteiligt: Telephonfabrik A. G. (Telefongyár R. T.) 14,8%; Magyar Cukoripar R. T. (Ungarische Zucker-Industrie A. G.) 13,9%; Hazai Fésűsfonó és Szövőgyár R. T. (Vaterländische Kammgarn-Spinnerei und Weberei A. G.) 57%; Magyar Rabbethge és Giesecke Magtenyésztő R. T. (Ungarische Rabbethge und Giesecke Samenzucht A. G.) 40%; Zichy Béla Gróf Urkuti Bányaművei R. T. (Graf Béla Zichys Urkuter Bergwerke A. G.) 81%; Zagyvapálfalvi Üveggyár R. T. (Zagyvapálfalvaer Glasfabrik A. G.) 24,5%; Dreher Kőbányai Serfőzde és Csokoládégyár (Kőbányaer Dreher Bierbrauerei und Schokoladenfabrik A. G.) 13,7%; Felten és Guilleaume Kábel-, Sodrony- és Sodronykötélgyár R. T. (Felten & Guilleaume Kabel-, Draht- und Drahtseilfabrik A. G.) 74,4%; Szegedi Kenderfonógyár R. T. (Szegediner Hanfspinnerei A. G.) 15,8%; »Klotild« Első Magyar Vegyipar és »Acetic« Vegyiművek Egyesített R. T. (Vereinigte »Clotilde« Erste Ungarische Gesellschaft für Chemische Industrie und »Acetic« Chemische Werke A. G)) 8,4%; Hazai Papírgyár R. T. (Vaterländische Papierfabrik A. G.) 20%; Délmagyarországi Villamos Áramszolgáltató R. T. (Südungarische Elektrische Stromlieferungs A. G.) 57,1%; Drávavölgyi Villamos Áramszolgáltató R. T. (Drautaler Elektrische Stromlieferung A. G.) 90%; Petőházi és Nagycenki Cukorgyárak R. T. (Zuckerfabriken A. G. von Petőháza und Nagycenk) 82,5%; Continental Szalagszövőgyár R. T. (Continental Bandweberei A. G.) 41,1%; Vasárugyár R. T. Sopron (Eisenwarenfabrik A. G. Sopron) 84,5%; Hartmann Testvérek Nyomdafestékgyára R. T. (Gebrüder Hartmann Druckfarbenfabrik A. G.) 40%; Hartmann Vilmos-féle Papír- és Papírforgalmi R. T. (Wilhelm Hartmannsche Papierindustrie und Vertriebs-A. G.) 82,6%; Magyarországi Odolművek R. T. (Ungarische Odolwerke A. G.) 50%; Schember Magyar Mérleg- és Gépgyár R. T. (Schember Ungarische Waagen- und Maschinenfabrik A. G.) 10%; Schmoll és Kallós R. T. (Schmoll und Kallós A. G.) 25%; Soproni és Ujpesti Posztó- és Szőnyeggyárak (Soproner und Ujpester Tuch- und Teppichfabriken A. G.) 89,8%; Piatnik Kártyagyár (Spielkartenfabrik Piatnik) 84,4%; Ipari Robbanóanyaggyár R. T. (Industrielle Sprengstoffe A. G.) 12%; Felsőmagyarországi Bánya- és Kohómű R. T. (Oberungarische Berg- und Hüttenwerks-A. G.) 21,1%; Hazai Likőr-, Rum- és Szeszárugyár R. T. (Vaterländische Likör-, Rum- und Spirituosenfabrik A. G.) 47,1%; Első Magyar Cipőrugany-, Szalag és Húzógyár Wellesz, Schwitzer és Társai R. T. (Erste Ungarische Gummizug- Band- und Strumpffabrik Wellesz, Schwitzer & Co. A. G.) 17,9%; Gerő Adolf Szövött- és Kötöttárugyár R. T. (Adolf Gerő Strick- und Wirkwarenfabrik A. G.) 50%; Székesfehérvári Légszeszgyár és Vegyiművek R. T. (Székesfehérvárer Gasfabrik und Chemische Werke A. G.) 90,3%; Ujvidéki Kábelgyár R. T. (Ujvidéker Kabelfabrik A. G.) 33,3%; »UWAG« Magyar Szövőgyár R. T. (Ungarische Weberei A. G. »UWAG«) 85%; Prometheus Szén- Fa- és Koksz- R. T. (Prometheus Kohle-, Holz- und Koks-A. G.) 15%; »Chemicolor« Vegyészeti és Metallurgiai R. T. (Chemische und Metallurgische A. G. »Chemicolor«) 30%; Kárpáti Villamosmüvek RT. (Karpatische Elektrizitäts-

Wie ersichtlich, überließ das ungarische Finanzkapital den Deutschen auch während des Krieges nicht die wichtigen Positionen und der Raumgewinn des deutschen Kapitals in der ungarischen Industrie erfolgte in erster Linie nicht auf Kosten der ungarischen, sondern vielmehr des österreichischen, tschechischen, französischen usw. Finanzkapitals. Der deutsche Einfluß machte sich aber in diesen Jahren auch durch andere Mittel, so durch den politischen Druck geltend und stellte die ungarische Industrie in den Dienst der deutschen Interessen. Für die ungarischen Finanzkapitalisten war das nicht unmittelbar nachteilig, erhielten sie doch mehr Bestellungen, vermochten ihre Betriebe zu erweitern, ihre Kriegsprofite zu erhöhen usw. usw. Die einseitige Berücksichtigung der deutschen Interessen verletzte aber die Interessen des ungarischen Finanzkapitals, da sie es gleichzeitig auf vielen Gebieten einschränkte. Die meisten nach Deutschland ausgeführten Waren wurden nämlich nicht bezahlt. Auch das war ein wesentliches Moment in der Ausplünderung unseres Vaterlandes. Außerdem blieben auch die ungarischen Lieferungen an die Deutschen sowie die für die Deutschen verrichtete Lohnarbeit usw. usw. ohne Gegenleistung, worauf wir später noch zurückkommen werden. Die an der Ausfuhr interessierten Unternehmungen gelangten nur so zu ihren Forderungen, daß auf Grund eines zwischenstaatlichen Abkommens teilweise unmittelbar die Nationalbank, teilweise die großen Geldinstitute ihnen Geldsummen vorstreckten. Obzwar auch die von den Geldinstituten vorgestreckten Summen vom ungarischen Staat mittels ungedeckter Papiergeldemission durch die Notenbank refinanziert wurden, blieb das für das Finanzkapital doch ungünstig. Das ungarische Finanzkapital strebte also im Zusammenhang mit der Begleichung der deutschen Schulden danach, die in deutscher Hand befindlichen ungarischen Aktien als Begleichung der Schulden zurückzugewinnen. Diese Absichten waren schon zu Beginn des Krieges offensichtlich. Ein Führer der GYOSZ, Sándor Knob, warf bereits Anfang 1939 den Gedanken auf, man sollte den nach Deutschland gehenden großen Ausfuhrüberschuß nicht durch Erhöhung der Industrieeinfuhr decken, sondern die Deutschen sollten dafür einen Teil ihrer, damals bereits auf 120—130 Millionen Pengő geschätzten ungarländischen Kapitalbeteiligungen der ungarischen Industrie überlassen.[74] In der ersten Periode des Krieges konnten diese Wünsche noch nicht verwirklicht werden. Um die weiteren Lieferungen aus Ungarn zu sichern und keine Störungen eintreten zu lassen, zeigte sich die deutsche Regierung seit

---

werke A. G.) 51% ; Magyar Fémdobozművek R. T. (Ungarische Blechemballagen-Werke A. G.) 50%. Darüber hinaus ist außer den zahlreichen kleineren Beteiligungen auch die bedeutende deutsche Beteiligung an der Bauxit-Ipar R. T. (Bauxit Industrie A. G.) bekannt, ferner, daß ein erheblicher Teil des einzigen ungarischen Schwarzkohlengebietes im Besitz der ebenfalls in deutscher Hand befindlichen Ersten Donau-Dampfschiffahrts-Gesellschaft (Első Dunagőzhajózási Társaság) war. Bekannt sind schließlich die ungarischen Tochtergesellschaften mehrerer deutscher Unternehmungen, so beispielsweise der Budapester Betrieb der AEG. usw.

[74] Magyar Gyáripar (Ungarische Industrie) Nr. 4. 1939.

Ende 1942 bereit, das in deutschem Besitz befindliche ungarische Aktienvermögen zu überlassen. In den letzten Jahren des Krieges, von 1943 ab, ist schon die Rückerwerbung eines Teils der in deutscher Hand befindlichen Aktien möglich geworden, da dies zur Vorbedingung der weiteren Lieferungen gemacht wurde. Die diesbezüglichen Verhandlungen sind im November 1942 in Wien aufgenommen worden, wo ungarischerseits auf einen Aktienbesitz von ungefähr 250 Millionen Pengő sowie auf die Pécser Bergwerke Anspruch erhoben wurde. Die Deutschen — obzwar sie in der gegebenen Lage zu Zugeständnissen gezwungen waren — wollten ihre unmittelbaren Beteiligungspositionen in der ungarischen Industrie und in den ungarischen Geldinstituten nicht verlieren und wollten deshalb entgegen den deutschen Ansprüchen nur die Überlassung einer Aktiensumme von 30 Millionen Pengő in Erwägung ziehen. Sie erklärten sich einverstanden nur 13% ihres ungarischen Aktienvolumens Ungarn zu überlassen, was lediglich 2% der deutschen Schulden beglichen hätte. Sie waren nicht bereit, ihre Aktienbeteiligungen an dem Rimamurányer Eisenwerk, der Ganz-Fabrik, den Vereinigten Glühlampen, der Dreher-Fabrik, der Ungarischen ZuckerindustrieA. G., der Gummiwaren fabrik usw. abzutreten. Diese Gegensätze führten 1942 zum Abbruch der Verhandlungen.[75] Schließlich kam eine Kompromislösung doch zustande, nachdem die Deutschen der Rückerstattung eines Aktienvolumens im Werte von 100 Millionen Pengő zustimmten. Tatsächlich haben sie den ungarischen finanzkapitalistischen Gruppen bis Februar 1944 Aktien nur im Werte von 34,75 Millionen Pengő zurückgegeben. So übergab zum Beispiel die AEG ein Ganz-Fabrik-Aktienpaket mit 86 000 Aktien im Werte von 6,5 Millionen Pengő und damit gelangten die Aktien der Ganz-Fabrik vollständig in die Hände der Commerz-Bank.[76] Der Aktienbestand der Ungarischen Allgemeinen Kohlenbergbau Aktiengesellschaft (Magyar Általános Kőszénbánya RT.) ging im Werte von 8 Millionen Pengő ebenfalls in den Besitz des ungarischen Finanzkapitals über. Im Laufe der sogenannten Aktienrepatriierungen erhielt die Credit-Bank-Gruppe Aktien im Werte von 16 Millionen Pengő, die Commerz-Bank-Gruppe im Werte von 17 Millionen Pengő (hauptsächlich Salgótarjáner [7,7%] und Rimamurányer [13,7%] Aktien) und die anderen Banken Aktien im Werte von nicht ganz 2 Millionen Pengő zurück.[77] Selbst wenn das nur einen kleinen Teil der deutschen Kapitalbeteiligungen in Ungarn ausmachte, so muß doch festgestellt werden, daß es dem ungarischen Finanzkapital auf einigen Gebieten doch gelungen ist, die deutschen Kapitalbeteili-

[75] ZWA. Creditbank. Deutsch—ungarischer Aktientausch.
[76] ZWA. Ganz-Fabrik. Protokoll der Präsidialsitzung vom 16.9. 1943.
[77] ZWA. Creditbank. Deutsch—ungarischer Aktientausch. 4.2. 1944. Während des Krieges erwarb das ungarische Finanzkapital gewisse schweizerische (Filtex, »HPS« Textilfabrik A. G.) und — trotz dem Dazwischentreten der Deutschen — auch einige belgische und holländische (Egercsehier Kohlenbergbau) Aktien zurück. Die letzteren als Entgelt für Lebensmittellieferungen.

gungen zurückzudrängen, was auf die Stärkung seiner wirtschaftlichen Machtpositionen hindeutet.

Im Jahre 1944, nach der deutschen Besetzung des Landes, war das deutsche Finanzkapital — die gegebene Lage ausnützend — bestrebt, seine Hand nach dem größten Betrieb Ungarns auszustrecken. In diesem Zusammenhang ist es besonders wichtig, daß die SS von der Familie Weiss die Manfred Weiss-Werke käuflich erwarb, ebenso auch die anderen Anteile dieser Familie. (Dadurch gelangte die SS auch in den Besitz eines 12% betragenden Aktienpaquets der Salgótarjáner A. G.)[78]

Im letzten Kriegsjahr kam es also schon so weit, daß das ungarische Finanzkapital gezwungen war, einen Teil seiner bedeutendsten Anteile den deutschen Monopolkapitalisten zu überlassen.

Die wirtschaftliche Entwicklung in Ungarn während des Krieges wurde in vieler Hinsicht durch eine nachdrückliche Betonung der deutschen Interessen bestimmt. Wie wir gesehen haben, wurden die Entwicklung der Industrie und die kriegsbedingten Veränderungen ihrer Struktur über die Ausfuhr von enormen Mengen von landwirtschaftlichen Produkten und industriellen Rohstoffen hinaus in entscheidendem Maße von den deutschen Zielsetzungen bestimmt. Die Unterordnung des Wirtschaftslebens des Landes den deutschen Interessen — in welcher Form es auch immer geschah — wurde zum Mittel der Ausplünderung Ungarns in der Hand Nazi-Deutschlands. Die Unterordnung den deutschen Interessen ist wirtschaftlich in Form von »reinen Außenhandelsbeziehungen« zutage getreten. Laut der verschiedenen Handelsvereinbarungen hätte die ungarische Warenausfuhr deutscherseits durch Warenlieferung oder in anderer Form beglichen werden müssen. Diese Vereinbarungen dienten schon an und für sich der Ausplünderung des Landes, da sie auf ungleichem Warenaustausch beruhten. Hinzu kam, daß die Mark während des Krieges im Vergleich zum Pengő aufgewertet wurde, außerdem sind die Preise der deutschen Importartikel in viel größerem Maße gestiegen, als die ungarischen Exportgüter. All das bedeutete aber, daß Ungarn in den Kriegsjahren für dieselbe Menge deutscher Waren viel mehr ungarische Exportartikel als vor dem Kriege liefern mußte. Allein infolge der Maßnahme, wonach die Deutschen das Verhältnis zwischen den Export- und Importpreisen bewußt zu ihren Gunsten abgeändert hatten, zahlte Ungarn bereits in den ersten neun Monaten des Jahres 1941 bei 100 Millionen Pengő des Außenhandels 5 Millionen Pengő drauf.[79] Bis Ende des Krieges betrug diese Einbuße bereits 29 Millionen bei je 100 Millionen![80]

[78] ZWA. Protokoll des Salgótarjáner Exekutiv-Komitees vom 12. 7. 1944.

[79] Bericht des Landesverbandes der Ungarländischen Fabrikindustriellen (GYOSZ) vom Jahre 1942. Budapest 1943. S. 21 und 22.

[80] Kállay, Nicholas: Hungarian Premier, a personal account of a nation's struggle in the second World War. New York 1954. S. 302.

Das wird auch von anderen Quellen bestätigt, die die Preiserhöhungen der ungarischen Waren bis Ende 1943 auf 117%, die der Deutschen hingegen auf 190% schätzen.

Diese Methode, wenn auch nicht in derart zugespitzter Form, ist im allgemeinen bezeichnend für die wirtschaftlichen und Außenhandelsbeziehungen zwischen den höher entwickelten imperialistischen Mächten und den rückständigen, abhängigen Ländern. Im Laufe des Krieges wurden derartige Außenhandelsbeziehungen sehr bald zum Mittel der offenen, hemmungslosen Ausplünderung Ungarns. Die nach Deutschland gehenden Ausfuhrtransporte — die ungefähr 60% der gesamten ungarischen Ausfuhr ausmachten — wurden von den Deutschen in immer geringerem Maße beglichen und die deutschen Schulden wuchsen dem ungarischen Staat gegenüber immer mehr an.

Die enorme Verschuldung der deutschen Regierung erfolgte zur Zeit des Krieges gegen die Sowjetunion. Der Außenhandelssaldo wies bereits in den dreißiger Jahren im allgemeinen kleinere deutsche Passiva auf, im Frühling 1941 wurde jedoch die Außenhandelsbilanz für Ungarn passiv: es blieb eine Schuld von etwa 30 Millionen auf der Clearing-Rechnung, die im Juni desselben Jahres beglichen wurde. Des weiteren hat sich aber die Lage geändert: die deutsche Regierung stellte die Bezahlung der ungarischen Lieferungen ein, und wälzte die Begleichung der steigenden Schulden immer mehr auf den ungarischen Staat ab. Anfangs wurde das so gelöst, daß die Nationalbank bzw. das Konsortium der Budapester Geldinstitute der deutschen Verrechnungskasse 300 Millionen Mark »lieh« oder an die ungarischen Kapitalisten auszahlte. Seit Sommer 1942 waren aber die deutschen Schulden so stürmisch angewachsen, daß zur Regelung der Frage zwischenstaatliche Verhandlungen erforderlich wurden. Die deutsche Regierung brachte es wieder einmal mit ihrer gewohnten zynischen Offenheit zum Ausdruck, daß diese Schuld in der Zukunft noch erheblich steigen würde, d. h.: die Deutschen seien nicht geneigt, die ungarischen Lieferungen zu bezahlen, sie wälzen das ganz und gar auf den ungarischen Fiskus ab. Ein führender Beamter des deutschen Finanzministeriums, namens Litter, erklärte, daß der Großteil der ungarischen Lieferungen ». . . eigentlich . . . als Kontributionen zur gemeinsamen Kriegsführung zu betrachten seien, deren Gegenwert verbucht werden würde . . . Die Regelung der derart eingetragenen Summen würde eine, erst nach dem Kriege entstehende und zu lösende Frage sein!«[81]

Mit Rücksicht darauf, daß die ungarische herrschende Klasse noch damit rechnete, daß sich diese Investition — in erster Linie durch die Teilnahme an der Ausplünderung der unterjochten Länder — später reichlich bezahlt machen wird, stieg die Summe der deutschen Schulden in den Jahren 1942 und 1943 rapid an. Ende 1941 belief sich die Summe der deutschen Schulden auf 140 Millionen Mark. 1942 sprang der Betrag auf 506 Millionen, was mehr als 800 Millionen Pengő entsprach. Wie groß diese Summe war, wird ersichtlich, wenn wir bedenken, daß der gesamte, durch Banknotenemission gedeckte

[81] L. A. A. M. Wp. S. Dossier über die deutsch—ungarischen Verhandlungen 1942.

eigene Bedarf des ungarischen Fiskus um 40% niedriger war. »Dem deutschen Fiskus kreditieren wir um 60% mehr als dem ungarischen« stellte der Präsident der Ungarischen Nationalbank fest. »Das ist also eine sehr große Belastung.«[82] Bis 1943 hat sich aber auch diese gewaltige Summe verdoppelt und ist auf 1035 Millionen Mark gestiegen![83] Im Jahre 1944 stiegen dann die deutschen Schulden in einem noch schnelleren Tempo weiter an, was noch dadurch gekrönt wurde, daß für die Besatzungskosten Ungarns das ungarische Volk fast 2 Milliarden Pengő aufbringen mußte.

Hitler-Deutschland war also Ungarn gegenüber in hohem Maße verschuldet. Vor dem Kriege gerieten im allgemeinen die Schuldnerländer in eine abhängige Situation und sie wurden von den Gläubigern in Form von Zinsen usw. ausgepreßt. Im Kriege hat sich die Lage geändert. Zahlreiche führende kapitalistische Länder, die früher Gläubigerstaaten waren, sind nun zu Schuldnern geworden, und zwar jenen Ländern gegenüber, deren Gläubiger sie ehedem waren. Diese Verschuldung trug jetzt aber einen ganz anderen Charakter, sie bedeutete lediglich, daß die Ausplünderung der abhängigen oder Kolonialländer neue Formen annahm. Die Verschuldung wurde die Hauptform der Ausplünderung dieser Länder, des unentgeltlichen Abtransports ihrer Rohstoffe, Produkte usw. Die Verschuldung Deutschlands Ungarn gegenüber bedeutete also, daß die rasch zunehmenden deutschen Ausfuhrtransporte zu dieser Zeit bereits sozusagen vollkommen unentgeltlich vor sich gingen, d. h. das faschistische Deutschland setzte die Ausplünderung Ungarns noch offener und in einem alles frühere übersteigenden Maße fort. Mit Recht konnte die illegale »Szabad Nép« feststellen: »Der Hitlerismus will unseren letzten Tropfen Blut aussaugen und damit sein Mörderleben verlängern.«[84]

Die ungarischen herrschenden Klassen leisteten dem deutschen Faschismus Vasallendienste und wälzten die enormen Lasten ihrer Politik auf das Land, auf die Schultern des ungarischen Volkes ab. Die auch ohnedies großen militärischen Ausgaben des im Dienste des deutschen Faschismus, entgegen den Interessen des ungarischen Volkes geführten Krieges wurden durch die unbezahlten deutschen Schulden nur noch mehr erhöht.

Die gewaltigen und immer mehr anwachsenden Ausgaben konnte der ungarische Staat aus seinen Einnahmequellen nicht mehr decken. Obzwar die Steuerlasten ungeheuer emporgeschraubt wurden, wurde die Proportion der Steuereinnahmen des Staates bei der Deckung der Kriegsausgaben immer geringer. Es genügte auch die Inanspruchnahme von inneren Anleihen nicht: der Staat griff zum Mittel der *ungedeckten Banknotenemission!*

Das umlaufende Geld war in Ungarn, ebenso wie im allgemeinen in den anderen Ländern, keine echte Banknote, sondern nur Papiergeld. Diese

[82] L. A. Protokoll des 42er Ausschusses vom 8. 4. 1943. XXXI. S. 384.
[83] Statisztikai Szemle (Statistische Rundschau) 1946, S. 131.
[84] »Az illegális Szabad Nép«. (Die illegale »Szabad Nép«) Szikra 1954. S. 31.

Die Kriegsausgaben des Budgets in Millionen Pengő[85]

Jahr	Ohne deutsche Schulden	mit deutschen Schulden	In % des Nationaleinkommens	
1938/39 ...	618,9	618,9	11,9	11,9
1939/40 ...	1845,7	1845,7	19,8	19,8
1941.......	1170,4	1496,4	15,5	19,9
1942.......	2041,7	2599,7	21,9	27,9
1943.......	3562,0	4525,0	27,6	35,1
1944.......	6915,8	9833,8	31,0	44,1

Beschaffenheit des Geldes sprang zur Zeit des Krieges, als das Geld nicht mehr auf Grund von Handelskrediten, sondern als dem Staate gewährte Anleihen in Umlauf gelangten, noch mehr ins Auge. In den kapitalistischen Ländern hat das Wachstum der Staatsschulden, d. h. die Verschuldung der Regierungen bei den Nationalbanken in den Kriegsjahren sehr große Maße angenommen.[86]

Die umlaufende Geldmenge schwankte in Ungarn in den dreißiger Jahren zwischen 400—500 Milliarden Pengő, in Auswirkung des sogenannten Győrer Programms stieg sie 1938 auf mehr als 800 Milliarden an und erreichte bis 1940, wenn auch etwas langsamer, die enorme Höhe von 1400 Milliarden Pengő. Es muß hinzugefügt werden, daß die Erhöhung des Banknotenumlaufes teilweise damit zusammenhängt, daß sich die Umlaufgeschwindigkeit des Geldes infolge der Kriegsverhältnisse notwendigerweise verlangsamt hatte. Die durch die Gebietseinverleibung erfolgte Bevölkerungszunahme machte eine Erhöhung der umlaufenden Geldmenge ebenfalls erforderlich. Schließlich muß berücksichtigt werden, daß die Produktion und der Warenumsatz zu dieser Zeit ebenfalls eine ansteigende Tendenz zeigten. Infolge des Eintritts Ungarns in den Krieg und infolge des stürmischen Anwachsens der deutschen Schulden nahm aber der Banknotenumlauf nach 1941 im schnelleren Tempo sprunghaft zu und wurde 1944, auf dem Gipfelpunkt der Kriegsanstrengungen und infolge der deutschen Besetzung sogar maßlos.

Die Erhöhung des ungarischen Banknotenumlaufs hat den Banknotenumlauf vieler anderer Länder — darunter auch in den meisten von dem deutschen Faschismus unterjochten Ländern — weitaus überstiegen, während der Banknotenumlauf in Ungarn mehr als auf das 14fache anwuchs, stieg er zur

[85] Zusammengestellt auf Grund der Daten von Schlußrechnungen. Hinsichtlich der deutschen Schulden s. auch : Sándor Ausch : A háború finanszírozása és az 1938—1944. évi infláció Magyarországon. (Die Finanzierung des Krieges und die Inflation in Ungarn in den Jahren 1938—1944. Közgazdasági Szemle. (Volkswirtschaftliche Rundschau) 1955. Nr. 10, S. 1204.

[86] Varga J.: A tőkés gazdaság a második világháború után. (Die kapitalistische Wirtschaft nach dem zweiten Weltkrieg). Szikra, Budapest 1947. S. 257—258.

Gestaltung des Banknotenumlaufes[87]

Jahr	In Milliarden Pengő	%
1938.......	863	100
1939.......	974	112
1940.......	1 386	160
1941.......	1 984	229
1942.......	2 958	342
1943.......	4 391	508
1944.......	12 180	1411

selben Zeit in Deutschland nur auf das Achtfache, in Japan beinahe auf das Fünffache und selbst in den meisten unterjochten Länder im allgemeinen nur auf das 5—6fache.[88]

Selbstverständlich könnte man aus dem schnellen Zuwachs des Banknotenumlaufs und der Menge des Papiergeldes allein noch auf keine inflatorische Erscheinung schließen, die Vorbedingung zur Entwertung des Geldes, zur Inflation wird ja erst durch einen mit der Verminderung des Warenverkehrs einhergehenden Zuwachs des Geldumlaufs geschaffen. Die Verminderung des Warenverkehrs begann aber bereits nach 1940, da die Industrie, und zwar nicht nur die Schwerindustrie, sondern größtenteils auch die Leichtindustrie, für die Armee bzw. für die deutschen Bedürfnisse arbeiteten. Es ist aber eine allgemein bekannte Tatsache, daß für die ungarische Bevölkerung auch von Lebensmitteln nur ein Minimum, manchmal und von einigen Bedarfsartikeln selbst das nicht gesichert werden konnte. Die rapide Zunahme der Papiergeldmenge, gleichzeitig aber die Verminderung der Warendeckung hatten eine bedeutende Preissteigerung zur Folge. Trotz der amtlichen Preisregelungen stieg die Preisindexzahl im Großhandel zwischen 1939 und 1944 nach amtlichen Ausweisen um 22%. Die Preiserhöhungen waren aber in Wirklichkeit viel größer.

Bei den statistischen Ziffern sind einerseits bewußt solche Komponenten berücksichtigt bzw. außer acht gelassen worden, die die Preiserhöhungen geringer erscheinen lassen, andererseits werden nur die amtlichen Preise berücksichtigt, obwohl ein ziemlich bedeutender Teil des Warenverkehrs, etwa 40%, auf dem Schwarzmarkt zu viel höheren Preisen abgewickelt wurde. Die Preise waren auf dem schwarzen Markt ungefähr zehnmal höher als die amtlich angekündigten Preiserhöhungen.[89]

[87] Auf Grund der entsprechenden Jahrgänge der »Magyar Statisztikai Évkönyvek« (Ungarische Statistische Jahrbücher).

[88] Magyar Statisztikai Szemle (Ungarische Statistische Rundschau) 1946. S. 122—123.

[89] ZWA. Generalratssitzungsprotokoll der Ungarischen Nationalbank vom 26. 5. 1943. Ansprache des Generaldirektors Richard Quandt.

Die Inflation, der Entwertungsprozeß des Pengő, setzte also die Kaufkraft der Löhne und Gehälter herab und bildete eines der Mittel zur Neuverteilung des Nationaleinkommens zugunsten der herrschenden Klassen.

Die Neuverteilung des Nationaleinkommens wurde aber durch den Umstand in hohem Maße beeinflußt, daß die Inflationspolitik in Ungarn nicht allein zur Abwälzung der zunehmenden Ausgaben des Landes, sondern — wie wir es gesehen hatten — in hohem Maße auch zur Deckung des Mark-Saldos, der unentgeltlichen Ausfuhrtransporte nach Deutschland betrieben wurde.

Die infolge der ungedeckten Ausfuhren enorm angeschwollenen deutschen Schulden beliefen sich in den Kriegsjahren auf 4765 Millionen Pengő. Der Zuwachs des Banknotenumlaufes betrug in der Periode zwischen 1938 und 1944 11 337 Millionen Pengő, d. h. 45% *des gesamten Banknotenzuwachses ist von den deutschen Schulden verursacht worden!* Wie bekannt, spielten die deutschen Schulden erst zur Zeit des antisowjetischen Krieges eine entscheidende Rolle, zwischen 1938 und 1941 noch nicht. Während also der Banknotenzuwachs in diesen Jahren ausschließlich auf die ungarische Aufrüstung zurückzuführen war, waren es zwischen 1941 und 1944 schon die deutschen Schulden, die bei dem immer schnelleren Tempo der Inflation die entscheidende Rolle spielten.

Jahr	Banknotenzuwachs	Zunahme der deutschen Schulden	Proportion der deutschen Schulden im Banknotenzuwachs (%)
	jährlich in Millionen Pengő		
1941.......	598	326	54
1942.......	974	558	57
1943.......	1433	963	67
1944.......	7789	2918	37

Auf Grund der angeführten Tatsachen kann mit Recht gefolgert werden, daß bis zum Jahre 1944 die Inverkehrsetzung ungedeckter Banknoten, die sich entfaltende Inflation in erster Reihe eine Folge der deutschen wirtschaftlichen Expansion und jenes Umstandes war, daß die führenden Politiker Ungarns dem deutschen Faschismus dienlich waren. Wenn wir dies auch betonen, müssen wir doch darauf hinweisen, daß die Behauptung einiger führender Politiker dieser Zeit, die die Inflation aussließlich auf den deutschen Druck zurückführen und die Rolle der eigenen Kriegsausgaben bagatellisieren, unrichtig sind; diese Memoiren wurden hauptsächlich verfaßt, um ihre eigene volksfeindliche Politik zu beschönigen und ihre eigene Verantwortlichkeit zu verwischen.[90]

[90] Kallay, Nicholas: Hungarian Premier, a personal account of a nation's struggle in the second World War. S. 299.

Das faschistische Deutschland deckte ungefähr ein Viertel seiner Kriegsausgaben aus der Ausplünderung fremder Staaten. Ungarn gehörte zu diesen Staaten. In der Hand des deutschen Finanzkapitals war also der in den Satelliten- und in den besetzten Staaten einsetzende Inflationsprozeß ein wichtiges Mittel, um sich einen Teil des Nationaleinkommens der betreffenden Länder anzueignen. In diesen Ländern also, und so auch in Ungarn, erfolgte die Neuaufteilung des Nationaleinkommens unmittelbar zu Gunsten des deutschen Finanzkapitals.

Die immer totalere Unterjochung und Ausplünderung Ungarns durch den deutschen Faschismus belastete in grundlegender und entscheidender Weise in erster Linie die Arbeiterklasse und die werktätigen Klassen, verletzte aber gleichzeitig auch die Interessen der ungarischen herrschenden Klassen bzw. einiger Schichten dieser Klassen. Nach der deutschen Niederlage bei Stalingrad, als es offenkundig wurde, daß diese »Investition« nach dem Kriege ihnen nicht entschädigt würde, tauchte auch in der Politik die Bestrebung auf, möglichst mit den Deutschen zu brechen, aus dem Kriege herauszuspringen, um dadurch das Horthy-Sytem herüberzuretten. Die sich um den Horthy-Klüngel gruppierenden herrschenden Kreise blieben aber infolge ihres tiefen Hasses gegen das Volk und gegen die Sowjetunion bis Ende des Krieges Hitler-Deutschlands treueste Vasallen.

Zur Krönung der viertelhundertjährigen, schändlichen Herrschaft ihres konterrevolutionären Systems und der deutschen kolonisatorischen Bestrebungen lieferten sie unser Vaterland vollständig der Herrschaft des deutschen Faschismus und seiner ungarischen Trabanten aus und stürzten damit das Land ins Verderben. Im Jahre 1944 versetzte die Sowjetarmee ununterbrochen Schläge den deutsch-faschistischen Armeen und ihren Vasallenheeren. Im selben Jahre, als die völlige Niederlage Hitler-Deutschlands schon unmittelbar bevorstand, setzten die deutschen herrschenden Kreise noch alles daran, ihren Untergang hinauszuschieben. In Anbetracht der doppelzüngigen Politik der Kállay-Regierung, ihrer lahmen Versuche, aus dem Kriege herauszuspringen, besetzten die Deutschen — von den extremen ungarischen faschistischen Elementen unterstützt — am 19. März 1944 Ungarn und riefen — mit Zustimmung der Horthy-Gruppe — die Sztójay-Marionettenregierung ins Leben. Nahm die Ausplünderung des Landes schon früher ungeheuere Ausmaße an und wurde sie auch bis dahin immer offener, so kam die deutsche Herrschaft jetzt, nach der Besetzung in unmittelbarer Form zur Geltung und die Ausplünderung des Landes wurde völlig unverhüllt, in Form des offenen Raubes weitergeführt. Die deutsche Besetzung bedeutete für die Werktätigen einen hemmungslosen Terror, gleichzeitig aber auch — wie wir bereits erwähnten — eine neue, schwere finanzielle Last von 2 Milliarden Pengő, da die ungarische Marionettenregierung die Kosten der Besatzung auf sich nahm.

Seit Oktober 1944, als die Befreiung unseres Vaterlandes durch die sowjetischen Truppen bereits ihren Anfang nahm, begannen auch die Deutschen und ihre pfeilkreuzlerischen Söldlinge — zur Vollendung ihrer bis dahin betriebenen Raubwirtschaft — mit der Verschleppung der Fabrikseinrichtungen der ungarischen Industrie nach Deutschland, im nichtverschleppten Produktionsapparat hingegen richteten sie eine barbarische Verwüstung an. Bezeichnend ist eine Äußerung des pfeilkreuzlerischen Regierungskommissars für Unterkunftswesen über die Umsiedlung der Industrie nach Deutschland. In dieser Erklärung hieß es : »Die Früchte dieser edlen Arbeit werden nicht nur die heute lebenden Ungarn, sondern auch die Generationen der ewigen nationalen Zukunft zu spüren bekommen und segnen.«[91]

Der sogenannte »Lähmungs- und Verschleppungsplan« wurde am 14. November 1944 durch eine Verordnung des Landesverteidigungsministers (Nr. 51673/eln. H. M. 3. oszt.) geregelt. Die Vorbereitung, Durchführung und Kontrolle oblag den militärischen Behörden. Die Liste der zu sprengenden oder auszuführenden Betriebe wurde deutscherseits vom Hauptquartiermeister der Heeresgruppe Süd, ungarischerseits von der gemeinsamen Kriegsindustriegruppe des Landesverteidigungs- und Industrieministeriums zusammengestellt, die Deutschen gingen aber auch selbständig vor, anhand der Angaben der Deutschen Industrie-Kommission in Ungarn. Nach der Einkesselung von Budapest zerstörten einige deutsche Truppenkommandanten eigenmächtig verschiedene Betriebseinrichtungen.[92]

Die Verschleppung bzw. Zerstörung der wertvollen Maschinen richtete in zahlreichen — insbesondere in den kriegswichtigen Betrieben — schwere Schäden an. In der Egercsehier Kohlenbergwerks- und Portlandzementfabrik A. G. (Egercsehi Kőszénbánya és Portlandcementgyár RT.), die im September noch in Betrieb war, sprengten die Deutschen bei ihrem Abzug die Elektrizitätszentrale und den Kohlenabschneider.[93] In der Ganz-Fabrik erschien am 29. Dezember 1944 ein »Lähmungskommando« und sprengte die Regler- und Schaltanlagen.[94] Der Großteil der wertvollen Maschinen der Ungarischen Optischen Werke A. G. (Magyar Optikai Művek RT.) wurde hingegen nach Deutschland verschleppt.[95] Ähnliches Los ist auch der Székesfehérvárer Anlage der Jagdpatronen-, Zündhütchen- und Metallwerkenfabrik A. G. (Vadásztöltény-, Gyutacs- és Fémárugyár RT.) widerfahren. Hier wurden 60—70% des modernen Maschinenparks unter der Anleitung der deutschen Todt-Organisation weggeschleppt, und nur die minderwertigen Maschinen sind geblieben.[96] Die Lage war auch in vielen anderen Fabriken, so z. B. in den Ungarischen Munitionswerken A. G. (Magyar Lőszerművek RT.) die gleiche.

[91] L. A. A. M. Material des Ausschusses für Friedensvorbereitung II/2—28/13.
[92] L. A. A. M. Material des Ausschusses für Friedensvorbereitung I/1—3/1—24/3.
[93] Geschäftsbericht des Egercsehier Kohlenbergbaus, Budapest 1946.
[94] L. A. A. M. Material des Ausschusses für Friedensvorbereitung I/1—3/1—24/3.
[95] L. A. A. M. Material des Ausschusses für Friedensvorbereitung I/1—3/1—24/20.
[96] Zentralwirtschaftsarchiv. Commerz-bank. Industrie 14. Vadásztölténygyár. (Jagdpatronenfabrik).

Ein ähnliches Schicksal haben die Deutschen auch der Ujszegeder Anlage der Ungarischen Hanf-, Flachs- und Juteindustrie A. G. (Magyar Kender, Len és Jutaipar RT.) zugedacht, deren beste Maschinen bereits eingeschifft wurden. Da sie aber infolge des Anmarsches der sowjetischen Truppen nicht mehr abtransportiert werden konnten, wurde der Schlepper mit Ekrasit in die Luft gesprengt.[97]

Es fanden sich im Lande kaum einige Betriebe, die durch die faschistischen Verwüstungen keine Beschädigungen erlitten.

Die ungarischen herrschenden Klassen haben also dadurch, daß sie das Land zum letzten Vasallen Deutschlands herabsinken ließen und es in einen Kriegsschauplatz verwandelten, dem ungarischen Volk die schwersten Leiden zugefügt und die ungarische Volkswirtschaft den Verheerungen des Krieges ausgesetzt. Der an Deutschlands Seite geführte Raubkrieg hat *eine 40prozentige Verwüstung des ungarischen Nationalvermögens zur Folge gehabt.* Die ungarische Industrie hat schwere Verluste erlitten. Der Schaden an Gebäuden und Maschinenanlagen betrug ungefähr 900 Millionen Pengő (Wert 1938), was soviel bedeutete, daß *ungefähr 50% der Anlagenfonds der ungarischen Industrie vernichtet worden sind. 75% der Arbeitsmaschinen,* ungefähr 33% der Energiemaschinen sind zugrunde gegangen. Mehr als die Hälfte der Fabriken ist beschädigt oder vernichtet worden, ihre Kapazität hat um rund 46% abgenommen. *Die Produktionsfähigkeit der ganzen Industrie ist demzufolge um 24% zurückgegangen.* Die in den Betrieben aufgestapelten Rohstoff- und Produktionsvorräte sind beinahe vollständig verloren gegangen, was der Vernichtung von mehr als einer Milliarde Pengő gleichkam. *Etwa 20% der kriegsbedingten Verluste der Industrie sind unmittelbar auf die hitlerfaschistischen und pfeilkreuzlerischen Verwüstungen zurückzuführen.*[98]

Auch die Landwirtschaft hatte erhebliche Schäden. Der während des Krieges erfolgte Verfall der Landwirtschaft machte — auf den Pengőwert des Jahres 1938 umgerechnet — 3,7 *Milliarden Pengő aus.* Die im Jahre 1944/45 unbebaut gebliebenen Felder verursachten einen Schaden von weiteren 200 Millionen Pengő. Der in den landwirtschaftlichen Produkten eingetretene Schaden belief sich auf 1320 Millionen Pengő. Der Schaden unter den landwirtschaftlichen Maschinen betrug 162 Millionen, der landwirtschaftliche Gebäudeschaden 218 Millionen Pengő. Den größten Schaden erlitt der Viehbestand, wo die Verwüstung anderthalb Milliarden Pengő betrug. 52,6% des Viehbestandes von 1942, 59% des Pferdebestandes, 46,4% des Schweinebestandes und 82,7% des Schafbestandes gingen zugrunde. Ungefähr 14% der

[97] ZWA. Englisch—Ungarische Bank, Sitzungsprotokoll vom 8. 4. 1946.

[98] L. A. A. M. Material des Ausschusses für Friedenvorbereitung II/2—44/45. Statistische Datensammlung der Verluste in der Industrie. Durchgeführt vom Statistischen Amt im Sommer 1945 und Közgazdasági Szemle (Volkwirtschaftliche Rundschau) 1954. Nr. S. 360.

Tierschäden waren unmittelbar auf die deutschen faschistischen und pfeilkreuzlerischen Plünderungen zurückzuführen.[99]

Zerstörte Betriebe, eine ausgeplünderte Landwirtschaft, ein zugrunde gerichtetes Land: das war die Schlußbilanz der deutschen »Südostraum-Politik« in Ungarn. Das war das Ergebnis der Politik der ungarischen herrschenden Klassen, die Ungarn und die ungarische Nationalwirtschaft in den Dienst der deutschen Kriegsinteressen gestellt hatten.

[99] Ebendort.

IV

"UNWILLING SATELLITE" OR "LAST SATELLITE" — SOME PROBLEMS OF HUNGARIAN-GERMAN RELATIONS

The title of the book of the former American ambassador[1] and the epithet echoed so often in the years immediately following World War II express the two possible poles of evaluating Hungary's role in the Second World War. Needless to say, *in grosso modo*, most of the memoirs written by the former politicians of the Horthy regime and its supporters took positions which, though they differed in some substantial matters, were nearer to the former formulation. On the other hand, the books and articles written by historians in postwar Hungary — even if they never accepted the brand "last satellite" — focused on the circumstances that had caused Hungary to become that, a German satellite which was unable to disengage itself from the war up to the very last minute. This dichotomy, however, cannot be regarded as merely expressing different approaches, intentions and judgements. These poles were not created after the war for purposes of self-justification or for casting blame on the regime which fell in with the Germans. In some sense, these poles characterized Hungary and her foreign policy from 1933 to 1944, and expressed the play between things as they were and things as they were wishfully perceived to be, expressed the various foreign policy trends in Hungary, and the different ideas as to how to carry these out. These were the poles of the Hungarian reality.

According to Macartney, after "Hitler had become chancellor of the Reich, and ... after fifteen years, a power was at last in the field which seemed both willing and able to smash the chains of the peace settlement. Many people expected Hungary at once to throw herself into Germany's arms."[2] If this was not really the case, then Macartney found four different reasons for it:

1. Hitler was far from being ready to help Hungary to integral revision.

2. Genuine fears for Hungary's independence, awakened by the reemergence of a great united Germany standing on Hungary's very frontier for the first time in modern history.

3. Simple calculation. While the army officers, almost to a man, were convinced of the invincibility of the German arms, many of the influential politicians believed that the West would win.

4. The nation was sharply divided by ideological questions, particularly the Jewish problem.

In the same foreword, Macartney described Hungary's position after 1938, "as a succession of short downward slides, in each case due to very strong propulsion from outside, and in each case followed by prolonged efforts, if not to regain the lost ground, at least to avoid further loss."[3]

I agree with Macartney's statement so far that there was a succession of downward slides with a perpetual attempt to control it. However, if we regard the whole story from the beginning (1933) to the sad end (1944), then I would put it in a slightly different and probably more complex way. Kossuth's definition of politics as the science of exigencies is true of foreign policy as well. Exigencies may not, however, be regarded as just the potentialities of a given situation. I would regard a government's freedom of action as a function of its own aims and means combined with the possibilities of action left to it by force of circumstance, or the pressures put on it by more major powers, or the great powers. According to these premises, German-Hungarian relations are to be examined in the context of this combination of forces, and although, undoubtedly, the force of circumstances (German pressure) became more and more the decisive factor in this relationship, we ought not to forget that the Hungarian government always had a stake in the relationship, almost to the bitter end.

The Hungarian interest in that alliance was focused on three main considerations. The first, which had a particularly great influence on the relationship with the Third Reich in the first few years after the Great Depression, was the economy. The second is almost too obvious to speak of. Hungary strove for the revision of the Treaty of Trianon which — *nolens-volens* — under the given international circumstances could not be achieved but with German help. This was an issue already at the beginning of closer German-Hungarian cooperation, and became a dominant factor in Hungarian foreign policy from 1938 to 1942, the years of Germany's successes.

Last but not least, in spite of substantial differences in the political, ideological and power structures of the two systems, they had certain affinities: both regimes were anti-liberal and anti-democratic; only Germany was Fascist, but Hungary was authoritarian. How far this affinity helped build up the alliance in the 1930s is a moot point. I myself do not regard it as a decisive element; however, I would allow it a certain degree of importance. But by the end, roughly from 1942 to 1944, nothing else — neither economic interest nor the prospect of revision — would have tied Hungary to Nazi Germany. German pressure was certainly the decisive factor at this period of the war, in spite of the tremendous differences which became more and more explicit in the course of the war. The features common to the two regimes — the antiliberal, retrograde political and social structure of both — contributed greatly to the paralysis of important Hungarian political forces, and contributed to the country's downward slide from the position of an unwilling satellite to that of those satellites which were unable to successfully extricate themselves from the war. The dilemma of the unwilling or the last satellite was her need to manoeuvre in the permanent crossfire of the force of circumstances, i.e. the power of Germany, and the need to assert her own foreign policy aims. These two were compatible from time to time, though finally they proved to be contradictory. Still, occasionally, even the attempts to preserve an independent foreign policy line reinforced Hungarian-German collaboration. As the war progressed, external pressures on Hungary came to dominate, and unwillingness to follow the German line came to characterize her. It was, in the final analysis, the force of circumstances that was decisive in Hungary's moving from her position in 1942 as the most unwilling satellite to her position in the fall of 1944 of being the last one. But Hungary's political aims had been such that a large number of army officers and politicians — who had a great influence on public opinion — continued as late as all that to consider this her only real option.

In my short paper, I wish to show the three different periods in the history of the German(Nazi)-Hungarian relations, the parts played by the three main considerations (economic, foreign policy, and domestic power structure) in shaping this relationship, and the effect on it of the growth of German power. In addition, I would like to show the effect that this relationship had on the possibility of Hungary's actually conducting her own foreign policy during the war. It is well known that after World War I, the political reorganization of Southeastern Europe was accompanied by the attempt on the part of the victorious Allied powers to gain economic hegemony over the countries of the area. However, the Anglo-French hegemony that developed at the beginning of the 1920s contained numerous contradictions. From 1928-29 onward, Anglo-French economic hegemony was in a state of continuous crisis, partly because of the conflict between British and French interests, and partly because of the objective demands of economic development, expressed in the difference between the related credit and market systems. The international economic crisis further undermined the unity of the Anglo-French hegemony, and when the attempts to resolve the economic difficulties of the countries of the Danube Valley by uniting them in some kind of economic block under French leadership failed the initiative — after a brief Italian interlude - was seized by Germany. It took almost a year for Germany to take the first real opportunity that presented itself. This year, decisive in the building of Hitler's totalitarian system, was significant also for Hungary's economy, which became more shaky during 1933, one of the reasons being that the volume of her agricultural export to Germany reached rock bottom. (The fall in the value of exports to Germany was roughly 14 per cent.)

On April 22, 1933, Gömbös, Prime Minister of Hungary, wrote a letter to Hitler in which we read the following: "Nationalist Hungary, now governed with a strong hand, has always looked to Berlin with some expectation and sympathy. It is, I believe, also in Germany's interest to prevent unstable economic relations from undermining this sympathy...

I would therefore request urgently that the German government take a decision to come to our assistance in matters of agricultural export. I am convinced that Your Excellency's strong will will be obeyed over this issue as well, all the more so as I know that Your Excellency holds views that are identical with mine: *viz.* that politics and economic policy should be co-ordinated as far as possible.

Agricultural export, as I view it, is not merely an economic problem but one which has a bearing upon politics; and ... my political line would be strengthened, if this were appreciated on the part of Germany ...."[4]

Early in 1934, on the occasion of a conversation with Mackensen, the German Ambassador, Gömbös expressed himself bluntly: "The necessity of maintaining Hungarian-German friendship is too obvious to require emphasis. The further development of these — at present very good — relations depends on the attitude to be taken by Germany regarding German imports of Hungarian farm products."[5] Formally, at this point, Hungary was supposed to choose between Italian or German political orientation and economic help. In spite of Italian pressure, Gömbös was reluctant to opt for Italy; and though there was a sort of balancing between the two countries, his preferences, for economic, political and military reasons as well, were increasingly for Germany. Germany, aware of this situation, made up her mind to profit from Hungary's economic needs and political retribution, and to manipulate circumstances so as to acquire Hungary as her first helper in the Danube Valley. The twenty page memorandum prepared by Counsellor Schnurre of the German Foreign Ministry briefly summarized Hungarian foreign policies, emphasizing that Gömbös was working with both Germany and Italy and was not bound by Italian-Austrian cooperation. He was strongly anti-French and anti-Little Entente, and he rejected all plans for a Danubian Confederation, whether an Austrian-Czech-Hungarian tariff union, or some wider cooperation as envisioned by the Tardieu Plan. "This Hungarian policy corresponds to the demands of German foreign policy and guarantees that they will not enter into any kind of Southeastern European combination without us."[6] Conclusion: We need to support Hungarian foreign policy and must tie the country to Germany economically, "which can be done by assuring a sufficient market for Hungarian products".

So, by early 1934, the Germans thought the situation ripe enough to move to prevent the deepening of the Italian-Austrian-Hungarian connection, and to start to stake Hungary out as a definite economic territory. On January 19, 1934, there was a conference with the participation of Foreign Minister Neurath, Finance Minister Schwerin von Krosigk, and the President of the Reich Bank, Schacht. By then, the decision "that from the political point of view a new form and special treatment are needed when regulating relations with Hungary" had been made. Foreign Minister Neurath addressed a letter to Kánya on January 13, 1934.[7] In it he explained that the improved German economic situation made it possible to begin discussions, in the spirit of the Hitler-Gömbös talks, about deepening German-Hungarian economic ties. A German economic delegation was to travel to Budapest for the purpose of detailed discussions.

It was clear to the German ruling circles that concessions would have to be made in favor of Hungarian agricultural exports during the discussions. This, however, no longer created much of a problem. The newly evolving German economic policy wished to place its agricultural point of gravity in Southeastern Europe anyway. These points of view emerged at the January 17 meeting of the Economic Ministry, where it was stated that discussions with the Hungarians were justified for the following reasons:

"1. In the course of our exchange of letters last summer, the Reich Chancellor made a promise to Hungarian Prime Minister Gömbös that he would consider the Hungarian request regarding trade policy. 2. The Italian government, as it is well known, is experimenting with the creation of an Italian, Austrian and Hungarian tariff union.

It is in our interest to create a strong position for ourselves in Hungary to counterbalance these aspirations."[8]

The meaning of the German decision was clear: "Germany's purpose in the treaty about to be concluded consisted of tying the Hungarian economy closely and inseparably to the German economy by means of increased exchange of goods."

The Trade Treaty of 1934 is too well known to be dealt with here. It is clear that it was extremely important for Hungary to establish close ties with a larger economic unit. Viewed from this perspective, German economic penetration appears to have brought temporary advantages for Hungary because it created favorable circumstances for overcoming the effects of the Great Depression, and satisfied the demands of Hungarian agriculture for markets.

After the signing of the treaty, German foreign policymakers expressed their satisfaction. "It may be expected that Hungary will not lightly risk the very considerable advantages granted her by Germany and will be mindful of this in her political attitude and also with respect to commercial policy."[9] Nevertheless, whatever the advantages of the Treaty for Hungary's economy might have been in the short run, in the long run, these connections brought political as well as economic dangers. Could Hungary have pursued any other kind of foreign economic policy under the given circumstances? The question is difficult to answer. After the total failure of a Danubian block of any kind — to which Hungarian foreign policy contributed as well — and after her total neglect by the Western powers, her freedom was very limited. A drowning man will not refuse the hand stretched out to help him for fear of blackmail in the future. However, one may ask if it would not have been better to grasp the Italian hand instead. Was turning to Germany just an economic decision, or was it more of a political one, as Gömbös had said: "We fellow racists of long standing, who hold a common ideology, shall understand and back each other on economic policy as well."[10] Anyway, there is no doubt that in this very early period of the history of Nazi Germany, Hungary opened her door to German penetration (as was to be done a few months later by Yugoslavia, and in 1935, by Romania), and she became a basic element of German foreign policy in frustrating any plans and possibilities which did not coincide with German foreign policy aims. German-Hungarian relation in that phase was still based on a community of interest (which, of course, are never of equal weight when the partners are a great power and a small nation).

As the time was approaching for the second element of the community of interest (i.e. foreign policy aims) to yield fruit, the built-in dangers of economic cooperation came more and more into view. However, even at this stage, material interests made a rather large and important part of the Hungarian land-owning class a strong supporter of strengthening German economic ties, and of selling more and more goods on her markets. (Naturally, the entire agricultural sector had a stake in this, but the peasants did not have any influence to speak of in shaping foreign policy decisions.) After 1938, of course, foreign policy issues became more important than economic ones due to the changes in the international agricultural market. The Hungarian politicians of the interwar period never shared the views of Gambetta, who, after the annexation of Alsace in 1871, had declared: always think of reannexation, but never speak about it.

Hungary's foreign policy aims, i.e., the complete revision of the Treaty of Trianon, had never been concealed. Let us disregard for now the very important issue of to what extent this foreign policy aim might have been justified by the absolutely anti-Hungarian territorial stipulations of the Peace Treaty. Nowadays, it is almost a commonplace that the victorious powers in general, and French politicians in particular, sowed the seeds of a new conflict, when, for a variety of reasons, they showed complete disregard for the ethnic lines of demarcation in the case of Hungary and a population of almost 3.5 million ethnic Hungarians (Magyars), roughly 35 per cent of Hungary's population, were ceded to the successor states. Just as obviously, Hungarian foreign policy aims were not confined to a revision along ethnic lines — which might, in the long run, have brought some kind of understanding among the Danubian countries — but proposed to restore the Kingdom of Saint

Stephen, i.e. all the old territories along with almost 8 million non-Magyars. There were some very characteristic (but absolutely unrealistic) plans for revision nurtured already in the early 1920s by Horthy and his government; but the first foreign policy program that was in the realm of possibilities was the one that regarded Germany as the likely ally in any revision. Bethlen had attempted already in the late 20s to forge closer links with Germany. He believed that any well-founded foreign policy left the Italo-German military alliance as the only effective choice for Hungary. But an Italo-German military alliance was still far in the future; and Germany was not willing as much as to associate herself with Hungary for either foreign or domestic policy reasons.[11] Things changed after Hitler's seizure of power. One cannot regard a matter of chance the fact that Gömbös was the first foreign statesman who paid Hitler a visit. In spite of the fact that some Hungarian politicians, among them Bethlen, quickly realized that Hitler's Germany was not the Germany they were looking for, Gömbös was obliged to write clearly in a letter (which Hitler never answered) that Germany had to acknowledge Hungary's leading role in the Carpatho-Danubian Basin.[12]

Nevertheless, the formation of German-Italian axis had been extremely well-received by the Hungarian government and by the Hungarian press. "Dès lors 'l'axe Rome-Berlin' est devenu pour les Hongrois la baguette magique dont on peut attendre tous les miracles, bientôt, pour ces gens toujours pénétrés d'esprit troubadours, la connivence politique, d'une atmosphère romanesque (sic). Défenseurs attirés de l'Europe chrétienne c'était à une croisade qu'ils marchaient avec l'Italie et l'Allemagne. Ils enrolaient certes avec un enthousiasme sincère au service de la bonne cause mais un élément de calcul entrait pourtant dans leur geste." This is how Maugras, the French Ambassador, characterized Hungarian foreign policy in one of his reports.[13]

I would like to emphasize the last sentence of his report concerning the element of calculation. It is not my intention to blame the policy-makers for this element of calculation. One of the things in which Hungarian foreign policy was always at fault was its lack of the certain necessary amount of calculation. The *élément de calcul* is connected with a few further remarks in this report by the French Ambassador. As he saw it, the enthusiastic voice of the press was directed mainly by Gömbös. Kánya, the Foreign Minister, was much more cautious. As to the questions of whether the Ambassador was really expecting any results from this new Holy Alliance, he answered: "Attendez-vous de moi, que je desavoue nos espérances nationales". Kánya reiterated the formal Hungarian statement that the revision was to be achieved by peaceful means; nevertheless he also acknowledged that even he doubted that it would be possible without waging war.

As Germany regained her former strength, built up her military forces, and won diplomatic successes, the two trends in Hungarian foreign policy became more and more recognizable. These two trends had always been connected with different social and political forces, with different politicians, and with different personalities. Nevertheless, the position which came more and more to gain the upper hand was that Hungary had to march along with Germany, which was proving very successful in her foreign affairs. According to this view, the element of *calcul* dictated support for a foreign policy based mainly on an alliance with Germany.

Doubts were certainly raised. Opposition politicians, themselves warm supporters of a foreign policy aimed at the revision of Trianon, urged more caution. Eckhardt stressed that Hungary had to leave open which camp she would join in case of war.

"Il faut que la Hongrie garde la faculté en cas de conflagration de marchander avec l'un et l'autre parti. Nous ne voulons pas nous asseoir encore une fois à la table des negotiations parmi les vaincus." [14]

Even French diplomats who, for obvious reasons, were not very fond of Hungarian foreign policy aims and methods acknowledged that the relationship between Germany and Hungary was far from being as good as it had been declared.

"La fête de Saint-Étienne a d'ailleurs elle-même mis en relief les différences que séparent les thèses politiques de l'Allemagne nationale socialiste de la tradition magyare ...

'l'idée stéphanistienne' apparait comme essentiellement humaniste et chrétienne par conséquent très éloignée des théories étroites et materialistes de la race... L'évolution des rapports germano-magyars est donc assez complexe. Il y a outre, à côté des facteurs pûrement docrtinaux, des considérations de politique extérieure proprement dîtes. La Hongrie ne croît pas pouvoir se presser de l'appui de l'Allemagne mais elle ne veut pas laisser dominer ni manoeuvrer."[15]

Of course, the report was signed in 1937 when, theoretically, Hungary was still able to defend herself against attempts by Germany to rule her, but not against being maneuvered. A few months after November 1937, when Hitler held out a glimmer of hope for real revision at the expense of Czechoslovakia, Darányi, who was certainly regarded as more moderate than his predecessor, Gömbös, gave his consent to Hungary's participatin in a scheme for an attack aimed at dismembering Czechoslovakia.

The possibilities of maneuvering deteriorated after the *Anschluss* and Munich. Top Hungarian politicians, who, a few months earlier, their revisionist aims notwithstanding, had been cautious enough not to give their unconditional support to an attack on Czechoslovakia, made a sudden *volte-face*. Others were either not willing to do this, or saw best to refrain from such gestures, for having led a foreign policy not entirely trusted by Hitler, their *volte-face* would have lacked credibility. They were dismissed from the government (Kánya, for example).

From 1938 on, when the possibility of revision was at hand, the basic element of Hungarian-German relations was given. Yet even during this honeymoon period, when Hungarian Foreign Minister Csáky took for granted that "the leading role of the Axis was assured for the next twenty-five years in Europe", there were several occasions when Hungarian foreign policy refused to follow the German lead unquestioningly. Hitler made it quite clear to Csáky in January 1939 that he would set the restoration of the Empire of Saint Stephen as the aim of the Great German Empire. The most courageous act of the Hungarian leaders was the famous letter Teleki addressed to Hitler in July, 1939, which, after declaring that his government was on the side of the Axis powers in every respect, stated that, for moral reasons, they did not wish to be party to the attack on Poland.[16] Hitler was certainly infuriated, and, after two weeks, Csáky declared that this letter had never been written. After that declaration, Hitler stated that he was not requiring Hungary's military assistance against Poland; her withdrawal had become more or less a formal act. But still, the obvious question remains to be answered: How was Hitler able to press for the repudiation of Teleki's letter in July of 1939? I would say that at this time, Hungary did not yet fear German military intervention. The most important element of the pressure Hitler brought to bear on the Hungarians was the threat of their losing German support for their revision plans.

In the following years of Paul Teleki's government, clashes of interest on many secondary questions were a permanent feature of German-Hungarian relations. The attempt to maintain a relatively independent foreign policy course was coupled with the intention of continuing to go along with Hitler as far as revision was concerned. During the first part of the Second World War, the balance of power between the two states shifted much more in favour of Germany. I would not attribute too much importance to Hungary's refusing to grant the German request to use a Hungarian railway line against Poland[17] because this was a second rate issue more to test Hungary and to apply diplomatic pressure. Germany certainly was not pleased by Hungary's granting asylum to almost 150,000 Polish soldiers and still trying to keep two irons in the fire. However, Hungarian foreign policy had to maneuver between the Scylla of maintaining a relative independence and the Charybdis of further revision at the expense of Romania. As a matter of fact, the two aims were not reconcilable. Hungary failed more and more to maintain a certain degree of independence on the one hand because Germany had won the war in the west and had almost become the master of Europe; on the other hand, Hungary's revisionist aims provided the opportunity for further German interference in Danubian affairs, and allowed Germany to become the supreme judge in political disputes among the countries neighbouring Hungary. The sheer contradiction of her foreign policy became more and more perceptible. Hungary's most important foreign policy success, the return to Hungary of the northern part of Transylvania with two and a half million inhabitants, became *eo ipso* the reward for limiting Hungary's independence from Germany, for putting Hungary in a kind of (willing or unwilling) satellite position.

Teleki saw quite clearly that Hungary would have to pay a high price for the second Vienna award. It was not mere coincidence that he handed his resignation to the Regent on the day following the award. In his letter, he referred mainly to domestic policy issues and to his government's disputes with the Chief of Staff and with the army; but there were many direct and indirect references to the main issue, which was, in fact, every aspect of his political method and ideology, and his relations to Germany. Part of the payment was stipulated already in the separate provisions of the Vienna award regarding the right of the German ethnic groups in Hungary to representation by the Volksbund as their sole party. Germany soon made the rest of the cost known to the Hungarian government through the Hungarian Ambassador at Berlin. Hungary was to integrate more fully into the new German economic order (*Großraumwirtschaft*). This was the purpose of the new agreement concluded on October 10, 1940, according to which Hungarian agricultural production was to be suited more closely to the German requirements.

On the domestic scene, a lot was happening: the remission of Szálasi's remaining prison sentence; the retraction of Decree 3400, which prohibited civil servants from joining the Arrow Cross Party; the proclamation of the Third Anti-Jewish Law; the formation of a new party strongly adhering to the German platform (Imrédy's Hungarian Revival Party); and last but not least, Hungary's joining the Tripartite Pact. But, in spite of the cost, the Vienna award can still be regarded as the last act in the history of German-Hungarian relations when Hungarian interests still prevailed (at least at the foreign policy level), when Hungary's aims and her decisions were still the decisive factors, and not her fear of German power. Nineteen forty-one can be established as the end of the second period in the history of German-Hungarian relations between 1933 and 1944. This year marked the transition into a new period when decisions came to be determined partly with an eye to

German power, and partly by fear of the political and social transformations which were envisioned as possible after the war. The increasing subordination of Hungarian interests is well illustrated by the three major foreign policy decisions made in 1941. The first of these, the plan for a joint attack on Yugoslavia, can still, in theory, be seen as a part of Hungary's own revisionist program. However, there is no doubt that Teleki's agreeing to the German proposal of a common attack, or to the German troops attacking from Hungarian territory was much more due to his fear of German military force than to his eagerness for a new response to his revisionist foreign policy aims. (There is no doubt that Horthy was influenced by different considerations; and the army leaders might well have had different priorities, too. I am not trying to pass judgement on to what extent Teleki's decision was influenced by domestic policy components; but it is important to mention that the opposite decision might not have been supported by a large segment of his party and of his followers.)

The declaration of war against the Soviet Union, which was to prove so fatal a step, was overwhelmingly a response to German pressure, and a policy flight forward, i.e. the decision to enter the war at a phase when this step could still be said to bear certain elements of voluntariness, at a time when German pressure, which was sure to be forthcoming was not yet acute. Hungary had no territorial claims against the Soviet Union, and her basic foreign policy from the outset of her friendship with Germany involved no belligerence against her, unless we take into consideration that after Romania and Slovakia were already. involved in the war, Hungary's continued aloofness would serve to deprecate her in the eyes of the German leaders. Of course, with regard to political systems, or sheer ideology, Hungary was much closer to Germany than to the Soviet Union; nevertheless, I don't regard that similarity as a decisive factor in leading Hungary into the war; German pressure was what predominated.[18]

Finally, the third act, the declaration of war against the United States in December of 1941, was merely obedience to Germany's will, and proof of Hungary's trustworthiness as an ally.[19] This act, which according to Kállay was the gravest error committed by the government,[20] marked the end of the process of transition. The relationship between Germany and Hungary entered into its third and final stage. Though a large percentage of Hungarians probably still believed that there was some community of interest, this was already the stage when the salient feature of German policy, even when it clearly contradicted the interests of the Hungarian government, was coercion.

Ribbentrop and Keitel visited Hungary after the German defeat in the battle for Moscow, demanding that the Hungarian army send large, well-equipped troops to the Soviet Union. These acts were plain evidence that the basic element in the relationship was, by that time, German force, and that the phase when Hungary had been a German satellite was over. She had been a satellite without any kind of privilege 14 months earlier, when she signed the Tripartite Pact, the pact that Germany referred to in demanding her declaration of war on the United States. We might find it ironic that Csáky had tried to express the hopes Hungary had attached to this pact with the formula *primus inter pares* i.e. the first German satellite in the Danube Basin.

The third period of German-Hungarian relations may be dated from 1942. It is certainly open to discussion to what extent the change of government and the replacement of Bárdossy with Kállay was a sign of a proper change. Kállay's instructions when he was appointed by the Regent were to reverse Bárdossy's policy. What did that mean? Did they really intend to dissociate themselves from Germany, as mentioned in the literature from time to time; or did they mean to adopt a more cautious policy: Bárdossy's had been to move further to the right domestically in the interest of retaining Germany's good will.

Many of Kállay's acts show that in the beginning, he really was following the second route. Many of his words, even a lot of his actions, certainly showed no clear signs of an attempt to dissociate from Germany, even if you admit, and one must admit, that under the given circumstances any top Hungarian politician had to operate with a large degree of dissimulation. I wonder whether the real turning point was not the spring of 1942 rather than the end of the year after El Alamein and Stalingrad. No doubt, during the period under discussion, Kállay refused

Hitler's demands for new measures against the Jews (including yellow stars, ghettos and a certain amount of deportation). But in 1942, he still had not ruled out the possibility of the war's ending at least in a draw; as a consequence, his policy was quite different after the turning point, when he no longer had any doubts about Germany's losing the war. "Hungary began to appreciate more promptly than the others ... what may happen" — we read in the *Times* of June 4, 1943.[21] "Hungary was the first satellite that already felt the lash of the German whip" said Cordell Hull in his statement after the German occupation of Hungary.[22]

No doubt, Hungary was the first satellite to look for a way out after the hopes of a German victory faded. Certainly, Kállay's main concern was to give in as little as possible, and to find an opportunity for disengaging the unwilling satellite as soon as possible. And yet he did not succeed. He not only failed, but Hungary was the last to leave the wrecked ship of the Axis coalition. What were the reasons for the missed opportunities: her geopolitical situation, awkward leadership, military force, betrayal by the West, fear of Bolshevism or just bad luck? Probably all of these, plus one more component to which I would attribute very great significance in any explanation of Hungary's remaining in the Axis camp. After the German occupation of Hungary, two letters were published in the appropriate section of the *Times*. The first one was written by Judy Listowel, who supported her thesis of Hungary's complete surrender to Germany by asserting that the ministers in the new government were mainly of German origin. In one of the next issues, an answer bearing the signature "*Times* correspondent" was published. In this letter, reference was made to the overall continuity of government personnel even after the occupation; in fact, the majority of the government was made up of politicians who had served in different capacities in several governments and during the previous 10 years, and had become part of the top Hungarian political elite.[23] In short, even in this last period of German-Hungarian relations, when the main features were sheer German force and Hungarian loss of interest in cooperation, a sufficient number of Hungarians with significant political influence were willing to stay on the side of the Germans for various reasons. Fear of the Soviets was one, but certainly not the only reason against dissociation. A great many people were willing to stay on the German side even when the German idea of Hungary's role was best expressed in the famous sentences of Vessemeyer: "Every Hungarian, whether a peasant, a worker, or a soldier, who by his activity reduces our burdens, strengthens the Führer's reserves within the Reich. Every Hungarian who bleeds for us, reduces our own losses and reinforces our own reserves for further military efforts..."[24]

There is no question that there were large and influential political forces in Hungary whose activity is very important to an understanding of Hungary's permanent move from the position of unwilling to last satellite. Of course, the resistance of these forces might have been overcome under circumstances which Kállay had expected but which had not ensued. Were these expectations merely a case of entirely unrealistic wishful thinking, or were they based on realistic assumptions? Neither the one, nor the other.

Until the end of 1943, there was a certain element of realistic calculation in Kállay's plans. Since the beginning of that year, Hungary slowly moved in the direction of disassociating herself from Germany. No more troops were sent to the Russian Front (except, of course, for the remainder of the Second Army, which returned to Hungary during the summer of 1943; the Hungarian troops which were involved as security forces were not withdrawn).[25] Preparations were made to give more freedom of expression and of organization to left-wing opposition parties. Even the peace feelers that were put out seemed to be successful; a preliminary agreement in Istanbul was signed to the effect that Hungary would change sides if the Allied (Anglo-American) troops reached the Hungarian frontier. The embarkation of Allied troops in Southern Italy made that kind of probability likely.

In early September of 1943, the Soviet troops were fighting farther from Hungary's borders than the British troops. The same day that Allied troops landed in Italy, Kállay refused a German demand to send Hungarian troops as security forces to the

Balkans. The background of this German demand was that they wanted to disperse their troops along the coastlines in the effort to ward off an invasion. Hitler and his military advisors were almost convinced by the end of 1942 that they would have to face an Allied landing on the Balkan Peninsula in the not too distant future.

According to Hitler's directive issued on December 28, 1942, the situation in the Mediterranean was such that an attack on Crete was likely in the near future, and consequently, also on German and Italian bases in the Aegean Sea and on the Balkan Peninsula. "It must be expected that this attack will be supported by uprisings in the Western Balkan countries. If the worst comes to worst, the Italian Peninsula can be sealed off Europe somehow. Above all, it is of decisive importance for us to hold the Balkan oil, copper, bauxite and chrome securely."[26]

During the last months of 1942, after the Allied landings in North Africa, the top political (Hitler and Mussolini at the meeting of 18 December, 1942) and military Axis leadership considered this territory as the next possible Allied target, and tried to take all the necessary measures to prevent a successful attack. The landing was expected in the spring of 1943, "after the Tunisian battle had been brought to certain conclusion".

According to a memorandum of Warlimont's written in captivity after 1945, "In May 1943, Hitler's fear of an attack on the Balkans took concrete form." At a conference on May 19, Hitler declared that "an attack on the Balkan Peninsula was even more dangerous than the problem of Italy". Even after the fall of Mussolini, and after the landing in Sicily and on the Italian Peninsula, he was afraid that the attack may have been just a camouflage, a diversion with the main offensive coming later on the Balkan Peninsula.[27] If Hitler was almost sure of a landing on the Balkans, why should Kállay have thought differently? After all, it was his only hope of a possible relief. General Szombathelyi, Chief of Staff of the Hungarian army, in a memorandum submitted to Kállay in February of 1943, stated that since the end of 1942, "We have had to reckon with a landing in the Balkans", "A landing is likely already from the end of March".[28] However, even at this time, Kállay was overconfident, and in making his calculations he disregarded some important factors which could interfere with the carrying out of his plans. One such factor was domestic, and it was referred to in the memorandum sent to Kállay by the Smallholders and the Social Democrats in August 1943: they warned him of the strong influence of right-wing ideas, of the unreliability of the army, and called his attention to the tone of the press, to the belief that Hungary had no choice but to go along with Germany, an idea that Kállay, too, had often paid lipservice to in his first year of office, if only by way of dissimulation.

The other factor which Kállay did not sufficiently take into consideration was the strategic role assigned Hungary in Germany's military plans, and Hitler's suspicion of Hungary's political moves. As far as I know, historians so far have failed to note a remark made by Hitler on the very day of Mussolini's fall. According to his *Lagebesprechungen*, at the first meeting with his chief military advisers after having received the bad news concerning Mussolini, Hitler had the following to say: "Wir müssen nur aufpassen, daß nicht hier bei den Ungarn noch irgendwelche Schweinereien passieren. Welche Verbände können wir unter Umständen kurzerhand da hereinjagen... Panther Abteilungen mag da noch irgend etwas herimprovisieren? Wenn da eine Schweinerei wäre..." [29] It was not accidental that, when faced with the first attempt by Italy to change sides, Hitler referred to Hungary as the next possible candidate. He was suspicious enough of Hungarian policy from the beginning of 1943 (it may not be an exaggeration to say that he was the *most* suspicious of Hungary of all his allies or satellites) to express his doubts during a meeting with Horthy in April of 1943 concerning the reliability of the Hungarian alliance.

"Die Hoffnung Kállays durch einen Stellungswechsel über die Türkei und England eine Lösung herbeizuführen sei naturlich Kállay trügerisch. Deutschland und seine Verbündeten, in einem Schiff saßen, der sich auf stürmerischem Meere befinde. Es sei klar, daß bei dieser Lage jeder, der etwa aussteigen wolle, sofort ertrinken würde." [30]

This reproach for Hungary's peace-feelers, and particularly for the negotiations conducted by Professor Szentgyörgyi on which he had quite accurate reports let Hitler go on with a long series of complaints, particularly against Kállay, which concluded with the remark: "Kállay durch sein Verhalten den Eindruck erweckt habe, daß Ungarn nicht mehr an den Sieg Deutschlands und seiner Verbündeten glaube." Horthy defended his premier during the conversation and repudiated the German charges a few weeks later in written form.[31] However, the German intelligence was so much better, and the Hungarians' conspiracy and peace-feelers were so badly organized, that German suspicions did not abate, and in the summer of 1943, it came to the point that the German Ambassador to Hungary, Von Jagow, received secret instructions to terminate all personal contacts with Kállay.[32]

It is not the purpose of this paper to trace the events which led to the German occupation of Hungary; the story has been told in different books, and one of mine in particular, was devoted exclusively to this topic.[33] This paper is concerned to find a proper explanation for Hungary's disassociating herself from Germany only later in the war, in spite of efforts to do so earlier. And in this respect, it is extremely important that from the German point of view, Hungary had a very important strategic role and was regarded, from the economic point of view, as of vital interest. For this very reason, Hitler was even less prepared to leave Hungary alone than his other satellites. Immediately after the defection of Italy, the Wehrmacht was requested to elaborate a plan for the occupation of Hungary. And the project proper was submitted to Hitler by the Wehrmacht Führungstab on September 30, 1943.[34] But while Germany was prepared to prevent Hungary's exit from the war, Hungary was ill-prepared to carry out such a withdrawal plan. Hitler was able to frustrate Kállay's plan through the occupation of the country on March 19, and he was able to do the same on the 15th of October. In a conversation with General Jodl on July 31, 1944, Hitler made it clear once again that he was attributing special importance to the control of Hungary: "Die notwendigste Sicherung ist und bleibt für uns zunächst die Sicherung des ungarischen Raums, ernährungsmäßig ein einziger möglicher Ersatz für das, was wir sonst verlieren; rohstoffmäßig eine Quelle für eine ganze Menge: Bauxit, Mangan usw... Aber vor allem verkehrsmäßig überhaupt die Voraussetzung für den Südosten, (ist) die Sicherung des ungarischen Raums von einer lebenswichtigen Bedeutung für uns, so wichting, daß man sie überhaupt nicht überschätzen kann. Man muß also sehr überlegen, was wir an Neuaufstellungen gleich entweder hineingeben können oder dort aufbauen, um jederzeit in der Lage zu sein, wenn notwendig, einem ungarischen Staatsstreich des Herrn Horthy vorzubeugen oder zuvorzukommen."[35]

Any judgement concerning the opportunities open to Hungary's policy-makers must bear in mind the special strategic position of the country, the fine possibilities this gave Germany to intervene, and her firm decision to do just that if intervention seemed to be necessary.

Last but not least, there is one more important point to be mentioned in connection with Hungary's attachment to Germany even during this final period, when German-Hungarian relations were based entirely on German interests. This is Hungary's relations with her neighbours, and the issue of the Trianon frontier. It is a well known fact that one of the pillars of Nazi foreign policy was the exploitation of the controversies between the Danubian countries. Ribbentrop did not even try to conceal this, as is shown by the cynical remark he made to the Bulgarian Foreign Minister in "proof" of the fairness of the second Vienna award: "Der Schiedsspruch sei beider Parteien gerecht werden. Dies habe sich bei seiner Verkündung ergeben, bei der rumänische Außenminister in Ohnmacht fiel und der ungarische Außenminister seinen Rücktritt erklären wollte ..."[36]

If in the first period of the Second World War this controversy helped the Germans to lure both countries into the war,[37] then in the second period it may have helped to keep them on Germany's side.

On November 19, 1943, Hitler, reflecting on a report presented by Keitel that the Allies had allegedly, concluded negotiations with both Hungary and Romania, and that both of them were going to ask for an armistice within a few days, had the following to say: "Beiden zusammen werden es auf gar keinen Fall machen. Einer wird es machen, und der andere wird auf Grund dieser Unruhen sofort einmarshieren. Wenn in Ungarn Unruhen kommen sollten, worauf uns die Rumänen aufmerksam machen, dann müßten sie uns bitten daß wir und sie gemeinsam die Ruhe in Ungarn wiederherstellen."[38]

These rivalries were well reflected by the fact that the Czechoslovak and the Yugoslav ambassadors to London were constantly expressing their concern lest British foreign policy make any concessions to Hungary.[39] This sort of policy also was reflected in the conversation of Benes with Stalin concerning the future of Hungary and Romania.[40] Though the Hungarian government was the first to explore the possibilities of peace negotiations, and though her preliminary armistice of September, 1943 was more far-reaching than any diplomatic step of any other Nazi satellite country, the definitive relapse or retreat in Kállay's policy (which occurred between November 1943 and February 1944, when Hungary did not meet the obligations agreed to in September) was to a great extent due to concern over the fate of Transylvania, to the fact that, unlike Rumania, Hungary was promised no territorial reward in case of disalignment.[41]

Playing off Romania against Hungary had a very important part in Hitler's successful occupation of Hungary, and in the failure of Kállay's attempts to preserve Hungary's relative independence and to disassociate her from Germany. Hitler's allusion to an eventual German-Romanian intervention to prevent Hungary's exit from the war became a built-in element of German military plans for Hungary's occupation. One of the versions of the so-called Margharete plan was based on the assumption that Romanian, Slovakian and Croatian troops would join the German army in carrying out the military campaign. Hitler proved to be not a bad prophet. In a conversation with Marshall Antonescu on February 26, 1944, he made a seemingly unusual remark at the close of the discussion, relating that he had received a letter from Horthy demanding the withdrawal of Hungarian troops from the Soviet front.[42]

During the rest of the day, the Romanian Prime Minister returned to Hungarian affairs: "Eine Million rumänischer Soldaten für den Kampf zur Verfügung standen, wenn erst einmal die ungarische Gefahr beseitigt sei." He went even further when he asked Hitler to deal seriously with the question of Hungary: "Müsse man gegen Ungarn einschreiten, und zwar möglichst bald, da bei einer etwaigen Verschlimmerung der Lage an der Ostfront ein unsicheres Ungarn im Rücken zu einer außerordentlichen Gefahr werden könne."[43]

To avoid the German occupation of Hungary was a permanent feature of Kállay's politics during his attempts do dissociate Hungary from Germany. If there was a genuine fear of a German occupation, then the possibility of a German occupation in alliance with the Romanians was regarded as a nightmare. Another reason for apprehension of a German occupation was the fear that it might strengthen the role of the radical elements in the event of a resistance. Horthy's final decision at Klessheim on March 18, 1944 to stay on even though the Germans were occupying the country was made in the hope that he could prevent Romania's participation in the campaign. A few days after the occupation of Hungary, Hitler told Antonescu, who was again paying him a visit: "Nach der illoyalen Haltung der ungarischen Regierung und nachdem sowohl Rumänien als auch Ungarn sich den Wiener Schiedsspruch innerlich nie zu eigen gemacht hätten und nachdem Italien jetzt ausgefallen sei, halte es Deutschland nicht für angebracht, weiterhin als Signatar des Wiener Schiedsspruchs zu fungieren. Er (der Führer) bäte Antonescu, die vorgenannte Erklärung zunächst niemandem gegenüber zu erwähnen; im gegebenen Augenblick würde er (der Führer) sie öffentlich abgeben. Zunächst aber liege es im deutschen wie im rumänischen Interesse zu versuchen, einen Partisanenkrieg in Ungarn zu vermeiden; denn es sei jede deutsche Division wertvoll, die in Ungarn nicht gebraucht wurde und an die Front geschickt werden könne."[44]

Antonescu was very pleased with Hitler's communication and warned Hitler not to trust the Hungarians. The next day Hitler told him that North Transylvania would be declared an operations zone ("Operationszone") and that the Hungarian troops would be withdrawn ("von ungarischen Truppen geräumt werden müsse"). Antonescu proposed to let the Romanian refugees from North Transylvania return; if the Hungarians started any kind of partisan war, they could be used to fight against them ("gegen ungarische Partisanenbanden eingesetzt werden könnten").[45]

Actually, the troops sent to Galicia in April and May 1944 were mainly from Transylvania; however, not all the Hungarian troops were withdrawn, for the Hungarian army was ready to compromise, and to amass again at the Eastern Front.

The German occupation of the country put an end to the story of Hungary as the unwilling Satellite. The event came after it was already on the road to becoming the last to stay in the Axis camp. What followed was the horror story of the deportation of the Jews at Germany's wishes, but by the Hungarian gendarmery; the story of the annihilation of the First Army; and the story of the Nazification of Hungary. In the five months which passed between March 19 and August 25, Hungarian foreign policy was almost non-existent, negotiations with the Allies ceased, and Horthy practically withdrew from politics and public life and was entirely passive. During this five-month period, Hungary's international credit deteriorated tremendously; the military situation changed completely, and all the other German satellites came close to switching sides. Horthy started his secret negotiations again only after the Romanian upheaval, proceeding along his old premises as if nothing had happened during the last months. But the very event that had inspired Horthy secretly to get in touch again with the Western Powers entailed significant changes in the military and political situation of the Danube Valley. The Romanian upheaval altered the situation: "The turning over of Rumania to the Allied cause has given the Russians a great advantage and it may well be that they will enter Belgrade and Budapest and possibly Vienna before the Western Allies succeed in piercing the Siegfried line. However desirable such a Russian incursion may be, its political effect upon Central and Southern Europe may be formidable in the last degree."[46]

Romania, Bulgaria and Finland were already out when Horthy finally turned to the Soviet Union for an armistice. But due to bad preparation, due to German unwillingness to leave Hungary alone, and due to internal forces which either were still most ready to fight for Germany or were not ready to draw the necessary lessons from what had transpired, even this attempt failed. Horthy was obliged to cede power to the Arrow Cross, and the armistice was signed with Hungary only in January 1945, when the others had already long been on the winners' side.

NOTES

1 J.F. Montgomery, *Hungary, the Unwilling Satellite* (New York, 1947).

2 C.A. Macartney, "Foreword", in N. Kállay, *Hungarian Premier, A Personal Account of a Nation's Struggle in the Second World War* (hereafter: *Hungarian Premier*) (New York, 1954), p. xxi.

3 C.A. Macartney, *op. cit.*, p. xxiii

4 Quoted by: I. Berend and Gy. Ránki, "German-Hungarian Relations Following Hitler's Rise to Power (1933-34)", *Acta Historica* (Budapest, 1961), p. 321.

5 Országos Levéltár (National Archives) KÜM (Ministry of Foreign Affairs) File 195, 29/34 Political Department.

6 National Archives Microfilm, German Foreign Ministry 10945/E 479975, Schnurre's note, September 1933.

7 National Archives, German Foreign Ministry 10945/E 674981.

8 Deutsche Zentralarchiv, Potsdam, Auswärtiges Amt, Abt II 41228.

9 Documents on German Foreign Policy, Series C. Vol. II, Washington, 1959, Bulow's note of March 13, 1934.

10 Gömbös's letters: April 22, 1933. Deutsches Zentralarchiv, Potsdam, Auswärtiges Amt, Abt. II 41288.

11 As a sentence of a letter Horthy addressed to Hitler in 1939 put it: "Even at the time when during the period of the social democratic régime a whole world separated us from the German government, we always entertained close relations to the Reichswehr." *The Confidential Papers of Admiral Horthy*, (hereafter: *Admiral Horthy's Papers*), eds. Miklós Szinai and László Szücs (Budapest, 1965), p. 126.

12 Documents on German Foreign Policy, Series C. Vol II. Gömbös's letter of Feb. 4, 1934.

13 Documents Diplomatiques Français 1932-39, Second Series Tome III, Paris, 1966, report of Sept. 4, 1936.

14 Documents Diplomatiques Français 1932-1939, Second Series, Tome VII, Paris, 1972, report of Nov. 13, 1937.

15 *Idem*, Tome VI, Paris, 1970, Chargé d'Affairs' Report of Sept. 1939.

16 *Magyarország és a második világháború* (Hungary and the Second World War) eds. László Zsigmond, Magda Ádám, Gyula Juhász, Lajos Kerekes (Budapest, 1959).

17 Ciano in his diary was of a different opinion. He wrote: The Germans will not forget the refusal, the Hungarians will have to pay for this one day... *The Ciano Diaries*, ed. Hugh Gibson, (New York, 1946).

18 This is not to underestimate the anti-Soviet ideological elements in Hungarian foreign policy. According to the report of the German ambassador, when he informed Horthy of the German invasion, "the old champion of the struggle against Bolshevism welcomed it with jubilation". Documents on German Foreign Policy, 1918-1945 D XII, Washington 1962, report of June 22, 1941. A possible attack against the Soviet Union was a favored topic of Horthy's in his letters addressed to Hitler. "Russian Bolshevism and Pan-Slavism are one and the same, as far as their military and political objectives are concerned", he wrote in 1936. "There is no rest, security and happiness for mankind until the Soviets have been knocked down." *Admiral Horthy's Papers*, p. 82. "After November 11, 1918, Marshal Foch made the official proposal that France, England, Italy, Germany and Austro-Hungary should all immediately march against Moscow", Horthy wrote in a letter of Nov. 3, 1939, "establish order there, break up into its component parts that gigantic empire composed of 118 nationalities which was a threat to all; then they were to return, sit down at the green table, and as comrades in arms conclude an eternal peace... this would have been the only practical way to save Europe." *Admiral Horthy's Papers*, pp. 127-128; also in Documents on German Foreign Policy, D VIII, Washington, 1954.

19 Britain declared war on Hungary. Some ideological elements in the official anti-democratic anti-liberal ideology of the Horthy regime certainly might have contributed to this declaration of war, but I think we can regard this element a negligible part of the actual process.

20 N. Kállay, *Hungarian Premier*, p. 64.

21 *Times* June 4, 1943.

22 *Times* March 29, 1944.

23 *Times* March 25-29, 1944.

24 Gy. Ránki, "The German Occupation of Hungary", *Acta Historica*, (Budapest, 1965), p. 261.

25 According to Himmler in 1943, "Sie haben anständig mitgemacht": *Hitlers Lagebesprechungen. Die Protokollfragmente seiner militärischen Konferenzen 1942-1945*, ed. Helmut Heiber (Stuttgart, 1962), p.

26 H. Hubatsch, *Hitlers Weisungen* (Stuttgart, 1960), Dec. 28, 1942.

27 F.W. Deakin, "The Germans and Allied Plans for a Balkan Landing" in *The Third Reich and Yugoslavia 1933-1945*, (Belgrade, 1977), p. 478.

28 *Admiral Horthy's Papers*, pp. 213-214. Szombathelyi's conclusion was not quite Kállay's: the general was counting on the defection of Romania; in his view, intervention against Romania was the first step to "preparing" the complete occupation of Transylvania and her defense.

29 *Hitlers Lagebesprechungen*, p. 332.

30 *Staatsmänner und Diplomaten bei Hitler*, ed. Andreas Hillgruber (Frankfurt, 1970), April 16, 1943, p. 238-259.

31 *Admiral Horthy's Papers*, p. 249.

32 *A Wilhelmstraße és Magyarország* (*Wilhelmstraße and Hungary*), eds. Gy. Ránki, Gy. Juhász, E. Pamlényi, L. Tilkovszky (Budapest, 1968).

33 Gy. Ránki, *1944 Március 19. Magyarország német megszállása* (March 19, 1944. The German occupation of Hungary) (Budapest, 1978).

34 *Kriegstagebuch des Oberkommandos der Wehrmacht* (Frankfurt, 1961), Vol. IV, p. 181, January 1944, May 22, 1945.

35 *Hitlers Lagebesprechungen*, p. 589.

36 Quoted in Gy. Ránki's "East Central Europe and World War II", *Acta Historica*, 1974, pp. 199-200.

37 The *Times* argued in an article of July 13, 1941 that one of the reasons Hungary joined the campaign against the Soviet Union was her rivalry with Romania for Transylvania.

38 *Hitlers Lagebesprechungen*, p. 424.

39 Public Record Office, Foreign Office 371, 349956681.

40 V. Mastny, "The Benes - Stalin - Molotov Conversation in December 1943", *Jahrbücher für Geschichte Osteuropas*, September, 1972.

41 I want to refer to the differences in British and Soviet armistice terms. The British demanded the evacuation of the Allied territories (Czechoslovakia and Yugoslavia), the latter demanded the evacuation of all *occupied territories* (Transylvania as well). Public Record Office F.O. 3II I. 34495C16684.

42 Hillgruber, *op. cit.* p. 354. Actually Horthy's letter was addressed to Hitler on Feb. 12, 1944.

43 Quoted in Gy. Ránki, "East Central Europe and World War II", *Acta Historica*, 1974, p. 199.

44 Hillgruber, *op. cit.*, pp. 391-2.

45 Hillgruber, *op. cit.*, p. 405.

46 J. Ehrman, *Grand Strategy* vol. V., (Aug. 1943 - Sept. 1944) (London, 1956), p. 402.

PART II

ECONOMY, SOCIETY, AND POLITICS IN INTERWAR CENTRAL AND EASTERN EUROPE

The three studies of this section exhibit our broadened interest and research orientation. From the mid-1960s we turned to comparative history and the modern economic history of Central and Eastern Europe. The first article belonged to the very first studies we published on the region as a whole.

The two studies of György Ránki from the 1980s belong to his matured complex approach to interrelationship between social, economic, and political trends.

V

THE ECONOMIC PROBLEMS OF THE DANUBE REGION AFTER THE BREAKUP OF THE AUSTRO–HUNGARIAN MONARCHY

In October 1918, the Austro–Hungarian Monarchy collapsed. The Monarchy had previously provided a broad framework within which a number of nations had undergone social transformation, and modern capitalist economies had come into being. The strains and tensions engendered by the internal economic contradictions characteristic of the twentieth century, and which were reflected in the level of economic development as compared with more advanced powers, were no doubt a contributory factor in the breakup of the Monarchy, but its main causes should rather be sought in the political and social contradictions of the time and their reflection in public consciousness.

After the 1914–18 war, the political map of Europe was completely transformed. The decay of the Austro–Hungarian Monarchy had significantly contributed to this. Instead of large areas, each uniform in colour, smaller units appeared, each of a different hue. These small countries with populations ranging from seven to fifteen millions, entered on the struggle for an independent existence. On the territory of the former Monarchy, three successor states emerged—the Austrian republic, the Czechoslovak republic, and Hungary. Other important sections of it were incorporated into neighbouring states: newly resurrected Poland, an enlarged Serbia, now Yugoslavia, and Romania. The enormous extent of this redistribution of territories and populations denoted in itself a radical transformation of economic conditions.

The changes in territory and population did not, of course, account completely for the changes in the economic situation of the countries concerned. The economic potential inherited by the successor states bore no relation to their inheritance of land and people. Czechoslovakia, for example, came into possession of a disproportionately large share of the Monarchy's industrial potential. From the statistical calculations (which differ in some respects), we can conclude that 70 per cent of the entire industrial capacity of Cisleithania was concentrated in the new Czechoslovak state: 75 per cent of the coal mines, 63 per cent of the lignite, 60 per cent of the iron industry, 75 per cent of the chemical industry, 75–80 per cent of the textile and shoe industries. With its 13.6 million inhabitants—hardly more than a quarter of the population of the defunct Monarchy—Czechoslovakia disposed of an economy on a western European level, and of a powerful industry producing a large surplus for export.

Table 1

Area and Population before and after the War

Country	Area in sq. km. 1914	1921	Population in 100,000 1914	1921
Austria–Hungary	676,443*	—	51,390*	—
Austria	—	85,533	—	6,536
Hungary**	325,000	92,607	20,900	7,800
Czechoslovakia	—	140,394	—	3,613
Bulgaria	111,800	103,146	4,753	4,910
Romania	137,903	304,244	7,516	17,594
Yugoslavia (Serbia)	87,300	248,987	4,548	12,017
Poland	—	388,279	—	27,184

* Including Bosnia and Herzegovina
** Hungarian Kingdom in the Austro–Hungarian Empire

Similarly, the economic structure of Hungary, which lost the regions inhabited largely by the national minorities, underwent considerable change. It gained in industrial strength, for within its new boundaries, which enclosed about a third of its former territory, there remained about 55 per cent of its industry, and 41 per cent of its population. There was, however, a marked disproportion between its sources of raw materials and its manufacturing capacity; in other ways, too, the internal economic balance had been seriously upset: for instance, only 11 per cent of the iron ore and 15 per cent of the timber was left within the new boundaries, while it retained 80–90 per cent of the engineering and printing plants. Thus, even from the territorial standpoint alone, the postwar economies of the states of central, eastern, and southeastern Europe were not just continuations of the prewar economic setup.

The creation of independent states in the place of great empires, the dissolution of large territorial and economic units, the contraction of some countries to a third of their former area and the expansion of others to twice or even three times their former size in land and population, the economic condition of countries pieced together out of territories at different stages of economic development and taken from different states—all these circumstances created a radically new situation. Even under normal circumstances, a considerable period of time, in fact an entire historical era, would have been required to complete the adjustment to new conditions, the integration into a unified economic whole, the opening up of new development possibilities and the attainment of a steady and sustained rate of economic growth. But history did not allow the problem to be presented in this fashion. The needs of the new order became apparent at a moment when the problems of the transition from a war to a peace economy were being added to the already difficult problems faced by an economy crippled by war, and all clamoured for immediate solution. The simultaneous appearance on the scene of all these problems brought about complete economic chaos, almost inextricable confusion, and a state of utter hopelessness.

The most difficult conditions were to be found in the countries which had suffered the worst upheavals, Austria, Hungary, and Poland. By 1917, it was already plain that the Monarchy's Austrian territories were at the end of their economic tether. In the summer of 1918, the economic experts were unanimously of the opinion that Austria could not face another winter of war. Agricultural production had sunk to about 50 per cent of its prewar level, and at their best the Austrian territories were far from self-sufficient; they had always been dependent on imports, especially from Hungary. Hungary, however, could not come to the rescue, for she was not even in a position to satisfy her own requirements.

In many industries, production fell because of the shortage of raw materials, and even those branches of industry—such as coal and iron—which were essential for the prosecution of the war did not reach prewar production levels. Hence the young republic of Austria, created in the autumn of 1918, found itself in a catastrophic economic situation. To add to these difficulties, food supplies in the country were at a dangerously low level. The bread and flour rations were—to quote Schuschnigg—too big to die on, but too small to live on. At the beginning of 1919, the consumption of milk in Vienna was only 7 per cent of the prewar figure. The supplementary foodstuffs sent in aid secured, at the best, a condition of bare existence; agricultural output even by 1920 did not exceed 50 per cent of what it had been before the war. For lack of coal, the railways had, for the most part, been brought to a halt. Furnaces could not be fired. In the summer of 1919, 200,000 factory workers were unemployed. Inflation had started long before as a result of the enormous war expenditure. By the end of 1918, the value of the crown, eroded by numerous war loans, had fallen by two-thirds. In 1919, the situation continued to deteriorate, for the country had been bled white and was now to all intents and purposes cut off from the other parts of the former empire. In these circumstances, economic decline could not be arrested; on the contrary, it grew worse: industrial production was hardly more than one-third of the 1913 figure.

Conditions in Hungary were similar. Here, agriculture was the main source of the national income, and because of labour shortages, the requisitioning of horses by the army, and the fall in the number of cattle, it had suffered a sharp decline. The production of grain fell from 142 million cwt. in 1913 to 84 million cwt. in 1918, maize from 96 million to 48 million. There was a comparable industrial decline. In 1918, many consumer goods industries, long deprived of raw materials and fuel supplies by the war industries, showed a fall in production of 60–70 per cent. Even coal-mining, essential to the prosecution of the war, showed as early as 1917 a decline in production of about 17 per cent, and by 1918 the output of iron and steel had fallen by a half.

By 1918, the decline had reached such a nadir that the needs of the army could no longer be satisfied and the civilian population had to endure severe deprivations. Expenditure on the war swallowed up 40–50 per cent of the national income and was financed largely by the issue of paper money. Inflation had become as rampant as in Austria.

The short lived success of the revolution had, naturally, hardly any effect on the economic difficulties, and after the counterrevolution had gained the upper hand in the autumn of 1919, conditions became even more chaotic. The Romanian forces in the country which had helped to overthrow the Hungarian Republic of Councils contributed to this situation by dismantling and carrying off a not inconsiderable quantity of machinery and rolling stock. By 1919, Hungary's agricultural output had fallen to about a third, and by 1920, to about 50–60 per cent of the prewar figure. In the autumn of 1919, industrial production was only 15–20 per cent of the peacetime level, and by 1920, it had risen to only 35–40 per cent.

Even Czechoslovakia, which started on its way in more favourable circumstances than any of the other states in the area, could not avoid a temporary recession. The utter exhaustion and the inflation which in 1917–18 were characteristic of the monarchy in its death throes, had, of course, also involved the Czech and Slovak regions of the empire. At the end of 1918, in the months following the creation of the Czechoslovak republic, industrial production was only half the prewar figure, and even in 1920 it rose only to about 70 per cent. (Of the more important products, steel production was around 78 per cent, iron about 72 per cent, and cement about 85 per cent.) Owing to its greater strength and its more favourable situation on the side of the victors, the Czechoslovak economy had access to quicker and better possibilities of rehabilitation. By 1921, when Austria and Hungary were just beginning to emerge from their critical economic condition, Czech industry was already reaching 75–80 per cent of its prewar output, and on this foundation the republic could successfully tackle the currency depreciation.

The whole production situation of the immediate postwar years, more especially the ubiquitous and steep decline in agriculture, dealt a heavy blow to the export possibilities of those countries in the region which were particularly dependent on foreign trade. Hungary furnishes a characteristic example: compared to prewar figures, it exported only 0.1 per cent of wheat, 0.3 per cent of flour, 2.1 per cent of cattle, and 2.5 per cent of meat. (By 1921, the figures were respectively 7.4, 33, 20, and 78.) Only the export of wine and feathers reached or exceeded the prewar volume. By 1920, the total export of agricultural produce reached 21 per cent, and in the following year 41 per cent of the prewar level. Given Hungary's economic structure, this enormous setback could not be compensated for by the export of manufactured goods; and in any case, industrial exports had also declined. In 1920, they scarcely exceeded 40 per cent, and in 1921 reached only 57 per cent of the prewar totals. A vicious circle hindered the development of the export trade. For the economy to function and for industry to be put on its feet, foreign currency and raw materials were essential, but these could be secured only by the export of agricultural produce, a thing then impossible; the place of these missing agricultural products could have been taken by competitively-priced manufactured goods, but to produce these was impossible without importing raw materials.

In the nations of East Central Europe, the crippling of foreign trade created a catastrophic situation, for they had emerged from the breakup of the Monarchy with a so-called export-import sensitive economy. When Austria, Bohemia, and Hungary were parts of the old empire they did not have to cope with export problems, for a considerable proportion of Austrian and Czech industrial products—for instance. three-quarters of their textile manufactures—where marketed in the agricultural regions of the Monarchy, and the same in reverse applied to agricultural produce. For example, 80 per cent of Hungarian agricultural exports (primarily grain and flour) had been marketed in the Austrian and Czech areas.

Thus, foreign trade—that is, exports to countries outside the Monarchy—had played a relatively subordinate role, given the variety of possibilities within the empire itself. In the new situation, the successor states disposed of one-sided, unbalanced productive capacities. Some of them had inherited relatively too much industry, others too little. But in both cases, within the new frontiers, only part of the commodities required to operate the national economy was present. Without these essential prerequisites, these economies could not function satisfactorily within the restricted national markets. For Czechoslovakia and Austria, this implied the export of manufactured goods and the import of agricultural products and many industrial raw materials; Hungary, on the other hand, had to export agricultural produce and import industrial raw materials and capital goods. Thus, for the successor states foreign trade became vitally important; all of them became to a large extent dependent on it.

The foreign trade problem in its turn posed in a new form the question of capital accumulation. The very importance of trade, the restricted outlets for exports, the unavoidable need for imports were in themselves enough to increase the need for capital to finance trade. But capital accumulation, which had always been small, sank even lower because of the decline in production and the rapidly spreading currency depreciation. The fall in internal capital accumulation was particularly marked in the case of Austria, which had formerly been a relatively big exporter of capital and had played a leading role in supplying the capital needs of the more backward regions of the Monarchy. Inflation, always a corollary of economic exhaustion, had wiped out a large part of its monetary capital. In 1913, the deposits in the leading Viennese banks and in the savings banks of the capital and the countryside, came to 2.2 billion crowns. In 1923, this figure—converted to its gold value—had sunk to 8.7 million. The extraordinarily slow pace of recovery is demonstrated by the fact that even by the summer of 1925, average deposits stood only at 11 per cent of prewar levels. All this was an inseparable part of the new problems of financing, and forced Austria as well as Hungary to seek large injections of capital from abroad. Their only means of recovery from the economic chaos of the postwar years was to tap foreign sources. Currency stabilization, based on credits from western countries and the loans which followed, became one of the most important factors in the consolidation of their economies. The situation in Yugoslavia, Romania, and Poland was very similar. Only Czechoslovakia, by its own unaided efforts, managed to extricate itself from the postwar confusion and to embark on a programme of independent development.

However, the results of the breakup of the Austro-Hungarian Monarchy stretched much further than the short-term manifestations of economic chaos, or the troubles and convulsions caused by adjustment to new conditions. The confusion, which lasted for several years, was such as could lead both to great progress and to a state of permanent regression. When the Monarchy broke up, it was by no means clear which of these two possibilities would be realized, for conditions in the Monarchy had influenced the economic development of its constituent peoples in very diverse ways. Living together within a large area had brought both advantages and disadvantages. It had, for instance, been advantageous to Austrian and Czech industrialization, to the development of Hungary's agriculture and agricultural industries; it had been unfavourable to Austrian and Czech agriculture and to Hungary's consumer goods industry. In addition to these reciprocal advantages and disadvantages, the Monarchy had embodied a system based on the inequality of its constituent parts, as reflected in the division of labour. The economic unity of the empire had rested on the integration of backward agrarian regions with others which had attained a standard of industrial development comparable to that of Western Europe. Apart from the splitting up of an economic community which had endured for half a century, and of the capitalist development which had held it together, the end of the Monarchy denoted for the newly emerging states a release from both the favourable and the unfavourable aspects of the system through which the division of labour had been carried out. Thus, the longer-term developments in one or other of the successor states were not merely the result of the empire's disintegration, or of the economic potential which had been inherited, but were largely dependent on the path followed after the breakup and on the success of the economic strategy that was planned and pursued. Therefore, attention should be focused above all on the economic strategy of the various countries of the Danube Basin between the two World Wars.

In the economic chaos of the postwar period, the first efforts of the new states were directed towards making a clean break with their old economic ties and towards attaining, as far as possible, complete economic independence. They regarded it as their main task to eliminate the last traces of the division of labour prevailing in the former empire, and to make themselves independent of even those regions which had up till then been their natural market for some goods and their main source of supply for others. The value of the goods exported by Austria and Czechoslovakia to Hungary in 1924—even taking postwar territorial changes into consideration—sank to 60 per cent of the 1913 figure.

The newly independent states quickly walled themselves in with import prohibitions and high protective tariffs. For in the twenties, the European states—especially in Central and Eastern Europe—vied with each other in setting up the highest possible customs barriers. At the turn of the century, Hungary had already raised the cry for its own tariff system, and she could now turn this slogan into a practical economic policy. Although, by the conditions of the peace treaty, the customs duties of the erstwhile Austro-Hungarian Monarchy as set forth in Law no. 53 of 1907 were still obligatory for Hungary, Law no. 21 of 1920 gave the government the power to impose by decree new regulations for foreign trade. From July 1921 onwards, one decree after another was issued, placing ever larger numbers of commodities which had formerly been freely imported onto the list of prohibited goods. This applied above all to products of the textile, iron, leather, and engineering industries. Compared with the prewar 10–20 per cent duty on consumer goods, the duty from 1925 onwards averaged 50 per cent *ad valorem* and thus kept the principal imports of former days out of the Hungarian market.

Of course, the Central and East European states intended these barriers around their national economies to act as a protection against all their trading partners equally. In practice, however, protection did not work in a uniform way; its impact was most marked on the neighbouring states. This was a natural outcome, for both in agriculture and industry these countries used less up-to-date techniques than did the more advanced nations; consequently, their goods were dearer and could not compete successfully on the world market. Thus, although at the Austrian and Czechoslovak frontiers the same duties were imposed on grain and flour irrespective of origin, these proved to be much more effective against Hungarian than against American produce, in spite of the higher transport costs of the latter. While the customs tariffs of the Balkan states imposed a heavy burden on imported machinery, they affected Austrian products much more than, for example, English and Belgian.

Thus, the barriers which had been erected to promote self-sufficiency unquestionably divided the Central and East European states more deeply from each other than from those of Western Europe. It is significant that between the wars, Yugoslavia's trade with its Balkan neighbours was quite small, exports and imports ranging between 5 and 9 per cent of the total foreign trade turnover. Although immediately after the war Czechoslovakia, maintaining its old economic associations, still sold more than half of its exports to the Danubian states, by about the middle twenties the percentage had fallen to little more than a third. This process was reciprocal: parallel with this radical fall in exports to the Danubian states, Czechoslovakia, at the end of the decade (and partly for political reasons) was importing more than half its flour from overseas and not from its agrarian neighbours. The same situation developed in Austria, which was already buying a third of its wheat requirements in America, and during the same period was unable to sell the products of its engineering industry to its agrarian neighbours. Midway through the twenties, the Balkan states were buying French and English machine tools and equipment for textile factories, at a time when Austria's engineering industry was producing hardly more than a third of its prewar output. In spite of geographical closeness, of historical tradition, and the existence of natural markets near at hand, trade between the eastern and southeastern European states shrank to a minimum: to about 10–15 per cent of their total trade. An additional reason for this was that they all consistently and rigidly excluded the Soviet Union from their economic life. A large part of what was now Poland had formerly been part of the Russian Empire, and the greater part of its market lay, so to speak, on Russian soil; yet only 1.5 per cent of Poland's export trade was carried on with the Soviet Union. Conditions were similar in Czechoslovakia; while in the other East European states, not even this figure was reached. Exports from East Central Europe were directed largely to Western Europe which, by the Second World War, took 75–80 per cent of their exports and supplied 70–80 per cent of their imports.

The economic policies pursued were naturally accompanied by the growth of autarkic tendencies. Austria and Czechoslovakia, for instance, made great efforts to increase their output of agricultural produce and livestock which they had formerly obtained from the agrarian districts of the Monarchy. In Austria, by 1934, the stock of pigs was almost double that of the postwar reconstruction period. About the middle of the twenties, home-grown wheat could hardly satisfy one-third of the domestic requirements, but ten years later, it was already covering more than half. In the middle of the postwar decade, Czechoslovakia's production of wheat came to about 20 million hundredweight; ten years later, it had reached 34 million. In a particularly favourable year, Czechoslovakia, ordinarily an importer of wheat, showed a surplus on its own harvest.

It is, therefore, not surprising that the markets which the Danubian countries could have offered each other shrank more and more as, following the 1929–33 overproduction crisis, still greater efforts were made to achieve self-sufficiency. After 1918, Hungary still sold a fifth or a sixth of its exports to Czechoslovakia; but by the middle thirties, this had fallen to 5 per cent. On the other hand, it used as much of its available capital as possible to develop those consumer goods industries which it had formerly lacked.

In comparison with prewar standards, production in the Hungarian textile industry had doubled by 1925, trebled by 1929, and by the end of the thirties, had reached four times the prewar figure; the import of textiles, which in 1913 accounted for 70 per cent of total home consumption, now covered only 2–3 per cent. The most striking example of this severance of the associations based on the earlier division of labour can be found in the way Austria and Czechoslovakia developed their own industries. In the Monarchy, most of the spinning for the textile industry was done in Austria, while the weaving was concentrated in Bohemia. Each country wanted its textile industry to become independent of the other, so Austria began to enlarge its weaving industry, and by 1925 had already set up 5,000 looms, while Czechoslovakia, for its part, built spinning mills. Those Balkan states which had enjoyed independence before the war now also strove to consolidate their economic independence, but they were so backward industrially that international economic ties were not of paramount importance. Their efforts were in many ways successful, helping to correct the one-sidedness of their economies and to promote industrialization.

Unfortunately, these methods of encouraging development were by no means the most efficacious. As the states—dazzled by national pride and driven by nationalist passion—began the all-round development of their economies, they paid no heed to the narrow and restricted basis of their economic potentialities as compared to those of the economic cooperation formerly practised with the neighbouring Danubian states. Thus, their venture proved to be not only extremely costly, but also led to much overlapping of effort and superfluous parallel capacity. As a consequence, much of the economic capacity created earlier, both agricultural and industrial, was wasted. By the time Hungary's textile industry was built up, or Austria expanded its weaving, and Czechoslovakia its spinning mills, the old Austrian and Czech textile industries had lost a considerable part of their markets and had fallen into a critical condition. The same thing happened to Hungarian agriculture and flour milling which, deprived of a large part of their share of the Austrian and Czech markets, had also sunk into a state of chronic crisis. Austria tried hard to promote the cultivation of cereal crops and to develop its own milling industry. It introduced state subsidies, and in 1930 created a special fund by levying taxes on sugar, beer, and alcohol. Hungary's milling industry had supplied the total requirements of the Monarchy, but between the wars it could never, even in boom periods, produce more than three-quarters of its former output. The giant Hungarian mills, which had formerly worked for the export trade, closed down one after the other; their assets were disposed of, their empty premises were sold for conversion into textile factories, or were simply razed. Thus, apparently insurmontable difficulties in selling their products was one of the most obvious consequences of the developments in the agrarian countries of Central and Eastern Europe after the First World War. The developed and even the less well developed countries soon discovered that part of their industrial capacity was superfluous.

This, together with the endeavour of each country to develop industries which already existed in neighbouring states at a level high enough to produce export surpluses hindered, indeed rendered impossible, the creation of national economies based on the newest technological achievements, or the development of modern industries capable of competing on the world market. In other words, the effort to achieve agricultural self-sufficiency in the more industrialized states and the industrial ambitions of the agrarian states had indeed contributed to their own economic development, but had, at the same time, aggravated the new contradictions in the economic development of the entire area.

True, the more backward countries, through state aid and protective tariffs, succeeded in reducing imports, and thus laid the foundations for the relatively rapid development of consumer goods industries. Throughout most of these East Central European states it was the textile and other light industries which showed the most substantial progress. In Hungary, as already mentioned, the textile industry was in a position to cover practically all domestic requirements, compared to the only one-third of former days. In Yugoslavia also, it was the textile industry which between the two World Wars showed the fastest development. In the first half of the twenties, textiles had accounted for almost a third of all imports; in the second half of the thirties, for no more than 10 per cent. On the other hand, the import of machines and factory equipment doubled. In Romania, before the Second World War, textiles represented more than a fifth of the value of the total industrial output.

This rapid advance in the production of textiles and other consumer goods undoubtedly gave a great impetus to the industrial development of Eastern Europe; but it served also to conceal the discrepancy between the obsolete manufacturing processes and the industrial needs of the age. For during the first half of the twentieth century, the textile industry, indeed, consumer goods industries as a whole, were, in the more developed countries of Western Europe, already entering a relative decline. For example, during the years immediately preceding the Second World War, the output of the textile industry in England sank from 19 per cent to 11 per cent of the total industrial production; and in continental Europe, from 18 to 11 per cent. On the other hand, the share of the iron, steel, metal-working and chemical industries rose in England from 32 to 44 per cent, and on the continent from 41 to 50 per cent.

After the First World War, industry underwent a radical transformation. Through the use of new techniques, it became possible to provide electricity much more cheaply; industry, therefore, used it on a steadily expanding scale, and electrical power entered on its triumphant course. The multi-purpose electric motor forged ahead in competition with the clumsier steam engine. At the same time, the second great factor in the transformation of industry was making itself felt: the internal combustion engine, the invention of which led to completely new methods of industrial mass production. The modern assembly line was used first of all in the automobile industry; it opened the path to modern factory organization and management techniques, and to new ways of increasing output. It is no coincidence that these new mass production methods quickly spread to other industries, first to the manufacture of machine tools, with a marked effect on costs of production. All these processes naturally caused changes in the whole structure of industry, and in the more advanced capitalist countries, heavy industry advanced by leaps and bounds. In Western Europe, its share of the total output rose from 25–30 to around 50 per cent.

The majority of the Central and Eastern European states could not keep pace with this development; it was only the light industries which managed to increase production, while the potentially dynamic heavy industries, where the new technology could and should have been adopted, stagnated. In this part of Europe, there was practically no country which could adapt its engineering industries for modern mass production; with their small and restricted markets, they were unable to take advantage of the new developments in industrial technology. If we measure the advance of modern industry by the per capita consumption of steel, the increase in England and Sweden between 1913 and 1938 was between 50 and 100 per cent; whereas even in Czechoslovakia and Poland, there was virtual stagnation.

The exclusion of certain types of commodities and the effort of each country to produce goods which had formerly been imported meant that the advantages following from the intense efforts to increase production in certain branches of industry were counterbalanced by the recession in others for the lack of markets. The example of Hungary is typical and highly instructive: while textile production quadrupled, heavy industry made no progress, and the food processing industries showed a substantial decline; as a result, total industrial production rose very slowly indeed, by not quite 30 per cent over a period of twenty years. Owing to the stagnation in agriculture, the annual rate of increase of the national income was only about 1.5 per cent. In Austria, the rate of growth was similar, while Poland, which had regained its longed-for independence, was, between the two World Wars, quite unable to reach even that minimal economic growth. One important reason for Central and Eastern Europe's slow economic development was that these countries—though unable to accumulate large amounts of capital from their own resources, and though foreign sources of capital were less plentiful than before—still persisted in attempting to make themselves independent economically, and thus dissipated even the restricted opportunities of development open to them. Their exertions to promote economic development and industrialization were, therefore, bound to have only limited success.

In all the countries of the region, the problem of employment was the gravest. It was quite impossible to eliminate chronic unemployment; in Poland, Romania, Yugoslavia, and Bulgaria a fifth to a third of the rural population could find no work, and industry was in no position to absorb them.

Given the slow pace of economic development and the serious internal contradictions, there was, of course, no possibility of attaining the much desired economic independence, and in the end, little had been done to overcome the general backwardness. Before the outbreak of the Second World War, 75–80 per cent of the population of Albania, Bulgaria, Yugoslavia, and Romania still earned their living on the land. Even in Poland, the rural population had only fallen from the 64 per cent after the First World War to 61 per cent. In Hungary, about half the country's population worked on the land.

As a result of the policy of exclusion and autarky, of the consequent restriction of markets, and of the slow pace of industrial development and its consequences for capital accumulation, the economies of the Danubian countries remained extremely vulnerable and unstable. During the second half of the twenties, generous foreign credits and relatively favourable world market prices had enabled them to consolidate their economies; they even enjoyed a moderate prosperity. But when the temporary boom broke and the economic crisis of 1929–33 struck the world, all the economic problems flared up again more fiercely than ever before. Czechoslovakia, which had developed well during the twenties and appeared genuinely industrial; Austria, industrialized but stagnating after the First World War; Hungary, stuck in its old agrarian-industrial pattern; and the Balkan states, no longer facing competition from the Monarchy and longing for swifter industrialization—all fell into the most severe social and economic crisis, which, in its turn, brought to the fore the basic problem of their existence and progress. The dead-end reached in the thirties left only the choice between continuing as they were, or adapting themselves to be the *Lebensraum* of the new and frightening Germany of Hitler. The defencelessness of the Danube-Basin countries in the face of economic crisis did, indeed, prove fertile soil for the determined advance of the Germans. The rapid growth of German influence and her economic domination prepared the ground for the *Anschluss,* for the subjection of Czechoslovakia, and finally, for the Second World War. The incompetence and helplessness of the states of the Danube Basin on the eve of the war reflected the fiasco of the political pretensions, of the nationalist economic policies and of the plans for industrial development which they had clung to for twenty years. The economic problems created by the breakup of the Monarchy remained unsolved between the two World Wars.

VI

"RANGE" AND "CONSTRAINT"

THE SMALL STATES OF THE DANUBE BASIN AND THE INTERNATIONAL POLITICAL AND ECONOMIC SYSTEM 1919—1945

When treating the historical development of small states in modern times, it seems useful to consider this process in terms of a mechanical metaphor, the complementary concepts of "range" and "constraint". The dictionary defines "range" in this sense as "the extent of the operation or action of something"; to "constrain", in mechanics, is "to control or limit the motion of a body or mass to some particular direction or manner". The two concepts together describe the possibilities of an actual instance of motion, and, figuratively, provide a convenient shorthand for the kind of historical development we are about to consider. While we are on definitions, the question of how to define the concept "small state" also arises. Dictionaries will hardly help us here, in part because it is only recently that social scientists have accepted the fact that the historical, social and economic development of a given nation is effectively influenced also by its size. Yet: what chance of independence has a small state really got? What means has it of securing its autonomy? What chance has it of holding its own given the complexity of the modern world economy? These are hardly questions that can be evaded. And does a state's being a small state not have its own special political and social ramifications? Once we concede that there are indeed a set of internal and external factors specific to the development of small nations, further questions naturally arise: What makes a state a small state? What are the definitive criteria: size, population, and population density, or is it rather some economic criterion: the per capita national product, or the gross national product?

The problem with the definitions to be found in historical works is that they are not easily generalizable, for they are mostly specific to one particular historical period. And though I propose to focus on the history of the small states of the Danube Basin, particularly between 1919 and 1945, nevertheless I cannot help referring to some general aspects of the question.

In two of his works, *The Unequality of States* and "The Analysis of Small Power Politics" D. Vital offers two definitions of a small state, both negative rather than positive.[1] A small state, he tells us, is one which, in the long run, functions only as a dispensable and non-essential complement to the political and military resources of a great power. This definition is quite in keeping with Max Weber's concept of power: "Power means that potentiality within social relations which allows of

[1] D. Vital: *The Unequality of States. A Study of the Small Power in International Relation,* Oxford 1967; and a study by D. Vital: The Analysis of Small Power Politics, in A. Schou-Arne, O. Bruntland (eds.): *Small States in International Relations,* Stockholm 1971

having one's will even against possible resistance", he writes.[2] Still, we cannot regard this as satisfactory from the point of view of our question. "Small states" as a category can be approached from a number of possible angles. We could, naturally, set up a more or less arbitrary quantitative order and then place the various countries within its limits. For a long time, a population of ten million was regarded as such an upper limit. But a definition of this type has at least three weaknesses. First of all, it ignores the factor of territory; consequently Australia, Luxemburg and Hungary all fit in one and the same category. Secondly, it disregards economic correlations, too, categorizing Switzerland and Sweden with not only the small states of Eastern Europe, but also some South American countries, and newly independent African nations. Finally, this quantitative approach has been rendered ineffective by the multitude of dwarf states that have resulted from decolonization.[3]

Another approach considers the foreign policy aims of a given state against the background of its actual resources, at the same time analyzing its relative weight in international politics. What is of interest in both correlations is how far the nation's foreign policy interests go beyond its immediate environment. Still, no strict system of criteria can be based on any of this, since it does not necessarily follow that the foreign policy ambitions of a country are in proportion to its objective possibilities. We can take as examples of this Poland's pretensions to great power status in the interwar years, or Hungary's foreign policy during the same period. Hungary aspired only to the status of a regional great power, but was generally unable to estimate her own strength so as to minimize her risks in case of conflict. Clearly, size, economic resources, the country's weight in international politics, and other factors all contribute to a state's being a small state, but just as clearly, whatever we accept as the decisive criterion, the concept still remains highly relative.[4] But that "small statehood" has specific political, economic, cultural[5] and sociological ramifications is beyond question.[6]

Although the problem of small states runs through history, as far as I know, the Treaty of Westphalia marks the first attempt to regulate relations between small and great powers on the level of international diplomacy. Clearly, in the feudal period preceding, the question had been practically irrelevant, for the Holy Roman Empire and the Papacy served as integrating forces and where they did not, there was feudal anarchy.[7] In the Treaty of Westphalia, we already find small states being treated as having a part in great-power politics, though the part allotted them in diplomacy was decorative, and they were allowed no real say in the main issues.

But the rise of the middle classes went hand in hand with the development of the nation state, and during the 18th century legal and historical works appeared one after the other all aiming to theoretically elucidate and to practically regulate the place of small states in the world system. In 1632, world peace was still conceived of

[2] Max Weber: *Wirtschaft und Gesellschaft, Grundriß der verstehenden Soziologie,* II, Köln—Berlin 1964, p. 678.

[3] *The Other Power. Studies in the Foreign Policies of Small States,* London 1973.

[4] O. J. Falnes *The Future of the Small States,* Washington 1944.

[5] As Masaryk put it in one of his works written during World War I: "In a smaller community there is a more intensive intercommunion of men, ideas and feelings;..." Quoted by G. Heckscher, in: *The Role of Small Nations—Today and Tomorrow* from T. Masaryk: *The Problem of Small Nations in the European Crisis,* London 1966, p. 30.

[6] We refer here to Durkheim's observation that a small community makes for intensive division of labour in human society: many functions must be filled by a few people.

[7] T. Fleiner: *Die Kleinstaaten in den Staatenverbindungen des zwanzigsten Jahrhunderts,* Zürich 1966, p. 23.

in terms of the Pope, the Sultan and the Christian rulers establishing world order, and imposing their will on any possible gainsayer. All 18th century writings, on the other hand, beginning with William Penn's *Essay towards the Present and Future of Europe* (a pamphlet written still in the previous century, in 1694), writings such as Hobbes' *Leviathan* ("Contracts without the sword, are but words"), Sully' s *Grand Project* (1713), Rousseau's *Eternal Peace* (1767), and finally a work of similar title by Kant studied the question of how to reconcile international order with the interests of small states, or, as Rousseau put it: "to harmonize the outside influence of a great power and the interest or attitude of a small state".[8]

Though preceded by the defeat of Napoleon and called by the reactionary Great Powers of the Holy Alliance, the Vienna Congress of 1815 was the first attempt at settling a European question with at least the formal participation of the plenipotentiaries of several states.[9] Of course, here, too, hierarchy among the states was preserved intact: the lesser questions were discussed by eight countries—England, Prussia, Austria, Russia, France, Spain, Sweden and Portugal—while only the four Great Powers decided on more important matters. There were states whose interests were recognized "in general" as it was put, and there were others whose interests were recognized only within limits.[10]

The rise of the bourgeoisie in the 19th century, and even more the dissolution of the Turkish Empire considerably increased the number of independent small states. By 1917–18 the other two multinational empires of Eastern Europe had also fallen victim to time. In 1919 as many as thirty-five countries sent their representatives to the Paris Peace Conference and wanted to have a say in establishing the new order of Europe. But the Congress had only five plenary sessions attended by the delegations of all the nations present. Though Wilson had committed himself to a Peace Conference at which peoples and countries would not be treated as mere pawns in a chess game, Nicholson was right in regarding these plenary sessions as purely fictitious.[11] The reality of the situation was much more clearly reflected by the fact that the Great Powers were represented by five, the smaller countries by three, and the newly formed states by only two delegates each. And though Clemenceau's scathingly ironic "We shall appoint a special commission and you can talk to them for a couple of hours. Now we had better have a cup of tea"[12] made to Kramar (who asked for the floor for half an hour after Beneš had spoken for nearly three on the question of Austria and Hungary) was typical of the Great Powers' attitude on a lot of questions, and though the Treaty of Versailles failed to follow the principles of national self-determination earlier declared, still it established a system of small states in the Danube Basin. Legally speaking, then, the political independence of the small states of Central and Southeastern Europe was affirmed at Versailles; in fact, however, their independent status rested on the defeat of the German Empire, and Russia's secession as an international power as a result of the Bolshevik Revolution.

The international power system that had confirmed the small states in the Danube Basin in their independence suffered from several weaknesses and contradictions, quite independently of the fact that its fundamental principle, the right of nations to self-determination, had been greatly undermined by the actual peace settlement.

[8] J. A. R. Marriott: *Federalism and the Problem of the Small States,* London 1943.
[9] J. Rappaport *et al.* (eds.): *Small States and Territories. Status and Problems,* New York 1971.
[10] E. Bjol: The Small State in International Politics, in: A. Schou-Arne, O. Bruntland (eds.): *op. cit.*, p. 30.
[11] H. Nicholson: *Peacemaking 1919,* London 1934.
[12] Ch. L. Mee: *The End of Order, Versailles 1919*, New York 1980, p. 82.

The newly emerged nations' turning into an anti-German and anti-Soviet *cordon sanitaire* mostly at France's initiative and with French support presupposed the weakness of those two countries on the one hand, and the power of France, on the other. This power, however, functioned not only as a safeguard against Germany and Russia, but also as dominance compatible with the formal political independence of the small states of the Danube Basin. It was compatible even though France did her best to take economic advantage of these countries through capital imports, and to make political use of them to further French foreign policy, generally as buffer states (e. g., Locarno). The French *cordon sanitaire,* thus guaranteed the independence of the countries of East-Central Europe. By reasons of geography, French power politics could represent no direct threat to the independence of these states; French hegemony rested on a power system in which the countries of Eastern Europe played a marginal role, and a role, to boot, which was of value in case of confrontation only if they retained their independence. One of the tragic contradictions of Hungarian foreign policy during these years was that, because of Trianon, it worked for the destruction of a power system which limited the country's options on the one hand, but on the other, allowed it to live.

The weakening of France and the relative indifference of England changed the position of the small states of the Danube Basin by the beginning of the 1930s; an increasingly ambitious Nazi Germany could not tolerate the independence of the small states, not only because this was incompatible with its ideology and political system, but also because in the world system she was aiming at, these states were to have another role, if they were to play a role at all. After all, though geopolitics misses much of the truth, it does not follow that geographical factors are indifferent in a country's politics. Germany intentionally put the small states under stronger pressure. German plans envisioned the small states of the Danube Basin not as tactical pawns in the hands of confronting sides, but as the No. 1 reserve of a totalitarian world system being developed; their economic function was to be not marginal, but central. And, of course, unlike the Versailles theorists, the German value system ascribed no value, either immanent or functional, to the idea of national self-determination.[13]

Formal independence does not carry the same meaning in the different world systems. The French hegemony was based on an international system which rested on some kind of balance, and whose structure contained liberal elements. Under French hegemony, self-determination was considerably limited; in the German system, it became meaningless. In the French system, though France dominated, the states of the Danube Basin were regarded as parts of this hegemony, and were thought to act as a kind of balance. German power politics, on the other hand, did not consider balancing factors necessary, for it was intolerant even of secondary counter-forces. In the French system, the Danube Basin was of secondary strategic importance, and was difficult to get to; for the Germans, it proved to be of great significance as the territory they could best secure militarily.

According to the French conception, it was precisely the independence of the small states of the Danube Basin that best guaranteed their ability to function as buffer states. The German Nazi regime could envision only dependence: the countries would either become satellites or be assimilated. It had no need of buffer states, for it wanted to annihilate whatever it clashed with. The Danube Basin was of secondary and of ever decreasing importance from the point of view of French

[13] T. Mathisen: *The Functions of Small States in the Strategies of the Great Powers,* Oslo—Bergen—Tromsö 1971.

aspirations; the Germans, on the other hand, did everything to secure the economic resources of the small states in the Danube Basin. The French conception left open a certain range of action; the German program implied only constraint.

The peacemakers at Versailles had made three capital mistakes. The first was to be found in the general principle of the treaty itself, which, as the Germans insisted, was dictated in every respect, but which was said by the victors to be based on Bentham's liberal doctrine. The world view of Bentham and Wilson alike can be traced back to the traditional liberal idea that, as in the economy, so in international relations, too, a harmony of interests prevails. In fact, the fallacy of this view had been demonstrated by World War I: it held true only when the number of interests was limited, the supply of raw materials and goods to be divided was seemingly unlimited. Even as the liberal world view and the liberal concept of the human rights gradually lost much of their meaning in the 20th century, so the world order conceived in liberalism proved to be less and less compatible with the actual conflicts of interest and the consequent system of conflicts.[14]

The second error concerned the supposed position of the small states in this system. The conception itself had already been formulated in a Foreign Office memorandum in 1916: "The new Polish State would be one of the most powerful units among the independent countries which are expected to come into existence upon the dissolution of Austria-Hungary. From the point of view of England and France this conglomeration of states would prove an efficient barrier against Russian preponderance in Europe and German extension towards the Near East because these states would be happy and contented in the realization of their national aspiration, and strong as regards their economic future."[15] Well, the states in Eastern Europe could not play the part assigned them in the absence of the essential preconditions. To have become effective buffer states among their powerful neighbours, they would have needed unity and strong social cohesion, something that was practically missing in the states in the Danube Basin. Besides the urgent social questions, the national conflicts which continued to exist in some form or other were a source of permanent domestic difficulty in all these countries (conflicts between the Czechs and Slovaks, the Serbs and the Croatians, the problem of the Magyar and the German minorities, the thought of *Anschluß*); while the Little Entente *vs.* Hungary confrontation undermined whatever common front the Danubian states had ever formed on the international scene. With the coming of the Depression, the social differences became more acute; and as the spirit of Versailles faded, there seemed to be little to keep national hostilities in check.

Gaining economic strength was out of the question for these countries; the peace settlement brought economic ruin even to those of them which had been prosperous earlier, without, however, giving the underdeveloped states enough for economic balance: and this was the settlement's third great mistake. The cutting of the earlier economic ties temporarily weakened the area's economic position still further. The idea that these countries would prosper within the framework of some kind of French economic hegemony proved unrealistic. For one thing, France possessed no resources adequate to ensure the permanent development of the states in the Danube Basin. And although French help was temporarily supplemented by English and American resources, once the Depression set in, it not only precluded any kind of prosperity, but further highlighted the internal economic difficulties of the small

[14] E. H. Carr: *Conditions of Peace,* New York 1943, p. 60.
[15] D. Lloyd George: *Memoirs of the Peace Conference,* New Haven 1939, I, p. 13.

states. Stresemann was right in saying that it made no sense to establish new states if one made no effort to integrate them within the European economic system.[16]

To define the concept "small state" in an economic sense again involves a lot of difficulties; classical economic theory never paid much attention to the correlation between a nation's size and its economic prosperity; and Marxist economics followed the classics for quite some time in this, too.

Size as an economic category cannot be equated with volume, though theoretically, small countries have quantitatively fewer and qualitatively less varied resources.[17] Restricted resources naturally suggest that a small state specializes in producing and exporting the goods best suited to its resources. Of course, it may be objected that resources are not evenly distributed, and that consequently their availability cannot be regarded as simply a function of land area. The supposition that it is also ignores the human element, the capacity fully to exploit the available natural resources.[18]

Alfred Marshall connects geographic size with exports.[19] He starts out from the geometrical principle correlating a given area with the length of its borders. For instance, a circle with an area four times smaller than another circle has a circumference which is only twice as small. A small state, thus, has relatively longer borders, which automatically means a greater volume of foreign trade; likewise, the nearest markets, domestic as well as the foreign, will generally be a shorter distance off. Several arguments may be brought up against Marshall's, which tend to overestimate the importance of transportation costs. The neoclassical school stresses productive capacity as a potential handicap of the small states: given a developed international economy, productive capacity can be defined as a country's liability—under circumstances of total specialization—to make the production of certain goods a function of its size.

Besides export specialization, the smallness of their markets and disproportionate production costs put small states at a disadvantage. Furthermore, their production is relatively unprofitable because of the limited home market, and this is another handicap we must consider. For though Adam Smith did not deal with the economy of small states, he attributed great importance to market size as a factor in economic development. The population figures were not decisive in themselves, for population size was a market criterion only in relation to the national income; and per capita national income depended also on productivity.[20]

It is, thus, difficult to accept any one of the above criteria as generally applicable to small states. This conceptual difficulty well reflects the complexity of the economic consequences of being a small state. At any rate, the geographical, demographic and economic considerations (land area and resources, population, and market size) taken all together will bring us nearer to the heart of the matter, and to the economic historian's approach. "Small state" in an economic sense has been defined by Marcy as one which, "while depending comparatively heavily upon foreign trade both for supplies and sales markets, makes only a modest contribution to the aggregate flow of international trade".[21] In other words, foreign trade, in

[16] G. Stresemann: *His Diaries, Letters and Papers,* III, London 1935, p. 619.

[17] P. J. Lloyd: *International Trade Problems of Small Nations,* Durham 1968.

[18] E. A. G. Robinson (ed.): *Economic Consequences of the Size of Nations,* New York 1960, Introduction.

[19] A. Marshall: *Industry and Trade,* London 1919, chap. 2.

[20] I. Svennilson: The Concept of the Nation and its Relevance to Economic Analysis, and S. Kuznets: Economic Growth of Small Nations, in: *Economic Consequences of the Size of Nations,* I.

[21] G. Marcy: How Far Can Foreign Trade and Customs Agreements Confer upon Small Nations the Advantages of Large Nations?, in: *ibid.*

spite of its relatively small volume, contributes a considerable part of the national income. True, one could adduce quite a few counterexamples—a warning that it is unwise to be too categorical in one's generalizations. And it goes without saying that the size of a country is only one of the factors determining productivity, growth rate and the stability of the national income. Yet we can hardly say that it is of no economic significance.[22] We will not be far from the truth if we say that a country's size is of economic significance primarily from the point of view of its position. Though there are examples to the contrary, there can be no doubt that the disproportionately large foreign trade rate of the small countries makes them more dependent on international prosperity, and, all other things being equal, decreases the multiplication effect of foreign trade. An export structure that is highly concentrated geographically or product-wise is more liable to instability. Concentrating on the production of just the few goods which gave the chief impetus to development in an export-oriented economy in a certain sense tends to slow down the country's long-term economic growth, and to intensify the cyclic fluctuations.

Little attention has been paid by economic theorists to how a country's size ties in with economic policies and politics. For instance, economic policy decisions disadvantageous to the small countries are not merely the consequence of their weak economic position; this weakness is due partly to their limited political and military strength, and even what would otherwise have been an economically strong position often carries no weight precisely because of their military and political weakness.

All things considered, then, even the fact that some small countries have, in fact, worked their way up among the richest countries in the world, the special economic difficulties the small states wrestle with remains a question that can not be ignored. Three things we can take as axiomatic: *ceteris paribus,* the bigger the economic unit (to a certain point) the lower the costs of production; a bigger market can support bigger economic units; greater resources and a larger population means a bigger market, since the diversification of production is partly a function of the diversity of the domestic resources.[23]

A small country, especially if it is underdeveloped and concentrates on a few export branches, can easily have difficulties balancing its budget, and balance of payments deficits tend to lead to overall economic troubles. The effects of prosperity or recession in other countries spiral in more easily, and a small country is more vulnerable to the economic dictatorship of its neighbour(s), since it is in greater need of external markets (of the external market of specific countries) than the other way round.[24] The indices of economic dependence are the percentage that foreign trade represents of the GDP, the extent of trade with various countries, or rather, the proportion they comprise of the given country's foreign trade, the role played by capital imports and their distribution among the country's various partners, the diversification of exports and of markets, and the world market price of the given country's chief exports, their income elasticity and the trend of the demand for them. A country can be regarded as dependent on foreign trade if foreign trade constitutes 20 per cent of its economy; if *one* specific country accounts for a third of a country's foreign trade, the economy of the latter is highly dependent upon the decisions of the former.[25]

22 B. Benedict: *Problems of Smaller Territories,* London 1967.

23 C. N. Vakel, P. R. Bruhmananda: The Problems of Developing Countries, in: E. A. G. Robinson (ed.), *op. cit.*

24 R. Triffer: The Size of Nations and its Vulnerability to Economic Nationalism, in: *ibid.*

25 M. R. Singer: *War, States and World Powers. The Dynamics of International Relationships,* New York 1972.

Almost all the economic weaknesses besetting small countries came to the fore in the period between the two world wars. We shall concentrate here on three aspects of this econo-historical complex: export sensitivity; the resultant balance of payments problems; and finally, the relations between the economically dominant great power and the small state.

It is well known that the collapse of the Austro-Hungarian Monarchy meant a sudden increase in the significance of foreign trade for all the successor states; more precisely, it became a matter vital to their economic development. *Mutatis mutandis,* the same went for the Balkan states, almost all of which had territories newly annexed from what had been the Austro-Hungarian Monarchy. Although the agrarian character of these territories and the survival of the traditional economy made foreign trade less significant in theory, in fact, if we look at the question dynamically and considering that all of the states regarded their newly won or newly confirmed independence as the *sine qua non* of their statehood, it will be obvious that they set a premium on economic growth as its best guarantee; and this called for increased exports, the main source of accumulation and of the investments needed for development.

The economic instability of the small states of the Danube Basin in the interwar years had both internal and external causes. The two sets of factors were closely interrelated, and reinforced each other so much that one can hardly treat them separately; nevertheless, it is necessary to do so for methodological reasons.

The international economic division of labour which had worked well in many respects before World War I was in a crisis. One of the factors making for the crisis was the expansion of the European economy to become a more complete world economy, one in which the extra-European territories played a greater part; this undermined the traditional division of labour between Eastern and Western Europe, depriving the former of almost all its traditional agricultural markets. The traditional balance between supply and demand was destroyed, and the small countries, dependent on foreign markets, found themselves in an even more subordinate position. The other, even greater catastrophe was the Depression, particularly the years between 1929 and 1933. All the factors which had allowed the small countries to get at least some benefit from the earlier economic prosperity were done away with: the channels through which the fruits of accumulation had seeped through to them were closed off, and even the source of accumulation dried up.

In the 1920s, this process took the form primarily of export difficulties. After the postwar reconstruction, the volume of foreign trade was far short of the prewar level. In Romania, the per capita export was 40 per cent, in Yugoslavia 63 per cent, in Hungary 30 per cent, and in Austria 30 per cent of what it had been before the war. And all this at a time when foreign trade had acquired extraordinary importance in these small, resource-poor countries, at a time when their governments' economic policies centred upon establishing the economic basis of their political independence, i.e. at a time of import-substituting industrialization, when the volume of certain imports grew, while other imports were cut. The export difficulties brought about a trade imbalance for which the only remedy was a temporary balance of payments surplus.[26]

[26] I. T. Berend, Gy. Ránki: Kelet-Európa gazdasági fejlődésének kérdéseihez a két világháború között (On the problems of East European economic development between the two world wars), *Történelmi Szemle* (Historical Review), (1975), No. 4.

The weaknesses of the system that became explicit at the end of the 20s were already perceptible before the Depression hit.

Surplus of exports or imports in national currencies (millions)

	Hungary	Romania	Yugoslavia
1925	−45.9		
1926	−82.3	+1,095	−194
1927	−346.3	+4,629	+878
1928	−385.4	−5,225	−13,387
1929	−25.2	−665	−3,227

In consequence of the serious foreign trade deficit, repaying the capital imported ran into great difficulties, and the countries fell further and further into debt. In 1926, 8 per cent of Romania's exports went to service her debts; within three years, the amount had risen to 20 per cent. More and more of Yugoslavia's exports also served the same purpose. The Depression showed the economies of the small countries in all their weakness, and, what is more, brought to light the fact that their weakness and vulnerability resided partly in their own policy decisions. Except on a limited number of issues, the conference of agrarian states held in Bucharest in July and August of 1930 was unable to come to any real agreement.[27] Certainly, it was by no means clear that the cooperation of a number of small states would have weight of sufficient consequence on the world market actually to be of help to the Danubian states. But after the narrow-minded, nationalist economic policies and the evidently irreconcilable political interests had won the day, and it became evident that the planned concerted action was only a pious wish, was mere talk, they were even tangibly at the mercy of the Great Powers.[28]

In many respects, the Depression presented a textbook case of the economic weakness and vulnerability of small countries in general. Dependence upon external markets, extraordinary dependence on international prosperity, lack of export diversification, vulnerability to the economic and trade policies of the Great Powers, the weakness of the domestic market, disadvantageous exchange rates and extreme indebtedness were all present simultaneously.

The shrinking of the world market greatly cut the export possibilities of the countries in the Danube Basin. Romania's export of animals fell by 45 per cent, and her wheat export by 55 per cent. Between 1929 and 1932, there was a 54 per cent decrease in the volume of Yugoslavian exports. In 1934, Hungarian agricultural exports fell 27 per cent behind the 1929 level. At its lowest level, Bulgaria's cattle export was 86 per cent less than before the Depression. Since export prices fell more quickly than the volume exported, foreign trade receipts fell more than the exports. In Romania, for example, the quantity exported decreased by 42 per cent between 1929 and 1934, while the income from these exports dropped by 73 per cent. Calculated at prices held constant, Hungarian agricultural exports fell by 27 per cent during the same period, calculated at current prices, by 60 per cent. Calculated in

[27] N. Vuco: *Agrarna Kriza v Jugoslaviji 1930—1934,* Beograd 1968; N. Jordache: *La Petite Entente et l'Europe,* Genève 1977.

[28] Gy. Ránki: *Gazdaság és külpolitika* (Economy and foreign policy), Budapest 1981.

tons, Poland exported 28 per cent more than before the Depression, but her income from agricultural exports fell by 56 per cent between 1928 and 1932.

One reason why these countries were so vulnerable in their foreign trade was that they all concentrated upon the export of a few highly developed agricultural products. The five most important export products comprised 81 per cent of all exports from Romania, 70 per cent from Bulgaria, 52 per cent from Yugoslavia and 35 per cent from Hungary. Even in those countries where the five most important exports were not predominant, there was little possibility for diversification, because agricultural goods and raw materials had an absolute preponderance in the export structure. Agricultural produce and raw materials constituted 97 per cent of all exports in Bulgaria, 70 per cent in Hungary, 97 per cent in Romania, and 82 per cent in Yugoslavia. Since there was a more radical drop in the prices of agricultural raw materials than in the price of industrial products, the overall terms of trade with the industrialized countries fell by some 30 per cent. All this makes it clear why exports declined so dramatically and why it took a third of Romania's and Yugoslavia's export incomes and nearly half of Hungary's in 1931 to service their foreign debts.

During the years of economic crisis, the annual foreign debts used up 22 per cent of Austria's, 48 per cent of Hungary's, 28 per cent of Romania's, and 29 per cent of Yugoslavia's export incomes.

The crisis, thus, brought to the surface all the disadvantages of dependence upon foreign trade, and revealed the instability that lack of product and export diversification and balance of payments deficits lead to. "Limited in its area and variety of natural resources, limited in the number of people within its boundaries, confronted with greater problems of security, the small nation is at a distinct disadvantage", Kuznets says.[29]

Clearly, it was the desire to overcome the economic disadvantages of smallness that repeatedly raised the idea of some kind of federation, or at least customs union, among the states in the Danube Basin. A number of plans—the Briand plan, the Tardieu plan, the Broochei System, the idea of an Italo-Austrian-Hungarian bloc, and the Hodzsa plan—[30] all hoped to overcome the acute economic problems of these small states by enlarging the territories, the resources, and the markets they had at their disposal for their economic operations. Without going into the questions of the actual economic advantages and viability of these schemes, I should like merely to point out here that these proposals, which had mainly French support, came to nought mostly because of the other Great Powers' objections. And though the economic cooperation of the small states was recognized as impracticable for political reasons as a result, the logic of things seemed to suggest that the only way for them to surmount their export and balance of payments difficulties was to join a bigger market.

In Germany it had been recognized well before Hitler's appearance on the scene that Germany's economic power gave her foreign policy leverage *vis-à-vis* the small states of the Danube Basin. "We must take advantage of international economic relations to show that we are still a great power; our foreign policy should rest on

[29] S. Kuznets: Economic Growth of Small Nations, in: E. A. G. Robinson: *op. cit.*

[30] M. Ormos: *Franciaország és a keleti biztonság 1931—1936* (France and eastern security), Budapest 1969; M. Ádám: *Dunai konföderáció vagy kisantant?* (Danubian Confederation or Little Entente?), Budapest 1977; L. Márkus: *A Károlyi Gyula-kormány bel- és külpolitikája* (The domestic and foreign policy of the Gy. Károlyi government), Budapest 1968.

our economic strength", Stresemann had emphasized.[31] Brüning saw Germany's position as the biggest importer of agricultural produce as her major strength: the German market was the weapon to be used against Southeastern Europe.[32]

The more evident it was that the small states of the Danube Basin were unable to overcome their economic difficulties, and the more obvious it became that the Western powers either could not or did not want to give them any real help, the more Germany looked to *Ergänzungswirtschaft* both as a theory and in practice. *Ergänzungswirtschaft* as an economic theory was based 1) on the *Großraumwirtschaft* theory, which saw small economies as unviable in themselves under modern economic and technological conditions, and in need of merging with, or assimilating into a larger controlled economy for their development; and 2) on an idea of Southeastern Europe which saw geographic, economic, political and cultural considerations as all arguing for a "natural" relationship between the countries of the Danube Basin and Germany. As it was formulated already in 1929: "Though the concept of *Mitteleuropa,* which, according to Naumann, means the region stretching from the North Sea to the Aegean, was born during the War, and died immediately thereafter as an outcome of its conclusion, the facts of economic policy and transport conditions all prove that other Great Powers, and especially France, are unable to attain their ends in this area. Though a number of small and medium-sized countries have been introduced, by way of a barrier, between Germany and Southeastern Europe, political goals cannot prove stronger than the natural economic ties between these two regions... That Germany and Southeastern Europe form an economic unit is a fact that cannot be mooted...".[33]

And though during the Weimar Republic this was not yet official policy, it soon became that after Hitler's rise to power. The correlation between Schacht's *Neuer Plan* and the *Großraumwirtschaft* theory is clear enough. Moreover, the Depression as well as the consequent economic collapse of the small states argued in proof of the theory. The German *Großraumwirtschaft* literature has as its main point of departure a fact that the Depression too, seemed to confirm, namely that world trade could not, in principle, be regulated. New methods, such as tariffs and quotas, designed to curb the uncontrollable forces of economic competition, could be employed only temporarily, and provided only momentary solutions.[34] For the economy to develop, planned cooperation was necessary in specific large areas. In future, the framework of economic development will be not state which was itself the product of the liberalism that was being so much deplored, but a large economic and geographical unit, the *Großraumwirtschaft.* An area of such size created its own demand, and was able to satisfy it through its own resources and production. Naturally, the main task of the new *Großraumwirtschaft* theory with its carefully elaborated legal and political ramifications was to guarantee Germany maximal economic security, and Germans the highest possible standard of living. The area's entire economy was to be adjusted to serve this end. It followed that Southeastern Europe was an organic part of the future German *Großraumwirtschaft.* For one thing, it was seen as an indispensable source of raw materials and food-supplies in

[31] H.-J. Schröder: *Deutsche Südosteuropapolitik, Geschichte und Gesellschaft* (1976), No. 1, p. 7.

[32] T. P. Koops: Zielkonflikte der Agrar- und Wirtschaftspolitik in der Ära Brüning, in: M. Mommsen, D. Petrin (eds.) *Industrielle Systeme,* Düsseldorf 1976, p. 18.

[33] A. Mitrović: Die Theorie der Ergänzungswirtschaft, in: *Yugoslavia and the Third Reich,* Belgrade 1981.

[34] I. T. Berend, Gy. Ránki: *Magyarország a fasiszta Németország "életterében" 1933—39* (Hungary in the *Lebensraum* of Fascist Germany), Budapest 1960.

case of war, for another, as the agrarian complement to industrial Germany's market, an area that was to avoid any future industrialization, and was to remain solely an agricultural area primarily serving Germany's needs.

I do not want to go into the well-known story of how and to what extent Germany bound the states in the Danube Basin to herself economically already in the 1930s. What I want to stress here is that economic conditions forced into economic partnership with Germany not only Hungary—which derived certain direct economic advantages from this partnership and had foreign policy incentives to it—but also Yugoslavia and Romania, whose foreign policy conflicts with Germany should have been quite manifest. Both of them had to put aside their long-range foreign policy interests and, what is more, to get into the German market, were bound to accept certain political conditions made by Germany, since it was clear that no economic concessions would be given to countries hostile towards her. Thus, economic considerations had a great deal to do with the policy which passively stood by, or even helped in the collapse of the French system of alliances based on political sovereignty so that the German system could take its place.

Thus, though by the end of the 30s the states in the Danube Basin had overcome one of the greatest weaknesses of their economic position, their passive balance of trade, their success was a questionable one, since they could hardly hope to sail by the Scylla and Charybdis of the various forms of dependence. Prices on the export markets, as is well known, were so far German dominated that—given that the world financial system did not work, that in the absence of credits only export increases could give an economy the necessary impetus, and that this economic domination was increasingly supported by foreign policy and military considerations, too—this domination necessarily involved the danger of grave political dependence.

Nevertheless, it would be quite misleading to conceive of all this in terms of stereotypes: to see the Great Powers as unscrupulous manipulators, wolves on the watch for their prey, and the small states as their hopeless victims. History does not show the small states to have been law-abiding, upright countries with solid democratic institutions, though it is true that the aims they could set themselves were often limited by the ineffectiveness of the means at their disposal. The small states often brought trouble on themselves in the 20th century through the political conflicts among them, and they did so whenever—in the name of equitable power relations in the Danube Basin, or the reunification of historical lands, or the peoples' right to self-determination or any other plausible slogan—they turned to one of the Great Powers for help in getting the better of one another.

Yet Machiavelli's injunction seems no less timely in the 20th century then it was in his day: "A prince ought never make common cause with one more powerful than himself to injure another, unless necessity forces him to it, for if he wins he rests in his power, and princes must avoid as much as possible being under the will and pleasure of others. One never tries to avoid one difficulty without running into another, but prudence consists of being able to know the nature of the difficulties and taking the least harmful as good."[35]

If we glance over the interwar period, repeatedly we find small states requesting or, if necessary, trying to buy the assistance of some Great Power or other against some neighbour; and we find again and again that however much had been paid for it, the Great Powers, naturally, handled the alliance to serve their own interests, until, sooner or later, a kind of unilateral friendship—as Hitler put it—was forced

[35] N. Machiavelli: *Il Principe,* Chap. XXI.

upon the weaker party: the Great Power was supportive only to the extent that it was in its interest to be so, and left its smaller confederates in the lurch whenever its interests were not vitally concerned.

France's entrance into an alliance with the Little Entente— preceded by similar approaches on the part of Hungary—which was costing her too much, and Hungary's attempts to win Nazi Germany in the 30s, as well as Romania's repeated efforts to gain Hitler's support against Hungary during the war were all prompted by the same abortive policy.

The leading politicians of the Little Entente, in the first flush of their Versailles victory, were so enchanted by their success, and so blinded by the fact that the triumphant Great Powers had guaranteed not only their independence but also satisfied most of their teritorial claims, that perhaps they themselves believed that they were seeing their dreams come true. They thought they were securing the peoples' right to self-determination (while they were the first to violate it), they believed that the 20th century would be the age of the small states in the Danube Basin as well. But in fact, the interwar period was but a breathing space in the centuries long historical process in the course of which the fate of the small states in the Danube Basin was again and again decided by the dominant Great Powers of the region. The year of 1918 brought about an extraordinary historical situation: the Ottoman Empire on the point of death for centuries, finally expired, and the Habsburg Empire, which had temporarily regained its strength after the serious operation it had undergone more than fifty years earlier, also collapsed. Germany, both economically and politically the most ambitious to possess the area for the preceding twenty-five years, had also become unfit to fight for a while. And, finally, the Russian danger, too, appeared to be over, for the Bolshevik Revolution seemed to be tending toward different historical and social movements.

True, France especially fell eagerly on the Danube Basin, and England, too, appeared again and again on the scene to preserve the balance of power, if for no other reason. But these countries wanted mostly economic hegemony, and for geographical, historical and power-policy reasons ensured the small states a considerably wide range of motion. Consequently, the small states were more likely to feel that their political independence was no mere formality, that their historical path was not simply an instance of constraint. But already at that time it was clear that since the Little Entente regarded France's assistance as a protection against Hungary's territorial claims, Hungary was ready to accept the patronage of any Great Power who would aid her against the Little Entente. Old injuries and new, the ethnic conflicts—not only the question of the Hungarian minorities but also the quarrels between the Czechs and the Slovaks, between the Serbs and the Croats and so on—all came in handy for any Great Power determined to challenge the peace treaties.

The 1930s, naturally, brought revaluations of the old value systems. The social, political and ideological effects of the Depression had undermined the self-confidence of the small nations. Lacking adequate social and economic grounding, the weak points of national independence became manifest. The fact that the effect was not a drawing of consequences, but rather nationalism turning into chauvinism, into autarky, a presentation of relative values as absolute ones, is due, besides the internal political systems of these countries, to international forces as well. The collapse of the world economy seemed to "justify" the trend to autarky, the failure of liberal democracy the attraction to authoritative and Fascist alternatives and the deterioration of the Western democracies the approaches being made to Germany. At the beginning of the 30s, it seemed that there would be more participants in the game of world politics, and that the complexity of the international situation as the multilateral balance of power were all working to expand the range of small-power politics. But, as it soon turned out, this was not to be the case. The rise of Germany did not give the small states more room to manoeuver; on the contrary, they fell more and more under the constraint of the German sphere of influence. German pressure on this region was too strong to be balanced by a defensive France. Clearly, conditions were not only generally favourable, but concretely favoured the country that would attribute special significance to this area, would exploit the economic advantages it offered, and which was strategically located and in the position to have the greatest influence on this area.

From the second half of the 30s on, then, since the countries of the area lacked the preconditions—such as friendly relations between them, a sense of priorities, internal social and economic stability, the ability to exploit the Powers' conflicts of interest, and the willingness to give up irredentist ambitions[36]—which would have enabled them to mount effective resistance to German pressure, there could be little doubt as to the area's incorporation in the German power system. Just how far the independence of the small states in the Danube Basin was compatible with this power system was an open question for quite some time, even if one draws one's conclusions from Hitler's *Mein Kampf* instead of from the German diplomatic statements of the 1930s.

Initially, the small states of the Danube Basin were deprived of their independence ostensibly for ethnic or rather ethno-historical reasons. Of course, the conquest of Austria and Czechoslovakia would have been a death-blow to the Versailles settlement even if it had not been followed by the outbreak of World War II within some months. In any event, Germany's power over the area in 1939 was hardly of the same sort as the English-French influence of the 20s. Germany's dominant economic position, her common borders with several of the countries, and her evident determination to encroach on their territories left even the independent small states extremely vulnerable, especially after Munich had made the possibility of any future assistance by the other Great Powers very questionable indeed.

Though the policy of appeasement seemed to work well at the beginning, they were soon faced with the "Catch-22" so aptly described by the great political thinker, Machiavelli: "Nor will it do for him to say: 'I do not care for anything I desire neither honour nor profit, all I want is to live quietly and without trouble', for such excuses would not be admitted. Men of condition cannot choose their way of living and even if they did choose it sincerely and without ambition they would not be believed, and were they to attempt to adhere to it they would not be allowed to do so by others."[37]

During the war, the states of the Danube Basin lost their independence one after the other. Some of them were completely defeated on the battlefield. The divisions among them made it easier for the triumphant Great Power to finish them off one by one often with their neighbours' support. Others did not fight, but sought to collaborate, trying to save their sovereignty through complete diplomatic and tactical identification. But they all met their fate. Hitler, moreover, did not like small states, and when it was in his political or military interests he put an end to the independence of both his confederates (at least what was left of the satellite states' independence during the war) and his enemies.

[36] A. Baker Fox (*The Power of Small States, Diplomacy in World War II.* Chicago 1959) gives these as possibilities that might have put the small states in a position to resist great power pressure.

[37] N. Machiavelli: *Discorsi,* Book III, Chap. 11.

Hitler's insistence on total subordination—first made explicit though as yet in a peaceful form in the course of the Romanian, Hungarian and Yugoslavian trade negotiations of 1939—implied not some kind of informal empire with German hegemony or dominant influence, but incorporation, exploitation and even plunder, if necessary. For Hitler, there were only two possibilities: either Germany would be a world power or it would cease to exist. After 1939, the kind of dictation in the Danube Basin that this delusion led to necessarily met with more and more domestic and international resistance. Hitler built up the German *Großraumwirtschaft* in a way that lacked all semblance of economic rationality: quite clearly, the end could only be the nemesis of National Socialist rule. Its power stretched to the utmost, Hitler's Germany subjected the area to military occupation and economic plunder, and itself brought about the historical circumstances that led to the overthrow of German hegemony in the Danube Basin.

As World War II drew to a close and it became evident that Nazi oppression was doomed, the question of the future of the Danube Basin became a pressing one. Similarly to other official statements, the Atlantic Charter, which the Soviet Union subscribed to as well, left no doubt that the genocide, the terrible political oppression and economic exploitation in the area had to be a thing of the past. But just as evidently, neither the pre-1938 political nor social *status quo* could be restored. True, the Allies intended to restore the sovereignty of all countries which had fallen victim to German advance, thus, the sovereignty of Hitler's first victims, the small states of Eastern Europe and of the Danube Basin as well. Nevertheless, there could be no real restoration of the past, for in the meantime several new factors had emerged which could not be ignored. The social and moral influence of the Left Wing had grown considerably in the course of the struggle against Fascism and Germany, and had created a changed domestic scene; international politics, the dominance of the Soviet Union altered the circumstances in which the states of the Danube Basin found themselves, with all the social international political consequences that this implied. The military situation indicated that, unlike at the end of the First World War, the chief military force on the continent was not the French army, but the Red Army. But there was also something else that we cannot fail to take into consideration: the interwar period of independence of these small states definitely proved to be far from a highlight in their histories. Nationalism came to preponderate in all of them, so that this part of the world became the scene of permanent intrigue, one against the other, as well as of a series of international conflicts. Moreover, despite all intentions to the contrary, the independent small states did not turn out to be stable elements of the old international system; they proved unable to play either an anti-Soviet or an anti-German part, so that their existence created something of a power vacuum which an ever stronger Germany could easily fill. No wonder the intellectual circles influencing English foreign policy modified their ideas on the nature of small states so thoroughly. During World War I, the keynote had been indiscriminate praise of the small states. Let me quote a few lines from one of the influential booklets published in the Oxford War Pamphlets series: "Almost everything which is most precious in our civilization has come from small states, the Old Testament, the Homeric epos, the Attic and the Elizabethan drama, the art of the Italian Renaissance, the common law of England. Nobody needs to be told what humanity owes to Athens, Florence, Geneva or Weimar. The world's debt to any of these small states exceeds all that issued from the militant monarchies of Louis XIV or Napoleon, or the present Emperor of Germany. The city state served as a school of patriotic virtue not in the men of the blustering and thrasonical type but refined and sublimated by every grace of instinct and reason. It further enabled the experiment of a free direct democratic government to be made with incalculable consequence for the political thinking of the world."[38]

During World War II, many people were of the opinion that the small states of the Danube Basin with the permanent conflicts between them had brought about a power vacuum that had facilitated the outbreak of the war, or at least, had made Nazi aggression easier. E. H. Carr, one of the finest of the liberal historians, had this to say: "The wielding of unlimited economic power by a multiplicity of small national units had become incompatible with the survival of civilization... Once the crabbing and confining effects of small national markets, small national political systems, and even small national cultures come to be felt as restrictions on a larger freedom, the days of the small independent national states, the embodiment of the ideals of 1919, are numbered."[39] Carr's view, shared by many others, was that "Britain and France proved to be unable to establish a lasting order in the Danube Valley in 1919, because they continued to pursue a principle of political and economic disintegration in an age which called for larger and larger units".[40] This idea became the official line of English foreign policy for a while: in 1943 several plans were elaborated for gathering the small states of the Danube Basin in various confederations after the Nazis' expected defeat.

The Soviet Union, on the other hand, did not share this view. The projects for joining the small states in confederations "reminded the Soviet people of a *cordon sanitaire* against the Soviet Union"[41] as one of the documents expressed it. The Soviet political leaders were of the opinion that "an early and a rather forced grouping of the countries into theoretically planned blocs involved dangers to both the small states and the future peaceful development of Europe".[42] The Soviet Union, thus, stood for the restoration of national sovereignty at the Moscow meeting of foreign ministers, and the same view was expressed in the decision to restore Austria's independence.

Of course, the question was not merely of theoretical significance: far more was involved than confederative proposals versus arguments for each country's independence. It was obvious that Russia's interwar years of weakness were over, and no country would be allowed to have its way in the area unless it coincided with Soviet interests.

Churchill, in any case, recognized this much earlier than most politicians of the Danube Basin, and the well-known agreement with Stalin was reached already on October 10, 1944. Today, there are several documents at our disposal which leave no doubt that this agreement did, in fact, take place, though its interpretation still gives rise to much controversy.[43] Churchill and Stalin divided the—politically independent—states of the Danube Basin into zones under English and Soviet influence. The proposed 50—50 division of Hungary which Churchill mentions in his book was modified already the next day. According to the English documents, in the course of the negotiations between Molotov and Eden, the Soviet foreign

[38] H. A. L. Fischer: *The Value of the Small States, Oxford War Pamphlets,* Oxford 1957.

[39] E. H. Carr: *The Twenty Years' Crisis 1919—1939. An Introduction to the Study of International Relations,* New York—Hagerstown—San Francisco—London 1964.

[40] E. H. Carr: *The Future of Nations. Independence or Interdependence?* London 1941.

[41] Gy. Ránki: Kelet-Közép-Európa második világháborús történeti irodalmának kérdései (Problems of the literature on the history of East Central Europe during World War II), *Történelmi Szemle* (1973), No. 3—4, p. 303.

[42] *Ibid.*

[43] C. Gati: *Seven Themes in Search of Reality. Political Life in Postwar Hungary, Hungarian Social History Conference,* Bloomington 1982; and V. Mastny: *Russia's Road to the Cold War,* New York 1979.

minister said the following: "Marshal Stalin thought that after learning of the considerable losses sustained by the Red Army in Hungary, the Army would not understand it if a principle of 50—50 were allotted. Molotov had been instructed by the Marshal (Stalin) to raise the question and to give his opinion." The extent of Soviet authority over Hungary, however, was closely connected with the problem in the other countries of Southeastern Europe. Molotov proposed a 90—10 distribution basis in Bulgaria as well as in Romania. Eden, on the other hand, was of the opinion that greater English influence was to be guaranteed in Bulgaria after the war than in Romania. Emphasizing that the "idea of percentages ... was worthy of consideration", Molotov soon came forward with the first of his proposed package deals, in which he suggested that the percentage distribution in the cases of Bulgaria, Yugoslavia and Hungary alike be 75—25 in favour of the Soviet Union. At the same time, he agreed to a 10—90 distribution for Greece, and 90—10 for Romania. When Eden quickly set this proposal aside, saying that "this is worse than the previous day's proposal" Molotov was ready to let the Western powers have greater influence in Bulgaria, "after the Germans had been beaten". Jumping at the opportunity, Molotov put forward a third package, proposing a 75—25 distribution of Soviet and Western influence in Hungary and Bulgaria, and a 60—40 in Yugoslavia. In his answer to the Soviet proposal, Eden underlined that the English Prime Minister "was greatly interested in Yugoslavia" and then put forward the one and only British counter-proposal of the day: Hungary 25—75, Bulgaria 20—80, Yugoslavia 50—50. On this proposal, the original agreement made by Churchill and Stalin would remain unchanged as far as Yugoslavia was concerned, while Moscow would have greater say in Hungary and Bulgaria. But for Molotov, even this was not enough. Setting Hungary aside for the moment, he answered that "he would agree to 50—50 for Yugoslavia if Bulgaria were 90—10". When Eden rejected this arrangement, Molotov immediately came up with another variation: 75—25 in Bulgaria and 60—40 in Yugoslavia.

The meeting adjourned without the parties' having reached a decision on Bulgaria and Yugoslavia; as far as Hungary was concerned, the Soviet Union agreed to a 75 per cent share of interest. But the next day it began all over again. The meeting continued in the Kremlin on October 11 (at the end of the day the American Ambassador, Averell Harriman, was also invited) and Molotov put forward what was clearly the last Soviet proposal: Hungary 80—20 (as against the 50—50 agreed on by Churchill and Stalin); Bulgaria 80—20 (as against Churchill's 75—25 proposal); and Yugoslavia 50—50 (in accordance with the Churchill—Stalin agreement). The English documents make no mention of resistance to the Soviet proposal. In the end, the Soviet Union had succeeded in increasing its influence in Hungary (Hungary was of less significance to the English) from the 50 per cent proposed two days earlier by Churchill and Stalin to 80 per cent, and in Bulgaria from 75 to 80 per cent. There was no change as far as Yugoslavia was concerned.

Of course, that was not the end of the story. The question of the small states came up again in the course of the negotiations to set up the United Nations, and also during a table-talk at the time of the Yalta Conference about the postwar settlement. Stalin argued that the three Great Powers which had borne the brunt of the war were also responsible for keeping the peace, and therefore should not allow the small states any rights inconsistent with great power interests. Roosevelt seemed to agree on this point, while Churchill was more careful, saying: "The eagle should permit the small birds to sing and care not wherefore they sing."[44] Of course, the

[44] Ch. E. Bohlen: *Witness to History, 1929—1969,* New York 1973.

Preamble of the United Nations Charter declares the United Nations "to reaffirm ... the equal rights ... of nations large and small", but I think this is to be understood in the spirit of Camus, who rated that only the most powerful have the right to absolute freedom. And absolute truth which does away with all contradiction, he added, destroys freedom.

Perhaps Churchill's idea is not the worst solution after all. Eagles should permit the small birds to sing as they like. An old American anecdote gives a good idea of just what this might mean: "The master presented a bottle of whiskey to his black servant, and asked whether he liked the whiskey given him for Christmas. When the servant replied that it was perfect, the master asked what he meant. The servant replied that had the whiskey been any better the master would not have given it to him; had it been worse, he could not have drunk it."[45]

We need to face certain facts. Reinhold Niebuhr, in his *Moral Man and Immoral Society* expressed the crux of the matter when he wrote: "The finest task of achieving justice will be done neither by the Utopians who dream of perfect brotherhood, not yet by the cynics who believe that the self-interest of nations cannot be overcome. It must be done by the realists who understand that nations are selfish and will be so till the end of history, but that none of us, no matter how selfish we may be, can be only selfish. The whole art of politics consists in directing rationally the irrationalities of men."[46]

In this sense, then, we need not lose faith. Perhaps an idea expressed in the course of wartime discussion on the possible value of small states is not utopian after all: "Small states succumb less rapidly to the allurement of power, to the deification of the state. Since they need not invest an ever increasing part of their national income in armaments for aggression, they can devote more of it to their achievement in all fields of science and of the arts. Since they need not have so much militarism and bureaucracy, the value of man and the dignity of the individual are more exclusively preserved." Furthermore, "small states provide excellent political laboratories in which to try out new social experiments and unfamiliar legislation".[47]

Д. Ранки

МАЛЫЕ СТРАНЫ ДУНАЙСКОГО БАССЕЙНА И СИСТЕМА МЕЖДУНАРОДНОЙ ПОЛИТИКИ И ЭКОНОМИКИ В ПЕРИОД 1919—1945 ГГ.

В статье дается определение малого государства и кратко освещается вопрос о том, когда и как встал вопрос о судьбе малых государств в системе международных отношений. Затем автор переходит к периоду между двумя мировыми войнами и на примере небольших придунайских стран показывает те своеобразные экономические, внутри- и внешнеполитические факторы, которые оказывали особенно большое влияние на историю малых государств.

С одной стороны, автор пытается определить, что означала «малая государственность» в системе французской и германской политической гегемонии, почему французская гегемония предоставляла относительно большой простор

[45] Ibid.
[46] R. Niebuhr: *Moral Man and Immoral Society.*
[47] A. Fenler: The Worship of Bigness. Are the Small Nations Doomed? *Social Research,* 1940.

и почему германская гегемония практически была настолько жесткой, что стремилась к ликвидации малых государств.

В статье рассматриваются те экономические условия, которые особенно отрицательное влияние оказали на придунайские малые государства в период большого упадка, те экономические компоненты, которые особенно затрудняли возможности малых стран приспособиться к новым требованиям: это прежде всего сильная зависимость от результатов внешней торговли, их второстепенная, подчиненная роль в мировых экономических процессах сильно мешавшая гибкому ведению хозяйства.

В заключительной части статьи автор анализирует проблемы придунайских малых государств в период между двумя мировыми войнами, заканчивая свой анализ рассмотрением соглашения, касавшегося малых государств, заключенного между Черчиллем и Сталиным в октябре 1944 года.

VII

State and Society in East Central Europe between the Two World Wars

IN OUR TIME, when the state in the majority of countries weighs heavily on society and the conservative criticism of Friedrich von Hayek in the defense of freedom attracts many new supporters, it is perhaps not superfluous to examine the role of the state.[1] Such an examination serves to illuminate the complexity and contradictory character of the process determined by concrete historical circumstances.

I

Liberalism, which theoretically wanted to limit the role of the state in society to a bare minimum, can hardly be harmonized, in a formal sense, with the Marxist conception of the state. Theoretically, the latter believed to have discovered in the state the instrument of suppression of the respective ruling classes, although Marxists admit that the state has (or can have) a compensative role in the alleviation of class antagonism and, at certain times, can even become autonomous and acquire its own functions. Despite their differences, there is a distinct similarity in the liberal and Marxist views of the state. Generalizing from the historical experiences and tendencies of the nineteenth century, both assume that the economic role of the state is minimal and tend to juxtapose state and society, whereby they see the hegemony of society as the classical historical tendency.

Instances that deviate from the assumption of the minimal economic role of the state, such as the well-known case of Germany, are considered as separate paths of development. These could have very serious long-range economic and political consequences leading, in individual cases, to historically distorted development, e.g. fascism. Odd as it may seem, the foregoing notion of separate paths contains the intellectual roots of the thesis of economic backwardness, which found widespread acceptance in the 1960s and which attributed the types and paths of economic development in Europe precisely to the differentiating role of the state.[2]

The twentieth century saw the development of a completely new interpretation of the role of the state, particularly after 1917–1918. In the 1920s traditional liberal concepts, which assumed the possibility of a return to the good old prewar times, occasionally attempted to turn back the theoretical clock. Advocates of such ideals hoped to restore a situation in which free economic and political competition predominated and the state continued to fulfill the economic function of a "night-watchman," to use the well-known characterization coined by Ferdinand Lassalle. If the facts could not be ignored, especially because they were stubborn facts, it was argued that the war and the subsequent revolutions had indeed interrupted the secular flow of events, but their course could not be permanently altered. With the end of the war and the ebbing of the revolutionary tide, the state would be driven back to the position it had before it was pushed into the forefront by the aforementioned events.

War and revolution could be seen as ephemeral (or even accidental) phenomena, but the deep rootedness and durability of their consequences soon became evident even in those countries that, to a large degree, had survived war and revolution intact. In the end, even the staunchest supporters of liberalism could not completely ignore the fact that their ideology was in many respects ridden with crisis, despite the fact that President Woodrow Wilson had adopted Benthamite international principles as his official program. Apart from the war, other serious social problems and numerous manifestations of modern society also served as indications of the deep-seated crisis of liberalism, the solution of which required increasingly severe forms of intervention and administrative control. In the chaos following on the heels of the war and subsequent revolutions, there arose a complicated cavalcade of political forces, of which parliamentary forces were only a part and not the most important one. Of equal importance were the traditional forces, such as the state church, the king, or the officer corps, which articulated their interests through traditional channels or through charismatic leaders in a renovated modern form. In addition, newly formed forces such as social and economic pressure groups appeared and the rapidly expanding role of the bureaucracy quickly exceeded its simple prewar ties to the ruling elite.

II

In East Central Europe the political and economic crisis of liberalism and the ensuing re-evaluation of values was linked to two essential factors. The first was the emergence of a large number of new nation-states as an integral part of the transformation of the old world order. This development, often ingeniously characterized in historical literature as the national revolution, had an especially severe effect on the region. Although these newly founded states were based on the Benthamite-Wilsonian principle of self-determination and were the formal product of a liberal world order, from the moment of their birth these late children of late-liberalism denied, so to speak, the leading principles of liberalism, especially in the form of the new or re-evaluated role of the state. The conviction soon became dominant within the elites of the new countries that liberal principles could serve as a midwife, facilitating the emergence of new states, but that they were insufficient to foster their growth and development. The primacy of the state—i.e., the nation-state—gained in importance in an environment that was strongly influenced by developments in Mussolini's Italy, where the omnipotence of the state had been unilaterally proclaimed. The existence of this ideological system further undermined the liberal world view, which was still reeling from the blows it had received from the victory and preliminary successes of the Russian Revolution. The ideas of the Russian Revolution exerted its strongest influence in East Central Europe, ranging from actual revolutions to attempts at revolution, and from the land question to the severe social problems of the urban proletariat.

We must emphasize at this point that the relationship between society in general and the state in this period in the history of Eastern Europe cannot be seen merely as a delayed though essentially identical phase corresponding to previous developments in Western Europe. Current research has convincingly documented the fact that the state in the East European countries has not been simply the "night-watchman" of modern economic development. Although it is both possible and necessary to differentiate between the respective economic roles played by the Austrian, Hungarian, and Serbian governments, it is sufficient for our purposes to point out the existence of those differences without investigating them more closely.

A further difference in the role of the state in Eastern and Western Europe is the fact that whereas the nation, i.e., the collectivity of the people, served as the foundation upon which the Western European state was formed, the exact opposite was the case in Europe; that is, the state formed the nation. Consequently, liberalism and progress were identified with that which the modern state advocated. However, it must be said that even in the comparatively liberal dual monarchy of Austria-Hungary the relationship between the governors and the governed was different from that in Western Europe, in that constitutionality was considered compatible with the strengthening of the empire's great power position. To a certain degree, the creation of the latter was seen as an essential preliminary condition for the former. Even more so the preservation of certain autocratic prerogatives of the crown in respect to the army and foreign policy, for example, appeared to be essential postulates.

If the emerging social and economic forces after the war led to a reappraisal of the function of the state in general, this reassessment fell on fruitful ground in Eastern Europe, although its beginnings did not point in the same direction in all states of the region. In the case of conservative counterrevolutionary Hungary following the reign of the "White Terror," which enabled the conservative and reactionary forces to regain control, many emergency laws passed during World War I continued in force, thereby permitting the government to further limit democratic rights. The state was presented as a guarantor of national unity, transcending society and, if necessary, establishing an autocratic system of rule in opposition to it.

In addition to new impulses, the reordering of the relationship between society and the state also incorporated important traditional elements. State intervention in Hungary, as well as in Austria and Yugoslavia, was not free of certain value preferences. The re-evaluation of the role of the state was not merely a matter of more efficient economic planning and social management, but also of assuring that all measures accorded with the preservation of the existing fundamentally capitalist order. The recognition of this situation is of limited value, however, if we do not examine how the enhanced role of the state strengthened the function of the bureaucracy and its ties to the dominant social class. In those views that emphasize the neutrality or the unequivocal subordination of the state apparatus, it is easy to discover and demonstrate empirically that the emerging bureaucratic elite associated with the growing influence of the state was closely tied to the ruling class by social origins and contacts. This does not mean, however, that the state as a system of exercising power (including the armed forces and the officer corps) does not represent a relatively autonomous social entity that, through its strongly enhanced role, is enabled to act in a highly independent manner. At the time when modernization as a goal arises, it becomes clear that a modern economy and society cannot dispense with administrative solutions and specific regulations. In that situation, the ideology of the leadership is one question, its realization another. There can be little doubt that the bureaucratic elite responsible for carrying out policy can achieve a dominant position independent of the ideology of the leadership.

III

In the Republic of Austria of late 1918, the Social Democratic party, as the predominant political force within the country, opted, several weeks prior to the institutionalization of the republican form of government, for a complete democratization of the state based on the sovereignty of the people, to be implemented through the election of a new parliament following the introduction of universal suffrage. Bipartisan parliamentary democracy was, at this time, considered the means whereby the will of society as a whole could find full expression and that a thus functioning democratic system could guarantee that only elected representatives of the people could exercise political power. Furthermore, the opinion seems to have predominated that all other (nonelected) governmental institutions, as well as the traditional bureaucratic structures, were thereby subordinated. "A free people in a free country," as the former Chancellor of the Republic Ignaz Seipel put it was, however, far from being realized, considering the fact that the Social Democratic and Christian Democratic interpretations of the concept "free" could not have been farther apart.

The fact that those forces hoping to increase democratic rights were held in check by a national bureaucracy, which, by virtue of its education, traditions, and functions, was by no means an advocate of the newly instituted system but rather a sympathizer with the past political setup, was not an exclusively Austrian phenomenon. This conflict between those social groups who based their authority on freely held elections and those whose power base was found in hierarchical structures, i.e., the contradiction between the bureaucracy and the parliamentary system of government, demonstrates the degree to which bureaucratic barriers can restrict the development of pluralist social institutions.

The escalation of political tension and the inability of one of the two major social groups to gain the upper hand strengthened the position of the governmental institutions. The murderous struggle between the two major political parties also enhanced the power of the state bureaucracy. The Social Democrats' influence was based on their ability to mobilize their vast membership, whereas the Catholic party could depend on the support of the government bureaucracy to shore up its shaky parliamentary majority and enable it to convincingly exercise political power. Nevertheless, the struggle for a democratic majority in favor of limiting state power would in any case have stumbled over the nearly insurmountable problems resulting from the economic crisis, which more or less forced an increase in governmental activity. The poverty, inflation, and the calls for a reordering of the economy, common in this period, all led to an increase in interest in state economic management options. The policy of the Social Democrats which, while limiting the undemocratic aspects of state control whenever possible attempted to expand the power of the welfare state, was of equal importance in this respect. This is exemplified by the activities of the Viennese city council during the 1920s and 1930s.

The increased polarization and social antagonism prevalent during the second half of the 1920s, forcing the country to the brink of civil war, did not lead, however, to a limiting or elimination of parliamentary democracy in this early period. Nevertheless the power of the government was further enhanced, and the presupposition that political democracy was not viable gained ground among the ranks of the Christian Social party, leading to a growing acceptance of authoritarian alternatives, which manifested itself in the ratification of the altered constitution of 1929. The amendments of the original constitution were in themselves minor, but they were imbedded in an ideological framework that assumed that state power was not of popular, but of divine origin, opening the door for the introduction of a corporatist social model. The ideals of the fascist system in Italy were inherent both in the growing strength of the Heimwehr as an additional political force, which existed independently of the official political parties, as well as in the various plans to organize a march on Vienna. Calls for the elimination of the popularly elected government and the introduction of an authoritarian state were becoming increasingly loud. The official Christian Social party line provided for a broadening of the power of the president of the republic, allowing him to exercise emergency powers and introduce dictatorial measures. The shadow of fascism was thus cast over the domestic political struggles of the day.

IV

Developments in postwar Hungary left no doubt that the relationship between the state and society was no longer the same. The two revolutions and the subsequent successful counterrevolution that followed on the heels of the military defeat of the Austro-Hungarian monarchy in World War I, thoroughly transformed the political system and enabled the state to establish its role as power broker. Although the counterrevolutionary regime introduced policies that were unparalleled in any other European country of that day in respect to their antileftist and antisocial thrust, at the same time it incorporated certain aspects of a new and far-reaching alternative, forming new structures through which the conservative state could enhance its hegemonic, political, social, and economic presence.

As of 1921, the Stephen Bethlen regime rejected the totalist approach to a large degree. However, this system did reappear to a certain extent through the integration of certain remnants of the old system into the new political setup. A "golden balance" was proclaimed between "unrestricted liberty and unrestricted dictatorship," while emphasizing that only the wealthy nations could afford democracy. Bethlen introduced a system of pragmatic *étatism* (state control) in which the unstable balance (a balance was never actually achieved in Hungary) between the executive and the legislative was tipped in favor of the former allowing the role and weight of the bureaucracy to reach previously unknown levels. Nevertheless under Bethlen the state, though playing a leading and perhaps dominant role, did not enjoy an absolute monopoly. Bethlen's regime shied away from trying to fully homogenize the entire spectrum of political activity. The various existing organizations were permitted to maintain their own respective structures and, what is more, their respective individual identities.

Andrew János classified the new political system instituted by Bethlen as being corporatist in nature, thereby introducing an important aspect into the discussion on the historical role of the state. According to János, politics plays a platonic role as guardian of the interests of the various separate social classes as well as the national interest as a whole and is thus able to retain a certain degree of autonomy.[3] This seems indeed to be the case as far as the smoothing out of the political and economic contradictions existing between the dominant social classes—primarily the upper middle class and the wealthy landlords—on the one hand and, on the other, the totalist forces among the state bureaucracy. Other social groups such as the peasantry or workers were excluded, however, from government "mediation," although the former were often the object of official propaganda. If corporatism is to be seen as a political system based on bureaucratic administration (as opposed to parliamentary debate), integrationist tendencies (as opposed to social atomization), and social fusion (as opposed to the exclusion of certain groups), then we must acknowledge that the corporatist regime under Bethlen integrated exclusively the interests of the upper and middle classes, while at the same time locking out and antagonizing others, such as the workers, and does not, therefore, fully fit the aforementioned description. The contradiction in the realization of different interests characteristic of the political system in Hungary in the 1920s was not yet strong and was tamed by the improving economic circumstances. Therefore, it posed no threat to the unstable coalition, which propped up the Bethlen regime. With the beginning of the worldwide depression the existing economic and social conflicts escalated, and the corporatist form of cooperation practiced by the dominant classes was increasingly undermined, so that the totalist tendencies inherent in the state bureaucracy could once again gain the initiative.

Julius Gömbös, a leading propagator of totalist developments, had stated at an earlier date that the exercise of force in the interest of the nation as a whole was only possible in connection with a "strong government [and] hierarchically structured society."[4] Antiliberalism had thus progressed to open antiparliamentarianism and anticommunism into opposition to democracy in general. The proponents of a dominant state were gradually narrowing the gap between themselves and the supporters of a totalist state.

V

The peoples of Yugoslavia who had, for the first time in their history, joined the community of states during the aftermath of World War I, had to deal with a very heterogenous inheritance. Faced with the fact that both the centrifugal and centripetal forces within the country were very influential, it soon became obvious that despite the existence of a shared language and common goals and interests the state remained the only true common denominator among the various South Slav peoples. Whereas in the past the Western European state served as the legal framework within which the national community could develop, in this period the Yugoslav state represented the very basis of national unity. The discrepancy between the two interpretations of the state is therefore tremendous. In the case of Yugoslavia, the state was by no means a mere framework that served the sole purpose of defining the limits of the newly established political entity, but rather an institution that penetrated all levels of social, political, and cultural existence. This state, founded as it was from above and from without, was endowed with the responsibility of guaranteeing the further existence of Yugoslavia as a united country. This led to the predominance of a centralist conception of the state, as opposed to the federalist alternative, thus automatically undermining the basis of parliamentarianism and increasing the power of the central government and other state institutions. The political culture in the country thereby took on an air of authoritarianism from the very beginning. The "Law to Defend the State," which outlawed the Communist party, prohibited strikes by government employees, and limited the rights of the trade unions, was a typical product of this period. Dictatorial tendencies increased in strength commensurate to the degree to which popular political opinion openly propagated the federalism and, more emphatically, the new, mainly Serbian bureaucracy, attempted to free itself of public control and even to subjugate society as a whole through the use of the power of the state and royal institutions, irrespective of the constitutionality of such action. This development reached a climax on 6 January 1929, as the king, with the backing of the state bureaucracy and the military, officially proclaimed the introduction of an authoritarian regime, thereby ending the short period of relative democracy in the country.

The parliamentary form of government had also been weakened by the local political party system. Few of the leading parties were supranational, the majority being organized along narrow national and local lines. This meant that the recurring clashes and differences of opinion became incorporated into a number of wider social, economic, and nationalist conflicts. Lacking a lasting power base, the government majorities were mainly the result of provisional and relatively unstable coalitions, leading to the establishment of twenty-four governments within less than ten years. The state, i.e., the executive, in coalition with the army and traditional bureaucracy, was therefore seen as the only force capable of holding the country together.

Although party pluralism was again established in 1931, the parties that were reactivated were largely "state owned" (*verstattlichte*) organizations in that they depended on the state for support. The parties did not grow out of society in order to guide and shape the state; they were created from above by the state for the purpose of directing society. Along with the trade unions, the numerous nationalist organizations, Yugoslavism with its expressly antiparliamentary and corporatist ideology, to say nothing of the openly fascist Ustasha, all were products of this strongly "nationalized" political life. This process was intensified by the effects of the worldwide economic depression, which influenced the thrust of the constitution of 1931, transforming the nature of the Serbian-Croatian-Slovenian kingdom and increasing political centralism.

VI

Irrespective of their status as victors or vanquished, all three Pannonian states were overwhelmed by the necessity of reorganizing their countries along new political and economic lines. The economies of the region were, as in the case of the respective political systems, in dire need of the guiding hand of the state.

The steps taken in the 1920s by the governments of the region were more or less free of ideological trappings, although nationalism was a key propaganda tool in all cases. The respective domestic authorities argued that the emergency steps taken in order to reestablish stability were only temporary, and that as soon as the international economic situation had improved and the political situation had returned to normal restrictions would be lifted. The main interventionist actions taken by the Yugoslav state aimed at reducing the inequalities existing between the various regions of the country, the unification of the currency, the introduction of necessary supraregional legal structures, and the reorganizing of the transportation system to link the newly acquired territories with the capital (Belgrade). Lacking adequate private initiative, the state was required to breach the gap and set up institutions which, in the long run, could guarantee national economic sovereignty. Thus economic and political nationalism went hand in hand with a further expansion of the role of the state.

The fear that continued economic dependency would sooner or later undermine newly won national-political independence led to an ideological fusion of the ideals of autarchy and autocracy. The increase in state power was seen as a prerequisite to national survival and served as the basis for yet another increase in government intervention. The dominant nationalist ideology held that all legislation and state action was to be judged according to its ability to strengthen national unity. As in Yugoslavia, this idea also seems to have strongly influenced conditions in

Hungary which, after four hundred years of various forms of foreign domination, had finally reestablished complete political independence, but was still reeling from the loss of its territories by the Trianon peace treaty. A powerful state was required as a panacea, which fit the needs of many who refused to acknowledge Hungary's diminished territorial position.

Nationalism did not play the same role in Austria that it did in the other countries of the region. Doubts shared by many citizens concerning the ability of the country to survive on its own and the particulars of domestic politics in the 1920s discouraged the development of an Austrian national consciousness. However, the economic woes that plagued the country in this period and the interventionist social and taxation policies of the influential Social Democratic party led to an increase in the economic power of the state. It is essential to emphasize that Hungarian and Yugoslavian state intervention was autocratic in nature, whereas the Austrian government followed policies which can only be characterized as an early form of welfare state. Nevertheless, the fact remains that economic conditions in all three Pannonian countries were indeed very similar, regardless of the political goals set by the respective local governments, and furthermore the role played by the national bureaucracies of these countries ran parallel. One of the main weaknesses of Austrian democracy in this period was the continued influence of unchanged bureaucratic structures. The results of the fierce class and party struggles in Austria presented sufficient "evidence" for those who believed that democracy was self-destructive and that only a hierarchically organized autocratic (as opposed to welfare) state could solve the country's problems.

Ideological advocates of a dominant state within the Austrian Christian Social party, as well as active supporters of these ideals, such as Othmar Spann, saw their theories, developed in the early 1920s, confirmed by the economic and social conditions resulting from the worldwide depression beginning at the end of the decade (1929–1933). The limited prosperity of the Pannonian region, resulting from years of slow improvement, was gone overnight and with it social stability. The economic crisis that affected all social strata—from the newly impoverished working and middle classes to the upper-middle and upper classes, was paralleled by an ideological crisis of enormous proportions. The liberal and democratic groups within the ruling elite were forced into retreat and were eventually completely defeated. This was accompanied by a steady increase in the influence of the dictatorial, fascist forces. Encouraged by the ultimate defeat of the liberal philosophy of free economic and social competition, these groups set out to restructure the function of the state, a state from which it was expected that it could reorder and revitalize the workings of the domestic economy, reorganize labor relations (possibly through the introduction of limited social reforms), and institutionalize the omnipotent role of the government in society. These radical changes, which to a degree had already been introduced in a more limited form in the early 1920s, were no longer seen as emergency steps to be rescinded at a later date, but as prerequisites to the achievement of social, economic, and political stability. As late as the 1927 international trade conference, protective duties and government trade policy were declared to be a mere framework needed to assist the self-regulation of free international trade and that such state intervention would soon be gradually reduced. The exact opposite proved to be the case. Not only were protective duties drastically increased, but a wide variety of protectionist measures, quotas, customs conflicts, various import barriers, and the like, threatened to change the very nature of international trade.

VII

The financial crisis of 1931 completely undermined the international economic ties of the three small states. Government intervention was required to avoid a widespread economic collapse. The Viennese Creditanstalt, which prior to World War I belonged to the leading European banks and which still enjoyed extensive influence domestically as well as in Hungary and to a lesser extent in Yugoslavia, was forced to fall back on state support in order to escape the threat of bankruptcy. The Hungarian government implemented a credit moratorium and blocked access to the banks for several days, thereby minimizing the effects of the crisis. A long list of decrees and regulations documented that the new function of the state was no longer limited to the creation of the social and legal framework of an otherwise free market, but rather that the state intended to bring the internal workings of the economy under its control. From this point on, foreign trade and foreign currency were brought under the control of the state through the introduction of a wide variety of measures, including the regulation of the currency rate, suspension of free convertability, credit barriers, the broadening of the powers of the National bank, and strict controls on foreign trade. The classical and neoclassical theories of a self-regulating economy lay in ruins, and John Maynard Keynes, who called attention to such eventualities as early as 1927, theoretically formulated the untenability of the classical theory of equilibrium.[5]

By propagating a moderate form of state intervention and the inflationary financing of increased demand, Keynes promoted the already existing quasi-intuitive economic policies to the status of an official doctrine. Thus state intervention was not only theoretically substantiated by enabling the dominant state to come out of the closet, so to speak, but Keynes opened the door to the linking up of his theories with those of individuals and groups holding the most varied social and political conceptions.

Although the actual application of state economic planning in Austria, Yugoslavia, and Hungary fell far short of the level of effectiveness reached following World War II, certain improvements were achieved. A complete collapse of the economy was avoided, and modest improvements were attained during the second half of the 1930s. The social system was ostensibly rescued and impending revolution detoured. The regimes were able to function and improve the economic situation to a degree. The Keynesian revolution, which followed this crisis, dismantled the last barriers existing between the state and civilian life, thereby allowing the state bureaucracy and state apparatus as a whole not only to act in the interest of the dominant economic strata, but also to directly influence their behavior. The dogma of economic growth replaced the holy creed of private ownership as the predominant ideology of the day. Society suffered a severe defeat as its relation to the state became fundamentally transformed. The most autonomous spheres of civilian society, including the economic sphere which in opposition to the political sphere had until then proudly announced its independence of the government, became enmeshed in the net of the state. When the state has so much freedom of action in the economy, no one could be surprised that its political role became evaluated anew, and that its relationship to civil society and its members became transformed in the course of the 1930s, or that authoritarian tendencies and fascist strivings became the dominant political current of the time.

The complete turnabout of events in Austria was indeed singular in realm. Whereas in the 1920s parliamentary democracy loosened control of society by the state, political developments during 1933 and 1934 led to a gradual introduction of authoritarianism. Government by decree was soon to be followed by a modification of the constitution. The so called May Constitution of 1934 marked the end of parliamentary government and the pluralist political party system, which were replaced by the corporate state.

Similar developments in Hungary were introduced by Julius Gömbös—the head of the traditionalist group of army officers that had dominated during the counterrevolution, the founder of the ultrarightist, race-purification opposition party, and the crony of the military establishment. The ninety-five articles set forth by Gömbös were based on the idea of the self-serving nation-state acting in the interest of the national community. The Hungarian government hoped that by adopting various aspects of Italian fascism, particularly the idea of corporatist state rule, it would further limit the influence of the already atrophied power of the parliament and advance and ultimately perfect its own extended power structures. Typical of this policy were the attempts to prohibit strikes and disband the trade unions as well as eliminate individual rights such as free speech and free assembly. These and other steps taken by the increasingly omnipotent state demonstrated that although total control over society was never fully realized in Hungary in the period between the two world wars, the balance of power did shift dramatically in favor of the dominance of the state.

In Yugoslavia, a royal dictatorship was introduced before the outbreak of the economic crisis. However by allowing for the existence of a plurality of political parties, the Constitution of 1931 checked somewhat the totalist tendencies prevalent at the time, although there were continuous efforts to increase the role of the state. The result of these opposing tendencies was a unique political mix of the political outlook of the traditional Balkan ruling elite, which accorded with the preservation of the predominant position of the old oligarchy and modern authoritarian impulses. The latter were represented in their most extreme form by Milan Stojadinović, who attempted to transplant to Yugoslavia the institutions of German and Italian fascism in both form and substance.

VIII

An analysis of the East European states demonstrates that, while different in many aspects, the respective national developments in the crisis-ridden period between the two world wars had one common denominator: the strengthening of the state or, to be more exact, the introduction of a new type of interaction between the dominant political circles and society as a whole. Highly influenced by historical circumstances particular to East Central Europe, developments in this region, however divergent they may have been, did reflect the general European crisis of social and economic liberalism manifest in the worldwide depression of 1929 to 1933. Kurt Schuschnigg, Austrian chancellor from 1934 to 1938, was correct in saying that the collapse of the Old Order of things following the Russian Revolution and the Peace of Versailles was the beginning of the totalitarian era in Central Europe.[6]

The twentieth century has seen the realization of the Hobbesian "Leviathan state." This bureaucratic beast seems indeed to be the product of advanced, industrialized civilization that, by necessity, has created its own political, social, and cultural set of values. If the Montesquieuian balance of power between the state and the autonomous sociocultural sphere is seen as the guarantee of liberty in modern society, then the new, extended role of the present state does present an awesome threat.

The interventionist state is indeed potentially totalitarian. This potential can, however, be checked. Although the traditional balance of power between the state and society has been eliminated through the historical events of the period between the two world wars, the Tocquevilleian contradiction between the desire of people to be led and their will to be free, does offer a basis for the maintenance of liberty under existing conditions.[7] This leaves us with two alternatives: (1) a welfare state, which redefines the relationship between the state and society, leaving enough room for a degree of social autonomy; and (2) the modern authoritarian totalitarian state, which either severely limits the scope of action within the social sphere or eliminates it almost altogether. The tragedy of the three East Central countries dealt with here, and of the region in general, is that during the 1930s they all trod the second path.

State and Society in East Central Europe

NOTES

1. Friedrich August von Haydek, *The Road to Serfdom* (Chicago: Chicago University Press, 1962).
2. Alexander Gerchenkron, *Economic Backwardness in Historical Perspective* (Cambridge: Cambridge University Press, 1962).
3. Andrew János, *The Politics of Backwardness in Hungary* (Princeton: Princeton University Press, 1982).
4. Sandor Konya, *A Gömbös Kormany* (Budapest: Akademia, 1964).
5. John Maynard Keynes, *The End of Laissez Faire* (London: Leonard and Virginia Woolf, 1926).
6. Kurt Schuschnigg, *Farewell to Austria* (New York: Putnam, 1946).
7. Alexis Tocqueville is found in E. Schapiro, *Totalitarianism* (Praeger: New York, 1972).

PART III

LIMITS OF REFORMING STATE SOCIALISM AND THE TRANSFORMATION AFTER ITS COLLAPSE

This section contains the studies of Ivan T. Berend, published during the 1980s and 1990s. His research closely followed the contemporary transformation of Hungary and Central and Eastern Europe. His analysis of reforms and their limitations became part of a struggle for radical reform. After the collapse of state socialism he took part in the international debate about transforming Central and Eastern Europe.

The first two studies cover the main reform measures of Hungary and their sever limitations. The third and fourth studies give a broad international picture on the end of century changes in economic thinking and policy and present a worldwide framework for a better understanding of the dramatic transformation and its sub-regional disparities in Central and Eastern Europe.

VIII

The First Phase of Economic Reform in Hungary: 1956–1957

In keeping with the socio-political changes that were taking place in postwar Hungary, a three-year plan was introduced in the summer of 1947, its aim being the economic reconstruction of the country after its grievous war losses. On January 1, 1950, the first five year plan was introduced; adopting the methods of the Soviet planned economy of the 1930s, it was based on Stalin's policy of industrialization and agricultural collectivization.

The bureaucratic war economy of the 1950s — accumulation was projected at 35% of national income and annual industrial growth rates of as much as 20% in some sectors were planned — which was designed to industrialize Hungary, an agricultural-industrial country, within five years, and to collectivize the peasant farms that had come into being with the land redistribution of 1945 in an even shorter time, proved unrealistic. Within a few years, the accumulation and the extraordinarily rapid growth rate had led to a fall in real wages of more than 20%. Shortages were the rule, and there were serious problems of distribution, so that the government was obliged to introduce rationing. There were no signs, however, of any change in policy: official propaganda spoke with obligatory optimism of plans successfully filled, and, oblivious to the harsh reality that no one could fail to perceive, even spoke of rising standards of living.

After Stalin's death, however, things began to change. In June of 1953, the Central Committee of the Hungarian Workers' Party [formed in 1948 through the fusion of the Communist and the Social Democratic Parties, and the country's ruling — and only — political party] came out with a forceful condemnation of a number of the mistaken policies of the previous years. Imre Nagy replaced Mátyás Rákosi as Prime Minister. The new party programme constituted a strong public criticism of the economic policies of the first five year plan. The changed atmosphere was conducive to economic analysis and economic debate. Between 1953 and 1956, the mistakes in the planning and control mechanism were convincingly demonstrated; proposals were made as to the principles on which reform should be based, and some tiny and cautious practical steps were even taken. [Early efforts of this kind were György Péter's pioneering economic study, János Kornai's critical analysis, and the corrective measures taken by the Planning Office]. Suffice it to say that by the autumn of 1956, Hungary's economists and *some* government circles were beginning to see the need for radical reform. This is well illustrated by a comment made by Miklós Ajtai on the occasion of the presentation of János Kornai's Ph. D. thesis. " The measures specifically taken to rationalize our economic system have been very successful in curbing its distortions and faults, and might continue to be so. These measures, however, are geared to deal not with the root of the problem nor with the original source of the difficulties, but rather with the consequences ". His survey of the economic debate, and the various contributions calling for radical change, ended in the following terms: " This detailed examination of the matter inexorably leads to our final conclusion: our economic system, as a coherent whole, is mistaken ".[1]

[1] Ph. D. thesis presentation, *Közgazdasági Szemle* (Economic Review), Nov.-Dec. 1956, p. 1483.

A month later, battles were raging in the country's streets. Our story really begins only after this, however, once the tragic autumn of 1956 had passed.

The plan for radical reform

The government headed by János Kádár that assumed power in the early winter of 1956 (with the help of the Soviet army) could have no doubt over the need for radical reform. It seemed that a great many things would have to be started anew. Hungarian communists closed ranks around a new platform, and under a new name: the Hungarian Socialist Workers' Party was now the ruling party in a one-party system. The party's new leaders had little to do with the policies of the previous decade; their first and most significant statement, passed by the provisional Central Committee in early December of 1956, reflected this: " The Rákosi-Gerö clique ... had adopted a sectarian and dogmatic economic policy ... and bureaucratic methods of leadership ". Among the things to be done, they emphasized the need for an economic system " which used financial incentives in every sphere: to encourage technical improvement, to promote better quality... Planning has not become less important, but it must address itself to different tasks: it must concentrate primarily on determining the ratios in which the various sectors of the economy are to be developed " ...[2]

Accordingly, when the Economic Commitee, the government's chief organ of economic decision-making, met in December of 1956, President Antal Apró declared that " there was a need for the creation of a comprehensive commission of economists, workers'-council members, and industrial and agricultural experts to work out for the goverment the problems

[2] *A Magyar Szocialista Munkáspárt határozatai és dokumentumai* (Resolutions and documents of the Hungarian Socialist Workers' Party), 1956-1962, Kossuth Könyvkiadó, 1964, pp. 13, 23.

relevant to economic policy planning and to economic management ".[3] Soon, the commission of experts was set up, with eleven sub-committees of 15 to 30 members each, to deal with the following areas: domestic and foreign trade, wages and labour, prices and material control, industrial production and organization, finance, etc. Two higher committees were to harmonize their work: the Commission for Industrial Production headed by György Péter, the President of the Central Statistical Office; and the supreme coordinating Economic Commission, whose president was Professor István Varga [the Director of the Institute for Economic Research before the war, and economic adviser to the majority Small-holders' Party during the years of coalition government just after], and whose secretary was István Antos, a member of the government. The composition and leadership of the commission left no doubt that this panel of experts would come up with a plan for radical reforms. This, obviously, was what significant forces within the party and in the government were, in fact, counting on, though others were inclined to regard the heterogeneous, " popular-front " composition of the commission as a tactical move, and wanted to channel its activities by directives, and so leave it out of the drafting and coordination of the final economic programme.[4] This, however, proved to be a minority view.

But let us stop here for a moment to consider an earlier

---

[3] Archives of the Institute for Party History of the Hungarian Socialist Workers' Party (hereafter: Party History Archives), 288 f. 23/1957, Minutes of the Dec. 10, 1956 session of the Economic Committee.

[4] According to István Friss' proposals of Dec. 12 and 15, " the Economic Committee should work out the shorter programme that is to serve as guideline... with a great many experts then taking part in working out the more detailed programme... Among the experts there should, if possible, be a great many non-party members, and older experts who had acquired their reputation before the war." The suggestions of the expert commission were to be co-ordination by the government Economic Committee, which was to work out " the entire programme ". Party History Archives 288 f. 23/1957, Proposal on the commissions to be set up to work out the government economic programme, Dec. 12, 1956.

event. Before the government commission of experts had even been set up, the Ministry of Finance had worked out its own very precise draft for the radical transformation of Hungary's economic system. *The contemporary issues of the planning and control of the national economy*, prepared on Dec. 5, 1956, had this to say: " The fact that the great majority of the means of production have been nationalized continues to make economic planning necessary. From this it follows that the national economy needs to be developed, and that a national programme specifying the correct proportions and relations must be worked out. However, the companies are now being run along plans that have been approved by the workers' councils. We have yet to solve the problem of how the national programme and the plans of the independent companies are to be brought into harmony... The general principle is that the national economic programme *must not be made company-specific.* The programme must be realized through influencing the companies by economic means. The companies must become independent, but certain spheres must remain under central control for the government which remains able to exert economic influence on them ".[5]

To this end, the draft proposed central investment, the central distribution of vital materials, and the central control — at least temporarily — of wages. (For instance, they proposed that the per capita average wage to be paid in 1957 be centrally specified).

It followed from the nature of indirect planning and control (operating without compulsory plan indexes) that " one of the most decisive problems of reorganizing the national economy involved the price system. What was needed was a price system that... was flexible enough to adapt to practical needs ". The draft proposed that consumer products should have centrally specified

[5] Party History Archives, 288 f. 23/1957, The timely issues of the planning and control of the national economy. Ministry of Finance, Dec. 5, 1956 (my italics).

set prices; the prices of the means of production were to be negotiable, with central influence in this case being exerted in the form of price controls on the most important raw materials.

A whole new system of economic incentives must also be worked out. " The new economic order must rely more on the profit motive... All this argues in favour of the introduction of profit sharing ". This was to be done immediately, and " was, at any rate, being pressed for by the workers' councils ". (It was also proposed that company profits go not only to the state budget but also into profit-sharing, and the investment, renewal, and welfare funds of the firms).

The draft worked out by the Ministry of Finance was linked with a more comprehensive work started jointly in December of 1956 by a group of 30-40 experts from the Ministries of Finance and of light and heavy Industry, from the banks and from the National Planning Office. They were ready with their proposals in early January of 1957, so that by the spring these were being debated in various forums. Opinions were greatly divided on a number of issues; it was to clarify their position that 6 members of the planning group published their views in the *Közgazdasági Szemle* (Economic Review) in April 1957.[6]

It is not my purpose here to go into the details of these proposals; the chief principles were in harmony with those expressed in the Finance Ministry's draft; as for the main ideas, these were adopted in the reform programme (which will be described in detail) presented by the coordinating Economic Commission. Let us, then, turn to look at it.

This — let us call it " interministerial " — commission started out with the idea that planning had to be made viable by doing away with the system that " broke the plans down " for mini-

---

[6] JÁNOS BOKOR, OTTÓ GADÓ, PÁL KÜRTHY, TAMÁS MEITNER, MRS. SÁNDOR SÁROSI, JENÖ WILCSEK: Javalast az ipar gazdasági irányitásának uj rendszerére (Proposal on the new system of industrial economic management), *Közgazdasági* Szemle, April, 1957, pp. 371-392.

stries and firms by compulsory directives; what was needed was a system of economic incentives to motivate the companies. The basis of economic activity and motivation in the new system was to be a " price system based on the law of value ", including non-fixed consumer prices as well.

The reform envisaged a special amalgam of central direction operating along with market factors. It seemed necessary " ... to get away from industrial production being primarily a matter of directives. At the same time, we do not think the introduction of some kind of purely market mechanism (free prices, production dependent on market demand, foreign competition, the absence of central direction) to be desirable either ". The main line of each company was to be determined by the ministry in charge. ' To start a new line, to change it, or to drop a line... requires the permission of the supervisory authority ". In the same way, certain basic materials were to be distributed centrally, and prices were to be a combination of fixed and free prices.

At the same time, suggestions were made for organizational and institutional changes that would foster the companies' independence. " It would be a mistake to believe, however, that this can be achieved while leaving the companies' present organizational framework untouched... The new mechanism requires that ... companies that have been forcibly broken up be reincorporated. Likewise we should consider the possibility of pooling some of the small companies that can function quite efficiently on their own ". The planners considered " some kind of agglomeration which would represent the interests of the industrial branch as a whole " as an important prerequisite of the functioning of the new mechanism. The reform programme worked out in December and January thus aimed at a balance between central planning and greater responsiveness to market influences.

The new approach to economic planning formulated in early December relied heavily, as we have seen, on the company workers' councils; in a way, their existence was the programme's point of departure: " Centralism, bureaucratic economic planning ", the preamble to the Finance Ministry's draft pronounced, " has been replaced on the workers' own initiative by the workers' councils and worker self-management. The new circumstances have made many aspects of economic planning problematic, and answers are urgently needed, at least on the theoretical plane ".[7]

For all that, I shall not be dealing with the issue of worker self-management. For one thing, it deserves separate treatment; for another, it was primarily a political, not economic issue: no really significant suggestion linked the proposed economic reforms with the workers' councils. True, their activity was always in the background, and all the reform proposals considered the workers' councils compatible with working of the proposed reforms. Nevertheless, the new economic system was treated as an independent matter. The interministerial committee, for instance, took a definite stand on the matter: "We cannot agree with those who think that the introduction of a new system is necessitated by the existence of the workers' councils ".[8]

The commission of economic experts called by the government had this to say: The Coordinating Economic Commission's suggestions for the new principles along which the socialist companies are to work, " the Commission would hold to be expedient even if no workers' councils were taking part in the companies' direction ".[9]

Before going on to describe the Commission's activities, let me just note that by the eve of 1957, Hungary's top political leaders — as the party's Central Committee's statement of December, 1956, well shows — were determined to introduce some

---

7 Party History Archives, 288 f, 23/1957, The timely issues of the planning and control of the national economy, Ministry of Finance, Dec. 5, 1956, (my italics).

8 Bokor, Gadó, Kürthy, Meitner, Sárosi, Wilcsek, *op. cit.*, p. 375.

9 Party History Archives, 288 f. 23/1957, The second proposal of the Economic Commission for the economic program of the Revolutionary Worker-Peasant Government, May 29, 1957.

radical changes. The preparation of the reform was considered as a political success, and was given a great deal of publicity.

Early in January 1957, an article appeared in the *Népszabadság* (People's Liberty) — the party's central daily — with the title: " What will the new method of economic planning be like? " Earlier economic mechanisms, " inasmuch as they directed everything from above, with masses of compulsory directives which suppressed the companies' independence... frustrated the potential as much as recognizing the real interests of the national economy ". The new " economic mechanism needed has been much talked about for some time now... However, there have been obstacles to getting the work under way, primarily because of the resistance of the former economic and party leaders with their stubborn devotion to the old ways... With the removal of these obstacles, work has been speeded up. The National Planning Office has set up a separate department for the working out of the guidelines of the new economic mechanism; ... the chief means of government influence on the economy are to be not compulsory directives but its planned influencing through economic methods ".[10] A week later, the newspaper noted that " the mistaken economic methods gave people no stake in production "; now that the companies are to be " treated as grownup ", people will have an interest in their economic operation.[11] In early February, a series of interviews reported on the government programme being prepared. György Péter gave an account of the work being done by the Commission he headed, of how " financial incentives and economic accountability " were to replace directives. Jenö Wilcsek reported on the plans for the new price system.[12] Another week later, the *Népszabadsàg* emphasized the work being done by these committees on the democratization of industrial management. " The democratization

---

10 *Népszabadság* (People's Liberty), Jan. 5, 1957.
11 *Népszabadság*, Jan. 12, 1957.
12 *Népszabadság*, Feb. 7, 1957.

of industrial management is an important precondition of the building of socialism, a requirement that we neither want to nor will give up ".[13]

There is no need to keep adding examples. Besides the newspaper articles meant for the public, however, it is interesting to look at the statements made by the trade unions, by way of directives to their activists. In February 1957, the National Council of Trade Unions gave the following impatient assessment of the economic situation: " As yet, we do not have as much as a clear outline of the new economic mechanism. The present economic situation might well temporarily necessitate a centralism that is even more absolute than before (for instance, in the distribution of raw materials and fuels), but the various ordinances and statements... are not explicit enough about the temporary nature of the momentarily justified centralized measures, but tend to emphasize, rather too strongly, the necessity of centralization in the future as well... All too often we identify the need for a planned economy with the destructive method of centralization... there is no more time to lose in formulating definite views on both the structure of the economy, and the new economic mechanism ".[14]

In the first months of 1957, there was considerable political pressure for the radical transformation of the economy. The government, or more precisely, the committees of experts delegated by its Economic Commission, had set to work immediately.

Each committee had to submit its suggestion within a month; accordingly, the body in charge of coordinating their findings and working out a final draft, the coordinating Economic Committee headed by István Varga and István Antos, was able to submit its proposals very soon indeed. The first comprehensive

13 *Népszabadság*, Feb. 17, 1957.

14 Party History Archives, 288 f. 23/1957, Economic Report of the National Trade Union Council, Preliminary bulletin on the January economic situation; February 11, 1957.

reform programme was ready at the beginning of March, 1957, and the first part of the programme was submitted to the government by the end of April. At the end of May, the second half was presented with the title " The planning of the national economy, and the factors and methods of plan fulfilment "; on June 1, an all-inclusive proposal was presented.

We can hardly overestimate the significance of these proposals, for they gave a comprehensive and systematic reform programme for every sphere of the working of the economy: organization, plannning and company activities.

The all-inclusive proposal [15] on which what follows is based was divided into three chapters. The first described the economic situation of the moment; the second the basic principles that were the points of departure of the new economic policy; while the third chapter described the new mechanism of economic control and planning. " Staying closely on the path of centrally-directed socialist economic planning ", the preamble declared, " we, too, must find those means and methods which will enable us to make our economic planning more flexible, but only for the sole purpose of making it a more effective instrument for realizing the centrally prescribed plans ". " There are areas in which immediate directives will always be necessary ", the document continues, " but the proper, deliberate use of indirect means of influence will make a significant proportion of the immediate directives superfluous ". " Annual plans will still need to be made on the basis of the long-range plans for the national economy, and the directing bodies will be responsible for their realization within their own sphere of influence. It is only by way of an exception, however, that the various concrete plans will be given a company-by-company breakdown: for the directing bodies will see to the fulfilment of the plans that fall

---

[15] Party History Archives, 288 f, 23/1957, The Economic Commission's all-inclusive proposals for the government's economic programme, June 1, 1957.

within their competence mostly by indirect methods. Thus the plans must define also the instruments and methods by means of which the directing bodies will be able to guarantee the fulfilment of the plan ".

The reform programme declared that the government "considered company independence one of the bases of the new system of planning ". For it to be that, however, it was vitally necessary for " the ratios of the factory prices in the price system to be an accurate reflection of the ratios of the corresponding production and social costs ".

The price reform was to affect everything from industrial factory prices through service costs to consumers' prices. Besides the introduction of fixed, maximum and free prices, it was considered inevitable that consumer price ratios should also be transformed to reflect real values: " At the same time as the new price system is introduced... the basic costs of living are to be made more proportionate in terms of one another ". Substantial increases were to be made within a period of 3 to 5 years in rents, public transport fares, and in service costs, with the consumers' expenses being compensated by wage rises (rent allowances) to come from cuts in the value-added tax built into the price of industrial goods. What was more, " Hungary's peculiar circumstances make it increasingly pressing for us to give adequate consideration to world market prices in working out our new price system. To be able to set proper prices on imports, what we need first of all is to determine a realistic exchange rate... The prices of imported raw materials must reflect the real costs of acquiring them ". At the same time, " the exporting productive enterprises must acquire an interest in selling abroad at foreign market prices. These enterprises must be paid the price at which the goods were sold abroad in forints calculated at the real exchange rate ". The entrerprises would, thus, have the market prices to orient them, and to give them an interest in production. In keeping with this line of thought, the proposal took a stand for the immediate introduction of profit sharing. For the enterprises to become independent, however, the systems of company investments and financing also needed to be altered. For this reason, "... we are introducing a system of supplying the enterprises with fixed and floating assets which puts an end to the present practice of their using fixed and circulating assets free of charge, and will require them to pay rent for the fixed assets, and a relatively high interest on the circulating assets they use".

The reform programme dealt also with the management of the economy. In the new system the National Planning Commission would be the chief managing body, which was to include, besides the various economic ministers and bank presidents, economic experts in every field. "The ministries are to be relieved of a great deal of their operational work". Their tasks were to be mainly the working out of development plans, preparing investments, gathering market information, and supervising the interprises. Direct management was to cease at the intermediate level too, its place being taken by pools and corporations coordinating related groups of enterprises, bodies which were to be in direct contact with the ministries. As an earlier draft of the programme put it: "We ought to examine whether after a certain transitional period it would not be better to set up one unified ministry of industry".[16]

In spite of the plans for radical changes, the reform programme contained an extraordinary number of safeguards to guarantee the effectiveness of central planning. Primary among these was the provision that investments were to continue to be allocated from a centralized budget.[17] The reform proposal considered

---

[16] Party History Archives, 288 f. 23/1957, Proposals on the shaping of the country's economic structure and mechanism, March 2, 1957, István Antos, István Varga.

[17] Increased company independence, therefore "can nowhere mean that central direction is abandoned or even slackened. Thus, for example, though the companies can make proposals regarding investments, ... the decision on what investments to make

the central allocation of materials likewise necessary for a long time to come, maintaining that it could be done away with only when goods were " plentiful ". Central control over prices was also built into the system, the free formation of prices by the market being envisaged only in certain areas, and even there only when goods were abundant.[18] In addition, the system of immediate economic directives was also declared to be tenable under certain — not precisely specified — conditions.

The commission of economic experts, much as they were committed to radical change, included realistic transitional measures in their reform programme, as well as guarantees of effective central direction. Although substantial structural changes were undeniably proposed by the all-inclusive reform programme submitted in the summer of 1957, there were definite signs of compromise, of an inclination to moderate the demands for reform. This is demonstrated by the letter written on June 17, 1957 by István Varga and István Antos to Antal Apró, president of the government's Economic Committee. In this letter the heads of the expert Commission informed him that four members of the Commission had submitted a minority paper along with the second report of May 29. By way of background, we read the following: " The original proposal was based on the idea that the system of compulsory plan directives is to be done away with (except in the case of investments), and that the fulfilment of the plan adopted by the government would be guaranteed through a system of economic incentives. In the course of the meetings of the Coordinating Economic Commission, this original idea underwent some alteration. The document enclosed here starts

---

is to be exclusively a central one. Failing this, there is no guarantee that the national economy will develop in the right direction".

[18] If there are no shortages, " ... it is possible that the price of the plentifully available goods will be made free... We must emphasize, however, that even in the distant future this can become practice only in the case of goods that are less important in production and to the consumer ". Staples, basic raw materials, basic industrial products and major services " ... will always have to be set maximal and minimal prices ".

out from the assumption that the system of compulsory plan directives is to be employed under certain curcumstances ".[19]

That there had, indeed, been a retreat is evident also if we compare the first draft of the reform programme prepared by the Commission and signed by István Antos and István Varga on March 2, 1957 (*Proposals on the economic structure and mechanism to be introduced*) with the all-inclusive proposal submitted at the end of May described above. In contrast with the strict limitation of the May proposal which considered free prices possible only in the case of goods of secondary importance, the draft of early March had as their basis the following idea: " Once goods have become plentiful, in all areas where there is no longer a shortage the prices of industrial products will be influenced by the law of supply and demand ". No provisos are attached to the following statement either: " State subsidies must, in theory, be done away with all along the line ".

Naturally, the proposals on the reform of the price system were closely tied to the idea that planning based on directives must be progressively done away with. " Enterprises " we read in the programme of early March, " will continue to function as planned economies. Each company will continue to make company plans, though these will not be of the nature of compulsory directives. The companies and the ministries and the National Planning Office will inform each other mutually, but the central plans will not bind the companies. " In managing the companies... greater rôles will be given to various economic means, for instance, the credit, price and tax policies ". In Appendix 1 attached to the proposal, the Committee on Industrial Organization put this same thought another way when it stated: " Among the new methods of the economic management of the existing enterprises, indirect, economic measures must gradually

[19] Party History Archives, 288 f. 23/1957, István Varga and István Antos's letter of June 17, 1957, to Antal Apró.

come to predominate; these must become the primary instruments of the working of the economy and market structures... Measures of this sort are the price system, and various forms of taxation, ... the credit system, and allowing the companies a greater financial interest in production through changes in the wage and bonus systems ".

By this interpretation, " the owner, the state, was leasing the company, i.e. the fixed and circulating assets, and the goodwill of the firm, to the company collective ". In return, the company was to pay 5-6% rent for the fixed assets it used; was to pay the interest rate it had bid for its share of the central renewal and investment fund; and was to pay an interest of 18-20% on the circulating assets it used. The residual profits, however, the company could use to create a contingency fund to insure flexible management, and to pay profit shares. Companies which were poorly managed and were unable to meet these requirements might go bankrupt. " In some cases ", the plan noted, " nonsolvent companies might have bankruptcy proceedings taken against them ".

As István Varga and István Antos had put it in the letter quoted above, this initial conception relegated direct central intervention to a single sphere: investment. It is same idea that we find in the early March plan: " Investment funds will continue to be allocated through detailed directives ". But even these centralized investments were linked with the idea of company independence, for " the new establishments are to be strictly planned, and the cost borne by the budget, not free of charge, however, but at an interest rate generally prescribed for the use of independent funds ". However, the starting of a new entreprise would be a company matter, with the company being incorporated and its managers appointed before the investments were started, the managers having an interest from the company's very inception in the most economic investments possible, and being themselves in charge of the investments. Though this system left room for investment from company profits, these would hardly be on a scale comparable to the amounts centrally invested from the budget.

In concluding this discussion of the comprehensive reform planned, we must note that the commitee of experts had in mind also the restoration of the country's economic equilibrium. The scarcity of goods being as bad as it was, they thought that a number of direct, central measures would, initially, be necessary, but that these could be gradually done away with once balance was restored, or, as they frequently put it, once supplies were " plentiful ". They thought that it would take all of 1957 and 1958 for the economy to get on its feet. It was with this in mind that they stated that the new " economic mechanism can be introduced but gradually ". At the same time, it had been made quite clear in the Appendix 1, referred to above, just what was meant by gradualism, and what was not: " Gradualism does not mean that the step-by-step introduction of these reforms should be, or can be put off for years. The old methods of economic planning cannot be continued, for they cannot solve our present grave difficulties... "

Counter-proposals aimed at partial solutions

Before going on to give an account of what happened to the proposals made by the government commission of economic experts, let me go back a bit to another angle of the story. From the beginning, as was to be expected, there was an extraordinarily strong group which argued the system of planning and control of the ' fifties had been basically appropriate, and who wanted only to do away with its " excesses and distortions ". This group was most energetic in its repudiation of radical reforms. They argued that the July 1956 meeting of the Central Committee of the Hungarian Workers' Party — which had recalled Mátyás Rákosi from his post as Secretary-General " for reasons of health " and had put Ernö Gerö, who had been second in command in his place as head of the party — had specified the way out of the economic crisis as well: the second five year plan (for the years between 1956 and 1960) was to have set the economy on the right track. It was this process that the events of October 1956 had interrupted. Now that political stability had been restored, ran this line of argument, nothing more needed to be done than to return to the path laid out in July. This view was clearly put by István Friss, Head of the Economic policy Department of the Central Committee of the Hungarian Socialist Workers' Party in the course of the parliamentary debate on planning and the budget in June of 1957: " ... After many healthy initiatives, in *June* of 1956 the party took a stand for what was essentially the right economic policy and method of economic planning: ... the democratization of economic life, a considerable degree of decentralization, greater local independence, and a better system of giving the individual an interest in production through economic incentives". And since October of 1956, " significant steps have been taken along this correctly chosen path ".[20]

Thus, while — in accordance with the decision brought by the Hungarian Socialist Workers' Party in December 7 of 1956 — the economic expert commission convened by the government set about working out the new system of economic planning and control as described so far, the adherents of this alternative conception were also busy detailing their solutions and trying to win it acceptance. Their stand was exceptionally well summed up in a memorandum of May 24, 1957, entitled *The Party's economic policy*. " We are firmly committed to the Marxist-Leninist principle of central direction and planning for the whole of the national economy... At the same time, we must, obviously, learn from the mistakes made, and must correct them... Central planning for the whole of the national economy, must be conjoined

[20] István Friss, Gazdaságpolitikai problémáink és az 1957. évi terv (Our economic policy problems and the 1957 plan), *Közgazdasági Szemle*, July, 1957, p. 704.

with maximal local independence, and the encouragement of local initiative. The party's decisions of July, 1956, point in this direction; we were on this road before the counterrevolution, and are continuing along it since the counterrevolution was defeated ".[21]

A few days later, a revised version of the memorandum added that "... Lenin's concept of democratic centralism be applied to the country's economic life ".[22]

Naturally, it would be fruitless to go into a theoretical discussion of how far the " Marxist-Leninist principle of central direction and planning for the whole of the national economy " was *not*, by the very nature of the thing, a theoretically grounded policy of planning and control, more precisely, to go into the fact that in the last years of Lenin's life, after the victory of the revolution, this " principle " had proved as compatible with the system of direct distribution used under war communism as with the market mechanisms operating under NEP. Even more fruitless would be a discussion of how far Lenin's theory of " democratic centralism ", a principle of party organization, was applicable to economic planning.

In any case, decentralization was an important principle of this approach to correcting the shortcomings of the functioning of the economy. Extraordinarily interesting in this regard was the work done during these months by the Economic Policy Department of the Hungarian Socialist Workers' Party under István Friss's direction, which aimed at the *rationalization* of the earlier system of planning. Thus, while the government commission of economic experts were finalizing their programme — whose main points had been public since the Spring — another reform project got under way, the two being completed at about the same time. Friss and his colleagues were analyzing how affairs

[21] Party History Archives, 288 f. 23/1957, The party's economic policy, May 24, 1957, Economic Department of the Central Committee.

[22] *loc. cit.*, May 27, 1957.

stood in 30 industrial companies in the spring of 1957. " This period ", concluded István Friss in his report, " was one in which the system of economic planning operating up to October 23, 1956, was no longer in effect, and no new methods of management had yet been introduced. Under these circumstances, it was the companies themselves which had to come up with the methods absolutely necessary for management, and adopt the ones they thought best. This in fact means that in industry — and in other branches of the economy as well — the past has been a period of nation-wide experimentation ".[23]

The findings were really interesting. As the director of the Csepel Auto Works reported, " In December of the past year, and in January and February of 1957, there was no central or ministerial planned economic management to speak of. Our company was given only one figure by way of projected volume of production, which set our value of output at a maximum of 60% of what it had been in the comparable quarter of the previous year. Just what goods were to make up this projected figure was decided by the company quite independently through getting into contact with the companies it cooperated with and with the buyers. It was on the basis of their demands that the production plans were made, that personal needs and production costs were estimated ".[24]

In the April 4 Machine Works the situation had been analogous: " The two chief indicators prescribed for the company had been the profit on the finished products and the export plan... All the details of satisfying these two central directives were left to the company to work out ".[25]

From all this, István Friss concluded the following: " One of the most positive results of the past period is without doubt

---

[23] Party History Archives, 288 f. 23/1957, Some contemporary problems of the direction and management of industrial enterprises, István Friss, July 8, 1957.

[24] Party History Archives, 288 f. 23/1957, report of June 18, 1957.

[25] *loc. cit.*, report of June 15, 1957.

that uniformity in planning, has been done away with... the plans made are more suited to the industry and company in question than before ".[26] The National Worsted Mill, for instance, had been given centrally set investment quotas, had had the quantity of finished goods specified, as well as the quantity of the raw materials and wool that could be used up, and had had the average salary and productiveness centrally set. The Köbánya Pharmaceutical Company had received directives as to the production quantity of three special products, had had the forint value of its exports (and the quantity of two main export products) set, and had had its wage fund, its gross profits, and the quantity it could use of the two most important raw materials specified. " Gross production value " was seldom prescribed, and then mainly in the food processing industry.

On the basis of all this, István Friss drew the following conclusion: " It follows from our findings about the present state of planning that it is a good idea to prescribe for the companies the quantity of the products that are most important to the national economy, to prescribe the export plan, to set a maximum on the use of the most important raw materials, to specify one factor regulating wages, as well as the company's productivity and total expenses. The company-by-company prescription of these indicators seems justified by a variety of circumstances... failing this, it would be a matter of chance how the various companies got a hold of the materials needed for their various products, to say nothing of the wave of speculation and corruption that would inevitably ensue ".

The proposal, however, was to let the companies keep the independence they had acquired, and to keep central direction less obtrusive: " This spontaneously developed situation ought to be made permanent, and steps should be taken to prevent the success of the efforts undoubtedly being made for the

---

[26] Party History Archives, 288 f. 23/1957.

ministries to restore all the earlier constraints of planning without exception".

From the point of view of the rationalization of planning, the above summary claimed that important lesson had been learned as it had not been in the days of detailed production plans. The ministries did not now prescribe company production lines, but left it to "the industrial and wholesale companies concerned to draw these up themselves", which resulted in a better satisfaction of consumer demand.

There were also a great many spontaneous changes in the system of wages.[27] It was during these months that wage planning shifted from the direct control of wages to the prescription of average wages. The companies were generally very critical of this step. "Average wage control is not very popular; the companies have come out very strongly against it. The chief criticism is that it prevents wage rises" and that "it results in intra-company unemployment, for they take unnecessary workers at low pay so as to get a low enough average. The measure tends to inhibit the growth of productivity... It is an impediment to the introduction of wages high enough to serve as an incentive to work". In spite of this, the proposal was categorical in its position: "It was necessary to prescribe average wages, and it continues to be necessary to keep central control over average wages, or else... wages would grow at very different rates. This would result, on the one hand, in a great fluctuation of manpower, and on the other, in too great a rise in wages in some places".[28]

[27] To October of 1956, two-thirds of the workers were paid by piecework; from November on straight hourly wages practically became the rule, the amount being set on the basis of the earnings for the year's third quarter. Subsequently, however, the companies experimented, with all kinds of solutions. Hourly wages tied to individual performance were introduced, as were task bonuses, and piecework and hourly wages combined. The earlier system of complete central control over bonuses practically came to an end, and the companies received their bonus funds in an absolute sum, part of it to be disposed over by the company management, part of it to be paid out upon the satisfaction of conditions specified by the ministries.

[28] The proposal argued that the system of profit sharing, also newly introduced, could

István Friss, thus, proposed a basic adherence to the old system of planning and control, with provisions for the correction of its mechanism.

The immediate practical economic adjustments

While the various reform programmes were being worked out, there was also the need for immediate practical decisions. Matters could not be put off under the given political and economic circumstances. A whole series of practical improvements was brought to the attention of the government, and its Economic Committee and other government bodies could hardly manage to review all the reforms being constantly introduced. Let us look now at some of the more important ones.

One of the first moves involved changes in the price system. As early as December 1956 the government Economic Committee was discussing proposals for the creation of a Price Office. As the proposal put it: " The democratization of our economic life, the introduction of the new economic mechanism necessitates our taking a stand on the role of prices and on price control... In the new economic system to be introduced, central price control need not apply to all areas of production and marketing, for the companies must have a significant role in setting prices, ... and indirect, looser forms of price control must be more extensively ".[29]

A month and a half later, the president of the new National Price Office was expounding the following to the Economic Committee in the proposal entitled *on the actual tasks of industrial price control.* " The Economic Committee has concluded that

---

not be adequately evaluated, for " ... increased company independence has become the practice at a time when prices do not properly reflect production costs, a circumstance that has led to a great many contradictions and negative results. Our investigations have, therefore, shown that it is time that the issue of factory prices was settled ".

[29] Party History Archives, 288 f. 23/1957, Proposal for the establishment of a Price Office made to the Economic Committee, Dec. 14, 1956.

the system of subsidized prices is not consonant with a socialist price mechanism, and can, thus, be maintained only temporarily. After industrial production and industrial cost prices have become normalized, industrial factory prices must be set by December 31, 1957, so that they might come into effect on January 1, 1958 ". The proposal linked the setting of value-prices with the demand for company independence, and the actual fact of worker self-management: " ... The withering away of economic incentives ", noted Béla Csikós-Nagy, " would come precisely at a time when we are hoping to make worker self-management a part of the economic mechanism ".[30]

At the same time, to protect consumer prices, the government temporarily set industrial price controls in March, emphatically emphasizing, however, that consumer subsidies " were not in keeping with a socialist price mechanism ", and would be kept up only until factory prices were settled.[31] In fact, work was already going on on the reform of factory prices, the goal being to make them value and/or cost reflecting in order that they might serve as economic guidelines and incentives.

The most significant and most consistent reforms, however, were in the field of agriculture. The decision behind them was, obviously, of a political nature: for the consolidation of power, it was vital to win the support of the peasantry, and this could not be done merely by putting an end to the forced collectivization and administrative molestations of the ' fifties. The hated compulsory deliveries had also to be done away with, all the more so since in October 1956, Imre Nagy's government had already completed the earlier modifications and ameliorations of the system by abrogating compulsory deliveries as such. Political considerations alone excluded a return to the old methods. Much

---

[30] Party History Archives, 288 f. 23/1957, The proposals of the President of the National Price Office made to the Economic Committee, June 31, 1957.

[31] Resolution 1029/1957 of the Hungarian Revolutionary Worker-Peasant Government, *Magyar Közlöny*, March 10, 1957.

the same could be said of the other method of central agricultural planning, the compulsory sowing plans.

In November, 1956, therefore, the government announced the abolition of compulsory deliveries and other obligations. With this, the foundations of the earlier system of planning in this branch were completely undermined. Here, it was not only this element or that of the old system that was replaced: instead of compulsory directives mediating between the government and the peasantry, their economic relationship was now essentially regulated by the market. Instead of prescribing compulsory sowing plans and setting compulsory delivery quotas, the government was left with setting agricultural prices high enough to serve as an incentive to production. Thus we find the Minister of Food observing in the Spring of 1958: " After compulsory deliveries were abolished, the relationship of the state and the peasantry ceased to be an administrative one and became primarily a trade relationship ".[32] The logic of the matter required not only the raising of the previous unrealistically low buying price to one more closely approximating to the real value of the goods bought, but also the abrogation of all administrative measures that artificially discriminated against small producers. Decree 3263/1957 provided for the introduction of a uniform agricultural price system.

Naturally, the government had to fight to win acceptance for its new agricultural policy. In Borsod county, for instance, in the summer of 1957 the Edelény District Council circulated " pledge-collecting " papers. " In some places ", the report prepared for the National Purchasing Committee noted, " we found dangerous practices being indulged in especially by the councils, namely, that they are using the old methods of pressure to realize the government's plans for buying up agricultural products on the

[32] Party History Archives, 288 f. 23/1958, Proposals made to the Hungarian Revolutionary Worker-Peasant Government, May 2, 1958, Minister of Foodsupply.

market, and thus are doing more harm than good... Excesses are to be found easily enough, and peasants have been compelled to "pledge" their products when the quantity thus obtained is insignificant... We must emphasize in particular that it is only now that the producers are beginning to believe that compulsory deliveries have ended".[33]

A variety of reforms was a day-to-day necessity in other areas as well. In March of 1957, for instance, the Minister for Light Industry urged the introduction of a mechanism best suited to serve the new economic goals. Nothing is a better illustration of the contradictory nature of the reform steps taken under the pressure of circumstances than this proposal. The old reflexes, the ossification of old economic practice into a so-called "socialist economic theory" were to be seen everywhere, as these lines from the Minister's proposal urging a flexible approach to incentives and profits very well shows: "... We must count on the probability that certain products which are less profitable to manufacture or would actually involve losses will be neglected by the companies. To avoid this, the directorates... will give directives for the manufacture of these products, and by way of sanction, should the companies fail to comply, will have the power to cut their profits".[34] Compulsory directive, thus, survived as the last resort. It was not only the ministries, however, that were prone to this view. The companies, too, felt insecure in the new milieu, and when, around the turn of 1956 and 1957, central planning became reduced to only certain compulsory indicators which left the companies with incomparably greater liberty than before (in the areas, for instance, of production line sales, and procurements), a great many companies — partly because the nature of planning had not really changed the fewer

[33] Party History Archives, 288 f. 23/1957, July 22, 1957.

[34] Party History Archives, 288 f. 23/1957, Proposals to the Economic Committee, March 26, 1957.

indicators notwithstanding, and partly because most of the company managers were more at home in a centralized economic system — required a return to more decisive central planning. Accordingly, " ... the ministerial and *company* managing bodies urged the restoration of disciplined planning as a precondition of plan fulfilment ".[35]

When the partial reform of the planning system was being discussed in 1956, there had been economists who had warned in no uncertain terms: "... we cannot hope to find the solution in purely quantitative cuts in the numbers of compulsory directives, reports, and administrative staff". Events were proving them right with uncanny speed. Just as true proved to be another point made at the time, namely, that such partial measures which left intact the essence of the mechanism of planning based on compulsory directives " can serve only to strengthen an unhealthy kind of spontaneity which will give rise to its own counter-tendency: the attempt to restore the abolished plan indicators and bonus specifications ".[36]

But contradictory as the situation was, the government set about introducing a whole series of reforms. Partial reforms were being worked on, for instance, for the regulation of foreign trade. In January of 1957, the Economic Committee discussed the proposals made by the Minister of Finance and the Minister of Foreign Trade for changes in the system of price equalization used in foreign trade till that time.[37] Even while the reforms were

[35] Party History Archives, 288 f. 23/1959, The changes of economic guidance since 1957, concerning industrial production. Appendix No. 1. National Planning Office. April 17, 1959 (italics mine).

[36] On the occasion of János Kornai's Ph. D. thesis presentation, Sept. 1956; cf. *Közgazdasági Szemle*, Nov.-Dec. 1956, pp. 1490-92.

[37] Party History Archives, 288 f. 23/1957, Proposals to the Economic Committee on modifications in the system of price equalization in foreign trade, Jan. 25, 1957, István Antos and Jenö Incze. Price equalization developed " ... as a part of an export policy that concentrated purely on the volume of exports ", and automatically made up the difference between the domestic prices and the price — however low — at which the goods were sold abroad (in 1955-56, money thus paid out from the budget

being worked out, the two ministers suggested, "... definite steps need to be taken to encourage more economical foreign-trade activity... all the more so as more and more companies are being given foreign-trade rights..." The proposal was to introduce a domestic surcharge from April 1957 on to make up for the difference between the unrealistic exchange rate in effect and the realistic exchange rate. "The present exchange rate... discourages exports and encourages imports". At the same time, the proposal urged that "the automatic settling of the occasional real differences in prices from the state budget be put an end to at once".[38]

Until comprehensive reform could be introduced, thus, temporary and partial measures were taken to eliminate undesirable effects and to make the economy run more smoothly.

Among the corrective measures was the revision of the earlier doctrinaire stand on the practically wholesale restriction of private enterprise. In agriculture and industry alike, the private sector was now thought to be both possible and necessary, and even within the cooperative sector, the cultivation of household plots for the market was encouraged. The change in attitude is well reflected by the report of the President of the National Planning Office of mid-December, 1956: "The National Planning Office started preparing the plans for 1957 of the basis of the following major considerations: ... private initiative must be given much greater scope than before in production and commerce alike; to this end, private investments of benefit to the national

came to over 10 billion forints). For this reason, the introduction of a price system and an exchange rate that reflected real values was absolutely necessary.

[38] The official exchange rate was 1 U.S. $ = 11.75 Ft; the suggested surcharge was to make up for the difference between this official rate and the non-official "shadow" exchange rate of 30 Ft to the dollar; instead of the automatic settlement of the price differences, the introduction of fixed price equalization rates was suggested, one which would not allow the companies to make claims on all their losses, but only on those permitted by the rates which were to be fixed by types of goods on the basis of past years' experience.

economy must be promoted".[39] Paragraph four of Decree 1014/1957.1.26 specified the conditions under which small tradesmen could work for the public sector.[40]

It was to encourage private enterprise that the government's Economic Committee made its decision of February 1, 1957 concerning the leasing of certain state-owned shops.

Those small retail stores and restaurants which were operated "as public enterprises only with great difficulty" were to be leased out to private enterpreneurs. This "is to be started as an experiment involving about 200 units; altogether, about 1,000 units, or about 6% of the retail network will be up for lease". Simultaneously, privately owned retail shops were also to increase in number. The proposal was to raise the number of private retail shops from the existing 9,500 to "at the most 20,000".[41] On February 19, there was a government decree to this effect.[42] The matter of nationalized housing was also reviewed.[43]

There seems little need to go on adding further examples of the variety of reform steps being taken. Many people believed that improvements of this sort could make the economy run more smoothly, and would prove to provide adequate answers to the problems at hand.

---

[39] Party History Archives, 288 f. 23/1957, The proposals made by the National Planning Office on Dec. 14, 1956, Árpád Kiss.

[40] "We must make provisions for small tradesmen to be able to get contracts from the public sector without restrictions, on the basis of competitive offers publicly made... The materials they need for doing these jobs have to be guaranteed them at the price they are available at to the other productive sectors." Party History Archives, 288 f. 23/1958, Proposal to the Hungarian Revolutionary Worker-Peasant Government on work done by small tradesmen for state bodies and companies, July 5, 1958, Mrs. József Nagy and István Antos.

[41] Party History Archives, 288 f., 23/1957, The decision taken by the Economic Committee on Feb. 1, 1957, and the proposal by János Tausz, minister, on Jan. 18, 1957.

[42] Decree 1022/1957 of the Hungarian Revolutionary Worker-Peasant Government, *Magyar Közlöny*, April 21, 1957.

[43] Law-decree No. 28, 1957 of the Republic's Presidential Council, Magyar Közlöny, April 21, 1957.

The assault on the plans for radical reform

Those who considered any substantial departure from the economic order of the fifties basically incompatible with socialism believed that the economy could be set on its feet with the more rational, practical solutions that day-to-day experience had necessarily given rise to. On this interpretation, these immediate solutions were not a transition to a more comprehensive, radical reform, but were in fact substitutes for it, for radical transformation was rejected on principle.

At the same time, the expert committees of economists appointed by the government all came out with proposals calling for unambiguous and immediate radical reform. The Economic Commission already much quoted explicitly emphasized that the introduction of just some elements of their reform programme could not possibly lead to any solutions. The proposals advanced by the inter-ministerial committee of experts in January came out strongly against gradualism and any attempts to introduce small, or partial improvements.

" As far as we can see, the introduction of the complete mechanism cannot be regarded as a distant goal to be realized sometime in the future... We must not forget that economic policy and the economic mechanism exert influence on each other ". " The right economic goals cannot be based on the present mechanism; in fact, this mechanism — which does not even let us see clearly in economic matters — will hardly let us develop a proper economic policy ".

At the same time, the experts noted: " The measures already taken to simplify central directives — and indicators — and to increase company independence have proven ineffective. At best, they have led to small quantitative changes, but to no qualitative change ".

The great majority of the country's economists shared these views, and were engaged in vociferous debates with those committed to partial improvements. With the consolidation of political power, however, this latter group started a determined counter-offensive.

Here, of course, it was not merely a matter of differences over the kinds of economic solutions evisaged. The counter-offensive against the " reformists " was a political and ideological struggle. Just how far this was the case is clearly indicated by a study dated May 24, 1957, written by Andor Berei, a member of the party leadership and president of the National Planning Office 1956. The study was meant for publication and was entitled *A call for ideological struggle against the revisionist economic theories.* It is indicative of the significance of the views expressed that the provisional Political Committee of the Hungarian Socialist Workers' Party felt it necessary to discuss the article. It will be worth our while to have a look at the main arguments of this rather lengthy study.

" Revisionist views ", the author started out, " were becoming ever more frequent in Hungarian economic writing before October, 1956... These views are influencing our economic life at the present, too, to no negligible extent. This article... is a critical analysis of the most fashionable form of economic revisionism in Hungary today, the trend that claims to stand for " a new economic mechanism ". Though its exponents start out by criticising real shortcomings, " they tend to exaggerate the shortcomings that there are, and to generalize them ".

After the preamble, Andor Berei put the question that was most important from the point of view of the argument: " Is it possible... to plan for the national economy in all its branches without compulsory directives involving every part of the country? At the present state of socialist economic development ", he immediately answered, " the nation's economy can be planned only through centrally elaborated state planning... These unified, central plans can be confidently and uniformly realized only through the use of state intervention, primarily through compulsory directives regulating production, marketing, etc. If the plans were not in the form of directives, they would no longer have a realistic chance of being fulfilled. On what grounds would we call " plan " an economic programme that was neither law nor directive...? "

After this strong stand for the traditional form of planning as the sole possibility, the author goes on: " The economists proclaiming the new mechanism say that the termination of the " system of directives " will not preclude the fulfilment of the nation's economic plans because the state will be able to influence the activities of the companies through financial and other indirect means... Financial, credit, and other instruments, however, cannot in themselves insure that thousands and tens of thousands of companies will produce and deliver goods of the kind required by the unified national plan, and in the quantity required... "

In this view, an end to compulsory company-by-company directives would be tantamount to a return to capitalism: " There is an unresolvable contradiction in the new economic mechanism between the theoretical recognition of the need for planning and its practical repudiation. With the termination of the dominant role of the socialist state in the economy, economic planning itself would come to an end. Willingly, the new mechanism is a return to anarchy in production, to the rule of " blind laws " ... and would serve to " reproduce " the capitalist elements in the national economy more and more every day ". " The revisionist critics of economic planning... have dethroned the peculiar laws of socialist development, and have set on the empty throne not a new idol, but a very old one, the law of value ". Berei's verdict is categorical and unequivocal: " The views and theories hallmarked by the name new economic mechanism, while they might be right in some matters of detail, are fundamentally the wholesale revision of the Leninist principles of building a socialist economy, of major theses of socialist political economy... We reject the new economic mechanism as a form of revisionism, as a mistaken theory that would set us on the wrong track... "

It cannot be considered a coincidence that Andor Berei thought it necessary to make a personal attack on István Varga, the head of the governmental expert commission feverishly working on the new reform programme: The new mechanism, Berei wrote, as " István Varga — who, with admirable candour openly confesses himself to be a non-Marxist economist — tells us, can work only when the national economy is balanced. ... The adherents of the new mechanism clearly hope that if this balance exists from the beginning, even their economic system will not destroy it... The final judgement on the new economic mechanism is pronounced precisely by the fact that a balanced national economy is something which this system can hope to achieve neither at the start, nor in the course of its existence ".[44]

I have dwelt on this article at some length, for it is an extremely clear expression of the views of those opposed to more radical reform. It is just as clear a stand for moderate improvements as opposed to a new economic mechanism: " The way to correct the mistakes that have been made ", wrote Andor Berei, " is not to destroy the foundations of economic planning, which alone are adequate to the demands of a socialist economy, but rather to eradicate completely the anti-democratic, bureaucratic. and subjective distortions that have attended the realization of the Leninist principles of a socialist economy... To the economist calling for another mechanism, we answer: not another one, but this one better! What we need is not a new mechanism, but that the system of economic planning now in operation should work better, more perfectly ". The conclusion followed from the logic of this kind of argument: " The revisionist views attached to the new economic mechanism not only do not promote,

[44] Party History Archives, 288 f. 11/85, The draft by ANDOR BEREI: " A call for ideological struggle against the revisionist economic views ", May 24, 1957.

but are actually one of the greatest impediments to the success of the extraordinarily necessary attempts being made " to find a way out of the difficulties... " The new mechanism is not an economic panacea, but one of the most destructive forms of revisionism. Convincing ideological battle must be waged against it ".[45]

Analogous positions were stated in a variety of forms from spring of 1957 on. In a debate held on March 19 at the National Planning Office, a number of those working at the Office argued against the radical reforms being urged by others, and for the retention of the system of central directives.[46]

In the April number of the *Közgazdasági Szemle* (Economic Review), Ilona Bieber, József Fábián and Emil Gyulyás's joint article essentially denied that the mistakes of the fifties originated in the system of planning and management: " We maintain that the mistakes in Hungary were rooted not in the economic base, in the relations of production, but in the economic policy. The economic policy was over ambitious... The correction of these economic policy mistakes does not necessitate qualitative changes of the sort that would involve the alteration of the socialist relations of production ".[47] We find the same kind of opposition of economic correctives and the new mechanism in

---

[45] *loc. cit.*

[46] Debate on the perfecting of economic planning held at the National Planning Office, *Közgazdasági Szemle,* May, 1957, pp. 568-577. Albert Katócs argued that since the goal was the development of a new industrial structure, and since this could be done only through planning, " we cannot afford to do without specific plans at this time ". István Bartos and Tamás Morva emphasized that " we need only quantitative changes to develop the economic mechanism "; a system of incentives based on the law of value can be auxiliary at best. Repeating this idea, Pál Füsti concluded: " Our task now is to correct the mistakes and not to dispense with planning ". József Soós put this question: " How could the mechanism guarantee the goods adequate to the buying power our plans provide for when the companies would, essentially, be producing what is most economical from their point of view? "

[47] Ilona Bieber, József Fábián, Emil Gulyás: Megjegyzések a Közgazdasági Szemle 1956. 11-12, számának vezércikkéhez (Some comments on the leader of No. 11-12, 1956, of the *Közgazdasági Szemle*), *Közgazdasági Szemle,* April, 1957, p. 396.

an article by Géza Ripp, " Economic planning or anarchy ", which appeared in the *Gazdasági Figyelö* (Economic Observer).[48]

Endre Molnár attacked the various articles in the *Közgazdasági Szemle* defending the new mechanism in the central theoretical journal of the Hungarian Socialist Workers' Party, the *Társadalmi Szemle* (Social Review). In his article entitled " Revisionist views on the economic role of the socialist state ",[49] he expounded the following: " In the course of the attempt to work out the new economic mechanism, an attack was launched on Stalin's observation that our plans are not prophecies, they are not guesses, but directives'. The proposals calling for the new economic mechanism have in common that they are attacking the strongly centralized state direction of the economy, a state direction which takes the form primarily of unified, compulsory plans which comprehend the national economy as a whole ". " The advocates of the new economic mechanism ", he goes on, " do not see eye to eye on everything. Most of them, however, agree in regarding compulsory planning and directives in the state management of the economy as a necessary evil, and, with nostalgia, exert themselves to reconstruct an economic mechanism in which prices and values, and a system of economic incentives automatically regulates " the economy.

The author is categorical in his rejection of such views: " If the economic activity of the companies is not regulated by compulsory state directives... if, that is, production is regulated essentially by the law of value and by the market (as it is in the capitalist economy), then the undesirable features characteristic of capitalist economy will also necessarily appear ".[50]

Thus, while Endre Molnár based his arguments on the international conflict of capitalism and socialism, since as he put it, " the need for a strong proletarian state, and for central leader-

48 *Gazdasági Figyelő* (Economic Observer) No. 4, 1957.

49 *Társadalmi Szemle*, June, 1957.

50 *loc. cit.*, pp. 51-54.

ship in the economic sphere, too, follows from the antagonism between the imperialist and the socialist camp ",[51] István Friss, we find, drew similar conclusions from precisely what capitalism and socialism had in common, namely, the trends in technological development. " Looking at the main effects of technological progress common to the countries of the various social systems... we want to call attention to one last fact. This is the growing importance of state intervention... In which direction the socio-economic effects of technological progress are pointing is essentially the question of whether technological progress is necessitating greater economic centralization or not... The facts give us an answer... that seems unambiguous enough. The growing weight of state intervention in non-socialist economies, the growing number of experiments made by non-socialist countries at developing a part or all of their economy on the basis of plans made for a number of years all show that the central direction of a nation's economy is more and more a necessity ".[52]

The last word in the public debate was the heated repudiati on of the reform programme worked out by the Commission of economic experts and summarized by Varga in the *Közgazdasági Szemle*. Edit Varga's criticism of the proposals was particularly unconditional: " István Varga's article, which contains numerous correct observations in matters of detail, is essentially and all things considered mistaken... István Varga says he wishes to promote... the consolidation of economic planning; the train of thought and logic of his article, however, leave the reader with quite the opposite impression... Under the banner of reforming planning, his thinking in reality leads us into the cul-de-sac of the impossibility of planning ". But Edit Varga sees no real reason for concern: " We have no reason to suppose

---

[51] *loc. cit.*, p. 57.

[52] István Friss, A technikai haladás társadalmi-gazdasági következményei (On the socio-economic consequences of technological progress), *Közgazdasági Szemle*, Nov.-Dec. 1956, pp. 1350, 1353.

that we shall not be able to get to know the laws of socialist economic development more precisely". For another thing planning is necessary to the dictatorship of the proletariat. "Planning is the chief instrument in executing the economic policy of a proletarian dictatorship... If the plans are realistic, and consonant with the laws of economic development, their fulfilment depends primarily on the activities of the socialist state. Is it possible to realize the economic programme of a proletarian dictatorship without directives? Clearly, it is perfectly impossible". István Varga had even had recourse to Stalin to prove his point, quoting Stalin's comment that "we must not forget that over and above the elements that planning can influence, the national economy has elements that are, as yet, independent of planning". Edit Varga, however, turned the tables on him, finishing the sentence that he had quoted only a part of, and showing that in fact it proved her argument. For the sentence ran on as follows: there are antagonistic classes, "which cannot be overcome simply by the national planning office working out plans"; thus, "questions that planning cannot influence must be solved through the class struggle".[53]

Official confirmation of this criticism came from István Szurdi of the party's Central Committee in his "Some comments on the ideas and proposals of the Economic Commission". This statement, which was discussed by the party's Economic Advisor Board, declared a number of the Commission's suggestions useful, but went on to state: "... We must make it perfectly clear here, that the planning of the nationalized companies through compulsory directives goes with economic planning as one of its basic features, and is the chief method of state control".[54]

---

[53] Edit Varga, A tervezés módszereinek megjavitása (Improving the methods of planning), *Közgazdasági Szemle*, July, 1958, pp. 699, 597, 700.

[54] István Szurdi, Néhány észrevétel a Közgazdasági Szakértő Bizottság elgondolásaihoz, javaslataihoz (Some comments on the ideas and proposals of the Economic Commission), *Közgazdasági Szemle*, July, 1958, p. 694.

The fate of the reforms

This, of course, brought only a temporary end to the debates. Hungary's economy consolidated with surprising speed after the grave disequilibrium, unemployment, and danger of inflation of late 1956 and early 1957.[55] This economic stabilization went with the concurrent and especially rapid process of political stabilization (and was, in part, its result).

Just as the shock of political collapse had necessarily strengthened the forces calling for radical reform, so the speedy economic and political consolidation undoubtedly went to reinforce the voices urging the retention of the old system of planning and control, with some partial corrections introduced.

It was in this changed enviroment that the decision had to be made whether to introduce radical economic reform, and risk all the possible chaos and difficulties of adjustment, or to stay with the old system and continue the process of improving on it which had already been started. Obviously, the decision was influenced by a number of practical political considerations, the desire to keep up the process of peaceful consolidation already under way being an important factor. Clearly, the ideological arguments were also of central importance. The effect of decades of dogmatism was felt in that the system of planning and control evolved under the particular historical circumstances of the Soviet economy of the 1930s was still identified with Marxist-Leninist theory, and the laws of socialist development. In the political leadership there was a clash of views, and it was at the summer session of the national meeting of the Hungarian Socialist Workers' Party in June of 1957 that the old dogmatic wing came on strongly to " rectify " the policy the new party leadership had been following. The main task at this point was

[55] Already in February, 1957, István Friss was able to note: " Our present calculations indicate that the country's economic situation in 1957 might be better than one would have thought possible either in mid-December, or even mid-January." Party History Archives, 288 f. 23/1957, The national economic plan of 1957, Feb. 5, 1957.

to protect the new political line. What was required, therefore, was not only a clear counter-offensive, but also tactical compromises in some areas.

Changes on the international scene during 1957 also influenced the shape events were to take. After the Soviet Communist Party's 20th Congress and the Chinese promise to let many flowers blossom, 1957 brought counter-effects everywhere. The Chinese situation, the Polish and Hungarian crises, the open attacks on socialism made most representatives of the communist and labour parties which met in Moscow in the autumn of 1957 see revisionism as the chief danger. Relations with Yugoslavia again became strained, and the principles of the Yugoslav party leadership — workers' self-management, and the reformed economic model — were strongly criticised as the embodiments of revisionism. " Struggle on both fronts " was again called for, and the Hungarian party leadership also emphasized — as Ferenc Münnich, the party's second man put it in his article in the *Társadalmi Szemle* discussing the Hungarian party's experiences — that " the Hungarian Socialist Workers' Party has regarded and still regards revisionism as the chief danger ".[56]

All this, it seems, decided the fate of the economic reform programme. This was already clear at the national party meeting in June. While the resolutions consistently spoke of the struggle on " both fronts ", in spite of the fiery debates, on economic matters the position was the following: " In connection with the system of economic planning, the party conference declares that it attributes decisive importance to central state control...(and) repudiates those mistaken views which deny the need for central state planning and control. Should these views be given free play... they would lead to anarchy, to the strengthening of capitalist elements, and to serious damage to the socialist economy

---

[56] Ferenc Münnich, Az MSzMP tapasztalatai a revizionismus elleni harcban (The experiences the Hungarian Socialist Workers' Party has gained in the fight against revisionism), *Társadalmi Szemle*, No. 11, 1957.

and the people. The party is conscious of the fact that in past years economy has been more centralized than necessary... A number of the measures making for excessive centralization have already been done away with, and work is being done to work out the most appropriate form of economic management ".[57]

This work, of course, was no longer to be done by the government Economic Commission with its programme of radical reform. Soon it was reported that the reform planning initiated by the government, by the Economic Commission, had been suspended. " The stoppage of work on the further development of the system of economic planning and control is common knowledge ", we read in a confidential report on the work of the Economic Commission in 1957. " The government had instructed the Economic Commission in January, 1957, to set about reviewing the system of economic planning — at the same time as it was working out the measures to prevent inflation — and to propose the means by which the system might be developed. Work was indeed started with the cooperation of about 200 experts, but their proposals were never discussed, and no detailed plans for their practical implementation were ever made. Except for some small economic measures, no real change ensured... " [58]

We get an even more precise picture of the fate of the Commission's reform programme from the following: " The committees finished their work and submitted their comprehensive proposals nearly a year ago. Since then, a great many things have changed in our economic circumstances, and we see many things much more clearly... Some of the proposals have been used in the government measures taken... " [59] The study goes on to

[57] A Magyar Szocialista Munkáspárt határozatai és dokumentumai, 1956-1962 (Resolutions and documents of the Hungarian Socialist Workers' Party) p. 75.

[58] Party History Archives, 288 f. 23/1958, Report on the work of the Economic Committee in 1957 (Draft), The Secretariat of the Economic Committee, Feb. 4, 1958;

[59] Party History Archives, 288 f. 23/1958, Comments on the Economic Commission's proposals.

list the proposals that had been acted on. Among the practical modifications, it mentions that more attention is being paid to reconstruction as opposed to new investments, and that profit sharing has been introduced. Other proposals — for instance, the adjustment of wage proportions — it considers to be something that might be acted on in the future. It then goes on to state, however: " The comprehensive proposals of the Economic Commission contain, besides the useful proposals listed above, a number of mistaken ideas as well, which are not in keeping with Marxism-Leninism, and diverge from the goals the party and the government have set... The members of the Commission had decisively and strongly dissociated themselves from the dogmatic approach and sectarian practices of the past, but can hardly be said to have done so completely from revisionist, rightist ideas and practices... " This was thought to be illustrated by the fact that according to the Commission, " compulsory directives would, for the most part, become unnecessary... (and) plans would be given a company-by-company breakdown only by way of exception ". " Significant steps have, in fact, been taken to increase company independence. Most of these have had the effects desired, but in some areas, for instance, in the control of materials and in investments, we even went too far... It would be well to return some of the economic factors entrusted to the companies to the competence of central authorities ".

As we can see, it was partial and gradual economic improvements that were opted for, with only some elements of the radical reform programme being adopted. A whole series of practical steps taken from the end of 1956 on testify to the victory of the gradualist approach. In retrospect, in the spring of 1959, the National Planning Office summarized these steps as follows: " In the years preceding the counter-revolution, a number of steps had been taken to simplify planning, steps which were supplemented with new measures in the plan approved in 1957. The basic aim of the measures taken in 1957 was to increase the effectiveness of planning through increased independence for the ministries and the companies. These measures involved further cuts in the number of compulsory plan indicators ".[60]

There can be no doubt that the system of planning and control that took shape in 1957 was different from the earlier economic system. The main change was that there were fewer government-specified indicators. For all that, we might want to review the areas in which directives were still compulsory, for these included the following: the total value of production; the quantity of the most important products broken down by quarters (the number of products affected, however, was only 17% of what it had been in 1954); the quantity that had to be produced for the domestic market (the total value, and broken down by quarters, but for only 25-50% of the goods that had been affected in 1954); the quantity and value of the goods to be produced for the foreign market (but here, too, only 25-50% of those specified earlier); supplies of the chief raw materials (a third of the materials formerly thus regulated); all wage funds; production costs per 100 forints of production value; investment funds (broken down financially and technically, and with central approval needed for the details of each individual investment); the proportion of the renewal fund that could go into building; average wages (given annually, and for the quarter with the highest average wages); and finally, the bonuses for technical and managerial staff.

The report prepared by the National Planning Office then goes on to note: " In presenting these types of indicators for approval to the Council of Ministers... an attempt was made to have planning operate through just a few of the most significant indicators, those most suited to the particular area ". The lower managerial level added only slightly to the scope of the central

[60] Party History Archives, 288 f. 23/1959, The development of economic management since 1957, with special reference to industry, National Planning Office, April 17, 1958.

directives; " however, besides the approved indicators, the ministries and directorates usually give other planning indicators as well for purpose of orientation ". The various ministries used different planning methods at times, and the number of the compulsory directives also differed. " The most radical cut in the number of planning indicators has been made by the Ministry for Light Industry ".

In the end, therefore, the most that could be said by way of illustrating the companies' greater independence was that the number of the goods marked as having high priority, and the number of plan indicators — especially the number of quantitatives directives — had been cut, and that the quarterly breakdown of production values had been abandoned. The views that had been expressed in connection with these changes were summed up by the National Planning Office report as follows: " There is no consensus among the companies, either, as to whether the decrease in the number of the indicators, the changes in planning and control have really made them significantly more independent. Some companies are, in fact, explicitly sceptical in this regard, emphasizing that although there are indeed fewer indicators, those that there are, because they apply to the company's chief activity, tie its hands as completely as had the plethora of indicators in the past. The lower managerial bodies and enterprises were given fewer compulsory indicators, but since they usually got also the ministerial or other detailed indicators for purposes of calculation, they hardly saw any difference as compared to the former practices... the companies feel that it is an indication of their lack of independence that there are no means at their disposal for the acceleration of their most important development projects ". Labour management had, in fact, become less centralized, for compulsory staff indicators were no longer prescribed (although staff quotas were indirectly set through controlled wage funds and average wages).

A similar attempt to make bureaucratic planning less rigid

was the cessation of central planning in certain areas, especially in light industry. " Production ", we learn from the National Planning Office report, " is related to demand, and is established through continuous discussions between the representatives of the industry and commerce ".[61] Material allocation, too, which had been comprehensive and exhaustive, was also restricted to certain areas.[62] The companies were also more likely to be asked to take part in the working out of the plans.[63]

By way of an experiment, certain companies were given direct export rights, in the hope that, having a greater interest in marketing, they would show greater interest in production. Foreign trade, too, acquired new impetus when the incentive was no longer the need to satisfy compulsory directives, but rather a system of price equalization.[64]

There were partial changes in the system of investment, too,[65] but not ones that substantially altered its mechanism, for " ... investment goods continue to be at the companies' disposal practically exclusively free of charge ". The companies, therefore,

---

[61] Instead of production according to directives, " specific agreements between industry and commerce took their place ", " exhibitions of goods by industrial branches, and contracts made on the basis of what was offered there ".

[62] While in 1954 the quantity of materials to be used in the production of 1,271 goods was specified, and even in 1956, 567 products were thus subject to nation-wide regulation, from 1957 on, " the number of goods affected was about 290 ", excluding the centrally regulated production of special staples.

[63] Some ministries, for instance the Ministry of Metallurgy and Machine Industry, had the companies work out the plans, others used the companies' proposals to draw up the plans jointly.

[64] In cases of price equalization more favourable than the price equalization rate specified for that type of product, the company got a share of the savings. At the same time, as the Planning Office noted, the interest of a company in production and in foreign trade was not really harmonized, for " ... even in the case of these companies (i.e. those with foreign trade rights) there is one set of incentives to production and another to foreign trade ".

[65] The companies could have up to 10% of their surplus profit, and could use it to set up a development fund. At the same time, the companies' opportunities for independent activity had improved in that they could use some of the funds available for reconstruction for investments that did not involve building.

" ... continued to try to get acceptance for as great an investment demand as possible ".

The system of incentives, too, became more rational in that the companies were no longer given an interest in the sheer quantitative fulfilment and overfulfilment of the plans (the latter a form of executing the so-called " gross production plan "). The companies themselves disposed of a part of the bonus funds, and bonus ceilings were lowered considerably (from 50% of one's total earnings). Profit sharing, which was based on genuinely productive company activity, was an attempt to give greater emphasis to qualitative as apposed to purely quantitative demands. At the same time, the economic milieu (including the price system and limited company management) being what it was, it comes as no surprise to read the following in the National Planning Office report: " ... The system of profit sharing is not what its name would lead one to expect: as it is today, one might just as well call it a collective bonus, or a director's fund calculated once a year ".

All these changes indubitably made the system of planning and control somewhat more flexible, and operated to resolve a number of its more prominent earlier contradictions. Similar correctives were to be made in later years as well.

New turning-point: the preparations for radical reform from 1964

As the first half of the 1960s showed, in spite of partial reforms the familiar difficulties of the system were reproduced and results quite the opposite of what the economic policy makers had hoped for: it led the companies to continue to strive for quantitative results, independently of whether the goods were of a marketable quality; induced them to use as much imported material, manpower and raw material as possible in production; to neglect considerations of economy and effectiveness, and to neglect technological development as well. The early sixties were years of great economic tensions (In this study I cannot discuss this in detail). Suffice it to say that the lack of adequate responsiveness in restructuring production, and indifference to the need for technological development and to qualitative demands made it impossible to balance the considerable volume of imports with exports that were marketable abroad; this led to the accumulation of debts so great that as early as 1962/3 the payments due amounted to twice the country's hard currency earnings from exports. A part of the industrial products manufactured to fulfil plan directives were of such a poor quality that they were unmarketable both at home and abroad. By 1964-65, the country's unmarketable stocks came to 8% of the national income, an amount more than twice greater than that spent on national defence. It was only in agriculture that the system of planning and control had undergone radical change, and served the country's economic policy goals; in industry and the other branches, the situation was practically unaltered. The theoretical arguments of 1957 were being decided by experience.

Yet there was also another kind of experience to fall back on in these years of economic tensions, the experience that reform, partial though it was, was possible and desirable. This change in attitude, and what had been learned from the economic experiments of the intervening years, stood Hungary in good stead. Her political and economic leaders were realistic and courageous enough to take another look at the programme for radical economic reform.

The intention to do so was first expressed in the February, 1964 issue of the *Társadalmi Szemle* in an article by Rezsö Nyers, the Central Committee's new secretary for economic affairs. "The methods of economic planning and economic incentives", he wrote, "must always be suited to the economic policy aims of the given period... It would be a grave mistake indeed to see any one system of planning and control as the essence of a socialist planned economy". The author then went on to say that he felt that the time had come " ... for us to reexamine the methods of economic planning and its incentives ".[66]

On July 21, 1964, the Hungarian Socialist Workers' Party's Economic Committee met to discuss proposals " On the direction of work on the development of economic planning, and its programme ". The Committee decided "... to start a comprehensive analysis of economic planning, including the mechanism of production, of incentives, of financing and of management, the price and monetary systems, and the structure of the economy... We must come up with a critical evaluation of the present economic mechanism and economic system, and work out a comprehensive plan for their reshaping ".[67] A committee of three headed by Rezsö Nyers was set up to coordinate the work which was to involve experts in every sphere touching the economy, and was to take two years. (István Friss, who had revised his earlier views on the basis of the experiences of the intervening years also had an important part in this work).

The initiation of such a reform programme was, obviously, facilitated by the fact that in the Soviet Union, too, the summer of 1964 saw the beginning of a public debate with articles by J. Liberman, V. Trapeznykov and others in *Pravda* on the need for economic reform. In 1965 the Czechoslovak government, too, started to prepare an economic reform programme headed by O. Sik. The need for change was, thus, in the air.

At the December 10th 1964 sitting of the Central Committee of the Hungarian Socialist Workers' Party the lessons to be learned from the current five year plan were discussed, with the following conclusion: " The Central Committee... considers it necessary that the present economic mechanism... be subjected to comprehensive and critical analysis, and that it be modified accordin-

---

[66] Rezsö Nyers, Az ötéves terv derekán (Midway through the five year plan), *Társadalmi Szemle*, No. 2, 1964, p. 19.

[67] Party History Archives, 288 f. 15, Minutes of the July 21, 1964 sitting of the Economic Policy Committee.

gly ".[68] Reform had been given a green light. On November 18-20, 1965, the Central Committee was already discussing " The first principles of the reform of the system of economic planning ".

The document that ensued was a radical change from the stand taken by the party and the government eight years earlier: " Critical analysis has led to the unequivocal and unanimous conviction that there is a need for fundamental change. The main shortcomings of the present system are obviously closely interrelated, and cannot be eliminated one by one, but only through complex and comprehensive action ". Speaking of the earlier, partial corrective measures, the Committee pronounced them " correct at the time ", adding that " today, more than this is needed... A basic problem ", the resolution went on, " is that our system of economic planning is still... greatly centralized; the companies have minimal independence, the economy is still regulated principally by strict and direct state intervention in the form of compulsory directives, market impulses and the law of supply and demand are permitted to have little active influence on the economy... Our economic mechanism as a whole is not sufficiently conducive to our taking advantage of the benefits of the international division of labour... Our present system of economic mechanism... has become incompatible with our economic policies, and retards their realization... *it is high time to change the present system giving a ministry-by-ministry, company-by-company breakdown of the national economic plan* ", declared the resolution. " All too often, such a breakdown far from helping to fulfil the plan, achieves just the opposite... A typical fault of our entire price system is that prices greatly — and, economically speaking, unjustifiably — diverge from the social cost of the product in question, and that ... prices are too rigid,

---

[68] *A Magyar Szocialista Munkáspárt határozatai és dokumentumai* 1963-1966 (Resolutions and documents of the Hungarian Socialist Workers' Party), Henrik Vass (ed.), p. 107.

and quite unsuited for harmonizing supply and demand... We have come to the conclusion that price relations and the law of value exist and operate in socialist economies as well, and that they must be made the best use of to promote progress. We must take steps to ensure that price relations and related economic phenomena — the market, prices, cost prices, profits, credit, etc. — will play a substantially greater and more active part in the socialist economy... *historically speaking, the organic unity of socialist planning and of active market relations is inevitable...* The main task of economic planning", we read in the 1965 resolution, in words reminiscent of the phrasing of the December resolution of 1956, "is to project the chief goals of economic development... and their proportionate weight;... we must give considerably greater independence to the nationalized enterprises... This can be done... through seeing that the plans are fulfilled not through various specific breakdowns. i.e. not through the administrative prescription of plan indicators, but through principally economic means..." [69] This is enough to show us that the government economic policy of 1964–65 was, in effect, a return to the radical reform program of December 1956.

The economic reform worked out and introduced in Hungary between 1964 and 1968, in spite of the compromises and internal contradictions that made it less effective, and in spite of the attacks soon made on it in the hopes of bringing about its defeat, nevertheless introduced a new type of planning, one which marked a historical turning-point in the development of the Hungarian socialist economic model.

Today, we are witnessing a new chapter in the development of this model, one that is still being written — amid the debates attempts to check it, and the compelling pressures of the 'seventies to keep moving ahead — by the day-to-day reality of Hungary's economy and economic policy.

---

[69] *Loc. cit.*, p. 278.

IX

THE CRISIS OF THE HUNGARIAN REFORM IN THE 1970s*

Successful reform and plans for further development after 1968

The reform decision made by the Central Committee of the Hungarian Socialist Workers' Party in May 1966 can be regarded as one of historical importance. It abolished the centralized bureaucratic planning based on mandatory targets and thus started the transformation of the functional and management system of the economy. Intensified interests and market incentives brought about a more flexible system which, important compromises notwithstanding, provided favourable opportunities for exploiting the prosperous trends at that time evident in the world economy. Accelerated growth, faster technological modernization, improvement in services, large-scale development of motoring and a surplus on the balance of payments (which had rarely occurred before) were all signs of successful adjustment to the international trends of prosperity. In this article, although I do not want to examine the frequently discussed questions of the results and effects of the economic reform, it does seem indispensable to briefly discuss the fact that the preparation of the "second stage" of the reform originally introduced with deliberate compromises and planned to be gradual, in other words, the preparation of a more consistent assertion of the 1966 reform conception began very soon after the introduction of the reform. The Economic Policy Committee, the highest economic policy body of the Hungarian Socialist Workers' Party, discussed a proposition concerning the "Subject matter of the further development of the economic management system, and the organization of the work" at its meeting of 30th September 1968. Consequently, it made the statement that "the functioning of the economic management system, its analysis, the strengthening of its influence and its further perfection necessitate two

*A true account on and evaluation of the debate necessitates a hint on two facts, not mentioned in the papers above.

1. The pioneering paper by I. T. Berend was written and published in Hungarian before the Party Conference in June 1988, that is, before the shift which made analyses of this type possible.

2. Beside the two articles rejoining the debate a third one has also been published in *Valóság*, the monthly that published I. T. Berend's paper, namely, by László *Szabó*, a well-known journalist, who is more than once cited in the debate. As his argumentation does not contain any relevant aspects of the questions disputed we did not find it necessary to include his paper in the presentation of the debate.

different lines of activity." On the one hand, it was seen to require "theoretical activity involving scientific analysis concerned with a long-term outlining of the means of economic management and the regulators needed to serve the evolvement and completion of the reform, and of its feasible variations." To guide this activity, a committee was formed with István *Friss*, Péter *Vályi*, József *Bognár*, Lajos *Faluvégi* and Tamás *Nagy* as members. At the same time, preparatory work was started on positive reform measures such as the "establishment of a uniform rate of exchange. . . (convertibility – uniform rate of exchange – domestic price system)". In addition, there began an analysis of questions concerning "the extent to which the administrative, banking and other organizations can come up to demands; according to which principles, and in which direction they should be further developed. . ." The following areas also became topics of research: "ways to improve the social control of the economy, the role of the supervisory committee. . . advantages and disadvantages of filling management jobs through competition, etc." [1].

The proposition of the Chairman of the National Board for Material and Prices, submitted in spring 1969. already contained a far-reaching new measure of the Economic Policy Committee concerning the price reform: "The task facing the long-term price policy arise exactly from the fact that the criteria providing the basis of the 1968 price reform have, so far, been only partly asserted." Lack of competition, exceptions integrated into the system of regulators, a wide gap between consumer and producer prices, and the restrictive effect of fixed prices were indicated as causes. It was stated that "these circumstances cannot be fundamentally changed within a short time", but further reform measures must be taken so that "world market relative prices should more definitely affect price formation. The aim is that, by the early 1980s, consumer prices which can in fact promote rational changes in demand and supply should be predominant."

The Economic Policy Committee made yet another far-reaching fundamental decision at the same meeting: "In the course of elaborating the price policy conception, it has to be taken into account that the convertibility of the forint, and a currency reform will be items on the agenda in the coming years. . . In the course of further perfection of the price system, efforts must be made to ensure that relative prices on the domestic market should more clearly reflect relative prices on the world market, thereby contributing to the restructuring of production. . ." [2]

From 1969 on, the large-scale plans for further development of the reform affected fields which had been untouched by the 1968 reform, on account of unavoidable compromises. One of these fields, particularly to be stressed, was the programme of institutional transformation, deliberately neglected by the reform. The Economic Policy Committee discussed the proposition concerning the "further development of large enterprise organization" in summer 1969. It made the following statement: "The monopolistic position must not be maintained in the production and trade of such consumer articles. . . where this position entails disadvantages for household supply and price formation." A decision was made supporting the principle which recommended the splitting up of a few large enterprises and trusts. It was also laid down that "it has to be investigated, in which fields and by what means small and medium enterprises using up-to-date equipment and functioning profitably should be established." [3]

When, eighteen months later, the implementation of this decision was reviewed, reports had already been made of a few minor investigation covering 70–80 enterprises (i.e. in 1970). [4] In that year, an exhaustive institutional reform plan for the restructuring of enterprise organization was drawn up.

The Economic Policy Committee stated that: "The enterprise organization, in the way it has developed in the past, has failed to provide the optimum organizational framework for the evolvement of the reform in several fields. It did not seem expedient to revise enterprise organizations simultaneously with introducing the reform. However, in order to improve the efficiency of the reform, it is necessary to carry out a revision and correction of the enterprise organizations.

Under the work programme of the Economic Policy Committee, we started a revision of organization in certain industries – building industry, transport and trade. . . In the course of the rush reorganization of 1962–64, many enterprises were fused into national large-scale enterprises to comply with the requirements of the central management. In a number of industries the large enterprise or the trust worked in a monopolistic position. . . Such a position developed in several such fields in which this structure is an obstacle to any sound competition. . . Large monopolistic organizations often play a role that is disadvantageous for consumer and producer prices. . . The crux of the problem involves the existence of unjustified monopolistic positions and. . . with a lack of the small and medium enterprises which are indispensable for satisfying consumer needs. . . competition must also be made possible by splitting up large enterprises and by organizing factory units into independent enterprises."

"In conformance with the guiding principles, the types of measures for the development of organizations are as follows: splitting up large economic units (the large enterprise and trust). . . cutting off units from monopolistic large enterprise organizations; . . . The establishment of direct relations between domestic and foreign trade on the one hand and producer organizations on the other, widening the sphere of those enterprises disposing of dependent foreign trade rights, and the creation of new organizational forms."* The appendix of the proposition also contained the detailed suggestions of each ministry for the abolition of enterprise monopolies and the splitting up of a few large enterprises.

*"In consideration of practical needs, monopolistic types of organization seem to be justified in certain public utility services, e.g. MÁV – Hungarian State Railways, the post office, if that is reasonable in view of optimum size (with regard to international competitiveness). This also applies to such fields where domestic and international load distribution requires direct operative measures (for example, electric energy industry, aluminium metallurgy, meat industry). The monopolistic position must not be maintained in the field of consumer articles and non-communal services in which such a position entails disadvantages for household supply and price formation." [5]

It may seem surprising how long I have dwelt on (not to mention the length of the passages quoted) the 1970 programme of the institutional reform, which aimed at splitting up the large enterprise organization. This is, however, justified by the importance of the envisaged reform measure and by the need to demonstrate the existence of a reform strategy encompassing progressive principles, and striving to assert itself gradually and consistently.

The work that was started between 1968–70 on further development of the reform (i.e. the preparation of the planned "second stage" of the reform) is of such significance that it justifies presentation of work accomplished in another field: that concerning capital and labour to flow more freely and, further, together with the top-level decisions made on the subject. Relying on the decision of the Economic Policy Committee, the Economic Policy Department of the Central Committee formed a work commission with the task of examining the flow of social capital. In the report of this work the following can be read: "The commission has made extensive analyses and drawn up proposals. . . for the temporary or definitive redistribution of the decentralized development resources and for the introduction of a partial commercial credit, for an increased variety of forms serving redistribution of the fixed assets of economic units, for the legal regulation of the issue of and subscription to bonds, and for the establishment of an institution that would organize and deal with the planned flow of capital.

The commission's proposals have been discussed and approved by the Economic Policy Committee. . ." In addition, the Commission considered it to be important that the freer flow of resources should start as a complementary form, in a decentralized manner.

"Legal rules that are in force have so far not allowed a temporary or definitive redistribution of the decentralized development sources in the sphere (and within the scope of authority) of enterprises." The commission, however, took a stand which enabled "the temporary and definitive transfer of development funds. This will allow development funds that are free for short or long periods to be allocated to areas in which they can be used more efficiently. Development funds can be definitively transferred for investment purposes or for financing permanent needs for working capital, and credits can be granted from such funds for the placement of commercial supplies. . . State-owned enterprises and cooperatives may transfer or let or freely lend to one another their fixed assets and material goods (machines, equipment, etc.). . . The Work Commission suggested that issue of and subscription to bonds be allowed, since this form of redistribution of social capital can be fitted into the Hungarian economic management system and it would entail economic advantages. On the basis of the decision made by the Economic Policy Committee, preparatory work began on the legal settlement of the question. According to the conception. the issuers will be the central organs of the state, certain groups of councils, large enterprises, cooperative centres and banking institutions; the subscribers will be the economic units (enterprises, cooperatives), councils and private individuals. The proposed bonds will be negotiable through the banking institution authorized thereto; this may involve the selling, or contracting of a loan against security on the bond. Bond issue will be subject to licence and, in order to acquire the necessary experience (after the legal settlement), in the first instance it will only operate in a narrow sphere, mainly with a view to satisfying local communal needs."

". . . As was suggested by the work commission, the Economic Policy Committee has decided to establish a Central Development Institute. . . According to the conception, the Institute will deal with grants and allocations in connection with the large-scale development of working enterprises ("increase of the capital stock"), their reduction or winding up ("withdrawal of capital"), foundation of small and medium enterprises, and investments (also involving favours und grants). Preparations for the establishment of the institute are under way, as is also the investigation of questions regarding the development of a rational organization of the banking system.

The Economic Policy Committee further considers it important that economic research pay more attention to the theoretical problems of the flow of social capital." [6]

In 1970, the economic management started work on the reform of the flow of assets and capital, the flow and mobility of labour, the wage reform transforming wage and income proportions in order to promote the former. In this respect, one important measure taken within the framework of the 1968 reform was now considered as only an initial step. This involved the abolition of the earlier applied strict penalties for "arbitrarily" leaving an enterprise, i.e. the liberation of the flow of labour, which had been put into practice by a modification of the Labour Code. The deputy ministers' meeting in the Ministry of Labour – charged with the preparatory work in restructuring wages and income relations and of forming concepts for a long-range income policy – reported on the progress of these preparations of further development in the following manner: "In the middle of the present year, the Economic Committee instructed the Minister of Labour to draw up a long-range programme for the transformation of income relations and to submit it to the Economic Committee before the end of the next year."

"On the basis of the known criteria and economic processes, certain questions must be answered. For instance, how should the difference between minimum and maximum earnings – in percentage and in absolute forint amounts – change? What role should qualifications play in determining relative earnings? In comparison with the present situation, what shift is necessary in the relative earnings? What does the notion of high earnings indicate? Is it possible at all to determine this in an absolute or relative sense? . . .

Analyses should be made of the direct and indirect prospects for, and the necessity of, influencing extremely high personal incomes." [7]

Thus it is evident that between 1968 and 1970 the development and further progress of a price system more reflective of relative values and international market effects, the preparation of an institutional reform of enterprise organization so as to improve the conditions of competition on the market, the preparatory works necessary for creating a convertible currency, the laying down of the conditions for the freer flow of capital and labour among enterprises and the establishment of the necessary institutions were already on the agenda and fitted into the existing strategy of a genuine further development of the reform. These measures would have eliminated many of the compromises and restraints which had been built into the 1968 reform. As such, they would have promoted a gradual yet essential further development of a more consistent mechanism of economic functioning, taking into account political and social conditions.

However, in the early 1970s, further development programmes were soon taken off the agenda.

Halt – adverse criticism of the reform

The preparatory works of an institutional reform came to a halt. It became quite clear that the further development of the solitary Hungarian reform and a consistent assertion of its principles were hardly feasible. The entire history of the Hungarian reform process demonstrates clearly that it was definitely influenced by the reform trends emerging in the socialist countries, the policy adopted in 1956 by the 20th Congress of the Communist Party of the Soviet Union, the 1964–65 Soviet reform initiatives (the so-called Liberman dispute) and the Czechoslovak reform decision. János *Kádár* could justly state at the November, 1967 meeting of the Central Committee: "Economic management reforms similar to ours are in the making in several countries. . . I think that is an international necessity urged by development." [8] However, after the introduction of the Hungarian reform, i.e. at the end of the 1960s and beginning of the 1970s, the situation radically changed. Reforms were not only taken off the agenda, but reform became increasingly suspicious of "reformism".

The Hungarian reform process (which the party leadership insisted on carrying further in spite of the radically changed international environment since the preparatory phase) elicited distrust. Consequently, it faced open or covert criticism from the end of the 1960s. Prime Minister Jenő *Fock* openly discussed the matter before the public at the national propaganda meeting in 1971. He talked of the unease in other socialist countries about the abolition of compulsory plans, the introduction of market elements, and the weakening of the omnipotence of the state. These developments were judged to be perilous to socialist conditions.

In December 1973 an article in the daily *Népszabadság* talked about the "fraternal worries" shown towards the Hungarian reform: "Although the instances are less frequent, we have seen in our friends not only trust but also worries with regard to our economic management system. What is a planned economy without compulsory plans for enterprises? How is the state's role asserted, if more than half of the investments are put at the disposal of enterprises? Such and similar questions have often been raised, especially in the course of disputes among economists." [9]

It is hard to judge and, at the present time, impossible to reveal in detail, what mass of direct and indirect criticism and pressure existed beneath the publicly known surface, it was just the tip of the iceberg that could be seen.

In any case, the criticism – expressed in various forms in the early 1970s – encouraged the Hungarian party leadership to adopt a defensive stance, forcing it to repeatedly declare that it did not want essential changes, that the reform that had been put into effect did not produce an economic management system different from that of other socialist countries, and that no "Hungarian model" existed at all.

In October 1972 the central party daily stressed in an inner editorial: "We are witnessing the increased use of *one of the latest methods of anticommunism: propagation of the various « models »* of socialism. . .

Its objective is . . . to stir up nationalism, encourage national separation, and give rise to distrust between countries that are building a new society. According to these dual efforts, the « models » themselves can be divited into two different groups. One comprises the so-called «types of socialism», and these are described as «democratic» and «humane», etc.; the other consists of "national types", such as «Russian» or «Hungrian» socialism. . .

The models of «national» socialism attempt to confront national particularities with the general rules of socialist building. . . They make use of the «models» to «justify» and promote national separatism, as well as to belittle the international significance of the Soviet experience in the building of socialism. *The purpose of the theory of different national models of socialism is to rouse nationalistic and anti-Soviet feeling.*

Bourgeois propaganda also proclaims the existence of a«Hungarian model», contrasting it with the work of other countries building socialism . . . In this respect, our position is clearly to refuse the unfounded conceptions surrounding a so-called «Hungarian mode.»" [10]

In spite of the first few successful years and further development of the "new economic mechanism", the hesitation of the reform process soon led to the emergence of even stronger anti-reform criticism and disputes. This was rooted mainly in the inner social conflicts had been deepened by the reform.

The reform, although quite extensive, had only partly been put into effect and this raised difficult new requirements, disturbed deep-rooted habits, and upset hard-set doctrines. There were also numerous misunderstandings. The latter were magnified by inexperience and the errors committed, as well as by the omission of necessary interventions. The functioning of the reform mechanism basically hurt earlier vested in various fields and on various levels. In other words, interests jeopardized by the reform were important factors underlying the tensions and the criticism. The principle of differentiation of incomes according to quality, value, and amount of performance worked against the interests of those refusing to increase their efforts, those seeking comfortable positions, or those unable to improve their performance. Such attitudes helped to produce average – or below-average – results, and thus the levelling off of incomes served their interests well.

That type of medium-level manager who was never compelled to make an independent decision, nor was capable of making one, who shifted responsibility on to higher levels, who rested content in a comfortable approach of "not doing anything will cause no trouble", and who put obstacles in the way of those "obsessed" with seeking new ways and taking risks – it is in the interest of such a manager to see that the environment gives him security (also strengthened through a few personal ties). The emphasis laid on competence alarmed the tens of thousands holding medium-level posts in the administration and the political leadership who had only political-ideological trustworthiness and good connections to their credit.

The reform obviously hurt a lot of interests. This intensified conflicts and elicited attacks.

More exactly, it provided opportunities to pretend to act in the interest of workers and the protection of socialism, to exploit the undeniably emerging social tensions, and to ensure a kind of mass support – all with the intention of backing up the political attack on the ruling power and the political trends. Accordingly, certain groups conjured up images of increasing capitalistic tendencies and talked of the discarding, or at least a serious weakening, of the planned economy. In the field of income policy, they pointed to the suppression of workers' interests and talked about a "private paradise". They were worried about state-owned industry because the agricultural cooperatives were becoming "over-pretentious"; they were anxious about socialist principles because of the levels of income differentiation and the trickeries that distorted it; and, against the "economist's" approach to efficiency, they laid emphasis on ownership, incomes policy, and the socialist way of life.

The situation was an intricate one, fraught with many confusions. For example, by giving priority to household supply, the reform intended to allow greater scope to small enterprise or to the small- and large-enterprise combination. This was inevitable, for state-owned big industry, the advanced state-owned network of services, and the socialist large-scale farms could not satisfy the demand for commodities (either in volume or the necessary range of choice) and indispensable services. Of course, such services were mainly in the interest of workers – who constitute the greater part of the population – for they eliminated, for example, meat shortages that had frequently occurred before, and provided mending and repair services.

It has to be added that the political leadership had to explain this interaction as early as the mid-1960s, at the time of the preparation and introduction of the reform. Party leaders made serious efforts at explaining to party members and to all workers that the recognition and assertion of the interests of agriculture and the peasantry represent, in the final account, a policy in the workers' interest. For example, in connection with the raising of agricultural procurement prices, Lajos *Fehér* argued in a public debate in early 1966 against, those who ". . . object to « the extent of support » given to the peasantry. Many even add that, «as a matter of fact, workers pay for the raising of the peasants' living standards.» A certain amount of anti-peasant feeling arises in town from time to time. Such feeling is now strenghthening." [11]

János Kádár stressed in a speech he delivered about the same time: "Such superficial statements according to which problems are solved at the expense of cities are much too biassed and fraught with emotional elements. It has even been said that peasants are not working but speculating. . . Party members must by all means understand that the measures taken are part of a well-considered conception which, in harmony with our previous policy, is to serve the interests of the working class and of the whole working people. . ." [12]

Beside the trustworthiness of these words, facts: a fast elimination of meat shortages and the general improvement of supply were genuinely convincing, at least for some time. After a few years, however, parallel with the development of income differentiation, anti-peasant and anti-intellectual emotions were again prevalent. Peasants' incomes were, namely, growing faster than workers' incomes, though the latter were growing at a higher rate than ever before. There appeared, of course, those "clever" people who grew rich in 2–3 years by exploiting the grave shortages of the capacities of the state-owned building industry, and by making use of the building boom brought about by increasing incomes. Yet there was a lack of measures which could have hindered the growth of differences and the exploitation of deepening social tensions. For example, there were no adequate measures of taxation.

Another opinion, which emerged and enjoyed mass support, claimed that "order must be made", the economy must be subordinated to incomes policy, household farming should not enable peasants to grow wealthier than workers, the outstanding incomes earned by intellectuals and managers in their main jobs and their extras should be limited, and these measures were to be implemented in such a way that, limitations notwithstanding, risk-taking initiatives would be encouraged along with the productive spirit, so that no recession should occur in any field. No adequate compromises were found, however.

The leading group of reform critics within the political leadership, who aimed to "cut off the excesses of the reform", opened a line of attack in autumn 1972. It will be the task of a coming generation of researchers to reveal the matter in full by poring over archival sources.* It is already a well known fact, however, that in spring 1972, when he was sixty years old, János Kádár offered his resignation to the Central Committee. The latter did not accept the resignation but asked János Kádár to retain his post. At the same time, certain conservative political groups increased their activities and, in their drive for greater power, they found the best ideological basis in the protection of "workers' interests" and "socialist values". It was clear that they had some international support.

Criticism of the Hungarian reform at home found ample support and a reference basis in the conservative circles of the other socialist countries, and in their distrust of the Hungarian reform. This criticism broke through officially and publicly, though only partially, in November 1972. The decree approved at the Central Committee meeting, while stating that "the economic management system put into force on the 1st January 1968 is an appropriate and efficient means of serving the socialist planned economy and of building socialism", stressed that the execution of earlier decisions had not been adequate in every respect, and, "what is more, it does not follow the desired course in certain fields, nor is it implemented in the desirable way." [13]

*At the time of writing this manuscript, the party archives were open to research up to the end of 1970; details revealing the divisions of 1970 were thus not available.

Two and a half years later, in his contribution to the 11th Congress of the Hungarian Socialist Workers' Party, Árpád *Pullai* – secretary of the Central Committee – said in reference to the November 1972 Central Committee meeting: "The party did not hesitate to examine the correctness of some of its earlier decisions. It had the strength and the courage to make corrections in accordance with society's interests and our principles. . . it corrected the trend where it was not satisfactory." [14]

Zoltán *Komócsin*, secretary in charge of the foreign affairs section of the Central Committee spoke even more plainly in his article "With unchanged politics" in *Népszabadság* in spring 1974: ". . . it was stated in the resolution of the 10th Congress that the Hungarian economic management system introduced in 1968 has stood the test. . . Yet we must *not* be dogmatic and insist *rigidly on every word that has been said. . . What was good yesterday may grow out-of-date today and it may need to be changed. . . let us learn* – the more the better – *from the approved methods of the other socialist countries. . .* It is a well-known fact that the economic management system of the European fraternal countries. . . is different from ours in numerous respects." The conclusion suggested that "*with constant adjustment and further development of practice in accordance with the changing requirements of reality*, we continue our way without wavering. . ." [15] Such reasoning expressed a need to revise the reform.

In autumn 1972 and in the ensuing years, efforts were made to release tensions and to carry out the corrections necessary for the sake of the reform, but attempts were also made to abolish the most important achievements of the reform. There was great confusion. Important groups of the political leadership maintained that the "two-front struggle" was the correct response in this situation and emphasized the risks confronting both sides in the debate. The editor-in-chief of the central party periodical *Társadalmi Szemle* thought it important in January 1973 to contradict certain rumours about the Central Committee decision "which say that essential opinions representing different platforms were expressed. Some say. . . that the followers of two basic conceptions, representing radically different objects, clashed. . . and continue to clash, and a battle between «reformists» and «dogmatists» has been mentioned." [16]

So much is in any case certain: that those against the reform were also compelled to make compromises. János Kádár repeatedly and very definitely made the statement in public: ". . . the Hungarian economic policy – including its agricultural policy – and the cultural policy are unchanged; we will pursue our well-tried economic management system. . ." [17] In the given situation, however, when conservative trends were also predominant on the international level, it seems that no way could be found to defend the reform line other than that of compromises and flexible retreat. Although the line was in a less advantageous and weaker form, the compromise at least enabled the fundamental achievements of the reform to be maintained.

The November decree of the Central Committee caused disappointment in certain anti-reformist circles. The editors of the central party periodical put questions to four leading party workers in early December 1972. "We asked them about the reception of the highly significant Central Committee stand taken. . ." One of those questioned – Pál

Romány, first secretary of the Party Committee of the Country of Bács-Kiskun – said, among other things: "Some expected a kind of «making order» . . . hoping to see it proved that errors can be made only «at the top» and that, consequently, the economic management system, or perhaps the cultural policy is to be blamed. . . Such expectations have not been fulfilled . . . those pressing for nothing but firmness and voicing pseudo-radical views wanted our party to retreat. . ."

A similar view was expressed by the first secretary of the Party Committee of the 13th District of Budapest: "Some expected the meeting to justify their opinion, which is that the economic management system has failed and that our policy was wrong." [18]

The central party periodical reverted to these questions some time later and, in an editoral, particularly stressed the point that «leftist» self-justifiers are mistaken in their expectations. . . our party has definitely blocked the way of retreat, i.e. the way back to a sectarian-dogmatic policy and its methods. . ."*

Retreat and recentralization tendencies

The fundamental institutions of the reform introduced in 1968 – economic management without compulsory plans, enterprises' market orientation, and the reliance of the state's control and influencing activities on economic regulators – were no longer to be eliminated. Yet decisions of fundamental importance were made which tended towards recentralization and, by virtue of corrections, there was something of a deliberate retreat. Among them, one statement deserves special attention. This says that "economic management organs should examine separately, and watch the activities of, the biggest 40–50 state-owned enterprises which produce the greater part of Hungary's industrial output and, where it is necessary, special measures must be taken to guarantee for them the necessary working conditions." As a result, the Council of Ministers in fact took the 50 biggest industrial enterprises and, in 1973, placed them under direct central control. These held 60 percent of Hungarian industrial assets, produced approximately a half of the country's industrial output, provided for more than 60 percent of exports and employed 700 thousand men. Although the general and mainly indirect market regulation of the economic management system remained valid for these enterprises, in fact important elements of the system of command management were informally smuggled back into their functioning. This was made obvious by declarations such as that of the Secretary of the Budapest Party Committee: "For us, the political purpose of the decision is the main thing, which is the consistent assertion of our working class policy." ". . . It is now possible for the economic management organs to receive direct and authentic information on the activities of these enterprises. . . Relying upon such information, they can maintain control more efficiently, if the work and interests of the

*Following a strictly "two-front" line, the editorial referred, in the same sentence, to a simultaneous repression of "all revisionist attempts." [19]

biggest industrial enterprises are in harmony with national economic interests, with national economic targets, and with the requirements of the economic policy of the party. Also, they can give immediate help to overcome the enterprises' unexpected difficulties.

It is the sectoral ministers who are mainly responsible . . . for executing the decisions. . . . I mention as an example the fact that the 1976–80 development conceptions of these enterprises will be discussed at a special meeting of the management and control organs concerned." [20]

Also, the Central Committee has ruled that the government should elaborate "an amendment of the economic regulators with a view to a planned development of the national economy. . ." [21]

The amendment of economic regulators started without delay and, in January 1976, corrections that were deemed necessary – along with the new rules which made use of lessons learned but also contributed to retreat – came into operation. In comparison with 1975, 5 percent more of the net income realized in the national economy was centralized. "This also involves a certain expectable centralization of decision-making and financing, in the course of the period," said Ottó *Gadó* about the amendment of the system of regulators. "The so-called large investment projects involving development loans, earlier planned and financed as enterprise investments, came within the central decision-making sphere." What is more, "informal" central interventions were institutionalized in the implementation process, so as to strengthen the role of control organs. This was in order that "the ministries could discuss and report on the important enterprise investment decisions." Through the reduction of import subsidies, and an increase of wage taxes, enterprise profit was reduced by 30–35 percent. In words still stressing anti-egalitarianism, the new regulation set strict limits to enterprises' incentive rewards. These were not to exceed 20 percent of the wages cost of the previous year (including the profit share at the end of the year). At the same time, taxation of the profit sharing fund was implemented in such a way that it reached into the 80 percent upper tax bracket since with "the payment of more than 40 days' profit shares development would be rendered impossible. . ." Through the new order of taxation, profit-sharing was to a considerable extent levelled – differences in fact could move between 15–18 and 36–42 days' wages. At the same time, the new wages regulation system placed a 600 percent payment obligation on average wage-increases over 6 percent, by means of the linear taxation of the average wage-increase.

"This system also «levels» and reduces dispersion" is the way Ottó Gadó summed up the situation in his description of the new regulatory system and he added that, "thereby a distortion of relative wages was rendered avoidable. . . although incentive was to some extent subdued."

Finally, a number of achievements of the reform were allowed to be impaired and overruled by the condition that, "if some objectives of the national plan cannot be attained with a suitable modification of the regulating system, and if it is justified in order to assert the interests of the national economy, ministers may avail themselves of the right of instructing the state enterprises, as laid down in the legal regulations." [22, 22a]

The corrections thus allowed a wide scope for direct central intervention, thus damaging enterprise independence. In autumn 1975 Árpád Pullai also stressed the importance of direct party control: "Such views and positions. . . have emerged which, though not expressly challenging the leading role of the party, would in fact repress it, should they be asserted. For example, some people thought, at the time of the introduction of the economic reform, that the regulators would somehow lead the economy quasi-automatically toward socialism. As a consequence of some erroneous views and a few incorrect measures, the leading role of the party was temporarily weakened in various fields of the economy – in factories, enterprises, and cooperatives. We, too, made a mistake when, at the time of the introduction of the economic management reform, we talked more of what the party organizations should *not* interfere with and less of what they should do. . ." [23]

Passions flared up about the issue. "It is difficult to render in words, to reproduce the atmosphere at the party meeting of the 13th District" the press report said in February 1975. "What is involved was made clear primarily by the party committee secretaries of the two biggest enterprises – given preferential treatment – of Angyalföld: the Hungarian Shipyard and Crane Factory, and the Láng Machine Factory. In their contributions, both levelled sharp criticism at the practice in which some of the central organs left the management of the socialist economy to the automatism of various regulators and considered direct control methods as outdated in the intensive phase of the development of the economy. This practice had, in recent years, given rise to several such economic decisions which, obviously, had disregarded the political consequences. Thus the collectives of large enterprises – of primary importance to the national economy – had been brought into an extremely difficult situation."

Referring to the long traditions of these factories as strongholds of the industrial workers, the contributors challenged the efforts which had been directed at the structural transformation of production. They had found that such efforts hurt their interests. In their judgement the decisions had brought "difficult times" to their enterprises and had caused uncertainty of existence, almost as if there was some anti-worker conspiracy. "That this has not succeeded is thanks to the November 1972 resolution of the Central Committee of the Party. . ." [24]

Among the reasons for direct intervention, however, the *protection* of the state-owned large enterprises, strongholds of industrial workers, played an important role not only on the enterprise level. "The development of state-owned large enterprises is not exclusively an economic question," Central Committee Secretary Béla *Biszku* argued in his contribution at the Party Congress "but it is an integral part of party policy. . . It can well serve the strengthening of the class base of a society that is building socialism." [25] Trade unions and trade union functionaries championed the same views on behalf of the workers of large factories, thus protecting their interests. These developments considerably strengthened the power positions of party and trade union officials.

In summer 1975, a newspaper article, reporting on the findings of party supervision, in large enterprises mentioned a favourable turn as compared with earlier years: "Some of the economic leaders thought at the time that it was enough if the party organization simply provided propaganda for the respective tasks, i.e. for their execution, and the rest was the economic leaders' business. . . Then, the party secretary could easily be reproached for «unauthorized interference» in economic managers' business". . . It rarely occurs today that one or another economic manager should question the right of the party organization. . . ' [26]

At about the same time, *Társadalmi Szemle* argued as follows: "Planned economic management. . . applies direct means in order to achieve the objectives that have been set. Some of the real processes are directly guided on the basis of the national economic plan, through central investments, instructions as to the fulfilment of special production programmes, the emphasizing of certain «expectations», the laying down of quotas, and in a few other forms as well." [27]

The intention to restore direct central intervention could not have been made more obvious by the Central Committee Secretary Árpád Pullai's remarks, made in Parliament in December 1972: ". . . every enterprise – the biggest included – is part of the country's economic processes. They are autonomous, yet not independent of what takes place from time to time in the national economy. The competent ministries must not leave these enterprises to themselves in their duties and difficulties to the extent that they have been in recent years. *Every large enterprise is responsible for its economic management. Yet every ministry is also responsible for the activities and development of the production units belonging to them.*"

"It is part and parcel of a planned economy that, *should any deviation from the current plan occur* – with a ministry, an enterprise, or a workshop – *all competent organs* and persons *should act with* competence and *determination.* In serving the purposes of the plan, operative action is not an artificial, «external» interference in the economy, but a part and method of normal activity." [28] (Let us remember: at the time of this official stand, there was no mandatory plan for enterprises.)

One measure of symbolic value, confirming central control, was the establishment of the National Planning Commission beside the Council of Ministers. This was intended to strengthen the role and efficiency of planning. [29] Another measure of symbolic significance was the raised status of the National Planning Office and the appointment of its president – who before had not even been a minister – to be deputy prime minister.

The November 1972 meeting of the Central Committee also deemed it necessary to effectuate changes in price policy. Although proclaiming the reform principles, it declared that "stability of prices must be guaranteed to a maximum degree. . . price control is to be extended and made stricter. The duty to give preliminary notice of intended changes in prices is to be extended. . . The ratio of limited prices in the building industry must be raised from the present 60 percent to 90 percent. . ." [30]

What effect the resulting change had on the price system of the 1968 reform – in which the objective effect of the changes in world market prices also had a part from late

1973 – is made clear by Minister of Finance, Lajos *Faluvégi*'s words two years later: "producer prices have lost much of their flexibility. . . again, profit fails to express the real efficiency of the enterprise, since prices and costs are not realistic, either. Prices are subsidized to no small extent. . . nearly 30 percent of budget expenditure consists of subsidies; more than half of the total of enterprises' profits comes from subsidies." [31]

Reform criticism was quite strongly directed at the enrichment of peasants, at the unscrupulous assertion of agricultural cooperatives' group interests as against the interests of "society as a whole." In the spirit of a working class policy, emphasis was laid on restraining the auxiliary industrial activities of agricultural cooperatives. The general policy emphasized turning the specifically Hungarian cooperative model, shaped during the previous reform process, back towards the classical "artiel-type" Soviet model, for ideological reasons. Central intervention was urged also in this field, and the local government organs (councils) were given an increased and more direct right of intervention in the affairs of independent and self-managed cooperative enterprises. Looking back on former years, the central party organs stated in June 1976; ". . . as the need has arisen to assert the central will more strongly, councils have been given an increasing number of production policy tasks, such as are *not specifically stated in legal regulation.* (These involve the promotion of special agricultural projects – for example, for cattle, sugar beet, and vegetables – as well as of specializations and unions.)" [32]

It is worth calling attention to the fact that the quoted resolution reflects the return to informal central intervention, i.e. recentralization. This was non-institutionalized, but easy to assert within the given socio-political framework. Such interventions gained special impetus from the "purification" campaign launched against profiteering and corruption. "Order must be made", "a strong hand is needed" – were the widely popular slogans. The leaders of several state farms and cooperatives were arrested and legal proceedings were started.

In the centre: attack against the "excesses"

Once again, I wish to emphasize strongly: there were abuses in abundance. Beside the sudden opening of possibilities, this was also due to uncertain feelings about the perspectives of enterprise and money-making, in consideration of the experience of former decades. Also, the complexity of the regulation and the infinite number of legal restrictions easily drove all kinds of economic activity to the narrow line between keeping the law and offending against it. In the course of the "purification" campaign, many real abuses were discovered. However, the treatment of such affairs, the form of making them public, their mass occurrence, manipulation, and the ideological-political bias accompanying them created an atmosphere in favour of restraining the reform mechanism. In February 1973, in the central daily paper *Népszabadság,* a series was started with the title *Oknyomozás árügyekben* (Investigation in price metters). The reporter had the task of inquiring into unjustified price increases. In one case he even blamed the party secretary of the price-raising cooperative, because of the latter's answer to the following question:

Was it indeed necessary to raise prices and, if so, was there a good reason for raising the price of a plastic shopping bag to such an extent? The answer was that "he was first of all concerned with the problems of the cooperative. That is to say, with group interests," the journalist added. [33]

About the same time, the same journalist described at length the private business disguised as official – of Univerzal, a new fodder concentrate. It actually was a typical case of profiteering. [34]

Similar disclosures proliferated in journals and a year later the proud statement was published: the number of disclosed criminal offences against social property fell from 34 thousand in 1972 to 29 thousand in 1973, due to increased external and internal control. [35] A highly illustrative case is that of the self-employed motor-schools, publicized in December 1963. In autumn 1972, papers reported that state-owned institutions could not satisfy the demand raised by increased opportunities for motor car driving and people were queuing up for motor-schools. *At the time,* the foundation of "self-employed work teams" was suggested as the only solution. "Well, since then a fair number of such work teams have been formed. In the meantime, however, they have not all earned good reputations: on the gates of two Budapest work teams, the inscription is there, symbolically: «closed because of cheating», and the «official winding up» of a third has also begun. . . The outsider. . . is easily led to think that *an evil spirit was released from the bottle* in 1971 by the Ministry of Transport and Communications when it made it legal to establish motor-schools on a self-employed basis." [36] In connection with this affair it was emphatically stated, of course, that the method itself was not to be eliminated. It was the control that needed to be tightened in order to prevent abuses. Yet the press campaign contributed – even in case of the correct treatment of individual cases – to the development of a definite political medium, and intensified distrust in general. This was the case in particular with agricultural cooperatives and state farms, where public attention was often drawn to "irregular functioning" and a number of police and judicial procedures were started against the heads of those state farms and cooperatives suspected of abuses. I think it is needless to prove that, as a consequence, not only were abuses discovered, but an increasingly chilly atmosphere surrounded the independent, flexible enterprising activities, such that they grew ever riskier.

Regulation, price policy, taxation and other instruments offered adequate possibilities for restraint. In 1974–75 the government made ample use of those instruments. However, the restrictive measures, and the propaganda which created an atmosphere of suspicion suddenly interrupted the upward trend of household-plot commodity production. In 1967, 220 thousand pigs were purchased from household-plot farms, whereas in 1974 the figure stood at 2.4 million. In other words, the pig stock of these farms increased more than tenfold as a result of the reform.

In summer 1975, however, a journalist of *Népszabadság* reported, after indicating the above-mentioned data, the following surprising news: "Yet all this is not to say that everything is all right about household-plot farms. A few of the cooperative leaders think that work on the household farming plots draws members away from the common activities. Therefore, these leaders *do not sufficiently help* household-plot production.

... What kind of troubles may arise... is demonstrated exactly by the change that took place in pig breeding last year. In the said year, the previous smooth development of household-plot farming broke, which is shown most clearly by the fact that by the second half of 1974, the number of sows in household-plots and auxiliary farms fell from 417 thousand to 290 thousand." [37]

So much is quite clear from that newspaper article that in 1974 the sow population of household-plot farms *fell by* no less than *a quarter.* The vague attempts at explanation were hardly convincing. A few weeks afterwards, further information on the matter could be read in the same daily in an article by Árpád *Pünkösti* under the title *Visszatér a múlt?* (Are times past coming back?): "In the village, beside transformation, progressive tax is the subject that has been upsetting people for some time. Let us see how.

Zoltán Szél and his wife have built up a nice little world of their own: mechanized household, mechanized farming... A horse, two cows, motorbicycle, Polski-Fiat car. Behind it, ten years of hard work. Zoltán Szél had two jobs: he did farming and transporting. His wife drove the plough till midnight, after midnight he continued... and then the pain and torment of being harassed.

... « Like this special tax now. I am not going to work to pay most of my income in tax», he says quietly but emphatically. A few days ago, his wife left her bed to sleep, through three nights, in the pigsty, so that the sow did not crush to death any one of the twelve piglets. Last year they reared that many porkers and two calves, but they will not do it any more. (Have similar decisions played a role in the fact that last year the number of sows fell by 30 percent in the district of Szeged?)

At Zákányszék there were 13 special tax-payers. Last year 51 farms were found to exceed the yearly Ft.50 thousand of net income. A great uproar!

... This is a difficult situation. Is it possible in today's world to simply bring back the past by a few measures? Some say that this is something similar to the kulak-lists, because it is as it was in the past, with the difference that the limit is not 25 cadastral yokes* but Ft50 thousand...

Zoltán Szél, therefore, steps out of the bracket of special tax. He will not work 14-hour days any more, he will have more time for choir-singing, theatre, etc. This is certainly good on the cultural side, but I do not think it is so good on the supply side." [38]

It can be seen that the tone of the press took a sharp turn in summer 1975, as a consequence of the frightening reaction to pig-slaughtering i.e. the menacing meat shortage. What we are interested in now is, however, not that, but the facts presented.

*14.25 acres was the limit above which peasants were classified as kulak. Ed. note.

The ideology of "development" of socialist ownership

The ideological basis for standing up against household-plot farming and auxiliary activities consisted in the consolidation of socialist production relations and the suppression of capitalist tendencies. This was voiced by Béla Biszku, second man in the party leadership, who lent the greatest emphasis exactly to this issue in his address at the national propaganda meeting, held at Balatonaliga in September 1975.

It is worth following his train of thought. He started by declaring that *state property* was public property, i.e. it represented *"a more developed form of socialist ownership."* "State property is public property in this country because it is not owned by a group or section of society, but by the whole nation. . . it serves the interests of the entire society, because its results do not benefit a group or a sector of society, but society as a whole." He stated that state property *"was to be considered as a higher form of socialization."* It is to be noted that Béla Biszku had already contradicted, at this initial point of his reasoning, the conclusion drawn from the historical review he had made in the introduction – namely, that the results achieved so far by Hungarian agriculture were inseparable from the clarification, after 1956, of "the most important questions of theory and principle concerning cooperative property." He justly recalled that "our theory had to be cleared of the distortions that had been spoiling it, especially in the early 1950s. One such distortion was to consider cooperative property. . . a lower-degree form of socialist ownership." This erroneous thesis was then "pushed to the extremes in practice."

He seemed to forget about this, however, when taking practically the same position as the one qualified as "distorted". In addition, paying little attention to the facts of life, he challenged the views that held "cooperative ownership to be more advantageous than state ownership", capable of more mobile and flexible functioning. He complained that "There were a few economists who. . . insisted that cooperative ownership was the more efficient form and that its fixed assets and live labour are better managed than in state-owned establishments. From this apparent «advantage» they came. . . to the conclusion that cooperative ownership was «more democratic» and «more social» than state ownership."

As against this, he rested content with making the following statement: "We are not faced with the actual or presumed advantages of the form of ownership, but with the form of economic management", which is "strongly limited". Yet what matters is that "these are exploited. . . exactly on account of the group-property character of the cooperative form of ownership. . . not so much in the interest of society as a whole, but in that of the group."

He indicated that the road of development of agricultural cooperatives involved "increasing the socialization of labour", leading it towards "gradually higher forms", and "confirming the socialist traits of cooperatives." What exactly was to be understood thereby was made clear by the ensuing theoretical explanation. This was to the effect that "household-plot farming is not to be considered a socialist form of farming." He polemized with those who argued that "in this country cooperative members' household farming plots are ever closer related to the cooperative farm and consequently draw the conclusion that these are «small socialist farms». This is nonsense. The household farming plot is not public property... its income is the member's, not the cooperative's." Although Béla Biszku stressed that support for household-plot farming was to continue, his starting-point concerned forms of ownership, and his emphasis on the strengthening of the socialist traits of cooperatives as a central task made it quite clear what the unambiguous perspectives of this policy were.

The other central issue surrounding the "strengthening of socialist traits" was expressed in the constraints imposed on the auxiliary industrial activities of agricultural cooperatives. "This activity," Béla Biszku stated, "began to produce several negative tendencies in the early 1970s... this situation also gave impetus to a negative process from the aspect of ownership. The cooperatives in which such auxiliary activities were pursued on a large scale realized considerable additional income." He spoke in more detail about fourteen agricultural cooperatives near to Budapest, which had been examined by the Political Committee. In these cooperatives, only 20 percent of the earnings had come from agricultural activities and, though "satisfying important national economic and, partly, household needs" through their various industrial activities, *"they had drawn thousands of former large enterprise workers away from the Budapest factories...* These subsidiary workshops could pay much higher personal incomes than large enterprises. This source of income, which is based on the cooperatives' enterpreneurial profit, cannot be considered as socialist distribution according to work... Rules and regulations must be adjusted in order that such phenomena should not spread, but rather be driven back." [39]

The stressing of the ideological elements provided the foundations for practical restrictive measures. For example, in spring 1973 a statement could be made, with satisfaction, about the effect of the measures adopted in the spirit of the 1972 decisions: "As a result of the central measures, the auxiliary industrial and trading activities of agricultural cooperatives now follow the line indicated by the decisions of 1972; earlier unfavourable accompanying phenomena have consequently been decreasing." [40]

In summer 1973, another editorial in *Népszabadság* discussed the need to reduce the subsidiary activities of cooperatives (or of cooperative partnerships): "Recently, the people's control committees in several counties have investigated the functioning of cooperative partnerships." It says in the editorial that they discovered such activities as were contrary to bye-laws: "Machine repair partnerships began to look for customers in other fields in order to make use of their capacities. Today they perform industrial, household, and trade services in an ever broadening sphere – in many cases *deviating from the objectives laid down in their foundation deed.*"

"A similar situation is emerging with the building industrial partnerships. Often they do not serve the aims for which they were once established, i.e. they do not work to satisfy the cooperatives' needs for construction, investment projects and maintenance... because they give preference to the orders of industrial enterprises, public institutions and private individuals. . . It is of general interest that the competent administrative agencies exercising official control over these partnerships demand regular functioning everywhere, and do not allow any deviation." [41]

The purpose of the constraints and restrictions, introduced in order to correct the excesses of cooperatives, was specified in the confirmation of the "socialist traits" of the cooperatives.

Béla Biszku described the task as follows: "approximating the state and cooperative forms of ownership" and promoting "the development of uniform communist public property, which is to grow out of the two earlier forms." He laid stress on the fact that "it is not a mutual approach which is meant", but "the development of cooperative property in the direction of higher socialization." Making reference to the establishment of the Soviet agro-industrial unions, i.e. to the fact that "under guidance of the sovkhozes (state-farms), the kolkhozes (collective farms) had formed . . . large-scale unions", he clearly determined the "further development" of cooperatives "in the direction of modern, unified large-scale enterprise forms. The positive forms of this development are yet to be laid down." It was upon this ground that he deemed it necessary to fuse cooperatives, i.e. to establish the largest possible units. [42]

These principles were also formulated by the 10th Congress of the Hungarian Socialist Workers' Party in March 1975. "We will carry on our agricultura policy, further strengthen the socialist character of agricultural cooperatives. . . the rational merger of agricultural cooperatives should continue." [43]

Catchword of distribution policy and labour policy

In addition to the affirmation of central planning and the development of socialist ownership, a further ideological weapon of primary importance was the demand for the consolidation and restoration of the socialist order of distribution. This included a higher-rate of increase of peasants' and intellectuals' incomes with special regard to eliminating "the chances of acquiring unearned income and of practising speculation and hoarding", and to a "general and proportionate sharing of the tax burden." Specific measures were put forward in the November, 1972 resolution, among other things with the intention of counterbalancing the income differentiation caused by the reform: "Of the fundamental working classes and groups, it is generally the workers, and especially the workers of large state-owned enterprises whose earnings have risen at a relatively low rate. . . The wages of the workers and foremen of state-owned industries must be raised. . . by an average of 8 percent from the 1st March, 1973."

"In order to put into effect an equitable sharing of taxation, the feasibility of introducing a comprehensive tax system covering unearned incomes (inheritance, gifts, etc.), movable property and real estate must be examined." [44] In 1973 death-duties and gift taxes were largely raised, and house-taxes for holiday home of more than two rooms were increased by 50 percent. On dwelling-houses worth more than Ft800 thousand and on holiday homes worth more than Ft500 thousand, a house value tax was imposed in addition to the house-tax. Highly progressive taxes were charged on profits earned through the sale of real estate; tax rates on additional incomes and personal property (cars etc.) were also raised.

Béla Biszku stressed: "Incomes must be regulated in such a way that they should not be allowed to accumulate in an overlarge measure... the sources feeding these non-socialist tendencies must be first narrowed, then stopped. At the same time, the social appreciation of work must be raised... Also, placing of the constraints on easy money-making must be seriously considered. It should not be left unnoticed that... quite a large number of young people... seek careers assuring fast and easy success, instead of desiring the plesure creative work can give... non-socialist traits have grown stronger in social thinking." [45]

The editor-in-chief of *Társadalmi Szemle* recognized already in January 1973 that a debate was necessary in order that negative social phenomena should not simply be ascribed to the reform: "Many are of the opinion that the spririt of selfishness and gross materialism did not exist earlier, or at least was evident in a much narrower sphere..." Two years later, the argument was a similar one: "Why do we not eliminate group interests? , I was asked at one place, and at another: Why had group interests «to be introduced»? ... Group interest was not invented by us, not introduced by us, and it is not just... the concomitant of enterprise independence." It was stressed, at the same time, that the policy of income restriction was not directed against certain groups of society: "Our fight is not against professions or groups, but against profiteering, hoarding, unearned or such large incomes as are not proportional with the social usefulness of the work accomplished." [46]

In spring 1974, however, the emphases changed in Béla Biszku's words: "In the first place, it has to be emphasized, as a characteristic trait of decisive importance, that the party policy is first of all a *worker's policy*..." Upon this ground, he justified the constraints placed on incomes earned through peasant and private activities. These included cases such as the auxiliary industrial activities of agricultural cooperatives, where "the market boom is exploited to an undesirable extent", or in the private sector which "can, as yet, adjust itself to certain social needs more flexibly than the big industries, and state-owned and cooperative trade. The result: some of those engaged in the private sector can earn incomes of higher value than their work accomplished. Thus excessively high incomes are also administratively constrained." [47]

In the spirit of the workers' policy, a resolution was formulated also in respect of the social composition of the party and its cadre policy. Among others, it made the following statement: "the problems encountered in the course of carrying out party policy in certain cases... hinder manual workers in associating with the party... The demand for raising the standards of know-how and of management is sometimes coupled with a view in which intellectuals and holders of various leading posts are ascribed greater importance within the party than is in fact necessary." [48] A veritable campaign was launched with the object of raising workers to intellectual and leading posts, at a fast rate, avoiding the consolidated institutional ways, such as the state school system. With this object in view, the entrance examination system of universities was amended by a revision of the measures made only a decade before which had been in the spirit of social unity and the elimination of discrimination. Accelerated one-year courses were started for young people of working-class origin so that they could enter universities without having acquired secondary school qualifications. Under this system, 200–300 young workers with no secondary school certificate were sent to university each year. [49]

The March, 1974 meeting of the Hungarian Socialist Workers' Party affirmed these measures, stating that: "The party considers it a political question, i.e. a question of principle, that the children of manual workers receive special support for their studies and graduate training."

On central initiative, a wide range of manager replacement courses were organized. The Party Committee of Fejér County organized a boarding-school course "mainly with the intention of training cadres for replacement." In March 1974 the Central Council of the Hungarian Trade Unions set up a five-month boarding-school course for worker-cadre training. KISZ (the Communist Youth League) launched such courses from 1976. The Central Committee Secretariat dealt with the issue at its meeting of 2nd February 1976 and "found that the number of managers who have been manual workers can grow at a relatively fast rate."*

Specialized knowledge, that had been strongly emphasized and upgraded as a result of the reform, now looked almost suspicious. A large number of ill-equipped and untrained economic managers had earlier been selected, on the criterion of political trustworthiness, to carry out the new tasks and now political requirements were again given primacy. *Népszabadság* said, in commenting on the government decrees concerning the political extension training of managers: "A resolution of the Council of Ministers has recently been formulated on the political extension training of top-level managers and the regulation of training for the replacement of managers. According to the resolution, the ratio of political information in education must considerably be raised. . . *it is one of the most general errors to put professional skill and talent in the first place* in such a way that political training and fitness are weighed only in the second or third place." [51] This was clear enough and, with the characteristic "overzeal" of local practice, masses of workers – first of all the worker members of the party committee of enterprises – were appointed as economic managers. This was objected against in summer 1975 even in the central daily of the Hungarian Socialist Workers' Party. Let me quote the introductory words of the article *Kapkodás nélkül* (Without haste): "A district party committee of the capital examined how the new worker members of enterprise party committees were helped in

*The Secretariat added, however, so as to dampen obviously over-zealous efforts: "In the long run, nevertheless, it remains preferable to make use of. . . the organized forms within the system of adult education. The purpose of the various initiatives is only to complement but not to replace state and party schooling. This was brought to the attention of the Central Council of the Hungarian Trade Unions as well as KISZ."

their function. It turned out that dozens of such committee members have been appointed to economic manager posts during recent months; there is even an enterprise in which nearly all members have been raised to such posts. . . the large number of workers hastily appointed to management posts gives ample grounds for assuming that a good many of them did not expect and, primarily, were unprepared for the honour. . ." [52]

Against the tendency of the assumed strengthening bourgeois mentality, ascribed to the reform process, and for the sake of evolving a real workers' policy, the central periodical of the Party published an article discussing the worker-intellectual relationship in its column entitled *Fórum.* The writer of the article started with the phrase: "the way we workers see it" saying that "in social life. . . there is a tension between intellectuals and other workers. This. . . may gradually grow into a grave conflict. As workers see it. . . *intellectuals are financially as well as morally overrated,* whereas labourers are considerably undervalued by society." It is said in the article, that if intellectuals think the wages of workers doing hard manual labour are too high, they should go and do such work themselves, and that "there are some who have done so but then «quickly fled back»". It also mentioned physicians who felt contempt for their patients, and believed themselves to be always overworked, except in their private office; "the address sir is slowly stolen back, its purpose being to distinguish", and *"these sirs begin to feel like «sirs» in the old meaning of the word."* [53] One of the contributors even added: "It is in the nature of socialism that the leading class, i.e. the working class must be cared for. . . this thesis has not been adequately observed in recent years. . . Thus a great many insults are now coming to light, and these are inflicted even in our days by intellectuals on manual labourers." [54]

In addition to laying emphasis on the workers' policy in various forms and by adopting wide ranging means, the ideological battle was also stepped up through direct administrative measures, in the spirit of the targets announced in November 1972. This was directed against "growing middle-class and lower-middle-class" views which were cited as being "alien to socialism." The cultural-political work commission of the Central Committee of the Hungarian Socialist Workers' Party took a stand "on the anti-Marxist view of a few sociologists" [55]. This was soon followed by a tidying up in the field of sociology.

The 11th Party Congress of March 1975 summed up the primary objectives of the political trend that was unfolding and increasingly asserting itself: "Our state is the supreme instrument of the building of socialism. . . Our socialist state's role is growing in the development of the national economy. . . In view of the increasing demands, central management and control must be made more efficient. Social interest is what is determinant: it is what group and individual interests must be subordinated to. The assertion of individual or group interests over the community's, i.e. the whole country's interests, must not be tolerated. The Congress maintains that socialist planning must be more strongly asserted; this is a fundamental task in the development of the national economy."

Among the keywords and statements of the unanimously approved resolution of the

Congress, the fundamental principle – which is clearly in favour of egalitarianism – is pointed out: "by means of a well-balanced wages policy and income regulation, disproportions which lead to tensions must be prevented. An important role is to be played therein by central wages measures."

Against acquisitiveness, wasteful consumption and the petty bourgeoisie

Ideology was also to contribute to the above purpose, its most important point being formulated thus: "our socialist perspectives must be more clearly outlined; the superiority of the socialist over the capitalist mode of life must be demonstrated." Therefore, a fight must be carried on against "the various reactionary middle-class and petty bourgeois views." [56]

A very powerful campaign was launched against "wasteful consumption" and wide ranging debates evolved on the need "to work out a model of socialist consumption and the socialist way of life." In summer 1975, *Társadalmi Szemle* gave an excellent summary of the debates: "The remnants of an earlier view, which embraced an ascetical nature and emphasized limited consumption. . ., devoted work, and sacrifice are still with us and often. . . are seen to embody exactly the principles of socialism. During the last ten years of improving material supply and growing consumption, distrust has also emerged. . . toward consumption. If protests in the name of socialist values against the so-called middle-class and petty bourgeois tendencies manifest in consumption. . . . . . the emergence and spread of certain new needs are interpreted as being an imitation of the capitalist consumption model", and this was followed by a demand "that a model of socialist consumption be worked out." Some think – the author says – that this is the main task nowadays, ". . . starting from the assumption that. . . the elaboration of the «consumption model» is a theoretical task; that theory will be able to solve such a task, relying on the values that have developed in the course of history and are inherent in the ideal of socialism (equality, collectivism, etc.)". If, however, such a model and such a scale of values are not present, and are not inculcated upon the masses by means of intellectual-cultural education, then the raising of living standards will only contribute to "the rising of material needs and the affirmation of the owner's attitude which concentrates on material goods. . . the so-called consumer approach and behaviour will be spreading. . . there is, at the root of several of the negative phenomena so often discussed nowadays, a «petty bourgeois tendency.»" [57]

In the months that followed, and for a number of years afterwards, papers and periodicals were flooded with writings that attacked petty-bourgeois ways and materialism: "Undoubtedly," one could read in December 1975, "the reform of the economic control and mangement systems has thrown wide open new doors before individual progress; such doors have, in general, offered possibilities which are in harmony with highly important social interests and socialist objectives. Nevertheless, complex and indirect forces have helped to a few other doors, through which petty-bourgeois selfishness and materialism has begun to infiltrate into our society." [58]

A few days later, the secretary of the Békés County Committee of the Hungarian Socialist Workers' Party talked in an interview about the profiteering president of a cooperative who had been duly punished. He concluded: "This case, however, teaches us a lesson of general validity. Thus I ask the question: does money, or the prospect of a higher income, necessarily lead towards socialism? " [59]

In October 1973, the writer of one article revealed the case of an economic manager who had travelled off the right path. He posed the question: what had led this man astray for he was one who "had gone through hundreds of difficult situations and crises, but never wavered in his political conviction and faithfulness to the party."? He gave the answer: ". . . The cause is nothing other than greed which can, at a point, exert an effect similar to that of a drug: it not only intoxicates but it completely perverts man. Can anyone in his right mind understand why a man should throw away his entire decent past and honour in exchange for a few fashionable clothes and a luxurious condominium flat?

No, it is a disease. It is like an insidious fever which conquers the organism slowly, gradually, almost unnoticed, and mercilessly eats away the last bit of one's energy." [60]

In summer 1973, a long series of polemical articles were published in *Népszabadság* on the subject of the "petty-bourgeois attitude". The contributors produced scientific arguments, philosophical and historical explanations, and personal examples to clarify their respective positions. On July 25 there appeared the letter of a woodmill worker of the cooperative of Ócsárd: "In my place, too, the petty-bourgeois attitude is a subject of lively debates. Some say that this means rightism, others that leftism is also the expression of petty-bourgeois views. It is also said that petty-bourgeois elements are middle-of-the-roaders. . .

I think one gets closer to understanding the petty-bourgeois character, if *the fundamental traits of the petty bourgeois are contrasted with those of the class-conscious large-factory worker. . .* In short, I have in mind the following as the fundamental traits of the petty bourgeois: *wavering* – always bending towards the class which is in a position of power: *comfort* – seeking the easiest possible ways in every-day life; *distrust* – since his individual effort is directed towards exploiting others, the petty bourgeois assumes the same about others; *selfishness* – his ideal is the capitalist bourgeois, therefore he is selfish and given to money-grubbing; *inward-turning*- he does not like to help in accomplishing common tasks which do not bring him direct gain; *imitation* – he likes to imitate the old ruling classes." [61]

In addition to scourging the petty bourgeois attitude, the petty bourgeois ideology was also caught in a crossfire of attacks. Setting rather wide limits, Géza *Ripp* made the following statement: *"The petty bourgeois ideology is manifest in the theoretical justification of the petty bourgeois phenomena just as it is the apparently over-radical criticism of the very same phenomena."* [62]

In an attempt to be objective, the editorial summary of the debate talked, among other things, of the "challenge of living standards", posed by the contrast between material progress and the shortfall in the development of human consciousness. "Thanks to socialism, we have overcome poverty – if not fully, but essentially – yet now we have to learn (or teach everybody) to live a new way of life, the socialist way." [63]

Once again it became a central issue of the debates that people must be taught the proper use of things, the consumption pattern characteristic of socialism, and the socialist model of a correct way of life.

It was within the framework of this same campaign that any preference given to group interests over the national economic interest was strongly attacked. László *Szabó* wrote that certain seemingly unjustified price increases made by various enterprises had not been countered even by the local party organizations, though ". . . by no means should we let ourselves be led by those who support local and group interests, to the prejudice of the larger social interests." [64]

A wide range of means were used to influence, to teach, to discipline, and to threaten enterprise and cooperative managers in order that they should not act solely in the interest of their enterprise or cooperative, but that they should observe the declared social interest.

Thus ran the arguments of the editorial of *Népszabadság:* "In today's situation, this is to be especially stressed, because there are managers on various levels who do not or cannot understand this: they make group interests absolute, and place them over the social interest, which in practice often amounts to infringing the law and bypassing rules. Their *own* enterprise, their *own* sector, their *own* field or organization are «god» to them; they will «use all their influence», prestige, and connections in order to assert the interests of their specific field; some even interfere with other organs' work, abusing their power, and do not refrain even from corruption and cheating, etc." [65] *Népszabadság* formulated the conflict and its solution, referring to the hierarchy of values that was to be set up in the spirit of asserting the "social interest" through external influence i.e. by means of teaching and discipline: "It is a fact that different interests exist and operate simultaneously in our society. Although to no identical measure, man's individual interest, the local or group interest of state-owned enterprises, institutions, and cooperatives, and the social interest (comprising and at the same time by far exceeding the former) appear, each one, as motive forces. Undeniably, these interests may from time to time conflict: one demanding priority over the rest. Such dilemmas can only be solved by always giving the green light to the social interest." [66]

Of course, in reality there was a many-sided approach to the tensions and conflicts. These by no means stuck to superficial phenomena, or the scourging of human weakness and natural interests. It is worth quoting at some length the reasoning of an article published in 1974 in the theoretical periodical of the Hungarian Socialist Workers' Party. In the course of campaigns conducted against petty bourgeois ways the author, Lenke *Bizám,* concluded – "it is first of all acquisitiveness that is pointed out: the petty bourgeois greed, money-grubbing, insatiable appetite for durable and less durable consumer goods. The conspicuous trait of his character is that value is only what he can actually hold in his hands. The same holds for his taste. . . instead of cultural needs, the petty bourgeois has only need for entertainment. . . that is why he always wants to relax, to get away from it all, instead of joining in something. . ."

The author, however, does not rest content with such superficial criticism. Her starting-point states precisely that "we encounter petty bourgeois phenomena in a much larger field than that occupied by the numerical proportion of small owners." The explanation, in that case, is to be found in everlasting bad human qualities, or in the "imported" influence of the West. Yet such explanations "would not only be insufficient, but mistaken in all respects." Opposed to these, the author does not start from the moral and the consumer's attitude, but from the producer's. She concludes that, the prevailing public ownership notwithstanding, masses of people "in fact engage in petty enterprise at «public expense». He grows from a public owner into a small private owner, as soon as. . . he can consider the machine, tool, desk. . . or field as a means to serve his private interests and can use them accordingly. . . It is he who – with his private interests – short-circuits the wide currents of the socialist production organization. . . In fact, he does private work instead of the productive activity which falls to him within the socialist division of labour. . . he tries to take as much as possible out of the factory. If tool and labour are underutilized, he will look for. . . ways. . . of drawing them into private utilization. . ." The author then sums up her opinion: "The petty bourgeois way customary in this country and very dangerous indeed, consists in a small owner's attitude towards the socialist public property. This can affect the building of socialism and where, in its economic bases, socialist distribution is not adequately asserted. . . the keyword for eliminating petty bourgeois ways is not contempt and the reduction of goods, but a genuine appreciation of goods and their argumentation through public ownership." [67]

In addition to "public ownership", attempts were also made to find the collective forms of spending one's free time. "We asked ourselves the question", the secretary of the Municipal Party Committee of Pécs said in an interview, "whether the individual, having obtained more free time from our state, can be expected to spend this time in conformity with the objectives of our society, i.e. to spend it in a useful, cultured manner. . . Ever more people spend their free time by working in their garden. . . working in the open air is not just recreation, it is by all means very healthy. . . Yet it cannot be denied that gardening separates the individual from the community." A solution is set forth, quoting the example of the "garden cooperative" organized in Komló. On a plot of land – which is state property – families do gardening, each on the patch assigned to them, without fences. "This is already community life." In a similar way, in a do-it-yourself workshop for all trades set up by *Hőerőmű Vállalat* (Heat Power Station) "there is opportunity for communal life in one's free time." [68]

Strong waves of demagogy stormed the widest spheres of social and political life. This was helped by the fact that criticism was not entirely groundless. The masses. that had for decades been accustomed to egalitarianism, strongly reacted to growing social and income differences, and in particular to unearned incomes and apparent trickery. Therefore, views that suggested that the "excesses" of the reform should be cut out, and "distortions occurring in the course of execution" adjusted, voiced certain real social tensions. They were even more popular among the workers, since practical measures were urged in their interest: wage increases, higher social prestige, a housing campaign, and managerial appointments, etc.

Such developments clearly contributed to the gathering of a political group around those objectives. This was all the more so as the supporters of the criticism and of the new initiatives were by no means all against the economic reform, but wished, instead, to see the elimination of certain undesirable phenomena which had not been adequately handled in the course of the reform.

There were many who engaged in the debate and argued against the economic view centred on income distribution and against the dogmatic approach to ownership, and the emphasis laid on "petty bourgeois ways". These voices were in favour of the reform. Their arguments and these forces, of which I shall not speak now, later on were to play an important role in subsequent policy changes.

From autumn 1972, however, the forces and views previously suppressed gathered strength, and this led to the bringing about of a series of definite and clearly restrictive measures. As a consequence, the reform process halted. The worst result was that the "second phase" of the reform, originally planned to take place in the 1970s, was entirely taken off the agenda and the reform stopped half-way. The further steps, postponed with a view to adopting a gradual form of development, but held to be important envisaged a release of most of the brakes and checks incorporated in the 1968 reform and aimed at the strengthening of market impacts. The inconsistencies of the reform which had soon become evident at the beginning thus became permanent, and they automatically intensified reactionary tendencies in the functioning of economy. This was mainly made obvious by the fact that, because of the lack of a consistently normative regulation, the masses of exceptions led to the reproduction of central directives by other means of regulation. More than that was involved, however, since the amendment of regulators, and the affirmation of other measures detracted much from the achievements of the reform which, from the outset, had already involved compromises. Examples of such measures include the implementation of direct instructions in a number of cases, especially in that of the large industrial enterprises, the centralization of an increased ratio of enterprise profits, and the turning back of the development of the agricultural cooperative model towards the traditional "artiel" type.

All this was accompanied by changes in leading personnel (affecting the persons who had played an outstanding role in the elaboration and introduction of the reform): Rezső *Nyers* and Lajos *Fehér,* secretaries of the Central Committee, Prime Minister Jenő *Fock,* and Deputy Prime Minister Mátyás *Tímár* were removed from their posts. There were also personnel changes in the non-economic sphere, and these affected the composition of the leading bodies.

The oil crisis and its consequences

The prevailing current was further strengthened during 1973–74 as a consequence of the crisis that shook the world economy.

The sudden rise in oil prices in autumn 1973, soon increasing fivefold on the world market, entailed a general rise in raw material prices. This put severe inflationary pressure on the Hungarian economy, being sensitive to foreign trade, and in particular to energy and raw material imports.

The excessive price rises led, namely, to increasing isolation from foreign trade, and to emerging protectionism in many countries. This situation hit particularly hard products of medium technological standards.

Therefore, during the first five years after the oil price explosion, the average rise in the prices of goods imported by Hungary amounted to about 70 percent, whereas the rise in the prices of Hungary's exported goods reached only 30–40 percent.

The balance of trade and the balance of payments, restored in earlier years, was soon upset. The deterioration of the terms of trade – amounting first to 20 then to 30 percent – led to loss-making in foreign trade, and the country raised credits of about $8 thousand million in five years to make up for the losses.

The situation was made worse by a lack of comprehension, i.e. by the erroneous judgements made in connection with the world economic shocks. For instance, in the beginning the opinion emerged – which, incidentally, the first government declaration on the subject also stressed – that the question was mainly about crisis phenomena of the capitalist economy. Thus it would neither affect Hungary nor any of the socialist economies, but would stop at the borders. Albeit with some delay it was recognized that what was involved was not transitory causes rooted in the political sanctions of the Arab oil-producing countries, but factors that affected the world economy vitally and which had, for a long period, been beneath the crisis phenomena and thus exerted an influence on the scope of movements of the world economy as a whole.

Because of this delay in recognizing the real state of affairs, Hungarian economic policy did not react at first, but continued its earlier path. Thus a fast growth rate was maintained (5–6 percent on a yearly average), there was a further increase of real wages although this was impossible to cover from domestic sources. The yearly 10–12 percent rate of growth of foreign trade necessary for the increase of national income was also forced. Because of the deteriorating terms of trade, the deficit also grew at a faster rate, and the accumulation rate of the credits – to bridge the lack of balance – rose so fast that by 1978 the credit stock was growing at a rate double that of the previous year.

The need to stem adverse tendencies, to restore balance and to adjust to the new requirements of the world market urged a most radical reaction. In such a situation, it was at first quite a natural reflex to try to strengthen central intervention. It was a kind of emergency, a very special situation, in which, even in a number of capitalist economies based on private ownership and thus unplanned, strong central measures were taken to ward off the crisis effects. Subjectively, therefore, the need for central measures and centralized solutions arose. The reform which proposed market crientation seemed justified in the mid-1960s, so it was said, but in this new market situation it presented risks, so that a reversal was necessary. Such views were even formulated according to which the fullest possible isolation from the world market was necessary, since its effects were clearly negative.

In addition to these subjective factors, the reform process was also objectively hit by the world economic trauma in that the warding off of the inflationary pressure of the world market, and the at least partial elimination of its impacts, finally destroyed the results of the 1968 price reform. Since the rises in world market prices were only partially incorporated in domestic prices, the latter were again rendered inapt by a complex and inextricable system of subsidies which distorted actual relative values. Enterprises bought oil and other raw materials at much lower prices than their real cost on the world market, and due to past practice were not even interested in economizing, although the need for this was daily proclaimed.

By the mid-1970s, therefore, the Hungarian economic reform had arrived at a crisis.

Survival of the fundamental achievements of the reform – a new turn

It has to be stated repeatedly, however, that all along the fundamental achievements of the reform survived – primarily the abolishment of the system of compulsory plans, and the institutionalized order of enterprises' market crientation. This soon proved to be of particular historical importance. Thus, the practical experiences of the five years following the oil price explosion made it increasingly clear that it was no longer possible to pursue further the previous development policy. The increasing difficulties could not be overcome, either, in the spirit of the "strong hand" and "let's make order." It was quite obvious that the Hungarian economy had to adjust itself to the world economy, and it became vital to transform the pattern of exports and of production, and to encourage competitiveness on the world market. The factors determinant in restoring the balance again intensified and multiplied the importance of enterprises' interest in the market, of a price system promoting this object, and of mechanisms working towards sensitiveness to market effects, with a view to flexible adjustment. These measures were considered even more important as it became more obvious that – and five years were enough to demonstrate it clearly – the shocks of the world economy were not transitory crisis phenomena hitting only the capitalist countries, and they could not be stopped on the border. In fact, they were the symptoms of a long-lasting structural crisis, compelling every country to react in one way or another. What is more, it depended on this reaction whether a country could keep pace, make up for its delay, or – if its reaction was partly or fully unsuccessful – it would finally be left behind. The preserved institutional continuity of the reform mechanism was soon able to provide a good basis for a new assertion of the reform tendency and for carrying on the reform process. The political and personal conditions of this turn – the inner motive and elements of which cannot be documented now, but only later, by future researchers – was created by the new "inner change of course" among the majority of the political leaders gathered around János Kádár. This ran contrary to the transitorily prevailing anti-reform tendencies, i.e. it took a stand again for the reform and, further, strengthened the pro-reform groups, removed influential personalities of the reform opposition, and made personal changes in the Political Committe and the secretariat of the Central Committee, including the post of the economic policy secretary. Mass support for all this was assured by economic experts on various levels, and by large groups of intellectuals supporting the necessary changes and continuance of the reform. The turning back to the reform began between autumn 1977 and 1979.

References

1. *A Magyar Szocialista Munkáspárt Párttörténeti Intézetének Archívuma* (Archives of the Institute of Party History of the Hungarian Socialist Workers' Party). (In the following: P. I. Archívuma) 288 f. 15/1958. 30th September 1968.
2. *P. I. Archívuma.* 288 f. 15/1963. Előterjesztés a GPB-hoz az árpolitika hosszútávú kérdéseiről (Proposition to the Economic Policy Committee (GPB) on the long-term questions of price policy). Országos Anyag- és Árhivatal. 17th May 1969; and the relevant GPB resolution.
3. *P. I. Archívuma.* 288 f. 15/1964. 28th June 1969.
4. *P. I. Archívuma.* 288 f. 15/1963. Jelentés a GPB részére a nagyvállalati szervezet továbbfejlesztéséről szóló 1969. évi GPB-határozat végrehajtásáról (Report to the GPB on the execution of the 1969 resolution of the GPB regarding further development of the large enterprise organization). 14th December 1970.
5. *P. I. Archívuma.* 288 f. 24/1970/3. Előterjesztés a Gazdaságpolitikai Bizottság részére a nagyvállalati szervezet továbbfejlesztéséről (Proposition to the GPB for the further development of the large enterprise organization).
6. *P. I. Archívuma.* 288 f. 24/1970/1. Tájékoztató a társadalmi tőke áramlásának ,tervszerű szabályozásáról (Information on the planned regulation of the flow of social capital). Hungarian Socialist Workers' Party, Central Committee, Economic Policy Department. 26th October 1970.
7. *P. I. Archívuma.* 288 f. 24/1970/34. Előterjesztés a miniszterhelyettesi értekezlet részére. Tárgy: A bér- és jövedelemarányok továbbfejlesztése (Proposition for the deputy ministers' meeting. Subject: Further development of wages and incomes proportions). 27th November 1970. Ministry of Labour.
8. Kádár, J.: Felszólalás a Központi Bizottság november 24-i ülésén (Contribution at the 24th November meeting of the Central Committee). *Társadalmi Szemle,* December 1967, p. 27.
9. Földes, I.: Fogadatlan prókátorok (Unwanted advocates). *Népszabadság,* 24th December 1973.
10. Pálos, T.: A negyedik dimenzió (The fourth dimension). *Népszabadság,* 15th October 1972.
11. Lajos Fehér's address at the festive council meeting of Gödöllő, on its receiving the rank of "town". *Népszabadság,* 4th January 1966.
12. János Kádár's statement on international issues, foreign and domestic policy, the situation of the Hungarian national economy, and the tasks of the year. *Népszabadság,* 1st January 1966.
13. *A Magyar Szocialista Munkáspárt határozatai és dokumentumai 1971–1975* (The resolutions and documents of the Hungarian Socialist Workers' Party 1971–1975). Kossuth Könyvkiadó, Budapest 1978. p. 377.

14. Pullai, Á.: A párt vezető szerepe, a pártélet kérdései (The party's leading role, questions of party life). *Társadalmi Szemle,* April 1975. pp. 106–107.
15. Komócsin, Z.: Változatlan politikával (With unchanged policy). *Népszabadság,* 23rd March 1974. (Italics mine.)
16. Benke, V.: Egységes értelmezés, kommunista kiállás, közös cselekvés (Uniform interpretation, communist stand, common action). *Társadalmi Szemle,* January 1973. p. 5.
17. *Társadalmi Szemle,* May 1974. p. 7.
18. Pártmunkások nyilatkozatai a Központi Bizottság novemberi határozatáról (Party workers' statements on the November resolution of the Central Committee). *Társadalmi Szemle,* January 1973. pp. 46, 50.
19. Kongresszusra készülődve (Preparing for the Congress). *Társadalmi Szemle,* May 1974. p. 7–8.
20. Üzemek a politika mérlegén. Beszélgetés Nagy Richárddal, az MSzMP Budapesti Bizottságának titkárával (Factories on the balance of politics. A conversation with Richárd Nagy, secretary of the Budapest Committe of the Hungarian Socialist Workers' Party. *Népszabadság,* 16th December 1973.
21. *A Magyar Szocialista Munkáspárt határozatai és dokumentumai 1971–1975.* Op. cit. p. 377.
22. Gadó, O.: *Közgazdasági szabályozórendszerünk 1976-ban* (The economic mechanism in Hungary. How it works in 1976). Kossuth Könvkiadó, Budapest 1976. pp. 40, 51.
22/a Gadó O.: *The economic mechanism in Hungary. – How it works in 1976.* A. W. Sijthoff, Leyden – Akadémiai Kiadó, Budapest 1976. pp. 157, 165.
23. Pullai, Á.: A pártélet, a pártmunka időszerű kérdései. Előadás az országos agitációs és propaganda értekezleten (Topical questions of party life and party work. Address at the national propaganda meeting). *Társadalmi Szemle,* November 1975. pp. 43–44.
24. Terényi, É.: Angyalföld neve kötelez. Jegyzetek a XIII. kerületi pártértekezletről (The name *Angyalföld* obliges. Notes of the party meeting of the 13th District). *Népszabadság,* 18th February 1975.
25. Biszku, B.: A munkásosztály vezető szerepe, a szövetségi politika és a szocialista demokrácia (The leading role of the working class, the policy of alliance, and socialist democracy). *Társadalmi Szemle,* April 1975. p. 64.
26. Terényi, É.: Segíteni a végrehajtást. A nagyüzemi pártellenőrzés tapasztalatairól (To promote implementation. The experience of the party supervision at large enterprises). *Népszabadság,* 2nd July 1975.
27. Földes, K.: Tervgazdaságunk szabályozási elvei, a szövetségi politika és a szocialista demokrácia (The regulation principles of the Hungarian planned economy, the policy of alliance, and socialist democracy). *Társadalmi Szemle,* June 1975. pp. 31–32.
28. Az 1973. évi költségvetésről tárgyal az országgyűlés. Pullai, Á.: A helyes döntések megvannak, most a tetteken a sor (The Parliament discusses the 1973 budget. Pullai, Á.: The right decisions have been made, now actions are needed). *Népszabadság,* 13th December 1973.
29. Resolution of the Council of Ministers No. 1023/1973 (30th June). *Törvények és Rendeletek Hivatalos Gyűjteménye,* Budapest 1973. p. 425.
30. *A Magyar Szocialista Munkáspárt határozatai és dokumentumai.* Op. cit. p. 379.
31. Faluvégi, L.: A közgazdasági szabályozás az V. ötéves terv időszakában (Economic regulation in the 5th five-year plan period). *Társadalmi Szemle,* August-September 1974. p. 18.
32. *A Magyar Szocialista Munkáspárt határozatai és dokumentumai 1975–1980.* Op. cit. p. 233.
33. Szabó, L.: Oknyomozás árügyekben (In quest of price affairs). *Népszabadság,* 18th February 1973.
34. *Népszabadság,* 7th January 1973.
35. Szabó, L.: A köztulajdon védelme (Defending public property). *Népszabadság,* 21st April 1974.
36. Medveczky, L.: Szellem a palackból: Mi van és mi lesz a „gebines" autósiskolákkal? (Evil spirit from the bottle: How do things stand, and how will they stand, with the "self-employed" motor schools?) *Népszabadság,* 30th December 1973.

37. Cserkúti, F.: A közös és a háztáji (Collective farming and the household-plots). *Népszabadság,* 4th June 1975.
38. Pünkösti, Á.: Mienk a dió? Visszatér a múlt? (Is the walnut ours? Are times past coming back?) *Népszabadság,* 13th July 1975.
39. Biszku, B.: A XI. kongresszus a társadalmi viszonyok fejlesztéséről (The 11th Congress of the development of social relations). *Társadalmi Szemle,* November 1975. pp. 10–13 (Italics mine.)
40. *A Magyar Szocialista Munkáspárt határozatai és dokumentumai 1971–1975.* Op. cit. p. 486.
41. Sólyom, J.: Az alapszabály szerint (Conforming to the foundation rules). *Népszabadság,* 8th August 1973.
42. Biszku, B.: Op. cit. pp. 14–15.
43. *A Magyar Szocialista Munkáspárt határozatai és dokumentumai 1971–1975.* Op. cit. 1978. pp. 917, 918, 926.
44. ibid. pp. 381–385.
45. Biszku, B.: A munkásosztály vezető szerepe, a szocialista demokrácia (The leading role of the working class, socialist democracy). *Társadalmi Szemle,* April 1975. p. 68.
46. Benke, V.: Egységes értelmezés, kommunista kiállás, közös cselekvés (Uniform interpretation, communist stand, common action). *Társadalmi Szemle,* January 1973. pp. 12–13., and: Benke, V.: Szocialista eszmeiség, művelődés, közösségi erkölcs (Socialist idealism, culture, community morals). *Társadalmi Szemle,* April 1975. pp. 82–83.
47. Biszku, B.: Pártunk politikájának időszerű kérdéseiről (On the topical questions of our party policy). *Társadalmi Szemle,* March 1974. pp. 3, 6. 7.
48. Az MSzMP KB Politikai Bizottságának határozata a párttagság létszámának növeléséről és szociális összetételének alakulásáról. 1972. november 21. (Resolution of the Political Comission of the Central Committee of the Hungarian Socialist Workers' Party on the growing number of party members and on the changes in social composition. 21st November 1972. *A Magyar Szocialista Munkáspárt határozatai és dokumentumai 1971–1975.* Op. cit. p. 394.
49. Resolution of the Council of Ministers No. 2026/1973 (8th August) on the university education of young people and skilled workers' qualifications. *Határozatok Tára. Gyűjtemény.* pp. 358–359.
50. *A Magyar Szocialista Munkáspárt határozatai és dokumentumai 1971–1975.* Op. cit. pp. 657, 908 909.
51. Terényi, É: Egyenrangú követelmények. Kormányhatározat a vezetők politikai továbbképzéséről (Equal requirements. Government resolution on the political extension training of managers). (Italics mine.) *Népszabadság,* 8th January 1975.
52. Komornik, F.: Kapkodás nélkül (Without haste). *Népszabadság,* 15th August 1975.
53. Nagy, B.: Munkásság és értelmiség (Workers and intellectuals). *Társadalmi Szemle,* April 1973. pp. 58–64. (Italics mine.)
54. Baráth, L.: Beidegződés vagy úrhatnámság (Habit or snobbery). *Társadalmi Szemle,* April 1973. p. 66.
55. *A Magyar Szocialista Munkáspárt határozatai és dokumentumai 1971–1975.* Op. cit. p. 456.
56. *A Magyar Szocialista Munkáspárt határozatai és dokumentumai 1971–1975.* Op. cit. pp. 920, 921, 927, 930, 933.
57. Szabó, I.: Szükségletek és érdekek a szocializmusban (Needs and interests in socialism). *Társadalmi Szemle,* June 1975. pp. 36, 42, 43.
58. Rózsa, L.: A pártban és a párton kívül (Within and without the party). *Népszabadság,* 17th December 1972.
59. Faragó, J.: Szigorú mércével. Beszélgetés dr. Szabó Sándorral, az MSzMP Békés megyei Bizottságának titkárával (By strict standards. A conversation with Dr. Sándor Szabó, secretary of the Békés County Committee of the Hungarian Socialist Workers' Party). *Népszabadság,* 29th December 1972.
60. Sólyom, J.: A szerzés ördöge (The demon of acquisitiveness). *Népszabadság,* 18th October 1973.

61. Vita a kispolgáriságról. Három vélemény (Dispute about petty bourgeois ways. Three opinions). *Népszabadság*, 25th July 1973.
62. Ripp, G.: A kispolgári ideológia szélsőségei (The extremes of the petty bourgeois ideology). Vita a kispolgáriságról (Dispute about petty bourgeois ways). *Népszabadság*, 5th July 1973.
63. A szerkesztőség összefoglalója (The board of editors: summary). *Népszabadság*, 23rd September 1973.
64. Szabó, L.: Politika és végrehajtás (Policy and implementation). *Népszabadság*, 26th November 1972.
65. Teljes szélességben (In full width). *Népszabadság*, 2nd December 1973.
66. Érdek, de kié? (Interest – but whose?) *Népszabadság*, 24th December 1973.
67. Bizám, L.: Mitől kispolgár? (What makes one a petty bourgeois?) *Társadalmi Szemle*, July 1974. pp. 44, 45–48.
68. Interjú Szentiványi Józseffel (Interview with József Szentiványi). *Társadalmi Szemle*, January 1973. pp. 60–61.

X

End of Century Global Transition to a Market Economy

– Laissez-faire on the Peripheries? –

Introduction

"Despite the fact", stated Giovanni Sartori in 1991, "that...a majority of the 175 countries...in official existence do not qualify as even minimal democracies, the *Zeitgeist* admits one and only one legitimacy, namely, that power derives from, and is bestowed by, the people. In today's modern world there is but one 'rightful government': freely elected government."[1]

The same could be said of free market economies. Although very few countries have a genuine free market economy, the *Zeitgeist* admits one and only one ideal legitimate economic system: a *laissez-faire* market economy without state interference, protectionism and public ownership.

After the fall of the Berlin Wall, the symbol of the division of Germany and the entire world into two opposing and confronting systems, an extreme though typical expression of the *Zeitgeist* was Fukuyama's vision of an 'end of history' which suggested the ultimate victory and unchallenged existence of a single, triumphant paradigm: liberal free market parliamentary democracy. Indeed, the entire world is on a spectacular march towards an 'ideal-type' *laissez-faire* system as described in textbooks by the Chicago School of Economics. Countries which had turned towards strong state interventionism, built a huge public sector and instituted centralized planning during the postwar period, now dramatically revised their policy and introduced privatization. Marketization became a leading trend through deregulation and the elimination of obstacles to free trade set up during the postwar decades.

What is the explanation of this historical trend? To understand the ongoing transformation, one would have to analyze the road which led to the present change.

1. Economic Models During Post-World War II Prosperity

Karl Polanyi's historical analysis "shows that never before our time were markets more than accessories of economic life...Where markets were most highly developed, as under the mercantile system, they throve under the control of a centralized administration which fostered autarchy...Regulation and markets, in effect, grew up together. The self-regulating market was unknown"[2] and first emerged in Great Britain during the 19th century.

---

[1] G. Sartory, "Rethinking Democracy: bad polity and bad politics." *International Social Science Journal,* August 1991. No.129. Blackwell Journals UNESCO. p. 437.

[2] K. Polanyi, *The Great Transformation. The Political and Economic Origins of Our Time,* Beacon Hill, Boston: Beacon Press. Fifth printing. 1964. p. 68.

"[A]s the transition to a democratic system and representative politics involved a complete reversal of the trend of the age," added Polanyi, "the change from regulated to self-regulating markets at the end of the eighteenth century represented a complete transformation in the structure of society...[I]t demands...the institutional separation of society into an economic and political sphere...Such an institutional pattern could not function unless society was somehow subordinated to its requirements." [3]

Though it triumphed as an aftermath of the British Industrial and French Revolutions, the self-regulating *laissez-faire* economic system enjoyed short-lived success and was consistently challenged from the early 20th century on.

Of course various attempts were made to replace free market economics with fascist state-regulated and state socialist non-market systems in the interwar period; but special attention should be placed on the fact that the self-regulated market was successfully restored after World War II by the United States and (thanks to Marshal Aid) some of the "core" countries of Western Europe. This definitely played a determinant role in what has turned out to be unprecedented postwar prosperity.

The second half of the 20th century was the scene of the most rapid economic growth in modern history. During the quarter of a century following postwar reconstruction, the world economy achieved a 3.8% average annual growth rate. No single economic model has, however, been responsible for this economic success.

The United States, Canada and some countries of the European Community possessed market economies based on policies of large-scale private ownership and free trade. But several European countries achieved the same or even better results by means of the creation of a state-regulated and partly state-owned mixed economy. France, Italy and Austria, for example, developed a huge state-owned sector comprising between 25% and 50% of industry. State planning was also introduced in France, and Austria based its socio-economic system on a so called *Sozialpartnerschaft,* which was an institutionalized agreement system between the state, entrepreneurs and trade unions.

The Asian countries followed strong state interventionist policy combined with autocratic and, in several cases, even dictatorial political regimes. These modernization dictatorships have been among the most successful actors in the international economy. Though developing a democratic system, India adopted essential elements of Soviet-type planning and economic policy. Latin America has been characterized by dirigist modernization dictatorships and pronounced state domination of the economy, including the creation of huge public sectors and a controlled market. Similar patterns were followed by most of the newly independent Third World countries of Africa.

The backward, peripheral countries were highly impressed by the Soviet model of modernization based on central planning, state ownership and forced industrialization. This blueprint, an explicit antithesis of *laissez-faire* capitalism, conquered nearly one third of the world. It was adopted and imposed in Central and Eastern Europe but also in other continents, first of all in Asia (the most important examples being China, North Korea and Vietnam) and also in some African and Latin American countries.

---

[3] *Ibid.* p. 71

Thus, various models existed in the postwar world economy, and they have competed vigorously with one another. Although these models were rather different, and, in a way, almost every country represented a special case, some generalization is still possible.

Taking a broad-brush approach, we may distinguish two major types: market and non-market models. According to this interpretation, the former may include the types of market economies that utilize state interventionism and often have a state-owned sector of the economy as well as some kind of planning. In these cases, however, state interference serves the market and counterbalances its shortcomings, rather than working against it. Countries employing regulated-market mechanisms sometimes have authoritarian or dictatorial political regimes as well. Hence, in addition to the classic *laissez-faire* countries, most of the European mixed economies and Asian state interventionist modernization dictatorships would fit into this category.

The second group consists of those countries where the market was destroyed, or where state intervention worked against the market, attempting to replace it with state activity. Beside the Soviet Bloc's central planning system, several Latin American, some Asian (for example India) and a number of African countries applied to this model.

Though there is some validity for distinguishing between these two basic types of economies, a differentiation among three models can offer a more accurate picture and a better understanding.

The author thus prefers to categorize the different countries into three models. In addition to non-market economies, a form which dominated one-third of the world in the 1980s, one may differentiate between two, somewhat different, types of the market economies:

- the *laissez-faire*, self-regulating free market economy, which is, as Karl Polanyi defined it, "an economic system controlled, regulated, and directed by markets alone...[N]o measures or policy must be countenanced that would influence the action of these markets...[O]nly such policies and measures are in order which help to ensure the self-regulation of the market by creating conditions which made the market the only organizing power in the economic sphere." [4]
- the regulated (often mixed) market economy, which is characterized by strong state interference and regulation. While the self-regulating market "subordinates the substance of society itself to the law of the market," [5] a regulated market is an "economic system [that is] absorbed in the social system." [6] A centralized administration influences the flow of money as well as supply and demand; and labor and land, meaning the society and its "natural surroundings," are often not subordinated to the laws of the market. In this model the economic system is controlled, regulated and directed by both the state and the market. State regulations assist as well as replace the market mechanism which is often incomplete.

After postwar reconstruction, in a quarter of a century, the non-market models enjoyed enormous success and a rather good reputation. Angus Maddison's calculations

[4] *Ibid.* pp. 68–69.
[5] *Ibid.* p. 71.
[6] *Ibid.* p. 68.

offer a broad view of the results and reflect the simultaneous success of the different economic models. Between 1950 and 1973, the Central and Eastern European planned, non-market economies achieved their best performance, an unprecedented 3.9% average annual per capita growth of their GNP which surpassed not only their previous rate of development – which had averaged 1% between 1913 and 1950 – but also the rapid growth of the market economies: the non-European "core" countries, including the United States and Canada, had an annual average growth of 2.2%, while the European "core", including several countries with the so-called mixed economies, reached 3.8%.

The highly 'statist' and regulated Asian market model's success was characterized by its 3.7% annual growth. Dirigist-regulated Latin America could boast a less impressive 2.5%, and the African countries 1.7%. Centrally planned Central and Eastern Europe almost quadrupled its interwar growth rate and began to catch up with the West during the most rapid growth period in history. According to Paul Bairoch, these countries attained a level that represented 66% of the European average per capita GNP in 1950, and 83% in 1973.

This brief survey may illustrate the fact that no one single model was responsible for the exceptional economic growth, and that the various models were indeed highly competitive. Hence, the lessons of post-World War II economic history do not reflect the unquestionable triumph of *laissez-faire* capitalism. On the contrary, different types of market and non-market, *laissez-faire* and state-interventionist (for or against market), social democratic, Soviet-type, Peronist, Keynesian and Asian-type, planning and public ownership dominated the economic arena in most parts of the world.

Thus, the roots of the recent victory of *laissez-faire* free market system are not very deep. They go back only as far as the major structural crisis of the 1970-80s.

2. Technological Revolution and Structural Crisis in the Last Third of the 20th Century

The structural crisis which became manifest after the Oil Crisis in 1973, followed by a similar jolt in 1980, was generated by a gradually-emerging and dramatically-expanding technological revolution which transformed the world economy. The change of the old technological regime began immediately after World War II. Its first milestones were the first mainframe computer (with its 18,000 vacuum tubes), invented in 1946 at the University of Pennsylvania, and a transistor that was able to magnify electronic messages, a product of the Bell Laboratory in 1947. Parallel to this communications revolution in the making, the service branches, which utilized computers, expanded with extraordinary speed. Automobile and air transportation, television and an endlessly-booming tourist industry accelerated a process that was already between fifty and seventy years old that had fostered the emergence of a broad lower-middle class, professional, white-collar society.

A historic turning point occured in 1956, when the United States, the world's most advanced country, was the first to reach the point where white-collar workers outnumbered blue-collar workers. As was often maintained, industrial society – the child of the Industrial Revolution – had ended, and a new age had begun.

It would take some time before the practical application of the new technologies and industries achieved a certain critical mass and could impact on everyday life. Indeed, as Daniel Bell observed, the new age actually opened only in the 1970s. At the beginning of this decade, the microprocessor, the "brain" of modern computers, was developed in the Silicon Valley, and this had both symbolic and practical importance, opening the road to further and further miniaturization and an increase in capacity. As a result, the cost-per-bit of computer memory decreased by 28% annually from the mid-1970s. The age of computerization had arrived. Until then, there existed only large computers owned and utilized by government, large companies and universities. But now microcomputers became popular and widely used. Further refinements of this new technology made it possible to link personal computers to large units, as well as to create data bases. Networking, together with a new variety of telecommunications technologies such as teleconferencing, cable television, teletext and videotext were the great new inventions of the seventies. "The technical advances in microelectronics that occured in the 1970s and 1980s," sums up Everett Rogers, "have spurred the Communication Revolution." All this was connected with an emerging new "high-technology industry..., one in which the basic technology underlying the industry changes very rapidly." [7] The most important high-technology industries, such as electronics and its sub-branch, microelectronics, centered on semiconductor chips, whose application was the main driving force of a new age of technology that included biotechnology, aerospace, advanced instrumentation and pharmaceuticals. Modern communications and computers penetrated virtually every sphere of the economy. According to some calculations, by the mid-1980s, roughly one-quarters of the American jobs were connected with computers as primary work tool. As a result, industrial employment continued to decrease in the United States. By 1980, only 2% of its active population worked in agriculture, and 22% in blue-collar industrial jobs.

The new technological revolution was characterized not only by new inventions, new technology, and new branches of production, but also by an entirely new industrial environment. To mention only some of the most important emerging new factors, the technical revolution was distinguished by an unparalleled complex of installments and production systems, coupled with a newly-refined division of labor. As one expert stated: "Refinement is perhaps the first apprehendable, moreover, measurable characteristic of those instruments, which are transforming the world. We are assessing the technological parameters of the electronic circuits, whose capacities are permanently increasing, in microns and fractions of microns. This is the determinant factor of their...fantastic capacity of storing and processing as well as speed... There is a permanent struggle for fractions of microns. Microns and ractions of microns characterizing modern processing technologies, the preciseness of machine tools, the interlocking of surfaces..." [8]

Another element of refinement is the quality of materials. The impurity of materials is measured by hundredth or millionth of percentages. Special alloys represent

---

[7] E. Rogers, *Communication Technology. The New Media in Society,* New York, London: The Free Press. 1986. pp. 14–15.

[8] T. Vamos, *Alamerult alepitmeny* (The Submerged Substructure), Budapest, 1991. (manuscript) p. 3. I am summarizing the following main characteristics of change on the basis of this paper.

connections of critical precision and require even higher quality standards. These demand the highest standards of hygiene within the industrial environment as a whole, a new requirement is, for example, the number of fragments larger than 1 or 0.1 micron allowed per one unit volume of air.

Complexity is the other most striking technological characteristic of the new technology. Recent electronic circuits already contain more than one million previously independent elements. A car or an airplane has several thousands, and tens of thousands, of components respectively. There are quite a number of products whose technological documentation is as heavy as the product itself. Huge international systems, such as telecommunications, air-transportation, or energy concerns, have an immensely-complex operational mechanism. The software for a new electronic trip-circuit may contain several million orders, and several hundred thousands machines can operate within one computer network. Complexity is even greater in production processes. A traditional product was easily processed if miniature measures and special tidiness were not required. Increased standards create myriad additional requirements. A half-size measure, a two-times refined surface, or two-times tidier product often require the fulfillment of five to ten times more factors. Several co-factors which might be neglected for the production of a traditional product would have to be counterbalanced. Production procedures are becoming much more complex; integral circuits have more than hundred working phases. The unparalleled complexity of the new technology characterizes the division of labor and demand rather than narrow specialization.

All these are immeasurably connected with a highly developed human-technological civilization and a new and advanced infrastructure of the information society. Since the highly complex system is in a permanent state of change and transformation, its interrelationships require a maximum flexibility. To adjust to this new environment and remain competitive implies thousands of social, organizational, infrastructural and technological prerequisites in all their complexity.

This "entire set of technological changes" led to the decline of previous technology and the branches which were based on it, while generating new leading sectors. This is what Schumpeter calls a "structural crisis" with its "creative destruction" comprising severe temporary turmoil, decline, or stagnation and other frightening symptoms of a sick economy with high unemployment, inflation and declining standards of living. In the late 1970s and early 1980s, the world had to face an unprecedented situation: stagnation combined with inflation ("stagflation"). Very few of the rich "core" countries remained immune, and most suffered temporary 10% to 12% unemployment with 10% to 20% inflation while the growth rate declined.

The relatively backward peripheries had a much more difficult time. Besides the painful experience of stagflation and increasing unemployment, they had to face an ever deepening debt-crisis and, in several cases, hyper-inflation.

In 1983, Brazil and Mexico accumulated debt of nearly $100–100 billion, while Argentina, India and Indonesia amassed roughly $30–30 billion. The unstoppable decline is reflected well by the fact that, in the late 1980s, Mexico had an annual trade deficit of roughly $20 billion. The total amount of debt in Brazil, Mexico and Argentina surpassed the level of their exports by three to five times, and the annual debt service consumed between 50% and 62% of their export incomes in the late 1980s.

Poland, Hungary, Romania and Bulgaria accumulated huge amounts of debts, varying from $10 to 30 billion. The net value of debts in the region as a whole increased from $6 to $79 billion between 1970 and 1980. Indebtedness became a self-generating process from that time on, and the 1980s led to a hopeless and devastating galloping of debt. By 1990 Poland accumulated $41.8, Hungary $20.3 and Bulgaria $9.8 billion of net debts, and indebtedness of the region jumped to $110 billion. At the end of the 1980s, Hungary's total debt was just over two times higher than its export earnings, while the corresponding figures in Bulgaria and Poland were three and even five times respectively. Additionally, most of the new credits served as repayment for the old ones. From the more than $20 billion that made up the Hungarian debts, only about $4–5 billion was invested into the economy. Most of the Central and Eastern European countries, as well as several other peripheral countries with a non-market system, were caught in the indebtedness-trap. Several countries of these regions, such as Argentina, Yugoslavia, and Poland, could not avoid an annual rate of hyper-inflation of between 1,000% and 1,300%. By the late 1980s, economic collapse was unavoidable.

Moreover, the structural crisis outside the advanced world became more acute and long-lasting than that of the "core" countries, lasting throughout the second half of the 1970s and the entire 1980s. Where the OECD countries, the most advanced of the "core" nations, achieved 3.6% growth between 1986 and 1989, and where Asian reached an annual average of 3.7% between the entire period of 1973–1987, and while the United States, after the severe recession of the late-1970s and early-1980s, experienced an unprecedented new boom later, the countries with non- or limited market economies were unable to cope with the crisis.

State socialist Central and Eastern Europe was strongly hit. According to World Bank figures, Hungary, which had an annual growth of 6% until the late-1970s, suddenly dropped to 1.6% and 0.0% in 1979 and 1980. Closely-connected with its political crisis, Poland witnessed a -10.0% and -4.8% decline in 1981 and 1982. Yugoslavia declined to 1.2%, 0.6% and -1.1% rate in 1981, 1982 and 1983 respectively. There was no recovery to come. In the crucial years of 1986–89, Hungary achieved mannual growth of 0.9%, with Poland putting on 0.2%, Yugoslavia 0.5%, and Romania 0.7%. East-Central Europe's growth, dropped to 1.9% between 1973 and 1987, less than half of its previous annual per capita rate of development.

Latin American, African, Indian, and other restricted market economies shared the same experience: African growth, slow as it already had been between 1950 and 1973, declined from an average of 1.7% in 1973 to 0.3% in 1987, while Latin America's growth decreased from 2.5% to 0.8%.

The crisis-ridden peripheral economies applied mostly non-market models, and their severe economic turmoil was thus a predicament of both the relatively more vulnerable peripheral economies and the non-market systems that had ceased to promote the "catching-up" process. Hence, once again, the gap began to grow dramatically.

The failure of the non-market systems was most spectacularly illustrated in the fact that the gap between Central and Eastern Europe and the United States increased from 1:3 to 1:4 between 1980 and 1989. In this single decade, the disparity between the region and the European Common Market doubled. Previously underdeveloped South

Korea, which could claim only one-half of the average per capita income of Central and Eastern Europe in 1980, had closed the gap by the early-mid 1990s. Concluded Eva Ehrlich and Gabor Revesz, two analysts of the process: "The development model of East-Central Europe, which aimed to catch up with the economically advanced countries, not only failed to realize this basic goal but led to an opposite consequence, the increase of the existing gap." [9]

There was, however, not only the question of the rate of growth and its evolving trends. The real and major difference was that the crisis occured in Central and Eastern Europe and in other non-market economies without a real adjustment and restructuring. Destruction, therefore, was not accompanied by creation.

In analyzing the reasons of their failure, one has to stress the somewhat complex coincidence of several factors: the non-market economies were not only traditionally peripheral, backward and subordinated to the "core", but had also sought to achieve a breakthrough through strong protectionism, by shielding their markets from international competition and attempting to create national or regional isolation. Additionally, several peripheral non-market countries heavily militarized their economies, in acts of aggressive confrontation or self-defense.

Protectionism and isolation from the world market definitely helped foster industrialization and rapid growth in the postwar world economy during its first quarter century. But when the harsh structural crisis made basic technological transformations manifest, and radical restructuring based on new technology became the most important requirement of the age, a country's isolation from the world market became a major obstacle to transformation and adjustment. The more militarized and protectionist the regimes became, the less able they were to adjust to the new situation.

The technological revolution and structural crisis of the last one-third of the century might serve to highlight the importance of a highly-flexible economy with market acting as an incentive and highly-motivated entrepreneurial interests prevailing. The advanced market economies were far better suited to the new economic environment than were the almost non-reactive, rigid and centralized bureaucratic regimes. In the age of the information-communication revolution, not only had the relatively backward peripheral economies lost their previous advantage to generate rapid growth but they were also incapable of crisis management and adjustment, in addition to being handicapped by obsolete infrastructures and policies of protectionist isolation, heavily controlled by a bureaucratic state or possessing a strong or dominant and protected state sector, and characterized by the complete lack of market interests.

3. The End of Prosperity – End of Leading Theories

The end of the unprecedented postwar boom that shattered the world economy undermined not only the peripheral economies and their tremendous efforts of catch up, but also called into question all the concepts and theories that dominated the academia and had influenced policy makers from the 1940s on. According to John

---

[9] E. Ehrlich-G. Revesz, *Osszeomlas es rendszervaltas Kelet-Kozep Europaban* (Collapse and change of the regime in East-Central Europe), September 1991. (manuscript) p. 103.

Kenneth Galbraith, in one of his lectures in Oxford in 1980, "nobody could gain a Ph.D. at Harvard in the 1930s who did not accept Say's law, while, similarly, nobody could gain the degree if did accept it from the 1940s on." Indeed, the ruling economic *Zeitgeist* of the 1940s in the West was a triumphant Keynesianism denying an almighty market-automatism and the validity of Say's assumed market equilibrium, which suggested that supply itself creates demand, and that every sale is potentially a purchase since the supplier and seller receive the income to satisfy their own demands. Smith's "invisible hand" creating and assuring a permanent market equilibrium was replaced by Keynes with an interventionist state, which itself was to create "additional demand." This was necessary, Keynes maintained, because the market was unable to guarantee harmony, given the fact that supply and selling does not always create demand, particularly when over-saving diminishes the total value of demand compared to supply. In contrast to the classical school of economic thought, Keynes and his followers stipulated that demand creates supply, and thus a force outside the market, the state, has to create extra demand by stimulating employment via public investment and consumption.

Several peripheral countries, however, went much further than this, copying Soviet-type planning which sought not only to correct and improve the market mechanism, but to destroy it entirely. They did so by banning or strictly limiting free enterprise (the main actor of a free market economy), by introducing central planning, fixing prices, and creating inexorable defense barriers against world market competition.

The leading competing paradigm of market capitalism, the economic concept of so-called Marxism-Leninism, the Stalinist version of Marxism, that was widely applied in a gradually expanding 'Socialist world system' which, in the end, dominated more than one-third of the world throughout the European, Asian, Latin American and African continents, and represented the most vigorous challenge. Several of its elements were adopted in non-socialist, peripheral, Third World countries as well.

But all these dominant postwar theories which seemingly worked in the 1950s and 1960s, clashed head-on with the changing realities of the 1970s. The emerging crisis thus became a predicament for these previously victorious theories as well. Keynesianism did not offer an antidote for stagflation, and the state socialist planned economies did not have the means and mechanisms to promote rapid adjustment to the changing technological regime and swift structural transformations of the economy.

In the critical period of a transforming world system when historical trends suddenly changed and traditional values suddenly questioned, one important factor had a profound impact on the theoretical and policy reorientation. This was a historical coincidence: the more backward a country was, the more its economy was characterized by state interventionism and a negation of the market. This was evident since these peripheral countries had sought to find an alternative model which would help them catch up without getting involved in futile competition with an overpowering "core". An inevitable outcome given the logic of peripheral backwardness, was that these countries and regions suffered the most during the structural crisis of the 1970–80s, and, as was illustrated above, they declined into a complex and endless depression. Poor and backward countries are always much less able to demonstrate the necessary flexibility to react adequately to major structural changes. What happened in the 1970-80s was thus yet another example of a well-known pattern in modern economic history: advanced economies react better and more effectively in historical turning points than do backward economies, and consequently the gap between them is further widened to a dramatic degree.

In spite of this fact, the failure of the peripheries was more often interpreted as a consequence of their 'statist,' anti-market policies than as an outcome of their limited peripheral abilities. In other words, the much deeper crisis of the peripheries was widely interpreted as regime- rather than region specific.

On the other hand, the much greater flexibility of the advanced "core" to react to the structural crisis by adjusting to the new technological era and its structural requirements was coupled with a successful propagation of free enterprise, market-orientation and *laissez-faire* ideology.

Hence, Keynesianism and the Marxist-Leninist Soviet model were effectively compromised, and a triumphant neo-classical liberalism replaced them as the predominate trend. Unable to find the ways and means themselves, and disillusioned with their own ideals, a desperate elite of crisis-ridden peripheries, began to believe that all the problems and all the economic turmoil had originated from a mistaken model. There was no resistance any longer: the Marxist-Leninist Soviet model was buried alongside with Keynesianism and social democracy in a huge mass grave.

The new *Zeitgeist* was determined by a jubilant Chicago school version of free market ideology. John Mynard Keynes was defeated by Milton Friedman who dominated the air-waves advertising his "freedom of choice," posing before television cameras comparing Hongkong with Red China and 'explaining' the difference between them by contrasting their policies and the models they had adopted. Leonid Brezhnev, Gustav Husak, Peronist-type Latin American generals and Mengistu-type African dictators were all easily thwarted by Ronald Reagan and Margaret Thatcher. The 'Reagan revolution' or 'Reaganomics' successfully promoted *laissez-faire* ideology and free market policies, offering the unparalleled American upswing that was taking place by the early- to late-1980s as an example to be emulated. Reaganomics was presented as a simple and quick solution to the world's complex economic ills. Similarly, Thatcherism offered a "vaccination" against the *Sozialpartnerschaft* and social-democracy, and initiated instant privatization in Britain.

The relatively successful adjustment of the "core" to the new technological and structural requirements of the 1980s, thus led to a triumphant vindication of free market ideology.

Although this victory was partly generated by several mere coincidences, the superiority of free enterprise was clearly not a mirage. In the epoch of an information, communications and service revolution which radically transformed the infrastructure and structure of production, the former declined dramatically alongside the spectacular rise of new leading branches, and the more flexible and reactive market mechanism that were the sign of affluent market societies proved to be much more effective than the non-market economies. Small-scale, highly market-sensitive firms played an outstanding role in most of the success stories. Market information is indispensable for orienting both investors and entrepreneurs. Consequently, state control and interference, let alone bureaucratic central planning, often proved to be counter-productive, for the state was simply unable to react fast enough. It is thus true that models that had worked relatively well and served a catching up process in the postwar decades were now rendered obsolete in the face of new realities.

The image of a free market system that is almighty and is the ultimate key of economic success, as well as the fact that it had indeed worked in some "core" countries and proved to embody an impressive potential for flexibility and an ability to react, influenced policy-makers, governments and international institutions to a great degree, creating an atmosphere of an almost dogmatic or religious belief in a single valid, uniform and universal model of an idealized *laissez-faire* system.

This ideology, combined with formidable technical and monetary skills, was conveyed by a group of Western economic advisers taking on the role of modern 'crusaders.' Dynamic, knowledgeable, ambitious, driven with a definite sense of mission and convinced of a single formula for economic success, these advisors arrived on the scene and quickly prevailed. As Alec Nove passionately noted: "Extremist neo-conservative think-tanks send missionaries to expound the gospel: roll back the *laissez-faire* is seen as the answer..." [10]

Moreover, one should not speak only of an intellectual atmosphere and a general *Zeitgeist,* because the impact was more direct when wielded by such powerful international institutions as the World Bank, the International Monetary Fund and several United Nations-related organizations. These, as well as the American administration and several other governments of the so called G-7 group of the most influential advanced countries, shared and represented an ideological belief in free marketism and suggested its application in all the crisis-ridden peripheral countries as a replacement for their previous statist models. Their 'suggestions' were much more than merely the friendly advise of senior partners. These governments and international institutions were the ones these countries were forced to turn to for aid and credit, and accepting these "suggestions" soon became a question of life and death, the only hope for survival. These governments and organizations were in the position of mandating the abolition of Cold War tariff barriers and restrictions. They could encourage private banks and companies to invest, partly by providing certain guarantees for investors. These were the powers who forgave debts and allowed a country's inclusion in the European Community.

The highly indebted peripheral countries, in several cases suffering from macroeconomic chaos, a lack of stability and hyper-inflation, sought any means to accommodate their potential saviors. Moreover, the World Bank and IMF, did not hesitate to prescribe conditions based on their ideological principles. Countries were practically forced to apply them, since this made it possible to stabilize their economies and encourage foreign investors. But, most of all, they believed they were paying an entrance fee to the European Community by accepting its conditions.

As Beverly Crawford rightly noted: "In 1989...the Commission of the European Communities was given the authority to direct and oversee bilateral assistance to Eastern Europe from EC members. In order to receive assistance from EC members, recipients were required 'to have pluralistic political systems...[and] to make rapid movement toward free market economies...and furthermore, 60 per cent of its lending

[10] A. Nove, *Economics of Transition – Some Gaps and Illusions* (manuscript), Berkeley, 1993. pp. 4–5.

is earmarked for private sector projects, directing capital away from the hands of the state. Conditionalities favors the radical over gradualist model of transition..."[11]

Indeed, as Mira Muc, head of the Slovenian privatization office stated in the early summer of 1993: "We gave our word to the World Bank for privatizing 400 firms in 12 months...without that there are no credits."[12] The international financial institutions represented a rigid stand regarding social policy and welfare programs. They always subordinated the social issues to "economic rationality," and pushed the governments to this direction. Governments of the countries of the region were forced to keep the budgetary deficit under 5% of GDP and cut social expenditure in a drastic way. In the fall of 1992, the newly appointed Prime Minister of Poland, Hanna Suchocka had to face crucial decisions since the IMF suspended credit to the country because its budgetary deficit surpassed the prescribed limit. Decreasing the deficit from 7.5% to 5.5% of the GDP, in accordance with the conditions of the IMF, pushed governmental policy toward harsh social conflicts in the summer and fall of 1992, which undermined the government. This policy of the international financial institutions led to a lack of social sensitiveness of governments which directed transformation. "Society...cannot be permitted to go bankrupt," stated Polish Deputy Minister Piotr Mierzewski, "because of health expenditures."[13]

"The actual economic programs of the governments," reported Federigo Argentieri, an Italian expert of the Central and Eastern European transition, "are more dictated by the International Monetary Fund than anybody else, leaving not too much place for maneuvering, except for nationalist and populist demagoguery."[14]

It would be, however, one-sided and unfair to condemn the IMF and World Bank and speak about an imposed blueprint of transition. These plans were relatively well-received by the new political elite, and they confused local economic experts.

There was, undoubtedly, a certain amount of logic in the advanced countries' advise, since the new governments were struggling with the difficult legacy of a bankrupt state-owned economy and therefore sought to replace it as soon as possible. To achieve this, a 180-degree change apparently seemed to make sense. A psychological approach may also shed some light here. In fighting against state socialism, and after years of analyzing and denouncing its structures, the former opposition emotionally bonded to the total negation of its legacy.

Moreover, the newly established parties and freely elected governments began to compete with each other in demonstrating their determination to follow the American-led Western world. The applause in the West that immediately followed was encouraging. The shock therapy definitely became the greatest propaganda success achieved by the former state socialist countries. The West awarded Poland with an

---

[11] B. Crawford, *Market, States and Democracy: The Transformation of Communist Regimes in Eastern Europe and the Former Soviet Union* (manuscript), Berkeley, 1993. (Crawford cited the U.S. Government Accounting Office's publication: *Eastern Europe: Donor Assistance and Reform Efforts.* Washington DC: US Government Printing Office, 1990; and A.Vanik, "A Forced March to Capitalism." *World Press Review*, February 1991.)

[12] *Napi Gazdasag,* June 5, 1993.

[13] *Rzeczpospolita,* February 22, 1993.

[14] F. Argentieri, "Hosszu gyotrelmes ut." (A long, painful road) *Nepszabadsag,* August 8, 1992. p.17.

unique and unparalleled gesture: it forgave 50% of Poland's official debt in April 1991, while the American administration took the spectacular step of reducing Poland's American debt by 70%.

"I understood the difficulties that we faced because of the Balcerowicz Plan," quoted Tadeusz Kowalik the statement of Bronislaw Geremek, one of the most influential Solidarity leaders, "but at the same time I knew that this was the only way that could secure the chances for Poland of getting place in the European economic order. In other words: without...a very painful renunciation...we had no chances to overcome the distance separating us from the threshold allowing us to start the process of integration. I was also aware that we must move very quickly...because Europe had frankly no intention to wait for us." [15]

The 'demonstration' effect of the shock therapy was strong. In competing for foreign aid and for easy access to the European Community, which was seen as a realistic possibility after the historic year of 1989, the Central and Eastern European governments became free-traders and anti-state interventionists to a degree surpassing the countries that were classic adherents of that policy. The new elite thus became the world's most ardent advocates of free trade ideology, and they followed it with neophyte bigotry and orthodoxy. Anyone who questioned this policy fell under suspicion and was arbitrarily accused of harboring nostalgia for the collapsed regime or of attempting to preserve certain elements of it.

4. Global Transition Towards a Private-Market Economy

In the midst of a devastating structural crisis and revolutionary technological and structural transformation, the North Atlantic community took the lead in conducting a successful adjustment. The new governments of Margaret Thatcher and Ronald Reagan launched an all-out attack against state interventionism, state ownership, social partnership, and cooperation with labor unions, while openly shifting the burden of the transformation to the lower strata of the society by means of radically-altered tax policy. Ideological hegemony was accompanied by the demonstrative practices of these governments.

'Reaganomics' was a massive, ideologically based commitment and action against both the legacy of 'big government' and the Democratic Party's traditional 'tax and spend' policy. Dramatic tax reductions and the withdrawal of the state from established responsibilities went hand in hand with contracting out, i.e. privatizing, key public services.

Although public sector agencies, having faced difficulties in performing key services because of labor shortages during the decades of the postwar boom, occassionally turned to private sector firms to undertake work which previously was entirely done by the public sector, it began to do so at unprecedented levels during the 1980s in several advanced countries. After the Conservative electorial victory of May 1979, several services previously covered by the Ministry of Defense and particularly the National Health Service (in its 2,000 hospitals) were contracted out in Great Britain.

---

[15] B. Geremek, *Rok 1989*, Warsaw, 1992. p. 365. Cited by T. Kowalik, in this volume.

From the early 1980s on, the Thatcher government initiated the privatization of state-owned industries. By 1985, nearly a dozen previously-nationalized firms had been sold to private investors. The sale of part of the stocks of British Petroleum began a process that led to the transfer of control to the private sector of North Sea Oil licenses, the majority of assets of British Aerospace, Associated British Ports, and British Telecom. The Jaguar car manufacturer, British Gas, Amersham International and other companies were entirely outright to private investors, while Hoverspeed and the National Freight Corporation were purchased by their own work force. In all, some 400,000 jobs were transferred from the public to the private sectors during the first half of the 1980s, and the value of the assets amounted to more than 5 billion pounds.

Britain's Conservative government privatized those firms that were nationalized by previous Labor governments particularly during the early postwar years. Other European countries had a longer tradition of state ownership and a mixed economy, though, and they too saw a massive outbreak of privatization thanks to the ideological triumph of *laissez-faire* economics.

The most interesting case was definitely France, where the tradition of a dominant state was not only due to socialist influence but to a kind of national tradition which spanned from Colbert through to De Gaulle. The latter, who nationalized Renault to punish Louis Renault for collaborating with the Nazis by producing tanks and army vehicles, carried out a major nationalization: "For reasons which are psychological as well as economic and moral," stated De Gaulle in November 12, 1947, "there was a need after the liberation of France to pursue a nationalization policy in the area of coal, electricity, and credit. This is what I have done." [16]

Until the early 1980s, therefore, France had a mixed economy with a strong state sector comprising 94% of energy industries, 83% of the telecommunications industry, 46% of the transportation industry, 44% of banking and 6% of other industries.

Unlike in the United States and Britain, France voted socialists in 1981. Francois Mitterrand became president as a result of the May elections while parliamentary elections the following month led to the formation of the Socialist government of Pierre Mauroy. Clearly, France was swimming against the tide.

Not only the United States and Britain but the entire advanced world, including Germany, Italy and Japan, were moving towards deregulation and denationalization. Germany privatized the Veba conglomerate and two dozen state-owned companies, while the Italy's IRI, the public holding company founded by Mussolini, privatized Alitalia, Autostrada, the Italian toll-roads, Elsag and nearly a third of Banco di Roma, altogether roughly one dozen major firms. The advanced "core" countries shared the values of neo-liberal economics.

Within twelve months, though, the Socialist government of France, had nationalized eleven major private companies and the remaining private banks. After this new wave of nationalization, 53% of the fixed assets of all French companies was held by public firms, which employed nearly one quarter of the nation's work force. In the energy, railroad, telecommunications and tobacco industries, the private sector entirely disappeared.

---

[16] Ch. De Gaulle, *Discours et messages,* tome 2. Paris, 1970. p. 154. quoted by B. Jacquillat, *Nationalization and Privatization in Contemporary France.* Hoover Institution-Stanford University, 1988. p. 16.

This proved to be, however, a short-lived trend in France. From the mid-1980s on, the Socialist president and the new Socialist government, led by Fabius, discontinued the previous policy and the country gradually and – after the electoral victory of Chirac – radically turned to the 'de-statization' formula of the other Western countries. The parliament enacted two privatization bills in July and August of 1986, and privatized thirteen major firms in a period of nine months. Within eighteen months, almost all of the nationalizations of the early 1980s had been re-privatized, along with some token companies of the traditional public sector.

The triumph of free market economy, deregulation and privatization in Europe was greatly assisted by the collapse of the South European dictatorships of Franco, Salazar and the Greek military junta. Coincidentally, these events all occurred during the the second half of the 1970s, when both the outbreak of an international structural crisis and, as a reaction, a general shift towards a private-market economy became characteristic. The new European democracies in the last stage of the Cold War were soon accepted by the European Community and began to adjust their political and economic regimes.

Although in Spain, a private economy began to flourish under Franco's political dictatorship, especially from the 1960s on, it was a strongly state-controlled and partly state-owned, mixed, dirigist economic regime. Similar to Mussolini's Italy, Franco's Spain also established its public holding institution, the *Instituto Nacional de Industria* (INI) in 1941, introduced centralized price and wage controls and also controlled all private business. The established public sector dominated the coal, electricity, transportation, ship building and telecommunications industries, and was also important in textile, as well as chemical and automobile productions. Roughly 20% of all assets were in the hands of the state until the end of the 1970s. Three major state conglomerates controlled the commanding posts of the economy: INI had a share in 700 firms, holding a majority of shares in 250 of them, where 210,000 workers were employed in 1984. INH controlled the majority stocks of thirty-one companies of the energy sector, and the Direccion General del Patrimonio del Estado, among others, monopolized the tobacco and telephone industries, and held a strong position in textiles.

In post-Franco Spain, the abolition of the dictatorial regime went hand in hand with the deregulation and liberalization of the economy. Price and wage controls and state regulations were abolished. As part of a national program of restructuring that was adopted in 1984, a major privatization campaign began to eliminate the state sector from the mid-1980's on. Within two years, a consortium of seven private banks liquidated or sold 350 state-owned industrial firms and 92 banks of the Patrimonio group. In 1985–87, two financial groups privatized the INI, including the holding company's crown jewel, the SEAT automobile factory, with its 23,000 workers, itself 6% of those employed in the public sector. In 1986–87, the privatization of the Patrimonio group took place in two stages.[17]

---

[17] *Les privatisation a l'etranger, Royaume—Uni, RFA, Italie, Espagne, Japon,* Paris: Etudes coordonnées par J.-J. Santini, La Documentation Francaise, Paris, 1986.; K. Asher, *The Politics of Privatization. Contracting out Public Services,* Macmillan, 1987.

Simultaneous to that taking place in the Western world, and, in some respects, in post-dictatorial Southern Europe, a market transition also gained ground in Latin America. One of the pioneers of the process was Chile, where marketization and privatization was also linked with the change of the regime. After the suppression of Aliende's socialist government, Pinochet's military regime began a vigorous privatization campaign from the mid-1970s, transforming the economy according to the concepts and personal advise of Milton Friedman.

A crisis-ridden Argentina, Mexico and Brazil soon followed. The governments declared a market transformation in the late-1970s and early-1980s. The public sector of the three countries had a 20%, 29%, and 34% share respectively of fixed capital formation (i.e., productive investments).[18]

Although privatization in Argentina already began under President Alfonsin in the mid-1980s, the process gained real impetus only at the end of the decade: between 1989 and 1991 the national telephone company, eight previously militarily-managed petrochemical firms, the national airline, power plants, two television stations, coal mines, 28 secondary oil fields, the port authority, the postal service and the Buenos Aires subway system was privatized. With just under $12 billion generated in the sales (and debt conversion) and a more than $11 billion guarantee of private investment, the significance of the rapid changes is clear.

Likewise, in the mid-1980s Mexico saw the beginning of a modest first wave of privatization under President de la Madrid, but it gained momentum only at the end of the decade: the national airlines, the Cananea copper mining company, the controlling interest of the country's telephone company, the leading steel plants and seven commercial banks were all sold. The state's petroleum monopoly subcontracted the exploration and development of promising oil fields, and, from early 1992, the privatization of privately-farmed but communally-owned land began as well. The fact that over $8 billion was generated and nearly $16 billion of investments were pledged showed how important this transformation was.

In Brazil a slow start in privatization in the 1980s – with the selling of six state-owned manufacturing firms for $500 million – was followed by an upswing from 1990 on. In two years four leading steel mills, fertilizer and petrochemical firms, heavy engineering companies and a shipping firm were sold for $3.2 billion, and the process was intended to continue until the end of 1993, generating projected revenues of $13 billion.

India's transformation was definitely one of the milestones of the international marketization process. With the introduction of a planned, mixed economy under Jawaharlal Nehru's Bombay Plan, India must likely possessed the most consistent non-market economy outside the communist world. The Industrial Policy Resolution of 1956 established a dominating state-owned economic sector, with only a subsidiary

[18] R. Floyed, C.S. Grey, and R.P. Short, *Public Enterprise in Mixed Economies,* Washington DC: International Monetary Fund, 1984.; T.J. Trebat, *Brazil's State-Owned Enterprises: A Case Study of the State as Entrepreneur,* Cambridge: Cambridge University Press. 1983. p. 122. (Cited by L.E. Armijo, *Policymakers' Motives to Privatize, with Illustrations from Recent Experience in Argentina, Mexico, Brazil, and India,* Paper prepared for the XVII International Congress of the Latin American Studies Association, Los Angeles, September 1992. p. 22.

role for private economy. While the commanding heights of the economy were in the hands of the state, private business was allowed in certain fields, though strictly controlled and guided. Private investments were regulated by a strict licensing system, and were thus allowed only when it suited government priorities. State regulation and licensing directed not only investments into newly-founded firms, but also in the expansion or diversification of existing ones.

Additionally, in certain areas, only small-scale private firms were allowed: 863 industrial items were reserved for small private business. Foreign capital investments were strictly limited by exchange regulations, limiting their possible share to 40% of equity capital and restricting their activities to certain fields of trade and commerce. The share of the public sector in domestic capital formation was 20% in the early 1980s, and almost the entire infrastructural network, including railroads, waterways, electricity generation and distribution, communications, and trade distribution networks, etc, were in the hands of the state.

Although Prime Minister Rajiv Gandhi was committed to market-oriented reforms and encouraged private business by granting it an "open general license," and though he had liberalized foreign investments into India's automobile industry by the second half of the 1980s, a marketization breakthrough occurred only, as in the Latin American case, at the end of the decade, and particularly in the early 1990s. The government of Narasimha Rao opened a new chapter after the spring of 1991, instituting, as B.V. Rao described it, "a dramatic U-turn from earlier planned strategies" in Indian economic strategy. The policy change was clearly marked by the government declaration on the New Industrial Policy of 1991, which replaced the one established in 1956, when it stated: "many of the public enterprises have become a burden rather than being an asset to the government."[19]

Deep in economic crisis and firmly in the indebtedness trap, India accepted the International Monetary Fund's assistance and conditions (a substantial IMF assistance was already offered in 1981, but was at that time rejected by the government). Following IMF and World Bank prescriptions, the country began major trade liberalization and deregulation. Import liberalization was initiated by allowing exporters to import up to the value of 30% of their exports and by reducing import duties. Within two years (in early 1993) and in two stages, India introduced full convertibility of its currency. Price and quality controls were lifted, licensing of private investment was abolished and foreign investments were encouraged with policies that included allowing foreigners to hold a 51% and, in some cases (sectors of strategic importance), 75% share of Indian industries. The government declared the beginning of privatization by disinvesting 20% of its equity capital in thirty-one state-owned industrial firms.

In Africa, the model-country which has followed IMF and World Bank reform programs first and most consistantly since 1983 on, is Ghana which gradually decreased import restrictions, ended most price controls, introduced tax reform and begun privatization by selling (or closing) roughly fourty state-owned companies.

Mosambique, Uganda, Benin, Malawi and Tansania joined the reforms but the initially optimistic forcasts on a five-seven year transformation have now been replaced by a much longer-term prediction, in some cases 15 years.

---

[19] B.V. Rao, in this volume.

In Turkey, another country with a mixed economy characterized by a huge state sector (35% of total manufacturing capacities and two thirds of bank assets were in state-owned companies) and five-year planning (introduced in 1963), the civilian government of Turgut Ozal initiated a transformation program to create a genuine market economy in 1983. The program, which had already been prepared in early 1980, envisaged the reduction of state intervention, and stipulated the removal of different regulations, the introduction of free market pricing and the liberalization of foreign trade. The government immediately began the privatization of state-owned industrial firms and banks and, as a consequence, nearly 500 major private joint-stock companies, or 3% of the firms, controlled 80–85% of all assets in the country.

Turning towards privatized free market economy was thus a global phenomenon which began in the late 1970s and continued throughout the 1980s and into the 1990s. Most of the advanced Western countries which had preserved mixed economies, those South European countries which were under dictatorial governments and had a state controlled economy until the mid-seventies, as well as the Latin American continent, India, Turkey and several other countries, began to privatize and abolish state regulations and protectionism and turned towards free trade, foreign investments, and the liberalization of prices and trade.

Although this process clearly began in the mid- to late 1970s, it remained in most cases relatively moderate until the end of the 1980s, gaining momentum mostly in the early 1990s. The reason for this is closely connected to the collapse of state socialism in Central and Eastern Europe and the Soviet Union. Their profoundly anti-market model represented an extreme alternative to *laissez-faire* capitalism and, as was documented above, this influenced several peripheral countries in most continents.

The death-blow to all non-market and mixed economic models was thus launched by the spectacular failure of the Marxist-Leninist alternative economic system based on isolationism and centralized planning.

Market-oriented reforms appeared already in the mid- to late-1960s in Czechoslovakia and Hungary, while the Hungarian reforms were radicalized in the 1980s and were accompanied by similar reforms in Yugoslavia and Poland. But, under Soviet control and one-party rule, all of these reforms remained half-measures.

The new governments of Central and Eastern Europe that emerged as a result of the *annus mirabilis* of 1989 inherited the legacy of a declining, bankrupt economy. The situation was characterized by stagnation spanning a decade and a half, a decline of the GNP, a deterioration in the standards of living, inflation, indebtedness, in some cases hyper-inflation and insolvency, and most of all a hopeless structural crisis and lack of adjustment.

The first freely elected governments, however, had a great advantage compared to their predecessors: besides their vile heritage, they enjoyed the overall sympathy of the population, were offered assistance by the advanced Western countries and commanded an internal legitimacy. Ideological taboos collapsed and Soviet domination disappeared, no longer hindering drastically-needed reforms in the various countries of the region.

Besides the urgent need for a macro-economic stabilization, the new governments immediately initiated the transformation of the centrally planned, state-owned economy. The lesson of the collapse of state socialism was that an economy must have market flexibility to be capable of adjusting to rapidly changing technologies and constantly transforming economic structures. Market prices thus had to be restored to reflect market requirements and assure a spontaneous measuring and selection based on market criteria. To achieve this, consistent deregulation was needed to sweep away all legal and institutional obstacles inherent to central planning and state regulations. A new legal and institutional framework was also needed, while the previous institutionalized isolation from the world market was to be swept away. The liberalization of imports and an opening of the domestic economy to international competition was the central issue from which to start.

The nucleus of marketization and "de-statization", however, was a steadfast privatization of an economy that was almost 90% state-owned or state-controlled and owned. Such a dramatic transformation towards a market economy had never happened before. The Central and Eastern European transformation to a private-market economy thus deserves special attention – and a more detailed description and analysis – as the most dramatic and important factor of the global transition process at the end of the century.

Because of her peaceful 'refolution', Hungary was the only country in Central and Eastern Europe to enter into the new era with well developed market reforms and a prepared plan to radically transforming its economy. In the summer of 1988, a large network of six specialist committees began to work on detailed long-term plans for a new economic strategy, including institutional and ownership reforms. Preparations for a transition towards a mixed market economy were led by the legendary reformist and "father" of the economic reforms of the sixties, Rezsö Nyers, Minister of State in the first post-Kádár government of Károly Grósz.

Working Committee No.1 was responsible for presenting a complex short-term program of transition between 1990–92. The 162-page plan, which, in the words of the head of the Committee in the introduction of the published program, was "not partial, weakened by compromises, over-gradualist in that it does not touch the foundation of the economic system, and not moderately corrective in aiming for a too long period of realization...but a complex, consistent reform which radically transforms the basis of the economic system,"[20] was on the government's desk in the early spring of 1989. The "half-market economy," asserted the program, cannot spontaneously develop into a proper market economy without a consistent process of reform. It has to include a drastic reorientation of foreign economic relations to make the Hungarian economy able "to develop according to the requirements and as a part of the world economy," by eliminating the differences (among them the different price systems) of the three existing markets – domestic, Comecon and Western. The plan also proposed "an immediate start of widespread privatization of property and a long-term leasing of state property, assisted by low interest credits"[21], the "attraction of foreign capital", the foundation of the Stock exchange and a whole set of deregulating measures.

[20] See the introductory remarks of the head of the Committee and editor of its published suggestions: I.T. Berend (ed.), *A Gazdasagi Reformbizottsag Programjavaslata 1990–1992* (The program suggestions of the Economic Reform Committee, 1990–1992), Budapest: Kozgazdasagi es Jogi Konyvkiado. 1989. p.11.

[21] *Ibid.* p. 160.

A three-year plan of import liberalization (of about 80% of imports) and a plan of monetary stabilization were also parts of the program. The last reformist government of Miklós Németh adopted and began to implement the transition plan; thus the freely elected Antall government inherited not only a plan but also an advanced process of transformation.

The government received a 'present' of another transformation plan, completed by a joint Hungarian-International "Blue Ribbon Commission." Its stated goal was to present a program of transition for the newly-elected government. Indeed, an ambitious plan, based on the Western pattern, was ready in April 1990 and was already on the new government's desk by the time it was formed.

The strategy of continuing what was already a long-established reform process was not questioned in Hungary. There were no advocates of "shock therapy" in this country, since it was evident that, based on the previous results of the reform and the major changes of 1988–89, a transition in certain basic spheres might be completed in three or four years.

In addition, the Hungarian Democratic Forum, subsequently the leading party of the governing coalition, had a somewhat ambiguous concept on economic transformation after its foundation. The first convention of the Forum in March 1989 stated that its goal was a "third road" between Capitalism and Socialism, and declared that "a strict market-based economy would only enrich a narrow group and impoverish the majority." Even the second convention in October 1989, which adopted a more detailed program, reformulated the typical populist third-road concept. "The Forum did not endorse total privatization," summarized a report, "and by privatization it did not mean ownership by individual private citizens...[T]he entrepreneurs...would not be individuals but groups." [22]

On the other hand, an uncompromising liberal opposition turned towards free market capitalism, but it did not challenge "gradualism" either, which in the Hungarian case did not mean over-cautiousness and delay. The newly-formed coalition government followed reform measures which did not lack the required "critical mass" for a fundamental transformation. Within two years, therefore, a market price system was practically complete, while subsidies were mostly abolished for industrial and agricultural products and substantially decreased for services. Marketization was established along with import liberalization between 1989–91: respectively 36%, 60% and then 86% of imports were liberalized during these years.

The retreat of the state and the advance of the market were closely connected to the development of a modern monetary system. The monopoly of the National Bank as the single creditor had already been eliminated in 1987, and thirty-six commercial banks were functioning in the country by the end of 1991. The 1991 law on the National Bank continued "de-statization" by reestablishing the bank's autonomy from the government. In the place of the previous monopoly of one single insurance company, two were in existence in 1986 and nine by 1990, with nearly one- third of them in foreign hands. Moreover, the role of middle-sized and small-scale banks are rapidly increasing.

---

[22] *Radio Free Europe Research.* Vol.14. No.48. December 1, 1989. Part IV of 4 parts. pp. 23–24.

The most radical change in the Hungarian reform process occurred with the privatization of what was basically a state-owned economy, which was one of the key elements of the transformation. The change of the system led to a dramatic breakthrough regarding privatization. The freely elected Hungarian parliament rejected re-privatization, i.e. restoring properties and firms to their genuine owners (or to their heirs), and has instead pledged to pay a certain (moderate) amount of compensation. The exception was forcibly-collectivized land, which was to be restored to the former owners, as well as schools and Church property (except landed estates). De-collectivization, which had been a particular focus of the Hungarian reform process since the mid-1960s in a rather successful attempt to combine private and collective farming, is now being drastically pushed further, with the new government predicting that private farming will, by 1993–94, be the dominant form. Property rights and the legal framework for unrestricted private enterprise, including unlimited foreign ownership of entire companies, had been granted already in 1988–89. Since private capital accumulation already had a decade-long history in Hungary, grassroots privatization, and the foundation of new small – and medium-scale firms, gained momentum from 1989 on. More than 40,000 private firms (with legal entity) have been established since that time, while the number of private enterprises without legal title (mostly small-scale companies) more than doubled between the end of 1988 and 1992. Their number reaching 532,000, according to a report of the Statistical Office. Moreover, according to several estimates, private firms are producing between 40% and 50% of the country's GNP. Some 40% of private business is engaged in trade, roughly one-quarter in manufacturing, and nearly 40% in services.

Foreign companies and joint ventures add up to more than 13,000 (compared to 1,332 in 1989), and invested capital totalled $2 billion in the summer of 1991 and surpassed $4 billion at the end of 1992. According to the Research Institute of Privatization, the share of foreign ownership in Hungarian firms in the middle of 1992 was more than 8%, a clear sign of foreign interest. With its earlier start, relative stability and more advanced market relations, Hungary has attracted more than one-half the Western investments into Central and Eastern Europe. The government, though, expected between 25% and 30% foreign participation; this has not been realized. Except for a few big multinationals, such as General Motors, General Electric and Suzuki, most of the investments have been small. In 1989–90, 90% of investments with foreign participation represented less than $130,000 each.

The most difficult part of privatization is the selling of big state-owned companies. Hungary decided to follow a gradual privatization plan and sell the companies piece by piece. The supervision of privatization is conducted by the State Property Agency, *(Allami Vagyonugynokseg)* which had been established in February 1989. As a prerequisite, state firms are first transformed into share holding companies. The Stock-exchange was reopened in Budapest so as to launch a domestic capital market. Though still in a somewhat embryonic state, it has nonetheless created a necessary institutional foundation. In 1991, the value of transformed companies was ten times more than it had been in 1990. Most of these firms, however, remained in the hands of the state. In March 1992, over 86% of the assets transformed to joint-stock companies remained in the hands of the State Property Agency, while only 2.5% belonged to private Hungarian investors and another 8% was purchased by foreign investors. The exact share of privatization thus did not surpass 10–13% of the former state-owned companies. Whereas in the early stage of a privatization 'gold rush', large established companies of the West were rarely attracted, investors with a small financial base were. (The average investment in foreign-owned companies or joint ventures has been $100,000). They hoped to withdraw with quick profits and in most cases had no interest in reinvesting. A significant portion of the investments was channeled into real estate and retail trade chains, fields that do not contribute directly to the creation of a competitive economy.

The car industry, however, emerged as a symbol of change. General Motor's open-field investment in Szentgotthard and cooperation with Rába led to the beginning of car production in Hungary. In March 1992, the first Opel Astra rolled off the assembly line; fifteen thousand will follow annually. Although only the assembly and painting is done in Hungary by fewer than 500 workers, and though all its parts are delivered from GM's other European plants, the enterprise still embodied a promising message. Even more exciting was the launch of Magyar Suzuki in August 1992, producing 60,000 cars per annum in its newly built factory in Esztergom, and employing 1,500 workers. Initially 40% of the components of the Swift cars will be Hungarian-made, but this might increase to 60%. With a total of 100,000 cars estimated to be built, the Magyar Suzuki plant would cover the demand of the domestic market.

In spite of its important results, the privatization process is rather slow. The State Agency has determined which companies would be sold (in the first round, twenty firms were put on the market) and has prepared every single case in typically centralized fashion. There were two reasons for doing this. First, the new political elite wanted to block what could be called spontaneous self-privatization and which received a great impetus in 1989–90, in order to prevent the former managerial elite from exploiting their positions to becoming part of the new capitalist class. In some cases, this type of privatization was accompanied by corruption, with the old managers selling the state company at an extremely low price to a private firm of which they were the co-owners, or to a foreign company that guaranteed them top management posts as part of the deal.

Hence, the government's plan to privatize about half of the state-owned companies in four or five years will definitely not be realized. According to the most recent projections, the government is planning a decade-long process. Based on its program, the state's share by the end of the 1990s would decline to 25% for banking and 20% overall.

The economic transition plans revealed certain similarities in Yugoslavia, another former pioneer of market-oriented economic reforms. Based on previous partial reforms, the government of Ante Marković a planned radical reforms in order to bring about real changes. The Croatian reform economist had already proposed a program of "new socialism" in January 1989. This aimed to combine workers' self-management with a proper market environment. Having been appointed in March, and witnessing the collapse of socialism in the neighboring countries, Marković a radicalized his plan even further. He presented the new program in December 1989 with the promise to build "a new economic and political system." The Federal Assembly passed seventeen laws from a package of 24 proposed by Marković a Six of the remaining seven were approved as "provisional measures" in December of that year.

The new reform was thus introduced and linked with a radical stabilization of the currency. At that time, Yugoslavia was suffering a bout of hyper-inflation. In March 1989, the inflation rate was 346%, and by December it had jumped to 2,600%. Macroeconomic stabilization and marketization were closely linked. The new Dinar (which was equal to 10,000 old ones) was introduced on January 1, 1990, the aim being to reduce inflation to 13% by the end of the year. For the first time in Central and Eastern Europe, a stabilized currency was made convertible by being firmly tied to the West German Mark (1DM = 7YD), and this served to push marketization even further by automatically implementing the world price system. At the same time, domestic price controls were also removed on almost 85% of all commodities (only the prices of certain basic services, raw materials and energy sources remained under control). Moreover, wages were temporarily frozen. Marketization was intended to be combined with a "pluralism of ownership", i.e. a mixed-ownership structure which would include private, public and mixed property as well as a uniform, and modern taxation system.

One week after the reforms were announced 900,000 workers went on strike. This included a 30-minute general protest strike in Belgrade in December 20. Their demand was wage increases of between 50% and 400%. But even more significant was the fact that the Serbian president, Slobodan Milosević, opposed the Marković government. The Slovenian Assembly also resisted any kind of centralized federal economic policy and offered several proposals for a new constitution. Yugoslavia was, however, soon engulfed in a civil war, and the peaceful transformation was smashed.

Transition followed a different pattern in Poland and Czechoslovakia. The catastrophic Polish economic situation, with hyper-inflation of 740% in 1989, an inability to pay back foreign credits, along with a severe shortage of food and consumer goods, required desperate measures; the new Solidarity government, which took office in September 1989 sought to adopt the most drastic transformation, a process that came to be known as "shock treatment" or shock therapy. The government took advantage of its popularity and strongly-based legitimacy, and was courageous enough to realize harsh and painful proposals. Radical reform economists who had already offered reform programs in the latter years of the Jaruzelski regime, now called for immediate change. The "Balcerowicz Plan", named after its initiator and the deputy prime minister of the Mazowiecki government, with the help and advise of the Harvard economist, Jeffrey Sachs, hurriedly prepared a combined macro-stabilization and marketization plan which was received by the International Monetary Fund with the greatest enthusiasm. Western governments and journals praised the shock therapy as the most appropriate measure and definite proof of the regime's determination and courage, while the advocates of the policy became international celebrities seemingly overnight. The plan was implemented by Januar 1, 1990. Subsidies on basic foods, housing and energy which accounted for more than 30% of budgetary expenditures in 1989, were cut to 15%. Expenditures on health and education were reduced. Strict wage controls implimented, pegging increases to between 20% and 60% of the inflation rate (based on the previous month, with a 500% penalty tax on those exceeding these limits). These were combined with a policy of comprehensive price liberalization. Consumption declined by almost 35%. "It is not surprising...that Balczerowicz," stated Andrzej Kozminski of Warsaw University, "wanted Polish society to swallow such bitter medicine as quickly as possible before the massive popular support for the new government evaporated and foreign help was diverted towards other Eastern European economies starting the transition process." [23]

The austerity policy was combined with monetary stabilization. The Polish Zloty was tied to a number of convertible currencies, and the exchange rate was kept relatively stable. The Polish currency was made partially convertible, which enabled enterprises and individuals to buy and sell currency on the domestic market. This caused the "black" exchange rate to disappear. Besides its financial impact, this helped link the domestic market to the world market and encouraged import competition, and internal marketization. Hyper-inflation was curbed, and the increase in consumer prices dropped to 250% in 1990 and to 70% in 1991.

Creating a market economy was, of course, inseparably linked to privatization. Grassroots privatization and the establishment of new private enterprises gained impressive momentum. Over 51,000 new private firms (with legal entity) were established, while the number without legal entity reached 1.5 million. By the end of 1991, in addition to agriculture, which was already in private hands, private industrial sales comprised 22% of the total, while private construction reached 44% and transportation more than 16%. Some 80% of the private firms dealt with trade, especially imports, and services.

The privatization of state-owned retailing networks (by open bidding) was relatively rapid; at the end of 1991, more than 85% had become privately-owned. The decisive question was, however, the privatization of large state-owned industrial firms, which, even in 1992, were producing nearly 70% of the country's industrial GNP.

Interest in purchasing these firms was almost non-existent. A total of twenty-six state concerns was sold in the first two years, while a number of surveys reported that only an additional 3–4% of the assets of state companies might find domestic buyers. Foreign investments also remained disappointingly limited. The first year was fairly promising: the number of joint ventures jumped from fifty-five (in 1988) to 2,480 (in 1990). The number of foreign-owned companies and joint ventures continued to increase and topped 5,000 by 1991, but the amount of invested capital reached only $353 and $670 million in 1990 and 1991 respectively, which was less than a third of the foreign capital invested in Hungary – itself somewhat limited.

There were a few major investments, such as Unilever's decision to buy 80% of the shares of Pollena Bydgoszcz, the leading Polish detergent producer. As part of the multinational empire, the company which was renamed Lever Polska, doubled its production with the help of a four million dollar investment. In addition, Pepsi-Cola announced a new $60 million investment in Poland. Most of the foreign or joint companies, however, represented a very small amount of investment. In 1990, some 66% of them had investments of between $50,000 and $60,000, while a mere 0.5% surpassed $3 million. Privatization, assisted by foreign participation, thus reached a dead-end, and further development promised to be slow.

[23] A.K. Kozminski, "Transition from Planned to Market Economy: Hungary and Poland Compared." *Studies in Comparative Communism,* Vol. XXV, No.4. December 1992. p. 320.

In June 1991, to accelerate the process, the government proclaimed the extension of shock treatment to the privatization strategy. In the framework of a Mass Privatization Program, the government announced the distribution of vouchers or investment certificates to all the country's adult citizens as a universal free citizenship grant. At the same time, the government set up a national investment fund which would manage the privatized firms. Each state-owned company selected for privatization by the government would allocate 60% of its shares to the funds and, in this way, to the public at large. An additional 10% of the shares would be distributed among the company's employees with 30% to remain under state ownership. The plan envisioned that Polish mass privatization taking about two years, with shares being made available only in 1994. Simultaneously, a secondary market of investment certificates and shares would be opened at the Warsaw Stock Exchange, since most citizens would, it was thought, prefer to cash in their vouchers rather than becoming share holders. It might take years until real, concentrated private ownership emerges in Poland.

Although the term "shock therapy" was linked with the Polish road of transition, the Czech government followed an even more consistent "Big Bang" strategy especially in its privatization drive. On January 1, 1991, after one year of preparation, Vaclav Klaus, the Minister of Finance and a free market ideologist, introduced radical marketization by liberalizing prices and imports. The first shocking effect was an almost 50% price increase in January and another in February, even though price increases did slow to between 2% and 5% during the spring. Consumption immediately declined by 37%. The market transformation, though accompanied by harsh criticism, continued unabated.

The Czech privatization schedule was even more radical. In October 1990, the Federal Assembly passed a law on restitution. Unlike those adopted in other countries of the region, the law guaranteed that those private properties which numbered about 70,000 units, that had been confiscated between 1955 and 1961 were to be returned to their former owners. In the same month, another law implemented so-called small privatization, which stipulated that 100,000 state-owned stores, hotels, and restaurants be auctioned to private bidders starting in January 1991. In the first round, 10,000 units were sold for $330 million. The overall calculated value of small businesses on sale was about $6.5 billion.

Grassroots privatization was highly successful for, by June 1992, there were 1.2 million private firms in the country.

In November 1990, the government also approved a draft law on large-scale privatization of about 3,000 large state-owned companies, which were first to be reorganized – the larger units being broken up into smaller ones – and then transformed into joint-stock companies. Their privatization was initially on a voucher scheme basis. Accordingly, each adult citizen was offered investment vouchers worth 1,000 points each for a nominal fee equal to $80. This authorized the citizen to buy thirty shares (since each share initially was priced at the same number of points) of state companies via the Stock Exchange, which opened in 1991.

By May 1992, the shares of 1,400 firms were already on sale, and the auctions of assets to a net value of $9.3 billion began. Some 8.5 million Czechs and Slovaks participated and, 56% of the shares on offer were allocated. The rapid realization of the program was unique in the region. "Almost overnight," reported The World

Bank's bulletin, "Czechoslovakia will boast the biggest private sector in Eastern Europe – and one of the highest rates of individual share-holding in the world."[24] A secondary market of shares was created almost immediately. In December 1991, a private investment fund (Harvard Capital and Consulting Fund) offered ten times more than the genuine nominal value for voucher points. Other investment funds followed. About 5.7 million people opted to sell their voucher-booklets, which resulted in the accumulation of about two-thirds of total voucher points in the hands of 420 private investment funds. By August 1992, the third round of auctioning had begun.

Although foreign capital is not a central factor in Czechoslovak privatization, some landmark investments may have a great long-term impact. In November 1990, 40% of the famous Sklo Union, the state-owned glass company and an important exporter, was bought by the Japanese-controlled Belgian Glaverbel. The following month, Volkswagen bought 31% of the shares of Skoda, the single most important Czech industrial firm, for $333 million. According to the terms of the agreement, Volkswagen will invest $6.3 billion (!) into Skoda over the next seven years, thereby acquiring between 70% and 75% of the stock. The transaction, if fully realized, would be the largest cross-border investment in European history, which may change the whole industrial environment of the region and, indirectly, the country as well. In two years, in September 1993, however, as Reuter riported, Milan Smutny, the spokesman of Volkswagen, declared that the company canceled the biggest chunk of its investment program and will not build the planned engine producing plant but accomplish only an assembly work in Mlada Boleslav. The investment project was cut nearly a half of the original one.

Although following different roads, the three pioneering countries of transition – Poland, Hungary, and Czechoslovakia – have achieved important results in the transformation towards a private market economy.

The Balkan countries, however, partly because of their later start, and partly because of a different political environment, have followed a more cautious and slower road in the same direction as their central European counterparts took, especially during the first period of transformation. Price liberalization and some sort of privatization were debated and introduced between 1990 and 1991.

The National Salvation Front in Romania initially had a definite Third Road concept. In the summer of 1990, Silviu Brucan, one of the leading ideologists of the front, argued that "Romania has a lot to learn from the example [of South Korea] if it wants to avoid becoming an exhausted half-colony of the West." This strategy, he argued, offers both "a great opening to Western investors and joint ventures, while maintaining a strong state sector and thus efficient control over development." He also advocated the combination of the South Korean with the Austrian models, especially the "social policy of Austria."[25]

President Iliescu himself often stressed the danger of copying foreign models and advocated for some special Rumanian road, labeled by some Western experts as "post-communist communism." In later months, however, the post-Ceausescu leadership of Romania turned towards Western social democratic concepts.

---

[24] *Transition. The Newsletter About Reforming Economies,* The World Bank. Vol. 3, No. 5. May 1992. p.3.

[25] D. Ionescu, "Quest of a Model: Development Strategies under Discussion." *Radio Free Europe. Report on Eastern Europe,* Vol. 1, No. 39. September 28, 1990. p. 28.

The Government Commission for the Transition to a Market Economy, which was set up in January 1990, presented its report in May of that year. The core issue was gradual price reform. According to the report, price liberalization implemented in three stages would take two years to complete. In other words, it would be in place by June 1992. The program was launched and subsidies were gradually cut. In September 1992, prices of staple foods doubled. As with the marketization process all over the region, Rumanian price liberalization led to a 228% price increase between June 1991 and June 1992.

In the summer of 1991, the government implemented a partial privatization of both the agricultural and non-agricultural sector of the economy. This was based on the idea of creating a mixed economy. For, the government intended to privatize 53% of the state's assets, about 6,000 "commercial" companies retaining the balance which were what were termed "strategic sectors" such as mining, transportation, armaments, and communications in a framework of reorganized, autonomous state-owned companies. The plan called for privatizing the "commercial" companies within seven years, partly by distributing "property certificates" or vouchers among adult citizens. Each voucher would comprise 30% of the assets, while the remaining 70% were to be sold by the newly established State Property Fund, by minimum 10% allocations each year on the market. But various limitations persisted, and even grassroots privatization had strong ideological restrictions placed upon it. Although the establishment of private firms was allowed in trade, services and tourism, the number of employees was to be limited to twenty. Thus, of the firms set up during the first eighteen months, 115,000 out of 145,000 were one-person family-run businesses.

Meanwhile in Bulgaria, the government opened the round-table talks of March 1990 by presenting an over-cautious plan for gradual marketization, which was opposed by those urging shock therapy. In October of that year Prime Minister Andrey Lukanov presented a program to the parliament entitled, "Accelerated Transition to a Market Economy." This program proposed that privatization begins in 1991. The government promised to devise a special plan for small-scale privatization by November.

Continued economic decline and an accelerated political transformation led to a stepping up of the transition process. In February 1991, a radical reform package was accepted, prices were liberalized on everything except energy products, the exchange rate was standardized and the currency floated on the free market. Liberalization of foreign trade also contributed to the establishment of a speedier marketization process, together with the elimination of the state monopoly on foreign trade. Persistent price adjustments to the world market resulted in a high inflation rate, generating a 120% increase in the month of February alone. The total price increases for 1991 was 334% although the rate of inflation did slow down in the spring and summer. A number of new laws were enacted to accelerate privatization. Reluctantly, Bulgaria reverted to radical measures: a restitution law guaranteed the return of residential, industrial, commercial, and landed properties that had been nationalized or confiscated after 1947 to their previous owners. This uniquely-radical step was the most important element of Bulgarian privatization: by June 1992, some 3,600 shops, along with 2,600 houses and apartments, 600 industrial sites, and 130 restaurants had been returned to their former owners, as had 85% of all eligible land.

The establishment of new private firms was also initiated and, by the end of the year, nearly 180,000 new small businesses had been registered, most of these in the trade and services sector. In June 1991, the government completed the first auction of state-owned shops and gasoline stations. Another 1,500 units were immediately prepared for a second round of sell-offs. Consequently, the role of the private sector in the Bulgarian economy rose from 5% to 25%.

The law of April 1992 regulated the privatization of large state companies. The Privatization Agency is responsible for selling the shares, and the employees of the companies have the option to buy 20% and 30% of them. In August 1992 the privatization of 65 enterprises began and was slated for completion by the end of the year. By early 1993, however, almost the whole of big industry, a total of 96% of assets, was still in state ownership. In contrast to the three hundred firms which had been prepared for privatization, the government sought to sell off 1,200 that is, one-third of state-owned companies in 1993. This extremely slow privatization process is partly connected with the fact that foreign capital inflow is almost non existant. Compared to the nearly $5 billion invested in Hungary, Bulgaria has received only $100 million in three years.

The history of the past three years in the former Soviet Bloc was essentially repeated in the Soviet Union after the failed coup in the summer of 1991 which was followed by the collapse both of the Union itself and the state socialist regime. An agonizing and chaotic political transformation in the successor states has been coupled with the dramatic collapse of a sick economy and an emerging hyper-inflation as well as an indebtedness crisis. Russia, still a great power in terms of its nuclear military capability, was seemingly incapable of consolidating itself without major foreign assistance, and prepared to follow the shock treatment approach. President Boris Yeltsin and Deputy Prime Minister Yegor Gaidar, in an entirely different political, economic and historical environment, attampted to follow the Polish path based on the advise of Western advisors such as Sachs and Aslund.

Hence, though facing tremendous political opposition and mass dissatisfaction, a market transformation based on the already-established Polish-Hungarian-Czech blueprint began throughout East-Central Europe, including the vast former Soviet empire and tiny Albania. Its progress, however, was not only relatively slow but also contradictory and ambiguous.

Although the future of the Russian and East-Central European transformation is far from clear, it is unquestionably true that the Soviet model of a non-market regime, along with its numerous variations on the theme, had collapsed completely. The alternative and compelling model which dominated one-third, and strongly influenced another one-third of the world through to the 1980s was now in ruins. The collapse of the model's East European stronghold led to an inevitable chain reaction: it breathed life into market transition and free-market ideology throughout the world, having a peculiar inpact in the peripheries, such as Latin America, Asia and Africa. As Richard Sklar stated:

"By the end of the 1980s, when Leninist one-party rule collapsed in Europe, its economic rationale for Africa had entirely disappeared. The avowedly Marxist-Leninist regimes of Angola, Benin, Congo, Madagascar, Mozambique, and Zimbabwe had become receptive to the logic of capitalist development long before their leaders finally embraced multiparty democracy, in each case between 1989 and 1991. Their basic economic practices were ideologically indistinguishable from those of other African regimes..."[26]

As the reforms that have taken place in China demonstrate, most of the Asian state socialist regimes are in rapid transition towards a classic Asian-type market-based modernization dictatorship, taking their cue from the most successful postwar models, the Japanese, the South Korean, the Taiwanese and so forth.

After reviewing the global trend towards a market transition based on a triumphant free market ideology, one has to address the most decisive question of our times: will global acceptance of the free-market ideology, and the new economic world system that is in the making, lead to a more effective catching-up process in the backward peripheries? In other words: will the replacement of the failed model with the economic formulae and ideals of the most advanced "core" satisfy the nations in transition?

This is the central issue of the age and will be that of the twenty-first century, since the history of the twentieth century has shown there to be a continuous revolt at the peripheries. The world has experienced nationalist upheavals that have unleashed the bloody forces of devastating world and civil wars, as well as attempts at rearranging borders and the world system, building or destroying empires, eliminating and replacing existant dominant powers. Major revolts and revolutions have erupted to destroy *ancien regimes.* Left-wing and right-wing rebellions have attacked the status quo, and powerful ideologies – Fascism, Nazism, Communism, as well as populist, nationalist, and religious fundamentalism – have risen and declined, only to re-emerge again.

In an unstable, strife-riven peripheral world, economic success and an emerging sense of well-being would be a miraculous weapon against self-destructive and internationally-explosive rebellion. As national decline (even in relative terms) and frustration unleash various types of devastating and revolutionary forces, a successful consumer society, as Eugen Weber once formulated consumes revolts and revolutions as well. Rising economic and consumption levels, as well as what might be called the 'middleclassization' of former class societies might serve as a solid basis for a new world order.

Will marketization, privatization, and the adoption of free market ideals unleash adequate market forces and sources at the peripheries to promote an effective adjustment to transforming technologies and economic structures?

It is of course too early to evaluate and generalize. We are in the middle or, rather, the beginning of a developing new trend, the opening of a new chapter in history. All forecasts and prognoses are uncertain and mostly biased. To envision a future for the peripheries based on the success of the free market economies in the "core" or the spectacular rise of some of the Newly Industrialized Countries, might be as mistaken as supposing a continuation of decline in the transforming economies that characterized the early years of the bumpy road to transition.

An historian could find ample reasons not to even try to analyze this process, maintaining that it is "not yet history!" but, sharing the view of Marc Bloch, there is no real reason to exclude the present from history. It is only a transitory point at the end of the

[26] R.L. Sklar, "The Future of Socialism in Africa. The Failure of Economic Statism." In: M. Cohen and M. Kilson (eds.), *Africa: Crisis and Change. Dissent.* Special Issue. Summer, 1992. pp. 399–400.

endless line of history and thus would be ununderstandable without the interpretation of the *longue duree* of the historical trends that produced it. Additionally, history *in statu nascendi,* in other words, a new chapter of history in the making, always provides an excellent opportunity for discovering some primery characteristics and determinants of the emerging new developments.

5. The Experience of Adjustment: Free-Market Versus Regulated-Market Models

What are the major economic lessons of the difficult years of the recent structural crisis and of the attempts made at adjustment? As illustrated above, some countries became, on the face of it, relatively successful in the wake of the stagflation of the mid-to late-1970s and the recession of the late-1970s to early-1980s. The increased prosperity of the 1980s in the United States, and in some other countries, suggested an end of the structural crisis in the developed world. However, the repetition of the recession in the early-1990s throughout the advanced world clearly shows that an adequate adjustment has not yet taken place. The "Reagan boom" was more a product of temporary phenomena than a successful structural adjustment. The $4 trillion deficit, accumulated mostly in the 1980s, one-quarter of which originated from foreign sources, demonstrates without a shadow of a doubt the bogus character of this past prosperity which went on to become an obstacle for future recovery.

In spite of repeated recessions, slow growth and high unemployment, as well as the eergence of hitherto unknown new economic phenomena such as 'stagflation' in the late-1970s and early-1980s, and the 'growth without job creation' in the early 1990s, the adjustment process of the "core" countries are definitely making progress.

Although some of these countries may decline and thus drop out of the "core" as a result of their not being able to adjust adequately, most of the affluent countries are going through the process of, to use Schumpeter's term, "constructive destruction." While suffering from the decline and collapse of some of their leading sectors, they are building up new branches based on the most modern technology. The slow-growth period of adjustment is thus pregnant with the promise of new prosperity.

The economic turmoil of the "core," as has already been noted, was accompanied by a far-reaching crisis in the peripheries. From the late-1970s on, decline in output, hyper-inflation, high rates of unemployment, and indebtedness crisis have had powerful impact within what have become the former state socialist countries, and well as in other peripheral economies. According to Angus Maddison's calculations, the critical period 1973–1987 reflect a slower growth rate of 3.4% (compared to the 5.1% achieved between 1950 and 1973) in the world economy, these figures being based on thirty-two countries from the various regions. The 'world' average, however, included below-average growth rates in the "core," with the OECD countries coming in at 2.4%, while Latin America was growing at 2.9%, and the Soviet Union at 2.1%.

The only region which achieved a continuously rapid growth was Asia, which registered a 5.9% increase. South Korea, Taiwan, and China put on 7.9%, 7.8%, and 7.5% respectively. In the 1980s, China achieved annual growth of more than 10%. "In Asian countries," writes Maddison, "the acceleration of economic progress in the golden age was even more marked. Eight of them achieved better (generally very much better)...growth rates than in the...earlier phases."[27]

Indeed, the average rate of GDP in the Asian countries at constant prices was only 1.7% in the period 1900–1913, 1.3% in 1913–1950, and then 5.4% from 1950 to 1973. Thus the highest rate (5.9%) was achieved during the recent structural crisis. Indeed, the IMF reported surprisingly high rates of growth in some of the 'developing countries' in the early-1990s, which reached 5% a year. China, with its reformed state socialist economy, recently achieved a record 12%.

While almost all "core" countries, as well as most of the peripheries, are suffering from the damage brought by the structural crisis, the Asian modernization models proved to be the most successful.

The Japanese government's five-year plan for the second half of the 1970s defined precisely the structural changes that needed to be made to the Japanese economy to enable it to adjust to the new requirements of the period. The state plan gave strong preference to the required percentage increase in the high-tech and aerospace industries, and guaranteed incentives and assistance to the strong market forces that were to help foster restructuring.

China has successfully combined consistent market reform, a rather special form of 'privatization' and structural changes based on political stability. Whereas the government has given the green light to private business, including foreign investment and joint ventures, and contributed to creating a more flexible market and export-oriented private sector within the state socialist economy, it has made no effort to privatize the state-owned economy.

The right to sell state-owned assets is still highly constrained, noted Andrew Walder, the Harvard expert on China. "[L]and, factories, and other enterprises are not freely bought and sold...and still generally remain under the de facto ownership of territorial-defined government agencies."[28]

The reforms, however, radically changed property rights by promulgating a "widespread downward reassignment of use rights within government hierarchies, and at the grassroots, from government agencies to households and individuals. The most dramatic such reassignment took place in the dismantling of collective agriculture."[29] The same principle was applied to collectively-owned assets in industry and trade. The lease-holder received the right to manage, along with increased autonomy. Victor Nee speaks about "informal property rights" in the reformed Chinese economy. As a result of these rights being delegated to managers, state-ownership became similar to that of modern share-holding companies, one fundamental aspect of which is precisely the fact that the running of the company is in the ends of an appointed management.

Between the state and the relatively small private sectors, the most characteristic intermediate sector which has increased dramatically since the late-1970s is the so-

---

[27] A. Maddison, *The World Economy in the 20th Century,* Paris: OECD. 1989. p. 37.

[28] A.G. Walder, Corporate Organization and Local State Property Rights: The Chinese Alternative to Privatization. In: V. Milor (ed.), *The Political Economy of Privatization in Post-Communist and Reforming Communist Systems,* Chapter 2. p. 11, (under publication).

[29] *Ibid.* p. 8

called collectively-owned sector in the rural areas and townships. This marketized, freely operating sector, which was owned by the local community and never belonged to the central state authorities became the main actor in the 1980s, absorbing nearly 60% of the increase of the labor force and achieving an annual 20% growth rate, which meant that its output doubled every three or four years.

Both the small size of the operations and the fact of non-exclusive property rights are linked with Chinese traditions. Since Western-style landownership never existed in the country, individual ownership was always constrained, property rights were complex, and small family-size firms traditionally dominant in the Chinese economy.

The Chinese reform model also embodies a cautious combination of domestic market protection and export orientation. The huge and very poor domestic market itself offers unlimited growth potential and the government is continuing to protect this market for domestic output.

This deliberate, far-sighted export orientation, however, has created special zones and forms, has attracted foreign capital, technology and expertise, and continuously has developed the export sector of the Chinese economy. The competitive export branches are being aggressively promoted. As a consequence, foreign trade increased five-fold between 1978 and 1988, and more than doubled its share of the country's GDP. It should be added that roughly one-quarter of exports are produced by the above- mentioned collective sector.

The entire market-oriented transformation of the economy was thus guided by the state, which also guaranteed political stability. Interestingly enough, the new impetus of reform and the high growth rate in the early-1990s was assured in the wale of the bloody Tienanmen Square massacre of 1989, when a mass demonstration and upheaval for democratic reform was ruthlessly suppressed by the use of tanks. As Andrew Walder argues, the Tienanmen Square events represent a turning-point in post-revolutionary Chinese history: in spite of using the traditional communist terminology, China is gradually turning out to be a classic Asian modernization dictatorship.

The future of China's reform, however, is still uncertain. Although it has been very successful and is generating not only astonishing economic growth but an equally impressive increase in consumption and living standards, including housing, the regime might ultimately be challenged politically and may even collapse. The country might disintegrate and decline into civil war. The major question is whether the inherent political stability of a dictatorship will survive marketization reforms.

Independently of a possible political disaster, however, the near decade-and-a-half of transition and rapid growth have, without a doubt, paved the road for a historically-rare market transformation and opportunity for catching-up.

The most successful example of adjustment to the new technological and structural requirements of the world's economy as well as the most spectacular example of catching-up, during the structural crisis in the last one-third of the century has thus undoubtedly been Asia's regulated-market economies. (China, which is gradually reforming away from state socialism into this latter category of Newly Industrialized Countries of Asia, is producing the strikingly smooth transition from a non-market, publicly-owned towards a mixed, regulated-market economy.)

The high degree of flexibility, combined with cautious and strong state participation aimed at overcoming the problems typical of an incomplete market and the lack of a market society has resulted in an increasing role for "new-style" Asia in the changing world system.

Replacing its traditional method, the United Nations published new calculations that counted the Gross Domestic Product on the basis of Purchasing Power Parity – calculations that shocked the world by proving that the assumed domination of the "core" countries was declining: rather than representing nearly three-fourth of the world's output, they actually had only a 54% share, at the expense of the rapidly-developing Asian countries. According to these new figures, China now has the second-largest economy in the world. Although calculations based on PPP are open to question, there is still a clear need to correct measuring techniques based on exchange rates. However, one cannot ignore the enormous and consistent advance and rapidly-growing importance of the Asian "success" countries such as Japan, South Korea, Taiwan, Honkong, Malaysia, Indonesia and, last but not least, China.

6. Anni Miserabiles in Central and Eastern Europe: a Laissez-faire System in the Periphery

Central and Eastern Europe, however, followed a different path after its *annus mirabilis* in 1989. As the most climactic and radical example of end-of-the-century market transformation in the world economy, its implications deserve special attention in this analysis. As was documented above, the region adopted the free market ideology of the Western "core" and began to rebuild its institutional and legal system, to reform ownership structures, and its economy based on the self-regulating free market model and property rights. Such an historic transformation, however, was bound to have unavoidable negative side-effects.

Closing down obsolete, non-competitive branches of the economy, ending subsidies to deficit-producing firms, or shedding part of the work force of over-staffed institutions are unavoidable steps in the transition process. The negative side effects are the decline in production and an increase in unemployment.

Adjusting to world prices and liberalizing imports is creating competition for heretofore protected and insulated Central and Eastern European economies, yet this is a prerequisite for market adjustment and introduces international market incentives. On the other hand, though, it is destructive for the obsolete branches and firms since it causes a loss of market, decline in output and an increase in bankruptcies. In an age of technological change and structural crisis, adjustment inevitably generates "creative destruction" as we have seen in the case of the advanced "core."

New and unfavorable external economic factors worsened the difficult transformation of the region. The complete collapse of the Soviet Union and the former Comecon market, a mini Gulf oil crisis in early 1991 and a severe recession in the United States followed by the Western world in general in 1991–93 has had negative repercussions on, and create additional barriers to, Central and Eastern Europe's transition.

Hence, the over-blown expectations and over-optimistic forecasts and promises inevitably came into collision with the harsh realities. Hope for a short, one- or two-year decline followed by a discernable recovery and real prosperity in four, or five years, was not well-based. Repeated government predictions of an imminent upturn in the national economy proved to be mistaken in 1990, 1991, 1992 and, in most of the cases, in 1993 as well. Official forecasts of a moderate, transitory decline in industrial output and domestic production, and calculations of a temporary increase in the rate of inflation and unemployment, have turned out to be grossly inaccurate. In the end, the deterioration of the economy has been much greater and has lasted much longer than originally expected.

The most educative case of instant market transition was that of former East Germany. The economic unification of East and West Germany was realized on July 1, 1990 with the elimination of the Ost-Mark, which made the West German DM the general official currency. A common German market was also created as a result of the removal of all the trade barriers between the two states, which were politically united on October 3 of the same year.

Seemingly overnight, the East German economy which had, up to that time, been managed along strictly orthodox, non-reforming central planning lines, had been a member of the isolationist Comecon, and had delivered the majority of its output to the Soviet and Central and Eastern European markets, became a part of the *laissez-faire* market economy of the Federal Republic of Germany. Drastic re-privatization was announced. Pre-communist ownership was legally restored. This was undoubtedly history's most uncompromising transition to a market economy, a shock treatment *par excellence.*

As a consequence, during the first three years of transition, East German production was cut to half its 1990-level, and 40% of all jobs disappeared. Describing the West German 'Economic *Blitzkrieg*' in East Germany, Roland Schoenfeld concluded: "East Germans are disappointed..., treated as second-class citizens... their life long endeavors failed and their economy – once eleventh among the world's industrial nations – in shambles." [30]

The total collapse of the former East German economy, once without a doubt the strongest and most developed in Central and Eastern Europe, might be taken as a test case. This is particularly apposite, since this part of the former Soviet Bloc received far more from external sources during the early years of its transition. The report of the Bundesbank in the spring of 1993 revealed that there had been a transfer of $250 billion from West to East Germany between 1990 and 1992. Nonetheless, instant marketization ruined the economy and the livelihoods of the majority of the adult generations of East Germany. It is significant that, in the early 1990s, a few – very extreme – but nonetheless relatively typical ideas emerged, calling for the de-industrialization of the *Ost-Länder* to make it into a tourism and recreation area. The belated and partial re-emergence of the post-war Morgenthau-plan, paradoxically enough proposed by the Germans themselves on this occasion, also typifies many of the gloomy forecasts made about this area, many of which maintain that the Eastern territories will be the 'undeveloped South' of a rich Germany.

One explanation for the collapse would certainly begin with the legacy of a vast but non-competitive, technologically and structurally-obsolete East German economy,

---

[30] R. Schönfeld, in this volume.

whose "principal industries," continued Schoenfeld, "were concentrated in 'rust-belt' sectors...with worldwide surplus capacities...and [with a] totally inadequate [infrastructure]." [31]

The dramatic collapse may also have been due to severe miscalculations and technical errors in managing the transition. Though this is certainly true, it cannot be denied that the dramatic collapse was, most of all, a consequence of the overnight introduction of a free market in a previously non-market society, integrating the isolationist, import-substituting economy into a *laissez-faire* West German and world economy. "When the hitherto totally protected East German industry was exposed abruptly to West German and international competition," explained the above-cited author, "its production collapsed." [32]

Despite the recent catastrophic economic collapse and the tragic human cost, including the loss of entire generations in their forties and above, and dispite the resulting political turmoil, re-emergent racism and murderous atrocities, East Germany's suffering will certainly be resolved in the framework of one of the world's strongest economic powers, Germany. The uncompromising marketization of former East Germany, however, clearly shows the devastating impact of replacing a non-market system with a free-market economy overnight.

Although the East German case is somewhat extreme, the situation reflects major similarities in the Central and Eastern European countries. The former Solidarity adviser Tadeusz Kowalik presents a dramatic picture of the post-1989 Polish situation: "Over the first year alone (1990) the national income declined not by the forecasted 3% but by 13%, distributed income declined by as much as 18%, and industrial production declined not by forecasted 5%, but by 23%. Real wages were lower by about one third. Personal consumption declined by 15%...And what is more disastrous, by the spring '92 the Polish economy...is still systematically declining. Thus, a severe recession is turning into a long-lasting depression..." [33]

The Polish "slumpflation", as Kowalik described it, actually worsened in 1991. While the government predicted a 3.5% increase of the Gross Domestic Product, in reality the decline continued at an accelerated pace: the Vienna Institute for Comparative Economic Studies published the shocking revelation that productive investments declined twice as much in 1991 than in 1990, industrial output and the Gross Domestic Product continued to decrease by more than 10%, and the electro-mechanical and chemical industries, which decreased production by 12.7% and 13.3% in 1990, fell by 29.1% and 14.3% respectively in 1991.

In the spring of 1992, the decline reached its nadir, with GDP and industrial output down just under 30% and 40% respectively. Unemployment, which stood at 6% at the end of 1990, surpassed the 12% mark a year later. This kind of "destruction" is not linked yet to any kind of "creative" impact. As one of the Polish experts summerized: "Productivity is going down and production cost per unit is going up, further undermining the competitiveness of Polish products. The percentage for costs in the total revenues of enterprises increased from 78.9 to 87.1% in the first half of

---

[31] *Ibid.* p. 68.

[32] *Ibid.*

[33] T. Kowalik, *Creating Economic Foundation for Democracy* (manuscript), 1992, pp. 5–6.

1991...It is clearly evident that continuation of the 'shock treatment' policies enhances further the cost driven inflation by increasing the cost of capital and further reducing demand."[34]

In Czechoslovakia, where a similar shock therapy was introduced in January 1991, the consequences were similar: instead of the projected decline of between 5% and 10%, the Gross National Product fell over the year by 16% and industrial output dropped by 23%. At the end of 1992, these figures had reached 20% and 36% respectively.

It pays to note and warn, however, that not only the economy but the statistical service of the region is in flux and one have to count with major miscalculations and mistakes.

In the analysis of Kowalik, Kozminski, and several other Polish economists, the reason for the continuous decline is the ill-advised, ideological shock therapy. "To a certain degree," stated Kowalik, "this is a consequence of the collapse of trade with the USSR, but undoubtedly the main reason was an orthodox, and very rigid, austerity policy."[35]

This argument, however, is contradicted by the fact that a somewhat similar decline occurred in more "gradualist" Hungary, where industrial output dropped by 9.6%, 18.8% and 10% in 1990, 1991 and 1992 respectively, while the GDP decreased by about 30%. After a slow start, unemployment, which was 0% had gone above 12%, with almost one in four workers unemployed in regions such as the North-Eastern base of 'heavy industry'. According to what look like robust government-issued calculations, a further dramatic increase of unemployment is still ahead.

Moreover, there has also a striking decline in agriculture. Since this was one of the former success branches of the Hungarian economy and a leading export sector, its decline demands special and more detailed attention. On an international level, Hungary used to be ranked as one of the top five countries in terms of per capita grain and meat production. In the fall of 1991, the area which was reserved for wheat decreased by 25%, and fallow land increased five-fold. Animal stock decreased dramatically: the deputy minister of agriculture reported in May 1993 that the number of cattle and pigs fell by 41% and 48%, poultry by 50%. He added: "The burden of change of the regimes was suffered most by agriculture."[36]

Agricultural production declined by 10% both in 1990 and 1991, but in 1992 it fell by a dramatic 23%. The use of artificial fertilizers drastically dropped to one fifth of its previous levels. So-called "side" activities of the cooperative farms, such as food processing, and various kinds of industrial and service ventures, virtually disappeared.

In addition, there has been a strong outflow of capital from agriculture. (In 1992, interest payments on savings accounts produced returns four times higher than investment in, for example, pig fattening.) In 1991, half of the amortization was not covered, and agricultural assets began to decrease. The state began subsidizing the slaughter of

---

[34] A.K. Kozminski, *Op.cit.* pp. 324–325.

[35] T. Kowalik, *Op.cit.* p. 6.

[36] L. Medgyasszay, "Dramai helyzet az allattenyesztesben (Dramatic situation in animal husbandry), *Nepszabadsag*, May 28, 1993.

animals. As a consequence, 137,000 people left agriculture in 1991. By 1992, only 440,000 people remained, half of those who worked in the sector a decade before.

In an analysis debated by the presidium of the Hungarian Academy of Sciences in early 1993, the authors maintained that "nearly one-third of the farms might be financially bankrupt in the near future...[and] there is a danger of a total disintegration of Hungarian agriculture."[37]

The first years of transition have thus caused more destruction in Hungarian agriculture than did the notorious forced collectivisation process.

Several factors have contributed to this destruction. In the first place, one should mention the legacy of a hidden agricultural crisis in the 1980s. Relatively high production cost did not cause perceptible consequences at the time, since export markets were available, and agriculture was heavily subsidized. But Hungarian agriculture, though very successful in its traditional activities, was unable to adjust to the world market's requirements. The hidden crisis became manifest from one year to the next after 1989.

Major mistakes were also a factor. The government, for example, accepted a re-privatization program of peasant farmland. This had been demanded by the Smallholder's Party, though (genuinely) rejected by all the other parties, including those of the governing coalition. The reconstruction of the old ownership structure, however, was being carried out in an entirely different historical context. Prior to the forced collectivisation, according to the census of January 1, 1949, some 56% of gainfully-occupied people worked in agriculture in Hungary. Today, only between 12% and 13% do so. In these circumstances, re-privatization could not provide an incentive for a renewal of agriculture, but rather, by creating a high degree of uncertainty, it would be likely to provoke a de-stabilization of agriculture. In addition, it coincided with an ideological crusade to eliminate cooperative farms, even though most of them have continued to operate.

The most devastating effect, however, was the elimination of subsidies. Not only budgetary tensions but also international requirements and an overblowen free-market ideology encouraged the government to do away with subsidies and open the domestic market. While Hungary earmarked a 10% state subsidy for its agricultural products in 1991, the European Community was providing 49%. Gyorgy Rasko, the deputy secretary for agriculture stated in an interview on December 24, 1992: "While the European Community has a 50% agricultural subsidy, Hungary, according to OECD calculations, has a negative subsidy...," by which he meant that Hungarian farmers paid out more in taxes than they received in subsidies.[38] Although the Community has an import tariff of 250% for beef, Hungary's is one of only 15%. Small wonder that food imports to Hungary from the European Community increased by 32% in 1991 and by 54% in 1992. On the other hand, Hungary could not exploit its increased agricultural export possibilities to the West (even though a 10% increase was granted for 1992). The first quarter of 1993 signalizes a continuing dramatic

[37] A. Sipos-P. Halmai, "Jelenkori agrarproblemak. Az atalakulo agrargazdasag feszultsegei es kibontakozasi lehetosegei (Contemporary problems of agriculture. tensions in the transforming agriculture and the possibility of ways out), *Magyar Tudomany*. 1993. No. 2. pp. 123, 127.

[38] *Magyar Hirlap*. December 24, 1992.

decline: Hungarian agricultural export decreased by 50%, while imports increased by 8% compared to same period in 1992.

A successful reorientation of Hungarian agricultural exports from the Comecon area to Western Europe was a major economic achievement, though there has been a high price to pay for it: "these exports are viable only at such a low price that it cannot entirely cover the cost of production." [39]

The same phenomenon battered Polish agriculture, where long-standing private farms had to face devastating competition from highly-productive Western agriculture. As Andrzej Olechowski, a close aid to Lech Walesa and member of several Polish cabinets expressed the religious belief: "even unilateral opening of the economy to the world is advantageous...Liberalization may be harmful...Nevertheless, the overall prosperity will increase." [40] As a consequence, reported Joel Haveman from Kaczewo in the summer of 1992: "The dairy cases of Poland's grocery stores are stocked high with butter from Germany and the Netherlands, so high that native son Brunon Wardecki cannot profitably sell butter even to his local market... When the Warsaw government engineered Poland's overnight transition to a free-market economy on January 1,1990, it virtually abolished tariffs on farm imports, making the country's agricultural market one of the most open in the world." [41]

Bulgarian agriculture, after re-privatizing land and re-establishing a maximum of 30-hectars peasant farms, dropped back to pre-industrial technology. In 1992, in addition, 1.9 million ships, 460,000 pigs and 253,000 cattle were slaughtered, since the small farms could not keep them.

The most dramatic decline, however, hit the traditional export sector of Bulgarian agriculture. The state monopoly of Bulgartabac used to be the world's Number One cigarette, and Number Two tobacco exporter. These two branches represented roughly one-half of the output of food processing. In 1992, tobacco production declined by 50% and the twelve processing, and nine cigarette producing firms worked at only 60% capacity. Bulgaria's share in the European market dropped to 10%. American export rose to twice the level of the previous Bulgarian record. Moreover, after halving tariff barriers, tobacco import reached 6.5 million kilograms, the amount produce of 10,000 Bulgarian tobacco farmers in one year.

Severe economic decline has been the most common characteristic of Central and Eastern Europe in the early 1990s. It was not only shock treated Poland or gradualist but consistently reforming Hungary that suffered the most massive losses. "The most dramatic output losses – measured output has fallen by more than half – have been in Albania...and the successor states of the former Yugoslavia," summarized two World Bank experts. "These extreme cases are attributable to special circumstances – in Albania, the disruptive disintegration of an unusually closed regime...and in Yugoslavia the civil war." [42]

---

[39] A. Sipos-P. Halmai, *Op.cit.* p. 122.

[40] "Integracji dzien powszedni." *Zycie Gospodarcze,* No. 44, November 5, 1993. Cited by: T. Kowalik, in this volume.

[41] J. Haveman, "Silver Curtain: Economic Decaying." *Los Angeles Times,* August 11, 1992.

[42] M.I. Blejer and A. Gelb, "Persistent Economic Decline in Central and Eastern Europe. What are the lessons?" *Transition. The Newsletter About Reforming Economies,* The World Bank. Vol. 3, No. 7. July–August 1992. p. 2.

As a matter of fact the Yugoslav economy was on the verge of total collapse by the summer of 1991. Industrial production had fallen by 30% and the GNP by 20%, tourism to the country plummeted from eight million visitors in 1990 to just a few thousand in 1991, which alone led to a loss of $4 billion, and the unemployment rate soared to a catastrophic 20%. In 1992, small-Yugoslavia's output suffered a further 30% decline and inflation rate reached 223% in the first quarter of 1993.

The downturn was substantial throughout the region. During the first one-and-a-half years of transition in Bulgaria, before the radicalization of the government's reforms, economic decline reached dramatic proportions: according to the Organization for Economic Cooperation and Development, decrease in output was close to 14% in 1990, one of the most abrupt in Central and Eastern Europe. In the first half of 1991, industrial production declined by 29% and production in general by 22.6%. The extent of the crisis was evident in the fact that exports dropped by 50% in the first half of 1991 (while trade in rubles fell by 75%). In addition, domestic consumption and production were crippled by a sharp drop in imports (from $4.11 to $1.59 billion). In 1992, Bulgaria's GDP decreased by a further 13%. In Romania, where moderate reforms were cautiously implemented, industrial production declined by one-third between the summers of 1991 and 1992, and unemployment reached 6.7%. The decline of the GDP in 1992 reached 15.4%, a rate surpassed only by the successor states of the former Soviet Union which suffered, on average, a 19% decline in their GDP.

Besides the particularly tragic case of Albania and Yugoslavia, and considering all the possible mistakes of statistics, the GDP of the other countries of the region certainly declined by an average of 20% to 30% and industrial output fell by between 30% and 40%. It seems clear that the year 1989, the *annus mirabilis* was followed by the *anni miserabiles,* in other words, several miserable years.

What was the reason of the extremely sharp and unexpected economic decline in the early 1990s?

In the case of Poland, explanations mentioned earlier attributed the crisis to shock therapy, which undoubtedly spurred the country's sharp downturn. But this interpretation cannot explain the general phenomenon of economic decline throughout the region.

In December 1992, Janos Kornai, one of the leading experts of the state socialist economy, provided another explanation for the decline of gradualist Hungary: "There were some factors, connected with international fluctuations, which contributed to the decline, but their role had a secondary importance. The primary explanation is the following: the severe decrease of production is a painful side effect of the healthy process of changing the system. Whereas several elements of the mechanism of economic decline seems on the surface to be similar to other cyclical phenomena and structural transformations ..., this is something rather different...its cause is the transition from socialism to capitalism."[43]

Kornai's point that the transition has several unavoidable, negative side-effects is of course correct, but nobody predicted a 30% to 50% decline. Furthermore, the proposed solution implicitly alludes to a concrete blueprint to be followed. If things go wrong, just proceed faster: "To end the decline," recommends Kornai, and his sugge-

[43] *Magyar Hirlap.* December 24, 1992.

stion postulates a single paradigm, the existence of only one road to follow, "one should not go backward, but forward, preserving the results of the transformation already achieved and accomplishing even faster the tasks still remaining."[44]

The "transformational recession," as Kornai called the economic decline in Central and Eastern Europe, has a multi-causal explanation. He speaks about six main factors behind it: "Shift from a sellers' to a buyers' market; Contraction of investment; Shift in the composition of output; Shift in the composition of foreign trade; Disruption of coordination; Enforcement of financial discipline."[45] In this interpretation even the "disruption of coordination" and "enforcement of financial discipline" are strong reasons for decline and economic chaos in Bulgaria and Albania, where the elimination of the old regime was not immediatelly followed by consistent reforms.

However, more and more experts are questioning the applicability of what David Stark formulated as "design capitalism." (He goes even further by challenging the term "transition" because the word implies a known end-result, and he prefers to use the "transformation.")

In addition, a third type of explanation has emerged. The drastic deterioration of general economic conditions, Domenico Nuti has observed, "is not [a] necessary concomitant of transition, nor a consequence of shock therapy..., but the unnecessary consequence of policy failures."[46] Nuti lists several policy failures, such as the dearth of liquidation and bankruptcy procedures, which had long encouraged firms to accumulate debt. He also criticized the lack of a "clear and coherent privatization program." But the primary focus of his criticism regards, "the failure in government management of the state sector."

Indeed, in most of the countries, the state sector was handled as if it were an instantaneously disappearing group of companies. State-owned big industry was written off, and served only as a source of state income. In most of the countries, state companies were, and are, overtaxed, unable to invest in themselves. They had used up their last reserves and had begun to concentrate on exporting to the West but, renounced by their respective governments, and unable to adjust to the rapidly-changing situation, they were, for the most part, doomed to oblivion. This "betrayed" ailing state sector, however, still represents the bulk of the responsible for between 50% to 70% of all domestic output, but there is little interest in revitalizing a part of it.

All the explanations, of course, contain elements of the truth. A certain degree of decline was unavoidable, the overly rapid transition caused even more damage, and policy mistakes contributed greatly.

The decline and extremely harsh disturbances, however, have deeper roots and causes. They are closely connected with an unquestioned, religious neo-liberal economic philosophy predominating in the region. The new believers are convinced that there is only one "design," an imagined, ideal *laissez-faire* capitalism without state ownership and intervention. All other options are to be rejected.

---

[44] *Ibid.*

[45] Interview with Janos Kornai, "Anti-Depression Cure for Ailing Postcommunist Economies." *Transition. The Newsletter About Reforming Economies,* The World Bank. Vol. 4, No. 1, February 1993. p. 2.

[46] D.M. Nuti, "How to Contain Economic Inertia in the Transitional Economies." *Transition. The Newsletter About Reforming Economies,* The World Bank. Vol. 3, No. 11, December 1992–January 1993. p. 2.

Unlike the period 1988–89, when a "Scandinavian model" and Austrian *Sozialpartnerschaft* were relatively popular in East-Central Europe, the new governments now enthusiastically copy "Thatcherism" and "Reaganomics." The highly-redistributive Scandinavian model is considered too *etatiste* and socialist. In the place of *Sozialpartnerschaft,* the regimes seek to crush the trade unions, which they view as being either "Red" or anachronistic to the changing times, and they frown upon union organizing as potentially threat to democratic order. The half-century triumph of West European mixed economies in France, Italy, and Austria, where the state had owned between 20% to 50% of the economy, was counterbalanced by a pronounced trend towards privatization in the 1980s. The most successful road of the East Asian countries, which in several cases combined market-oriented modernization with dictatorship, and in all cases utilized strong state interventionism, has not even been considered in Central and Eastern Europe.

This ideological approach has also been the source of other serious mistakes. Since the neo-liberal paradigm is based on the assumption of an ideal equilibrium and a perfect market and market mechanism, the followers imagined that the rapid introduction of this type of market would automatically resolve everything.

Alec Nove, in a study of the gaps and illusions of transition, critically cited Marek Dambrowski and Vaclav Klaus as resisting "interventionist pressures" and "the demand for a kind of government investment policy." As Nove points out, any kind of resource allocation for restructuring, any "state influence on the branch structure of the economy," or any "priority in government (economic) policy" over the market mechanism is rigidly opposed. "No industrial policy, no energy policy, no investment strategy. All will come about by itself if and when macro-economic stabilization is achieved."[47]

During the years of transition, the hierarchy of economic goals was, in a way, turned upside-down. In the beginning, marketization and privatization were initiated in order to provide adequate market incentives to assure successful adjustment. During these early years, however, a religious "de-statization" became a primary goal in itself, and not economic restructuring and the attempt to generate an adequate response to the challenge of the world economy, which were 'temporarily' pushed aside.

Schumpeter's term of "creative destruction" had certainly never been used more often that during those two or three years in Central and Eastern Europe. By the end of 1992, however, there had been an unexpectedly striking amount of destruction, but the creative aspects of the transition were still to be seen.

"The fall in output," stated two World Bank experts, "does not seem to have been accompanied by the radical economic restructuring that many expected as part of the reform process."[48]

The first three years of the transition, which led to a spectacular breakthrough in the transformation from a planned, state-owned system to one that is privatized and market-oriented, and which achieved impressive results in coping with the former shortage-ridden economies, could not yet generate significant results in restructuring

---

[47] A. Nove, *Op.cit.* pp. 5,10.
[48] M.I. Blejer and A. Gelb, *Op.cit.* pp. 2–3.

the economy. The core issue of the structural crisis, the need for a structural-technological adjustment, is yet to be addressed. State socialism was unable to respond because of the rigidity of the planned economy, and the lack of adequate interest in a state-owned economy. The first results of the economic transformation, however, were not sufficient to initiate a major restructuring. There are structural changes regarding the share of industrial and services branches, the size structure of enterprises, and on a micro-economic, i.e. product level. The lack of governmental economic policy to initiate and assist the macro-economic restructuring has certainly been a contributing factor to the lack of adequate transformation. But state interventionism is still rejected by the new political elite of Central and Eastern Europe. The first minor small steps toward the needed structural changes – at least in macro-economic, i.e. branch level – are linked, almost without exception, to a few isolated large-scale investment projects of several Western conglomerates such as Volkswagen, General Motors, General Electric, Unilever and Suzuki. But very few have shown genuine interest in the area, and those who have mostly did so at the beginning of the transition period. Some other Western giants prefer to build profitable Pizza Hut and Kentucky Fried Chicken chains. Philip Morris has invested in Czech tobacco industry. Needless to say, however, neither the German and Austrian retail chains Bauerkleider and Meinl, nor PepsiCo can possibly generate major structural changes.

Foreign investments, in general, are rather limited. Western investors have found most of the countries in the region not to be investment-worthy. This is clearly illustrated by the fact that roughly $10 billion have been directly invested into the Central and Eastern European countries (excluding the former Soviet Union) in a three-year period, which is only one-sixth of the $60 billion invested in Latin America during the last eighteen months, or one-half of the amount of American capital that flowed into Mexico in the single year of 1992. What is even more telling is that, in 1992, Kazahstan itself received as much foreign investment (because of its oil and raw material sources) as all twelve of the Central and Eastern European countries in transition.

Moderate domestic sources and small foreign enterprises had no real impact on the development of competitive export branches, partly because of a lack of financial strength, partly because of their preference in investing in trade and services. Hence, the real causes of the dramatic economic decline recall the experiences and lessons of the past: lack of adjustment has typified and continued to typify peripheral regions. The structural crisis of the 1980s generated somewhat similar processes in Central and Eastern Europe and Latin America. Their reaction was not very different from that during the structural crises of the 1870s and 1930s.

The poor peripheral countries of Central and Eastern Europe were unable to adjust at that time to world technological and structural changes, and sought a way out by increasing their traditional exports without restructuring their foreign trade. They succeeded only in finding a safe shelter in a regional agreement system, which was isolationist and was set to maintain regional self-sufficiency outside the scope of the world market. The self-sufficient imperial unit of the Austro-Hungarian Monarchy helped conserve the obsolete structure of the Hungarian economy and its grain-producing agriculture by counterbalancing the devastating effects of the world market – which had a dramatic 30% decline in terms of trade for the European grain producing and exporting countries. Effective agricultural protectionism ensured that the Dual Monarchy was the market for Hungarian agriculture and granted higher prices and an increase of over 30% in the terms of trade for Hungary.

Although the Habsburg Monarchy was able, by means of protectionism, to avoid the devastating effects of the structural crisis of the 1870–80s, it was, at the same time, untouched by the challenges and inspirations offered by the world market, and this contributed to its retention of obsolete structures and hampered adjustment to the new.

This pattern of "non-adjustment" was repeated during the structural crisis of the 1930s. This time Nazi Germany created an isolationist trading block with *Südosteuropa,* signing a set of agreements with Hungary, Romania, Yugoslavia, and Bulgaria in 1934 and 1935. On a bilateral basis, the countries of the region kept their trade from the world by using a clearing system employing barter arrangements which thus avoided hard currency payment. This type of trade was directed entirely by the state, which also set and subsidized the artificially-fixed prices, the money for which was raised by special bilateral tariff reductions. The safe, protected market undoubtedly helped the crisis-ridden Central and Eastern European countries to cope with the devastating impact of the Great Depression but, once again, the price paid for this short-term advantage was rather high, in part because it meant an increasing economic and political dependence on Nazi Germany, as well as the preservation of the old, unchanging structure of output and exports.

The 'non-reactive' (or regressively reacting) attitude of the peripheral countries led to the collapse of the self-regulating market economy during the interwar years. It should be added that this system was in a deep and continuously deepening crisis throughout the world in those decades. "Market economy, free trade, and the gold standard...broke down in the twenties everywhere," noted Karl Polanyi, "in Germany, Italy, or Austria the event was merely more political and more dramatic."[49]

In Polanyi's interpretation, the self-regulating market – an institution of the 19th century and an invention of Great Britain – had "only haltingly functioned since the turn of the century," was wrecked by the War and the treaties that followed. Still, "the tendency of the times was simply to establish (or re-establish) the system commonly associated with the ideals of the English, the American, and the French revolutions... [However] in the early thirties, change set in with abruptness. Its landmarks were the abandonment of the gold standard by Great Britain; the Five-Year Plans in Russia; the launching of the New Deal; the National Socialist Revolution in Germany; the collapse of the League in favor of autarchist empires...[B]y 1940 every vestige of the international system had disappeared..."[50]

Albeit in an immensely deformed way, "fascism and socialism... were live forces in the institutional transformation,"[51] and it is small wonder that most of the European peripheries in the East and South turned towards some version of fascism or socialism during the stormy 20th century. They did so because they preferred something other than the self-regulating free-market system, which they felt would be of no use to them in their drive to catch up with the West.

---

[49] K. Polanyi, *Op.cit.* p. 30.
[50] *Ibid.* p. 23.
[51] *Ibid.*

Polanyi, however, was entirely mistaken when he buried the free-market system, declaring its demise to have taken place in the 1940s. The free-market system, with the direct contribution of the United States, triumphantly reconquered the advanced European "core" and worked very well after World War II. Moreover, it became an internationally-recognized and ideologically-formulated ideal at the end of the century.

Conclusion

Central and Eastern Europe, which is presently going through history's most dramatic and spectacular transition process of marketization and privatization, is also suffering the most destructive consequences of that transition. The lessons to be learned from this case are historically important.

In addition to various factors of decline, the major reason for this tragic deterioration was a premature opening of the countries' market without even a partial technological and structural adjustment to the world economy having been made. This "opening of the greenhouse door" – which involved exposing the contents of what had, until that time, been a carefully-protected hot-house – in the middle of the harshest winter, in effect destroyed a large percentage of the 'greenery.' The more sudden and radical the opening of the door, the more serious was the destruction.

In addition, a premature and over-emphatic 'de-statization' was used in the attempt to set in motion market-automatism which had not even existed nor, where it did, functioned properly in the non complete-market economies. As a result of a lack of effective state guidance – to directed investment in a cautious way, to devise a labor and structural policy – not only did the adjustments and the structural changes not take place, but some very negative consequences occured.

All of the mistakes and difficulties are connected to the erroneous choice of the model of transition. To avoid any misunderstanding, allow me to reiterate that replacing a non-market with a market, economy was an unavoidable prerequisite for adjusting to the technological and structural transformation of the world. Privatization of an almost-entirely state-owned economy was inseparable from marketization. But a transformation to a regulated mixed-market economy would have been more 'organic' and much smoother than one to an imagined free and self-regulating *laissez-faire* market system. History rarely tolerates U-turns. Revolutions, which introduce new calendar in a theatrical fashon, have always carried the heavy legacy of the very past they rejected and this, against the will and dreams of revolutionary radicals, has often pushed them to take courses of action that they, in their heart of hearts, had rejected.

Moreover, as we have seen above, the peripheries have never had a successful free-market system. This could not work in a backward economic environment and in non-market societies, and in fact has never worked outside the advanced "core" countries.

Over and above all this, the last one-third of the century has shown that *laissez-faire* economies themselves have had relatively serious problems in coping with the adjustment that have been called upon to make. The two major recessions – one at the end of the 1970s and the start of the 1980s, and the other at the early 1990s – clearly reflect the difficulties inherent in this adjustment.

By contrast, the most successful adjustment and growth have been produced by regulated mixed-market economies, that is where a protected domestic market is teamed with an aggressive export drive. These countries have strong, interventionist states which deliberately assist and, if necessary, replaced the market mechanism (as history proves, even *laissez-faire* countries tend to turn toward regulation and state interference during major structural crises or periods of economic turmoil).

The irony of history is that the attempted model of a free- market economy in its Chicago School text-book form does not exist in the more pragmatic reality of the "core" countries, which often protect their economically-sensitive branches and subsidize their politically-important sectors.

The Central and Eastern European political elite obediently and enthusiastically sought to introduce the *laissez-faire* system, whereas the 1992 American elections had already expressed the need for correcting such an approach. The Democratic candidate won the election because of his promised job-creation program and his plan to revitalize the ailing economy. The middle class recognized the need for certain sacrifices and, when it comes to health care and educational policy, for reform along the lines of a Welfare State. Hence, the reforming Central and Eastern European countries were striving for a system that was already being questioned in its country of origin.

Instead of a religious-ideological free-market approach, a more pragmatic, organic transformation via a regulated mixed-market economy would have more easily delivered up a relatively smooth and successful period of change and structural adjustment – one with a relatively large publicly-owned sector, strong state direction, and intervention in labor, investment and structural (industrial) policy, as well as a combination of liberalization and, in certain fields, protection of the domestic market.

Has the future of the region already been determined by the transition policy that has been adopted? According to certain views, the damage caused by the mistaken choice of policy is already irreversible. The decline is devastating and it may take decades for these countries to recover. Privatization, in the form chosen, has imposed unbearable burdens on state budgets, since the "crown jewels" of these economies – valuable and promising firms with great potential – were sold for small sums during the first wave of privatization. Meanwhile, the hopelessly-bankrupt ones which used to be subsidized from the profits of the more successful firms, which have been sold off, have remained in the hands of the state, which stands no chance of selling them. The dilemma – whether to subsidize or shut down – creates an insoluble problem for the respective governments. The alternative is high inflation and a budgetary crisis, or a drastic increase in unemployment, possibly somewhere between 30% and 40%.

The premature, suicidal opening of the domestic market has even destroyed branches that used to be successful. Moreover, the $3.1 billion surplus of the European Community's trade with five Central and Eastern European countries in 1992 clearly shows that, despite the rethoric on assistance, the "core" is profiting much more from free trade with the region than are the transforming counties.

Although the devastation is wide-spread, it would be premature to forecast an irreversible decline of the region. Policy changes and a model correction may reverse unfavorable economic trends. A more skilful combination of regulations *and* market may soon revitalize the ailing economies in transition.

One might also not exclude the possibility of an eventual acceptance of some of the region's countries into the European Community. In this case, the high price of adjustment to Europe's institutional-economic system would indeed be a worthwhile entrance fee to dear Europe. In reality, and based on historical experience, however, only a few countries of the Western rim of Central and Eastern Europe have any chance of achieving that aim: those which, using the metaphor of Endre Ady, the early 20th century Hungarian poet, have been "ferry-boat countries" in their thousand-year-long history, sailing towards the West part of the time and then sailing back to the East. They may now have a new historical opportunity for setting sail.

Not only Central and Eastern Europe but the entire world economy is in flux, though. The countries that are, and will be, successful are those that find a pragmatic way, based on their own circumstances, to adjust to a rapidly-changing international environment.

The Chicago School market ideology may not prevail. Frank Hahn's prediction, made during his lecture at the British Academy in February 1992, may be proven correct by the turn of the century: "I hope I may have convinced you that the problems raised by incomplete markets are real...Keynes...has been declared out of date and wrong by the very simple device of ignoring and assuming away all of the difficulties which he thought to be important. But they will not go away. When, as now appears to be the case, they are again recognized, economists will again become more circumspect in their judgement of market economies...The General Theory...will again seen as pointing to the right questions." [52]

History teaches us that the roads lending up to, and down from, the "core" are equally passable during the trying and demanding times of major structural crises. There will be new "victor" and new "victim" countries, rising or declining depending on their response to the challenges of the world economy.

On the other hand, history also proves that the starting position of the "core" and peripheral countries are far from equal. Though a few former "core" countries may decline and a few former peripheral countries may rise and join the "core," the bulk of the periphery will remain where it is, unable to compete and adjust. The poorest 20% of the world's population receives only 1.3% of the global income, and has a 0.9% rate of participation in world trade. This part of the world will continue to decline. This is certainly true for much of Eastern Europe as well.

An emerging new world economic system may rearrange the inter-relationships, structures and strength of countries and regions but it also reproduces a great deal from the old system. It appeares that, following the marketization trend at the end of the 20th century, the differences and conflicts between North and South, and East and West – though changed and in somewhat modified form – will nonetheless remain.

---

[52] F.V. Hahn, *Proceeding of the British Academy,* 80. 1991. Lectures and Memoires. Oxford University Press. 1993. p. 217.

XI

From Regime Change to Sustained Growth in Central and Eastern Europe (The 1990s)

As a critique of the laissez-faire concept in interpreting Central and Eastern European transformation, I would suggest that the process does not end with systemic change. Laissez-faire interpretations maintain that economic growth, prosperity, and catching up are automatic outcomes of marketization. The reality is different. Systemic change, in the sense of economic transformation, would be senseless without creating the potential to respond to the challenge of the technological-structural revolution of the age. Successful restructuring cannot be the mere result of marketization and privatization. It cannot happen without the massive participation of transnational companies. Their investment, however, is not guaranteed and might be a mixed blessing. Appropriate international and national environments are required to generate a spin-off effect and avoid the rise of a dual economy with advanced foreign enclaves in an environment of continued peripheral backwardness. The first decade of transformation clearly reflects two, rather different possible outcomes of transformation and different responses to technological-structural challenges in the diverse areas of Central and Eastern Europe.

State socialism collapsed in Central and Eastern Europe a decade ago. In most cases the change of the regime was quite peaceful since the Soviet Union gave up control of the area, and the communist elite lost its self-confidence and hope to be able to solve the towering economic problems. In the decisive Polish and Hungarian cases significant opposition emerged from without and/or within the ruling party to either attack the regime or to reform it radically. A stormy and spectacular transformation began and characterized the entire period of the 1990s.

From the very beginning, a vast literature of 'transformatology' came into sight. Advisers of newly appointed governments, scholars, and experts of various international institutions worked out hundreds and thousands of studies, recommendations and critical analyses alike. A broadly accepted set of criteria for a reform program, the so-called Washington consensus of 1989, originally applied to less developed, crisis-ridden Latin American countries, was offered as a blueprint for the process of Central and East European economic transformation.[1] This prescription was offered for former state socialist countries by the international financial institutions: the International Monetary Fund, World Bank, and the American administration. Its central elements were macroeconomic stabilization those countries with significant inflation and indebtedness; the building of new institutions, and legislation necessary for a market economy; price and trade liberalization, and radical privatization of the previously nearly complete state-owned and operated economy.

Most of the 'transformatology' literature, covering these above-mentioned topics, is based on the explicit or implicit assumption that the elimination of deformed non-market economies, a restoration of market, and private ownership, paired with a laissez-faire free market system would automatically solve all of the major economic and even social problems of the transforming countries. The transition from plan to market is, thus, the key to the door of prosperity, and catching up with the West. 'The economic reforms,' stated Jeffrey Sachs in 1991, 'will set in motion a sustained process of economic restructuring… Once market forces are unleashed, there should be a strong pull of resources into the previously neglected [service] sectors… Agriculture is another area where we should expect major restructuring… The third major trend that we should expect is a complete restructuring within the industrial sector, from energy-intensive heavy industry to more labor-intensive and skill-intensive industries that can compete on the world market… Western firms…are likely to set up operations…for the sake of export production, in the same way as European firms are investing in Spain…'[2]

This assumption was in the air of the age. The competition of advisers and new governments in radicalism and the attempt to make a *tabula rasa,* to unleash almighty market automatism was partly a consequence of lack of experience in an unbeaten road, but most of all, of the *Zeitgeist* of the 1980s and 1990s, dominated by a Chicago school version of laissez-faire ideology, or, as George Soros named it, *market fundamentalism,* which 'disregard social values' and

---

[1] J. Williamson, 'The Washington Consensus Revisited' in: L. Emmerij (ed.), *Economic and Social Development into the XXI Century* (Washington D.C., Inter-American Development Bank, 1997).

[2] J. Sachs, 'The Economic Transformation of Eastern Europe: The Case of Poland,' in K. Z. Poznanski (ed.), *Stabilization and Privatization in Poland* (Boston, Kluwer Academic Publishers, 1993), pp. 208–9.

'seeks... to impose the supremacy of market values...'[3] 'Reaganomics' was presented as an overall, quick solution to economic ills. Thatcherism successfully undermined the concept of *Sozialpartnerschaft.* These ideals, advocated by the great powers, the international financial institutions, and hundreds of experts, and advisers, penetrated Central and Eastern Europe and the entire world. No doubt, if accepted, they served propaganda and public relation goals well, received headlines and tremendous applause in the West. Provided that this program represented *the only successful road* towards an automatic economic restructuring and prosperity generated by the introduction of market economy, it was logical to urge fast and radical strokes of market reforms. The speed is important if you have to go through the 'valley of tears' (Dahrendorf). The faster one concludes transformation, maintained the advocates of this concept, the better it is, because the pain of transformation will disappear and one can reach the other end of the valley of tears earlier. As Michael Mandelbaum of Council on Foreign Relations most characteristically phrased it, 'If the people... can endure the hardship that the policies of stabilization, liberalization, and institution building inflict, they will emerge at the other end of the valley of tears, into the sunlight of Western freedom and prosperity.'[4]

Thinking in the framework of the laissez-faire paradigm, the dramatic decline in output and GDP during the early 1990s was not as bad as the people of the region thought, because, things first had to be worst to get better later. The dramatic economic crisis is nothing else, as János Kornai interpreted, than a 'painful side effect of the healthy process of changing the system.' A 'transformational recession,' caused by a transitory 'shift from the sellers' to a buyers' market; contraction of investment; a shift in the composition of foreign trade; disruption of coordination, enforcement of financial discipline.' The appropriate cure of the *malaise* is to 'accomplish the task [of market reforms] faster'.[5] Jeffrey Sachs similarly warned in 1991: 'The time in the valley [of tears] depends on the consistency and boldness of the reforms. If there is wavering or inconsistency in economic measures, it is easy to get lost in the valley. Argentina

---

3 G. Soros, *The Crisis of Global Capitalism* (New York, Public Affairs, 1998), pp. XVII–XVIII, 196.

4 M. Mandelbaum, 'Introduction' in: Sh. Islam and M. Mandelbaum (eds.), *Making the Markets. Economic Transformation in Eastern Europe and the Post-Soviet States* (New York, Council on Foreign Relation Press, 1993), pp.11, 15.

5 J. Kornai, 'Anti-Depression Cure for Ailing Postcommunist Economies,' *Transition. The Newsletter About Reforming Economies,* 1993, February, p. 2.

has been lost for forty-five years.'[6] He, as well as many others, advocated 'comprehensiveness and speed in introducing the reforms' which 'can and should be introduced quickly, in three to five years.'[7] He also maintained that 'macroeconomic stabilization can also be achieved relatively quickly.' However, he added, restructuring that follows reform will take 'presumably a decade or more.'[8]

In sum, if you marketize and privatize fast, not only will systemic change and marketization be concluded in a decade or so, but also the restructuring that automatically follows and generates prosperity. This concept *implicitly* suggests that Eastern European *backwardness is a mere consequence of the planned economy* and state socialism. If this was the case, indeed, it would be enough 'to return to normalcy' by introducing Western type of market economy by bold and radical reforms.

In reality, the backwardness of the area and the failed attempt to catch up with the West has a long history. During the second half of the 19th century most of the area adopted the *Zeitgeist* of laissez-faire, free trade and export-led industrialization, and joined the international European economy. That attempt, however, failed, or, at least met with only limited success: Central and Eastern Europe remained agricultural, rural, and traditional, compared to the industrialized and urbanized West. [9] After World War I, in a radical departure from the past, the countries of the region turned to economic nationalism, introduced high protective tariffs, strong state interventionism, some kind of planning, and replaced export-led policy with import-substitution. The result, nevertheless, was the same semi-failure and continued backwardness.[10] The planned economy of state socialism was, from this respect, only a new, bitter, and extremist version of economic nationalism, or better to say, a modernization dictatorship. State interventionism and autarchy served to avoid hopeless competition, and reach the Western level. Behind the shield of an oppressive state, forced state capital accumulation served massive investments and rapid growth. The effort, again, failed. In other words, Central and Eastern Europe,

---

6 J. Sachs, 'The Economic Transformation of Eastern Europe: the Case of Poland,' in K. Z. Poznanski (ed.), *Stabilization and Privatization in Poland. An Economic Evaluation of the Shock Therapy Program* (Dordrecht, Kluwer Academic Publishers, 1993), p. 210.

7 Ibid., pp. 198–9.

8 Ibid., p. 198.

9 I. T. Berend – G. Ránki, *Industrialization and the European Periphery 1780–1914* (Cambridge, Cambridge University Press, 1982).

10 I. T. Berend, *Decades of Crisis: Central and Eastern Europe Before World War II,* (Berkeley, University of California Press, 1998).

consequently, is not in a position to simply reject the unpleasant and unsuccessful intermezzo of the last half a century and 'return to normalcy.' Rebuilding a private-market economy with all of its institutions and legal prerequisites, i.e. systemic change itself, cannot simply produce a mechanism of successful sustained growth, leading to catching up. This mechanism *has never worked* in this area. A brief comparison can illuminate the *longue durée* of economic trends in the region:[11]

Central and Eastern Europe's per capita GDP as percentage of the West

Regions	1870	1913	1938	1973	1989
Western Europe	44	44	44	45	40
Overseas West	32	30	35	38	32

The aggregate, comparative index of economic development levels, GDP per capita, clearly shows that during the three-quarters of a century, between 1870 and 1989, market and private economy could not generate automatic prosperity and the catching up process. Central and Eastern Europe's relative position vis-à-vis Western Europe and the overseas West remained unchanged. Ironically, state socialism with its planned economy generated a slight transitory catching up between 1950 and 1973, followed by an even steeper decline. Ultimately, the region landed on a lower peripheral level than ever before, or, using Jeffrey Sachs' metaphor, 'was lost in the valley of tears' for all of the modern era.

The transitory strength, and, in some places, popularity of state socialism emerged partly from guaranteed social security for the entire population, and partly from its promise to cope with historical backwardness, reach prosperity and high living standards. The regime, in the last analysis, collapsed because security became endangered during the 1980s, and the regime could not fulfill its program and did not lead to the Promised Land. Instead, a seemingly unsolvable and deepening crisis emerged. The regimes' legitimacy, based on its temporary success, was undermined; a deep disappointment penetrated the masses and even the elite.[12] The peoples of the area longed for a change, and, as the leading slogan of 1989 clearly reflected, wanted to 'join Europe.' As the demonstrators,

[11] A. Maddison, *Monitoring the World Economy 1820–1992,* (Paris, OECD, 1995), p. 212.

[12] I. T. Berend, *Central and Eastern Europe 1944–1993: Detour from the Periphery to the Periphery,* (Cambridge, Cambridge University Press, 1996).

welcoming Secretary of State, James Baker, in Tirana airport, expressed on their posters: 'Albania wants to be like America!'

The change of the regime, however, is far from equivalent to an automatic beginning of sustained growth and catching up. As an economic historian of the region, I strongly argue against the implicit assumption of a great deal of transformatology literature suggesting that sustained economic growth and catching up with the West is an automatism which starts to work when a country adopts the Western market model.

At this point, I must return to the often-analyzed question of economic decline, or 'transformational recession' in the early 1990s. Was it, indeed, a merely unavoidable consequence of changes from the plan to the market, as, among many others, János Kornai interpreted?[13] In my view, the 'transformational recession,' as Kornai named it, was only *one element* of a long, deep, and complex economic crisis in the area. One should not forget that the crisis had begun much earlier, basically from the mid-late 1970s, when the steam had already run out of the economic drive of forced industrialization in Central and Eastern Europe. Growth slowed significantly – from an annual 3.1% and 3.5% between 1950 and 1973 to 1.3% and 1.2% between 1973 and 1989 in Czechoslovakia and Hungary respectively.[14] Between 1978 and 1983, Polish GDP declined by more than 10%. During the second half of the 1980s, Romania experienced 0.7%, Yugoslavia 0.5%, and Poland 0.2% annual growth, compared to the 3.6% growth rate of the OECD countries. Aside from this, the terms of trade for the state socialist countries began to deteriorate: during the first decade after the 1973 oil shock, they suffered a 20% decline, and for some countries even a 26–32% decline of terms of trade. Foreign trade deficits dramatically increased, and almost all of the region's countries dropped into an indebtedness trap. At the time of the collapse of the regime, Poland accumulated nearly $42 billion, Hungary more than $20 billion, Bulgaria nearly $10 billion, the state socialist countries altogether $110 billion in debts. Debt service consumed a substantial portion – 40% to 75% - of the countries' hard currency income.[15] Quite a few countries started to lose control over inflation. That was an overall

---

[13] J. Kornai, 'Transformational Recession. A General phenomenon Examined through the Example of Hungary's Development,' *Discussion Paper No.1. Collegium Budapest, Institute for Advanced Study*, June 1993.

[14] A. Maddison, *Explaining the Economic Performance of Nations* (Aldershot, Edward Elgar, 1995), p. 97.

[15] I. T. Berend, *Central and Eastern Europe 1944–1993: Detour from the Periphery to the Periphery,* pp. 230–231.

economic crisis characterizing the last one and half decades of state socialism. Transformation, however, except in Hungary and Poland, was not on the agenda yet. This crisis, needless to say, did not end with the collapse of the regime, but continued; moreover, it became even more serious.

We have witnessed a long economic crisis in Central and Eastern Europe from the mid-1970s on up to now. A quarter-century long crisis is not unknown in economic history. This is a kind of *Great Depression*, Europe experienced during the last third of the 19th century, then in the interwar decades, then again, during the last third of the 20th century. The phenomenon is well explained by economic cycle theories. I prefer, as the most convincing and proven, Joseph Schumpeter's theory on *structural crisis*. Caused by a major 'set of technological changes,' the replacement of the old technological regime by a new one, leads to the decline of the old leading sectors and export branches based on old technology. This generates a wide-ranging slowing down and decline, and causes an economic crisis even in rich, advanced countries. It happened at the end of the 1970s and early 1980s, when, even in the West, double digit inflation and unemployment, and a significant decline in output exhibited the destruction of the structural crisis. However, rising new technology, 'the technical advances in microelectronics,' as Everett Rogers stated, 'that occurred in the 1970s and 1980s have spurred the Communication Revolution... [connected with the emergence of new] high-technology industry... one in which the basic technology underlying the industry changes very rapidly.'[16] A new infrastructure emerged, as Daniel Bell called it, a 'post-industrial society,' with an increasing number and share of white-collar employment in the ever-growing service sector. The adjustment to the new technology led to the emergence of new industries, new leading export sectors. The structural crisis, as Schumpeter explains, led to a 'creative destruction,' paving the way for new technology and prosperity. This adjustment created, indeed, solid ground for an impressive new boom in the United States and some other advanced countries.

The structural crisis in the backward areas, however, has a somewhat different outcome. It is definitely destructive, but lacks the creative impact. The peripheral countries of the world economy suffer more because of the severe decline of their terms of trade. Prices and markets for their export items, less processed and much less sophisticated than those of the core countries,' drastically decline. They do not have sufficient sources for research and development, know-how and financial sources to follow closely the new

16 E. M. Rogers, *Communication Technology. The New Media in Society* (New York, Free Press, 1986), pp. 14–15.

technological-industrial revolution, build up new leading export sectors. In other words, they suffer all the negative consequences of the structural crisis but are unable to catch the stormy wind of technological changes in their sails. The 'peripheral structural crisis,' as I call this phenomenon, is *destruction without creation.* Central and Eastern Europe experienced this situation three times from the 1870s to the 1970s–1990s and had only a 'backward' exit. The countries of the region preserved their obsolete economic branches and export sectors, and sold the otherwise unsaleable old products in a safe and highly protected regional market. That was guaranteed before World War I in the framework of a multinational empire (Habsburg or Russian). In the 20th century, in an alliance system led by a nearby great power (Hitler's Germany, then the Soviet Union).

After the collapse of state socialism, this type of 'backward' exit from the structural crisis was blocked. Without technological adjustment, the only shield against competition on the world market, although counterproductive in the long run, was Comecon isolation and regional self-sufficiency. After 1989, however, the countries of the region lost the protective shield of the safe and undemanding Comecon market, were forced to enter the world market and compete with the advanced countries, which have already adjusted to the new technological age. Moreover, they had to compete not only on the world market, but also on their own, opened domestic market. As a consequence, the peripheral structural crisis, prolonged since 1973, not only continued but also became much deeper during the 1990s.

Serious policy mistakes also contributed to the economic drama of the early 1990s. Richard Portes noted 'serious macro-economic policy errors... [such as] initial excessive devaluation of the currency.' Instead, he recommended, 'do not devaluate excessively; peg initially: then go to a crawling peg.' Another major policy mistake was that 'the opening to trade with the West – with convertibility, low tariffs, and few quantitative restrictions – was too abrupt...'[17] Domenico Nuti rejected the interpretation of economic decline as a 'necessary concomitant of transition.' In his view, it was an 'unnecessary consequence of policy failure.' Most of all 'the failure in government management of the state sector.'[18]

---

[17] R. Portes, 'From Central Planning to Market Economy,' in S. Islam – M. Mandelbaum (eds.), *Making Markets. Economic Transformation in Eastern Europe and the Post-Soviet States,* 1993.

[18] D. Nuti, 'How to Contain Economic Inertia in the Transitional Economies?' *Transition. The Newsletter About Reforming Economies* (The World Bank) Vol. 3, No. 11, December 1992–January 1993.

Although the march towards Europe and the reform from plan to market, in the long run, are very positive changes in the region, and this is the only promising road after the failure of state socialism. The economic policy during the first part of the transition period was, however, in many respects, mistaken. The difficult transformation process required a pragmatic and ideologically non-biased approach to reality. The countries of transformation should not have had to attempt to jump directly from a centrally planned to a laissez-faire economy, from an entirely state-owned to a one hundred percent privatized economy. State regulations and government policy were needed in the difficult transformation process when self-regulating mechanisms were not yet developed and market imperfections and non-market friendly behavior among the players was the rule. A regulated market, instead of a self-regulating market, a mixed economy with a restructured and efficient state-owned sector for at least a period of time, and a 'fine mixture between market and state'[19] would have been a more natural transition from plan to market. This approach, however, was immediately rejected and most of the transforming countries rushed to join the Reaganites and blame 'big government,' and state intervention. It caused unnecessary pains, led to the collapse of a great many old companies, which lost the bulk of their value and had to be sold for a fraction of their previous value. All these contributed to mass unemployment, a sharp decline in living standards, especially for certain rather vulnerable layers of the society. People in poverty, those with incomes less than 35% to 45% of the average wage, increased from 14% to 54% in Bulgaria, from 4% to 25% in the Czech Republic, from 25% to 44% in Poland and from 34% to 52% in Romania during the early 1990s.[20] 'Living standards of 57% of the population of Russia,' reported the journal of the World Bank in October 1999, 'are below the minimum subsistence level... the average life expectancy does not exceed 61.7 years.'[21] Social polarization, an emerging mortality and health crisis, sharply declining life expectancy – all of them phenomena typical for 19th century 'wild capitalism,' or, very late 20th century

---

[19] G. Kolodko, *Transition to a Market economy and sustained Growth: Implications for the Post Washington Consensus*, p. 45.

[20] *Central and Eastern Europe in Transition: Public Policy and Social Conditions: Crisis in Mortality, Health and Nutrition,* UNICEF, Economies in Transition Studies, Regional Monitoring Report No.2, August 1994, p. 2.

[21] *Transition. The News Letter About Reforming Economies*, The World Bank, Vol. 10, No. 5, October 1999, p. 35.

'bandit capitalism,' as two leading economists, N. Stern and J. Stiglitz named it.[22]

Can all these be considered unavoidable negative side effects of a positive transformation, or, the economic and social decline became much steeper and deeper because the 'transformational recession' was deepened by severe policy mistakes? Peter Murell's theoretical explanation hit the head of the nail: 'Economic and political decisions,' he maintains, 'are circumscribed by limits in social knowledge… inherited from the past… If one attempts to eradicate all… characteristics [of existing organizations] immediately, then one invites economic collapse… Large changes in the legal and policy framework produce highly dysfunctional outcomes…'[23] Not only speed and scope, but the inappropriate adoption of the laissez-faire market model also caused 'highly dysfunctional outcomes.' Grzegorz Kolodko, arguing against laissez-faire policy,[24] quotes three genuine authorities, George Soros, the World Bank, and IMF's Stanley Fisher: 'The untrammeled intensification of laissez-faire capitalism and the spread of market values into all areas of life,' warns Soros, 'can cause intolerable inequities and instability.'[25] 'Establishing a social consensus will be crucial for the long-term success of transition,' argues the World Bank in its report on 'From Plan to Market,' since 'societies that are very unequal in terms of income, or assets tend to be politically and socially less stable and to have lower rates of investment and growth.'[26] Stanley Fisher argues in the same way: 'adjustment programs that are equitable and growth that is equitable are more likely to be sustainable.'[27]

Regulation, state intervention, and a mixed economy are among the requirements for Central and Eastern European transformation. After a decade, it

---

22 N. Stern – J. Stiglitz, *A Framework for a Development Strategy for Market Economy: Objectives, Scope, Institutions and Instrument.* European Bank for Reconstruction and Development, Working Paper 20 (London, European Bank for Reconstruction and Development), April 1997.

23 P. Murell, 'Evolutionary and Radical Approaches to Economic Reform,' in K. Z. Poznanski (ed.), *Stabilization and Privatization in Poland,* p. 222.

24 G. Kolodko, *Ten Years of Postsocialist Transition. Lessons for Policy Reform.* Working Paper 2095. (Washington, The World Bank) 1999. (The next three quotations are from pp. 14, 17.)

25 G. Soros, 'The Capitalist Threat,' *The Atlantic Monthly,* February 1997.

26 *From Plan to Market. World Development Report 1996* (Washington D.C., The World Bank), 1996.

27 S. Fisher, 'Opening Remarks,' Conference on *Economic Policy and Equity* (Washington D.C., The International Monetary Fund) June 1998, p. 1.

is clear that all of the transformational economies are mixed economies, and this fact, provided that they adopted good policy, did not block the road for successful transformation at all. In Hungary, one of the success stories of transformation, 'under the privatization law, 92 firms will remain in permanent state ownership.'[28] In one of the most successfully transforming countries, Slovenia, 'the state still owns more than 50% of total assets in the economy.'[29] The state needed and still needs to guide the extremely complex process of transformation. In 1997, the World Bank called the attention to the important role of governments in various fields where market automatism will not work.[30] Governments have a role in macroeconomic policy, investment in basic social services, education, training, and infrastructure, creating and keeping a strong social safety net in order to prevent disastrous social side effects for the most vulnerable parts of the society.

The unavoidable 'transformational recession,' together with the avoidable policy mistakes, adoption of laissez-faire concept and policy – although more visible on the surface – were additional factors in the prolonged peripheral structural crisis, the basic cause of long-term decline. The interpretation of the East European economic crisis as basically a long depression of non-adjustment to a changing world economy, a peripheral structural crisis (deepened by transitory factors), might be strengthened by comparing it with the strikingly similar performance of other peripheral but non-state socialist countries in the world.

Latin America offers a telling parallel: from the mid-late 1970s on, as in Central and Eastern Europe, the same economic troubles emerged. Growth significantly slowed from an annual 2.5% to a 0.8%. The terms of trade had a similar 20% to 30% deterioration than in Eastern Europe, and the trade deficit became unbearable. Mexico had an annual trade deficit of about $20 billion throughout the 1980s. Indebtedness, however, was only a temporary solution and became a long term trap and disaster: Brazil, Mexico, and Argentina accumulated billions in debt which surpassed their exports by three to five times and the debt service consumed 50% to 62% of their export income. The striking similarity between Latin American economic performance and the East

---

28 *Transition Report Update April1999,* European Bank for Reconstruction and Development, London, 1999, p. 38.

29 Ibid., p. 44.

30 *The State in a Changing World. World Development Report 1997* (Washington D.C., Oxford University Press for the World Bank).

European one clearly exhibits the *region-specific*, and thus the *peripheral character of the crisis*.[31]

Believers in an almighty market automatism, however, argue that consistently reforming Central Europe is already elevated to the stage of sustained growth, while the hesitantly reforming Balkan and post-Soviet countries are still 'lost' in the valley of tears. The European Union, evaluating economic transformation, announced on July 15, 1997: 'Hungary can be regarded as a functioning market economy. Liberalization and privatization have progressed considerably... Hungary should be able to cope well with competitive pressure and market forces within the Union in the medium term... Hungarian enterprises are already competitive in EU markets...' The same was said about the Czech Republic, Poland, and Slovenia.

Regarding Romania's preparedness, although 'considerable progress in the creation of a market economy' was recognized, 'prices have been almost fully liberalized,' the European Union criticized, among others, the 'still fragile legal system' and the lack of coherence of policy making on economic issues.' Furthermore, 'much of Romania's industry is obsolete and agriculture needs to be modernized. The low levels ...of skills among the workforce also suggest that the economy needs a number of years of sustained structural reforms,' thus 'Romania would face serious difficulties to cope with competitive pressure and market forces within the Union.' [32] Similar statements could be made about several other Balkan and post-Soviet countries.

In the group of at least six Central European countries – Croatia, the Czech Republic, Hungary, Poland, Slovakia, and Slovenia – market economies are functioning, economic decline and rapid inflation are over, the annual economic growth is impressive. The 'well functioning market economies' basically recovered the early decline and mostly reached the 1989 level of per capita GDP.

---

[31] I. T. Berend, 'End of Century Global Transition to a Market Economy: Laissez-faire on the Peripheries?' in I. T. Berend, (ed.), *Transition to a Market Economy at the End of the 20th Century* (München, Südosteuropa-Gesellschaft, 1994), p. 14.

[32] 'Agenda 2000. Summary and Conclusion of the Opinions of the Commission Concerning the Applications for Membership to the European Union Presented by the Candidate Countries. Strasbourg-Brussels, 15 July 1997,' in Th. Veremis and D. Triantaphyllou (eds.), *The Southeast European Yearbook 1997–98* (Athens, Hellenic Foundation, 1998), pp. 333, 339, 344, 349.

GDP % change from previous year; last column = 1999 as a % of 1989[33]

Country	1990	1991	1992	1993	1994	1995	1996	1997	1998 *	1999 **	%
Croatia	-9.3	-28.7	-11.7	-8.0	5.9	6.8	6.0	6.5	2.5	1.0	79
Czech R.	-1.2	-14.2	-3.3	0.6	3.2	6.4	3.9	1.0	-2.7	0.0	95
Hungary	-3.5	-11.9	-3.1	-0.6	2.9	1.5	1.3	4.4	5.0	4.2	99
Poland	-8.0	-7.6	2.6	3.8	5.2	7.0	6.1	6.9	4.8	3.0	121
Slovakia	-2.5	-14.5	-6.5	-3.7	4.9	6.9	6.6	6.5	4.4	1.0	101
Slovenia	-4.7	-9.3	-5.5	2.8	5.3	4.1	3.3	3.8	4.0	3.8	107

*estimated, ** projected.

It is important to clarify that reaching the 1989 economic level in 1999 does not prove that these countries have arrived 'to the other end of the valley of tears' and already enjoy the 'sunlight of Western freedom and prosperity' (Mandelbaum). They hit the bottom then recovered the deep decline. Additionally, industry recovered only in two countries, Hungary and Poland. Real industrial output reached the 1989 level in these countries in 1997–98, while the Czech Republic, Slovakia, and Slovenia recovered only by 75–80% until 1999.[34] But we might not forget that the gap between them and the West, in that single decade increased from the nearly 1:2 level in 1989 to a 1:3 and 1:4 difference in 1999. The gap between East and West, as a consequence, is broader than ever in modern history.

In some countries, decline reemerged or continued, and they remained increasingly behind, nearing non-European standards. Bulgaria and Romania, after the severe decline of the early 1990s and a partial recovery of the mid-1990s, experienced a new crisis when output and GDP declined again. In Russia and Ukraine as well as several other successor states of the Soviet Union, decline has continued without stop throughout the entire decade. As a consequence, in 1999, Bulgaria and Romania reached only 66% and 74% of their 1989 GDP level respectively. Russia (53%) and Ukraine (35%), and the entire Commonwealth of Independent States (former Soviet Union) (53%) arrived only

---

33 For 1990–91: *Wiener Institute für Internationale Wirtschaftsgeschichte Research Report*, No.207 (Wien), July 1995; For 1992–99: *European Bank for Reconstruction and Development Transition Report Update* (London), April 1999, p. 6.

34 *Economic Survey of Europe 1998*, No.2, (New York, United Nations, 1998), p. 146–8.

at half of their 1990 level in 1999.[35] In 1989, the ratio between the GDP of Russia and Poland was about 7:1, by 1998; it was roughly 3:1.[36]

The utterly different performances of Russia and the Balkans, compared to Central Europe, are often explained by the lack of determination to pursue radical reforms. This certainly has relevance. However, the major difference between the economic performance of Central Europe, the Balkans and Russia has important causes in addition to hesitant reforms. Besides pursuing systemic change, the countries in transformation also have to *adjust to the structural crisis,* by restructuring the economy according to the requirements of modern technology, and, on this basis, reach *a sustained and higher than average growth.* Restructuring and adjustment, i.e. technological and structural transformation of the economy are central elements of the transformation, and, in some sense, the end and essence of it. However, only a few countries have begun doing so, while very little or nothing has been done in two-thirds of the region's economies.

The potential for adjustment to modern technology and new economic structures are not automatic outcomes of marketization and privatization. Even consistent reforms are unable to guarantee success; they represent only the very first steps in a long process of required adjustments. 'Only a part of the multi-layer transition process, namely liberalization linked with stabilization, can be executed... in a radical manner,' stated Grzegorzg Kolodko, one of the main architects of Polish transformation. 'As for structural adjustment... and behavioral change, they will take a long time under any conditions.'[37] It needs, argued Peter Murell, a different social knowledge and behavior, since 'socioeconomic mechanisms are information-processing devices... a society's stock of personal knowledge is acquired through a long historical process shaped by the institutions and organizations of that particular society.'[38] Transformation is not only 'a process leading from plan to market,' as Marie Lavigne argues, 'it could also be... a process leading from under-development to development.'[39] Transformation, without development, is quite senseless. If the countries remain in a backward state on the periphery of Europe, with huge masses in poverty,

---

35 Ibid.

36 G. Kolodko, *Transition to a Market Economy and Sustained Growth: Implications for the Post-Washington Consensus,* 1999, p. 74.

37 Ibid., p. 28.

38 P. Murell, 'Evolutionary and Radical Approaches to Economic Reform,' in K. Z. Poznanski (ed.), *Stabilization and Privatization in Poland,* pp. 219, 221.

39 M. Lavigne, *The Economics of Transition. From Socialist Economy to Market Economy* (New York, St. Martin's Press, 1999), p. 276.

systemic change results only in inefficient capitalism instead of inefficient socialism. Both had a long history in the area, moreover, they generated each other. Transformation, thus, must lead to sustained growth and catching up with Europe.' When is transition over?' asks Marie Lavigne. When the transforming countries approach the economic level of the least developed members of the European Union. According to Stanley Fisher (and his co-authors) and Tsuneo Morita, if they achieve a growth rate in the range of 4.5% to 6.0% annually against an assumed 3% growth in the low-income countries of the EU, it may take, in the best possible scenario, about 30 years. The Czech Republic may reach that level in 10–15 years, Hungary, Poland, and Slovenia in 20–25 years, Lithuania and Romania in 35 years, and Albania in 65–75 years.[40]

The way towards sustained growth and catching up leads through structural adjustment. Reforms and systemic change, no doubt, have already triggered such a development. Deregulation, the elimination of previous state socialist restrictions, triggered an elemental private initiative in some of the countries. A widespread business-like behavior and entrepreneurial attitude were revitalized, and domestic capital accumulation increased. It became the prime mover of economic growth and also a major factor in economic restructuring throughout the region. It required certain traditions and legacies, carried partly by the older generations but, in a way, transmitted to the younger ones. Reforming state socialist countries had tremendous advantages in this respect because entrepreneurial skills and business-like behavior have already became a part of the accepted value system. However, the social-political environment during the transition period also played an important role. An optimistic view on the future of the country, a belief in the potential of economic recovery and future prosperity, was an important prerequisite for domestic accumulation. The lack of national self-confidence in a humiliated and frustrated society generate a capital flight to the save haven of prosperous foreign countries. (Capital outflow from Russia is amounted to about $150–200 billion during the 1990s.)

The most spectacular result of privatization and domestic accumulation was the foundation of millions of new, mostly family, enterprises. These investments generated the most important structural change to date: the rise of the previously neglected and backward service sectors in Central and Eastern Europe. During the first half of the 1990s, the share of services in percentage of

---

[40] S. Fisher, R. Sahay, C.Végh, 'How Far is Eastern Europe from Brussels?' *International Monetary Fund, Working Paper* No. 53, April 1998; Ts. Morita, 'The Hidden Growth Potential of EU Candidates,' in *Transition. The News Letter About Reforming Economies,* World Bank, Vol. 10, No. 5, October 1999, p. 9.

the GDP in Hungary, Poland, and the Czech Republic increased from 55%, 36%, and 32% in 1990, to 63%, 56%, and 53% respectively by 1994.[41] This trend became characteristic even in the more backward regions. In Bulgaria, the share of services in GDP increased from 30% to 47%.

Hand in hand with this process, radical change occurred in the size-structure of enterprises as well. The previously existing well-known 'upturned pyramid,' the top heavy structure of enterprises, with absolute domination by huge companies and the relative lack of small-scale units was replaced in a few years by a normal pyramid structure.[42]

The key elements of adjustment, however, the adoption of revolutionary new communication technology, high-technology industries, and the building up of a competitive, highly productive export sector, in most cases, have not been achieved. This process has just started in Hungary, Poland, Slovenia, the Czech Republic, and Slovakia. The Balkan countries and Russia, with her partners in the Commonwealth of Independent Countries, about two-thirds of the former Soviet Bloc, are not even close to launching a successful technological-structural transformation and have descended into a continuous and deepening crisis.

Central and Eastern Europe, similarly to other peripheral regions, has never been able to pioneer technological revolutions. Insufficient resources for research and development, lack of knowledge and know-how, mediocrity and other cultural factors have always been obstacles to innovation and have never allowed a pioneering role in technology for a peripheral country in modern history. Many scientists and inventors, from the turn of the century on, left these areas to realize their dreams and became successful in one of the rich countries.

Although peripheral countries have made, in the best cases, minor contributions to technological innovation, in appropriate historical circumstances, they were able to adopt Western technology, accommodate themselves to technology leaders, and follow their footsteps. Since the 1870s, this was mostly connected with direct foreign investments resulting in the establishment of new firms and the introduction of modern Western technology and know-how.

---

41 P. Marer, 'Comparative Privatization and Restructuring in Hungary, Poland, and the Czech Republic, 1998–1995' in I. T. Berend (ed.), *Long-Term Structural Changes in Transforming Central and Eastern Europe,* p. 140.

42 E. Ehrlich, *Shift in the Size Structure of Manufacturing Establishments and Enterprises: An International Comparison.* Working Papers, Budapest, Institute for World Economics, 1993, p.18.

During the last third of the 20th century, the extreme harshness of the structural crisis in Eastern Europe mostly emerged as a consequence of total inability to adjust to the new world economy under state socialism. During the half century after World War II, the Central and Eastern European countries, could less than ever before accommodate them to the Western technological and structural transformation. This extreme situation resulted partly from the import-substitution policy of the Soviet Bloc, the lack of entrepreneurial and market incentives, and its self-isolation from the 'capitalist world market.' However, a major, if not *the* major, factor of the Soviet Bloc's incapacity was the economic warfare at the Cold War inspiring a strict Western embargo on modern technology transfer to the East.

The National Security Council of the United States concluded in December 1947: 'US national security requires the immediate termination... of shipments from the United States to the USSR and its satellites... which would contribute to Soviet military potential.' The intent of the policy was 'to inflict the greatest economic injury to the USSR and its satellites.'[43] NATO, and, a few months after its foundation, the new Coordinating Committee for Multilateral Export Controls (COCOM), established in November 1949, institutionalized this policy. Even the export of products of 'secondary strategic significance' such as steel rails and trucks, the export of between two to three thousand commodity categories was banned. The Bucy Report of February 1976, enforced in August 1977, recommended the ban of any kind of assistance in infrastructural development, building entire factories, and selling advanced technology in general. 'The widespread use of computers, even in commercial applications, enhances the 'cultural preparedness' [of the communist countries] to exploit advanced technology.'[44] From 1979 on, the export of all new technological achievements was strictly forbidden: computer network technology, large computer system technology, software technology, telecommunication technology, microwave component technology, advanced optics and sensor technology. The list 'contains a virtual roll call of contemporary techniques, including videodisk recording, polymeric materials, and many dozens of others.'[45] The traditionally accommodating economies of Central and Eastern Europe, consequently, could not buy and introduce modern communication

---

43 W. J. Long, *U.S. Export Control policy* (New York, Columbia University Press, 1989), p. 15.

44 M. Mastanduno, *Economic Containment. COCOM and the Politics of East-West Trade* (Ithaca, Cornell University Press, 1992), p. 194.

45 Ibid., pp. 213–5.

technology and were totally unable to follow the technological revolution of the 1970s–1980s.

The window of opportunity slowly opened after1989. Although domestic capital accumulation and good economic policy can make a difference, successful adjustment to the transforming world economy, and an appropriate response to the challenge of structural crisis is impossible without massive *Western investments and the participation of transnational companies*, the main carriers of modern technology and innovation.

The role of direct foreign investment and transnational companies is, however, often more than ambiguous. A sharp debate emerged about imperialism and the role of foreign investment at the turn of the century. On the one hand, it was often stated that capital exports are vehicle of exploitation and dominance. Especially in the case of very backward countries where capital needs were limited, this led to sheer economic invasion. Capital exports accelerate uneven development: the exporter countries develop at the expense of their subordinated peripheries. Capital exports and imports is a zero sum game. The participants either gain or lose and the winner, in the contemporary world, is the transnational company, while the losers are the exploited peripheries. In the globalized world, it may also lead to 'serious erosion, if not a total elimination, of national policy autonomy.'[46]

On the other hand, liberal and neo-liberal economics maintain the positive role of foreign investments as the main generator of development and prosperity. According to this view, both parties gain from the interrelationship, and economic growth and the standard of living increase faster in the poorer countries. Foreign investments, thus, generate a worldwide convergence.

Regarding the turn-of-the-century situation, 'the conclusion we can draw from the history of the European periphery,' I stated in a book written with G. Ránki in the early 1980s, 'permit no facile generalizations.'[47] The result of foreign investments in some cases, as we proved, was very positive and in others, negative for the recipient countries. In recent debate, J. Crotty, G. Epstein, and P. Kelly argue in a similar way: 'direct foreign investment is neither inherently good nor bad,' and the outcome of the activity of transnational

---

[46] H. Chang, 'Globalization, transnational corporations, and economic development: can the developing countries pursue strategic industrial policy in a globalizing world economy?' in *Globalization and Progressive Economic Policy* (D. Baker, G. Epstein and R. Pollin, Eds.),(Cambridge, Cambridge University Press, 1998) p. 107.

[47] I.T. Berend and G. Ránki, *The European Periphery and Industrialization,* (Cambridge, Cambridge University Press, 1982), p. 140.

companies and their investments 'will strongly depend on the overall national and international context within which capital mobility occurs.'[48] G. Myrdal rightly stressed the importance of the transportation and communication potential of the receiver country, its educational level, and its value system, which determine the positive effects of 'centrifugal spread of economic expansion.'[49] Others note the importance of the nature of the domestic and international rules of the game, the role of institutions and competition, and the traditions and entrepreneurial skill in a given country. In some situations, foreign investments may generate a spin-off effect and even a catching up process. In others, just the opposite happens.

The question, on the one hand, was whether the technology leaders were ready and interested to invest and transfer the new technology and knowledge to the transforming countries, and, on the other hand, whether countries of the region were prepared to receive and use these investment for generate a genuine spin-off effect and economic progress.

The inflow of capital immediately began in 1989–90, but until 1995, nearly half of the $23.2 billion direct foreign investment to Central and Eastern Europe was channeled only to Hungary ($11.4 billion). Hungary, in that period, received more than the successor states of the Soviet Union together ($6.4 billion). During the second half of the decade, however, capital inflow significantly increased in a few other countries as well:

Foreign Direct Investment in Central and Eastern Europe[50]

Country	Total inflow, 1989 in bn $	Inflow per capita in $
Czech Republic	13.5	1,350
Hungary	18.3	1,830
Poland	24.8	653
Central Europe & Baltics & Balkans	72.1	566
Former Soviet Union	23.7	84

48 J. Crotty, G. Epstein, and P. Kelley, 'Multinational corporations in the neo-liberal regime,' in *Globalization and Progressive economic Policy,* p. 119.

49 G. Myrdal, *Economic Theory and Underdeveloped Regions,* (London, 1957), p. 34.

50 *Transition Report Update April 1999* (London, European Bank for Reconstruction and Development, p. 12; *Transition. Newsletter About Reforming Economies,* Vol. 10, No.5, October 1999.

This amount of less than $100 million in a decade is rather small compared to the amount of international direct investments, which reached roughly $2 billion in that period. However, as a new peculiar characteristic of direct investment at the end of the century in the globalized world, in 1989, when the opportunity arose in the region, the investor countries invested mostly in each other's countries: 75% of these investments went into the five most developed countries. Moreover, as A. Bhaduri notes: direct investment 'accounts for only a tiny fraction' of the volume of transactions of foreign exchange in currency and other financial assets, which, as the main characteristic of economic globalization, reached nearly $1.3 trillion per day in the mid-1990s, (compared to $15 billion per day in 1973).[51]

Nevertheless, foreign direct investment played an important role in the region, but only in the three frontrunners of transformation, and in the small Baltic countries and Slovenia. The Czech Republic, Hungary, and Poland received nearly three-quarters of all investments in Central and Eastern Europe, including the Baltic countries, and more than half of the total investment in the East, including Russia and the other successor states. Western investors, counting on a per capita basis, also preferred some of the small countries such as Estonia ($947), Latvia ($634), and Slovenia ($596), especially during the second half of the decade. During the last years of the decade, annual foreign investment reached 3–4% of the GDP of the favored countries, while in Russia it remained only a fraction of 1%.[52] The comparative attractiveness of a country for foreign investors, measured by the stock of direct foreign investment relative to GDP, shows the unquestionable lead of Hungary and Estonia with a 39% and 35% share respectively. They are among the leading foreign investment recipients, while the Czech Republic and Latvia surpassed the world average of 15%. Slovenia and Lithuania are on the world average, while the Balkans' stock of foreign investments reached 5–6% of their GDP.[53]

Not all of these investments have contributed to restructuring. Some of them served only to enlarge the investors' markets. Major American film distributors bought up movie theaters in order to screen Hollywood movies.

---

[51] A. Bhaduri, 'Implications of globalization for macroeconomic theory and policy in developing countries,' in *Globalization and Progressive Economic Policy,* p. 152.

[52] *Transition Report Update April 1999,* (London, European Bank for Reconstruction and Development) p.12.

[53] 'Foreign Direct Investment: New Trends in Transition Countries,' *Transition. Newsletter About Reforming Economies* (The World Bank), Vol. 10, No. 5, October 1999, p. 8.

Retail chains were acquired: the Austrian-German Meinl took over a great part of the former state-owned Hungarian supermarket network. The Danone Group, one of the world's largest producers of dairy products, established a series of subsidiaries in Poland, the Czech Republic, Hungary, and Bulgaria during the first half of the 1990s. 'In strategic terms,' stated the Chairman of the company in his annual report in 1994, 'we persuade a very active acquisition policy... targeting markets outside Western Europe.'[54] Quite a few multinational companies also gained access to local and regional markets. Major tobacco companies, Colgate-Palmolive, PepsiCo, Nestle, and Ikea, and many others invested only in order to enlarge their markets. Quite a few of them gained monopoly position in the region. In spite of the short-term advantage of substantial investments, and the significant improvement of supply, market acquisition weakened the domestic market for domestic producers in the long run, and is therefore counterproductive from a local point of view.

Key investments were made, however, in the most backward infrastructural sphere, especially telecommunication that serves as the basis for any kind of technological progress to date. In a few rapidly changing countries, some of the world's telecom leaders began investing and modernizing. Hungary went the farthest by selling 67% of MATÁV, the formerly state-owned telecom monopoly of the country to Ameritech International and Deutsche Telecom. Only 6.5% of the ownership remained in the hands of the state. Estonia sold 49% of Estonia Telecom Ltd. to BalTel, Litvania 60% of Lietuvos Telecom to Amber Teleholding. Poland sold the first 25% of TPSA at the end of 1998. Three international telecommunication companies, AT&T, Alcatel, and Siemens gained ground in Poland. In many other countries of the region, state ownership of telecommunication remained dominant (74% in Slovenia, 51% in the Czech Republic), or remained untouched as in Bulgaria, Romania, Slovakia, and the successor states of the Soviet Union,[55] and foreign investment did not generate modernization.

Direct investments revolutionized Hungarian telecommunication. In 1990, only 9.6 main telephone lines existed per 100 people, in 1995 this improved to 18.5, and the number increased to 33.2 by 1997. Meanwhile, between 1990 and 1998, the number of mobile cellular telephone subscribers increased from 0.03 to 8.4 per 100 inhabitants and is rapidly approaching the Western level. In 1990,

---

[54] M. Koparanova, 'Danone-Serdika J.S.Co.' *Eastern European Economics,* Vol. 36, No .4, July-August 1988, p. 28.

[55] E. Ehrlich, *The Communications Infrastructure of the Central and Eastern European Countries* (Budapest, Institute for World Economics, February 1999).

the Hungarian telecommunication system was 45th among 56 analyzed countries. In 1995, ranked 34th, near to the medium standard, and by the end of the decade, it rose to the top third. While the Czech Republic, started at a higher point (15.8 main phone lines per 100 people in 1990), Slovenia, and Estonia reached more or less the same level as Hungary, and most of the others are behind. Moreover, the ranking of Russia (43 to 52), Bulgaria (28 to 48), Romania (41 to 54), and Ukraine (50 to 53) declined to the bottom of the 56-country sample. Starting from virtually zero, the number of internet hosts (varying between 25 and 50) and internet users (varying between 100 and 200) per 10,000 inhabitants, reached the medium Western level in the Czech republic, Estonia, Hungary, and Slovenia, surpassing France, Italy, and Japan already by the mid-1990s. On the other hand, Bulgaria, Romania, Russia, and Ukraine have hardly moved from 1 to 2 Internet hosts and 5 to 15 internet users per 10,000 people.[56]

Foreign investors slowly began creating modern industrial branches and competitive export sectors in the Czech Republic, Estonia, Hungary, Poland, and Slovenia. Until the mid-1990s, however, only one-quarter to one-third of foreign direct investment went into industry in the Czech Republic, Poland, and Slovakia. Hungary has a unique position with a nearly 80% proportion of industrial investments.[57] As in the spectacular Spanish and Irish economic miracle between the mid-1970s to the 1990s, when traditional local industries developed only slightly but transnationalization generated an unparalleled growth in modern sectors, here too, the transnational companies are the main actors. A few major companies sought to exploit the low wage level of the qualified labor force, quite a rare combination in less developed countries. The wage level in the Czech Republic and Hungary is less than one-tenth of the German level. As Anna Krajewska maintains on Poland, 'a mean wage of US $250 is one of the important motives in making direct investments... especially in labor-intensive industries.' The labor cost in Portugal, with the lowest labor cost level in the European Union, is three-and-half times higher than the Polish one.[58] Using the region as a low cost basis for exports, and gaining an important market share within the region, leading transnational companies have moved to some of these countries. Besides, Central European countries have a geopolitical

---

[56] Ibid.

[57] M. Szanyi, 'Experiences with Foreign Direct Investment in Eastern Europe,' *Eastern European Economics,* Vol. 36, No. 3, May-June 1988, p. 35.

[58] A. Krajewska, 'Transformation of the Polish Economy,' *Eastern European Economics,* Vol. 34, No.1, January–February 1996, p. 15.

advantage as well: their closeness to the West and well-developed transportation systems. These countries also have a historical-cultural closeness to the West, an environment suitable for Western economic activity. Late 19th–20th century experience, traditional economic connections, especially with Germany, also helped the renewal of cooperation. Central Europe belonged to the German *Grossraumwirthschaft* during the 1930s–40s, and Germany became the number one trade partner and investor in most of these countries in the 1990s.

The high- and relatively high-tech branches of industry, consequently, gained ground in those countries where foreign investment was substantial. The share of electrical, optical, and transportation equipment in total industrial output increased from nearly 13% to more than 25% in Hungary, from 12% to nearly 17% in Poland, and from 10% to more than 22% in Slovakia during the 1990s. This was in sharp contrast to the Bulgarian and Romanian situation, where the share of these branches declined from 10% to 8% and from nearly 14% to 11% respectively.

Structural changes went hand in hand with impressive developments in labor productivity. Foreign companies introduced Western management and paid somewhat higher wages, but required a higher productivity as well. As a consequence, productivity increased much more rapidly in those countries where foreign investment played a bigger role: Hungary, from one-third of the Austrian level in 1991, reached two-thirds of it in 1998. In Poland, labor productivity increased – compared to the Austrian level – from 30% to 50%, and in the Czech Republic and Slovenia from 40% to 50%, but the Bulgarian and Romanian levels stagnated around 30% of that of Austria.[59]

The Volkswagen Werke, Audi, Bayer, Siemens, and Henkel, main players in Central European investment, stepped in rather early. European and American companies also played a role. Thomson, the worldwide number two television tube producer established its firms in Warsaw and is selling the products via its European sales network. Philips transferred part of its battery production from Belgium to Poland, and exports more than half of the products in the European Union. Asea Brown Boveri founded 70 affiliates employing 23.000 employees in the region after 1990. Half of the machine tools the company uses in power plants for the South-East-Asian market are produced in Central Europe. Fiat integrated its long-existing Polish subsidiary into its global network and concentrates the production of Fiat Uno exclusively in Poland. Three-quarters of

---

[59] M. Landesmann, *Structural Change in the Transition Economies since 1989,* Paper presented at the conference on 'From Plan to Market: the Transition Process After Ten Years,' UN Economic Commission for Europe, May 2, 2000, pp. 11, 12, 27.

the output are sold to the parent company. The German Continental tire manufacturer in its Czech firm produce more tires than in its other branches, while basic tire parts (modules) are produced in the Czech Republic and Hungary, then shipped to the market for assembly.[60] Slovenia also attracted direct foreign investments into its industrial sector: by the mid-1990s, half of the foreign investment stock was invested in manufacturing, with the biggest share in the auto (14%), paper (10%), and electrical machinery (9%) branches. Leading multinational companies, Renault, Bayer, Henkel, Siemens, Semperit, and others sought to exploit the low wage level of otherwise well-developed Slovenia. Two outstanding projects were Renault's investment of a 54% share in the Revoz car factory for 54 million dollar, Danfoss International's investment in the largest Slovenian enterprise, Gorenje GA and jointly established the Biterm Company to produce thermostat in 1994. Characteristically enough, however, the Danish multinational Danfoss did not make the most modern type of thermostat available. Research and development also remained in Denmark. 'Danfoss does not allow Biterm a lot of initiative in the field of technology and R&D.'[61] This attitude of multinational companies is rather common. In February 1991, the German Linde firm bought 52% of the Czech Technopolyn, and, in 1995, it became the sole owner of the Czech gas, metallurgical and chemical plant. 'Since the foreign partner's entry, the subsidiary has ceased to do its own research and development. These activities are carried by the Technical Application Center and a modern laboratory in Höllriegelskreuth near Munich on a centralized basis...'[62]

Transnational companies made substantial investments in their East European firms. By the mid-1990s, foreign companies owned 12% of the Czech manufacturing firms, but their share of industrial investment was 25%; in Poland and Slovakia, also with 12% ownership in both countries, their participation reached 30% and 36% respectively. In Hungary, foreign share in industrial investments was nearly 80%.[63]

---

[60] A. Enzmann, 'Investment Promotion in the Czech Republic, Hungary and Poland,' in J. Bastian (ed.), *The Political Economy of Transition in Central and Eastern Europe* (Aldershot, Ashgate, 1998), pp. 47–8, 58.

[61] M. Svetlicic, – M. Rojec, 'Biterm d.o.o.' in *Eastern European Economics*, Vol. 36, No.5. September–October 1988, p. 84.

[62] M. Bohatá, 'Linde Technopolyn a.s.' in *Eastern European Economics*, Vol. 36, No.4, July–August 1998, p. 95.

[63] M. Szanyi, 'Experience with Foreign Direct Investment in Eastern Europe,' in *Eastern European Economics*, Vol. 36, No. 3, May–June 1998, p. 36.

One of the best results in restructuring occurred in Hungary, where a few major greenfield investments created new and modern factories and industrial branches. General Motors, Ford, Suzuki, and Audi established a previously non-existent car industry in Hungary with $1.3 billion investments (until 1996), partly producing partly assembling cars, engines, and parts. Philips, Guardian Glass, IBM, and Fuchs Metalwerke also made altogether $420 million greenfield investments for producing electronics parts, glass, and metal products. In 1995, 34% of foreign direct investments went into greenfield projects. In 1998, as a single example in the region, 94% of investments financed greenfield projects.[64] The single most successful investment case was the privatization of the Hungarian light-source producer, Tungsram, which had 2–3% share of the roughly $12 billion world market, and a 5–6% share within Western Europe. The American transnational company, General Electric, acquired 50% of the shares of Tungsram for $150 million in 1990, then virtually the entire company (99.8%) in 1994. General Electric integrated Tungsram into its global operation, invested about $600 million by early 1995, rationalized the company by closing down certain production lines and branch subsidiaries, and specialized production, mostly toward high-margin products, including new energy-saving compact fluorescent lamps. In 1994, they started the production of a revolutionary new product, Genura, the world's first compact reflector lamp using induction technology. From 1995 on, 90% of GE's European output was concentrated in Hungary, while several newly acquired West European facilities were closed down.

Tungsram's restructuring led to a double-digit annual increase in productivity. The number of employees was reduced from 20,000 to 9,000, and the company spent $30 million annually for retraining and redeployment. Moreover, 'this is the only example where a global multinational... decided to concentrate its worldwide R&D capability in a transforming economy in Central Europe,' stated Paul Marer and Vincent Mabert, the analysts of the GE-Tungsram case.[65] Out of the eight major research program sponsors by GE worldwide, four are at GE's Nela Park headquarters in Cleveland, the other four in Budapest. About half of GE's professional R&D personnel work in Hungary. Tungsram became the world's largest producer of light-sources, which sells,

---

[64] *Transition. Newsletter About Reforming Economies* (The World Bank), Vol. 10, No. 5, October 1999, p. 7.

[65] P. Marer – V. Mabert, 'GE Acquires and Restructures Tungsram: the First Six Years (1990–1995),' in *Performance of Privatized Enterprises: Corporate Governance, Restructuring and Profitability,* (Paris, OECD, 1996).

using GE's commercial network, 40% of its product in Western Europe, 30% in the Middle East and Asia, another 15–20% in the United States, and only 10% in Hungary and Eastern Europe. The earnings from its export are nearly $300 million in 1994, making Tungsram Hungary's largest industrial exporter.[66]

As in the Hungarian case, transnational car producers made one of the greatest investments in the region. The Volkswagen Werke with the largest Czech investment, Fiat, Renault, and General Motors are the leaders, but Daewoo and Suzuki are also present. Toyota and Isuzu are preparing to invest in Poland. In five years, Volkswagen may replace the Russian AvtoVAZ (Lada) company as market leader. According to the London based Economist Intelligence Unit's report, by 2005, car production in Central and Eastern Europe may increase by 30% and reach 2,88 million cars. Three-quarters of output, according to the report, may come from the Czech Republic, Poland, and Russia and 60% of the cars might be sold in Poland and Russia.[67]

As a result of creating internationally competitive industrial sectors, the transnational companies have started to play an important role in some of the countries of the region. In Western Europe their role is well represented by the fact that one-third of American exports and two-thirds of imports were intra-firm transactions by the late 1990s. One-third of the British, French, and Dutch industrial output is produced by transnational companies, and they financed 25 to 40 percent of the countries' research and development expenditures. Hungary, at the same level as Ireland, is far more 'globalized.' In these two countries, foreign affiliates produce more than two-thirds of industrial output and finance roughly 70% of the research and development expenditures.[68]

Hungary's exports, as a consequence, increased by 238% between 1989 and 1999, and by the second half of the 1990s, more than 45% of the country's exports consisted of machinery and transport equipment. Hungary was the only country in the region, which significantly increased its machinery exports (from 26% in 1990) during the 1990s. Although the Hungarian performance, from this respect, is quite unique, other Central European countries, as a clear indication of the progress of restructuring, are exhibiting similar trends: Poland increased its exports by 243%, the Czech Republic by 223%, Slovakia by 330%. Slovenian

---

[66] Ibid.

[67] *The Automotive Industry of Central and Eastern Europe: Perspective to 2005* (London, Economist Intelligence Unit, January 2000).

[68] *Measuring Globalization. The Role of Multinationals in OECD Economies,* OECD, Paris, 1999.

export more than doubled up to 1997. In all of these cases, machinery and transportation equipment represented between 20 to 35% of total exports.

The export development took place during a rather difficult regional restructuring of foreign trade. About 40% to 75% of the foreign trade of the Central and Eastern European countries was Soviet Bloc trade before 1989. The collapse of Comecon and the Soviet Union drastically decreased the Eastern markets. The countries of the region turned toward Europe, and, as early as 1995, the European Union became the main partner of the Central European countries: Poland, Hungary, the Czech Republic, and Slovakia sold 63%, 51%, 46%, and 38% of their export products in the European Union. Small wonder, 50% to 60% of their European exports still consists of primary products, i.e. food, beverages, unprocessed raw materials, fuels, and basic manufactures, mostly intermediate goods.[69]

Important investments, thus, had a significant spin-off effect in some of the Central European countries. They generated the growth of domestic business, which is itself an important contributor to economic growth, especially in Poland. Small domestic business, however, is rarely able to become technology leader. Various deals between local governments and transnationals contained clauses of compulsory reinvestment of part of the profit, mandatory use of domestic products and sub-contractors. Big transnational business, thus, often initiated small local business activities. Sometimes, as in the case of Volkswagen's Czech investment, various suppliers of VW also moved to the Czech Republic. Transnational companies play a significant positive role in Central European restructuring and sustained growth.

Russia, the successor states of the Soviet Union, and most of the Balkan countries exhibited minimal progress in restructuring. Foreign direct investment was minimal in this area, and mostly went into the extracting branches of oil, gas, and raw materials. Consequently, export is not the main vehicle of economic development as in Central Europe. Moreover, a sort of dual economy emerged: only the extracting branches belong to dynamic export sector – with or without foreign investments, and generate one-quarter of the GDP in Russia, while the processing industry produces non-competitive products for the domestic market. In this part of Eastern Europe, restructuring, in terms of producing competitive modern products based on new technology, hardly made any important steps. Transnationals are present but do not trigger any significant spin-off effect, and, in some cases, remain a foreign enclave, extracting and exporting critical raw

[69] H. W. Hoen, *The Transformation of Economic Systems in Central Europe* (Cheltenham, Edward Elgar, 1998), pp. 136–9.

materials, without developing modern processing industries and export branches, similar to the early 20th century situation in Romania, Serbia, and some other countries. This area, consequently, was unable to adjust to the late 20th century technological revolution and declined into a continuous peripheral structural crisis.

*

In those Central European countries, where impressive foreign direct investment assisted technological-structural adjustment, and the domestic institutional, legal, social environment, and attitude were appropriate to generate a general spin-off effect, economic transformation was paving the way to sustained growth and catching up with the West. These countries became members of NATO and are candidates for European Union membership. These decisive institutional changes might accomplish progress towards an equal partnership with the West, or perhaps, the road from the periphery to the core of Europe. Two-thirds of this large region, however, have taken only the very first steps towards, and cannot even meet the basic requirements of transformation into the new age of the Communication Revolution and the 21st century. They remain seemingly outside the integrating continent, behind a new 'Poverty Curtain' as a pruned, deeply disappointed and explosive periphery of Europe.

INDEX

In preparing this selected index, names and expressions, which occur almost on every page, or only marginally, are omitted.